The Perfectionist Turn

In Aristotle's eyes, ethics does not begin with thinking of others; it begins with oneself. The reason is that every human being faces the task of learning how to live, how to be a human being, just as he has to learn how to walk or to talk. No one can be truly human, can live and act as a rational man, without first going through the difficult and often painful business of acquiring the intellectual and moral virtues, and then, having acquired them, actually exercising them in the concrete, but tricky, business of living.

Henry B. Veatch, *Rational Man:*
A Modern Interpretation of Aristotelian Ethics

THE PERFECTIONIST TURN
FROM METANORMS TO METAETHICS

Douglas J. Den Uyl and Douglas B. Rasmussen

EDINBURGH
University Press

Edinburgh University Press is one of the leading university presses in the UK. We publish academic books and journals in our selected subject areas across the humanities and social sciences, combining cutting-edge scholarship with high editorial and production values to produce academic works of lasting importance. For more information visit our website: www.edinburghuniversitypress.com

Edinburgh University Press Ltd
The Tun – Holyrood Road
12(2f) Jackson's Entry
Edinburgh EH8 8PJ

First Published in hardback by Edinburgh University Press 2016

Typeset in 11/13 Sabon by
Servis Filmsetting Ltd, Stockport, Cheshire,
and printed and bound in Great Britain by
CPI Group (UK) Ltd, Croydon CR0 4YY

A CIP record for this book is available from the British Library

ISBN 978 1 4744 1334 3 (hardback)
ISBN 978 1 4744 2843 9 (paperback)
ISBN 978 1 4744 1335 0 (webready PDF)
ISBN 978 1 4744 1336 7 (epub)

Contents

Preface   vi

Introduction: What Is Ethics?   1

Part I: Making the Turn

1. An Overview of Individualistic Perfectionism   33

2. The Search for Universal Principles in Ethics and Politics   65

3. Tethering I   96

4. Tethering II   137

Part II: Facing a New Direction

5. The Perfectionist Turn   171

6. Because   201

7. Toward the Primacy of Responsibility   246

8. The Entrepreneur as Moral Hero   284

Afterword: Big Morality   320

Index   333

Preface

After having completed a work on political philosophy, our hope was to do a work on ethics. In thinking the matter through, however, we found it was not so easy to simply begin a discussion of ethics. We discovered that although everyone pays lip service to the notion that ethics and politics are distinct, understanding how and why they are so is not so easily accomplished. Indeed, it turns out that the structure of typical ethical arguments today is integrally like the structure of most normative political arguments. Both tend to culminate in what we call a juridical form of normativity. The sort of ethical theory we desire to advocate, by contrast, takes on a different structure. We were thus required to say more about political theory in order to find a space for ethics. In our work on political theory, *Norms of Liberty: A Perfectionist Basis for Non-Perfectionist Politics* (University Park: Pennsylvania State University Press, 2005), we link politics largely to what we call "metanorms"—or norms that provide a context for the exercise of actions in accordance with ethical norms. Such norms do take a juridical form. But how to move from metanorms to norms? That, we argue, requires a fuller appreciation of the nature of a perfectionist ethics. To make that turn, it was necessary to traverse still more political theory, because rather than taking its cue from ethics, almost the reverse seems true today: ethics is taking its cues from the political.

Hence, besides laying out our framework, much of the early part of this book is involved in showing how what we term "individualistic perfectionism" can be employed as both an alternative ethical theory and as a basis for criticism of other political and ethical approaches. By contrasting our individualistic form of ethical perfectionism with some currently predominant frameworks, we can expose the doubtable assumptions and implications of these other approaches to ethics and politics while making room for our own approach.

In the second half of this book we attempt to defend the foundations we have employed in the first half and to give some indication of their meaning in practice. Although we do not offer ethical advice on particular ethical problems, we do indicate that the locus of such solutions lies not with some impersonal rule, but within a deeply personal perspective. That personalism, however, is itself rooted in a naturalism which is the source of normativity in ethics. The doctrine is "perfectionist" because its norms, grounded in human nature, contribute to our flourishing and depend upon the idea of human perfectibility. While both personalism and naturalism can be controversial, they have the advantage of keeping ethics from lapsing back into the political, by offering standards that are not purely a function of the political. So in the end, we do achieve our goal of producing a work on ethics; but in the intellectual climate of today, space had to be cleared for that goal to be achieved.

It would be a mistake, however, to leave the impression that we deny *any* link between ethics and politics. Making room for ethics is not the same as claiming there is no connection between ethics and politics or that one's ethical theory has no effect upon the type of political principles one advocates. We believe that our ethical theory is consistent with our political theory and that politics needs an ethical connection. Both our ethics and politics are used in our analysis of alternative theories and doctrines. But in the end, our purpose was still to focus upon ethics, and we hope that, whatever the reader's opinion of our specific arguments and conclusions, it will be seen that we do offer an alternative to much of mainstream ethical theorizing.

It would also be quite false and arrogant for us to suppose that we could have arrived at any of our goals without the help of others. We owe a good deal to many individuals who have contributed to this project along the way. They are: Jennifer Baker, Daniel Beresheim, Alessandro Biasini, Carrie-Ann Biondi, Michael Bistreich, Peter Boettke, Brandon Byrd, Rosolino Candela, Paul Gaffney, David Gordon, Stephen Hicks, Irfan Khawaja, Shawn Klein, Mark LeBar, Michael S. Lopato, Tibor R. Machan, Eric Mack, David Miller, Fred D. Miller, Jr., Mathew Moya, Ellen Paul, Jeffrey Paul, Daniel Russell, Aeon Skoble, Emily Soares, Chris W. Surprenant, Jacob Traugott, Ed Younkins, and Leonidas Zelmanovitz. Also, special thanks go to Catherine G. Sims for keeping us on target with her suggestions and to Jonathan Jacobs and Elaine Sternberg for their incisive and probing comments on different parts of the manuscript. Finally, very special thanks go first to Jared Meyer for carefully reading and insightfully commenting on early and late versions of the manuscript and second to Roger E. Bissell for his extraordinary philosophical and editorial assistance. Yet, of course, none of these good folks are to be held responsible for any errors in this work. That responsibility remains with us.

We would further like to express our appreciation to the following associations, centers, foundations, and universities for their support and assistance: American Association for the Philosophic Study of Society; Association for Private Enterprise Education; Charles Koch Foundation; Liberty Fund; Social Philosophy and Policy Center at Bowling Green State University; Center for Ethics and Entrepreneurship at Rockford University; Department of Philosophy at the University of New Orleans; Politics, Philosophy, and Economics workshop at George Mason University; Department of Philosophy at the Università Ca' Foscari in Venice; and St. John's University.

Finally, we gratefully acknowledge permission to use material from works previously authored by us jointly or singly. These are:

Norms of Liberty: A Perfectionist Basis for Non-Perfectionist Politics (University Park: Pennsylvania State University Press, 2005);

"The Importance of Metaphysical Realism for Ethical Knowledge," *Social Philosophy & Policy* 25.1 (Winter 2008): pp. 56–99;

"Liberalism in Retreat," *The Review of Metaphysics* 62.4 (June 2009): pp. 875–908;

"Homo Moralis," *The Review of Austrian Economics* 22.4 (December 2009): pp. 349–85;

"In Search of Universal Political Principles: Avoiding Some of Modernity's Pitfalls and Discovering the Importance of Liberal Political Order," *The Good Society* 19.1 (2010): pp. 79–86;

"The Perfectionist Turn," *Social Philosophy & Policy* 30.1–2 (Winter 2013): pp. 69–94;

"Why Justice? Which Justice? Impartiality or Objectivity?" *The Independent Review* 17.3 (Winter 2013): pp. 441–60; and

"Grounding Necessary Truth in the Nature of Things: A Redux," in *Shifting the Paradigm: Alternative Perspectives On Induction*, ed. Paolo C. Biondi and Louis F. Groarke (Berlin: Walter de Gruyter, 2014), pp. 323–58.

Introduction: What Is Ethics?

> Many are the arts among human-beings ... that have been discovered
> experientially from experience, for experience makes the course of life
> pass along the path of art, and inexperience along the path of luck.
>
> Plato, *Gorgias*, 448c4–7

Perhaps nothing seems clearer to us and more pervasive in our lives
than ethics. We live constantly with a sense of our obligations and
duties, and with whether we have failed or succeeded in living up to
them; and it is generally not considered bad form to remind others of
their own. We are taught from our earliest ages that it is important
that we "be good" or "do the right thing." Unlike some concepts
that can be difficult to understand, ethical norms seem to be readily
cognizable. Indeed, we believe they need to be of such a form that
virtually anyone can follow them. Of course, at the same time that
we recognize how pervasive ethics is in our lives, we also recognize
that there are many complicated ethical questions that do not seem
to lend themselves to easy answers. Yet, for all the potential difficulty
in finding some answers, we seem readily able to comprehend the
nature of those difficulties in a way that would not be true of, say, a
problem in theoretical physics. And although we at least sense that
complicated ethical theories may occupy the time of philosophers,
we also believe that philosophers are considering matters we generally understand, and which are not themselves simply products of
the philosophers' own reflections. Ethics is something real for us all,
not a theoretical construct.[1] It would still be of concern to us even if
ethical theorists did not exist.

Whatever else might be said about ethics, then, its universality is
palpable. We have phrased this last sentence carefully. We are saying
that ethics *is* of concern to all of us—not that it should be, or that the
world is a better place when it is, but that it is *in fact* of concern to

---

[1] We will discuss the realistic (and non-reductive naturalistic) character of ethics in
  Chapters 5 and 6.

all of us. The first question, therefore—and, we would venture to say, the last, as well—is simply: What is it about which we are so concerned? This question, simple enough in itself, is somewhat complex to answer. We could be concerned about something because the very presence of others continuously demands that we be so concerned. As an example, this might take the form of recognizing the need for rules governing relations among persons, while also responding to pressure to follow those rules. Or, what we are so concerned about might relate to the very nature of becoming who we are, irrespective of the demands that arise from the presence of others. As it turns out, these two types of concerns match the two basic approaches to ethics that we wish to outline here; and their tension animates much of the reflection on ethics both in ordinary life and in theorizing about ethics. The former sort of concern, where the necessity of living among persons is taken to be the principal reason for developing norms of conduct—even with respect to ourselves—we shall designate as the *template of respect*. The latter sort of concern, where the source of all norms—even those concerning our life among others—derives from the existential fact that we must make something of our lives, we shall designate as the *template of responsibility*.[2] We offer these approaches as fundamental, alternative frameworks. While there can be overlap between them, in the sense that particular prescriptions consistent with one framework might also be so with the other, one must nonetheless choose a starting point and understand any "overlap" in terms of one or the other of the two basic templates. One must make this choice because particular moral prescriptions do not exist without a context through which they are understood, appreciated, and developed. At some level of fundamentality, we get a context which is basic. The two templates just mentioned seem to us to be the basic orientations within which to frame thought about ethics.

---

[2] We have tried to employ terms for each position that sound positive and are attractive in themselves. "Responsibility" and "respect" are also terms employed within each framework; that is, within the framework of respect, one can speak of responsibility and vice versa. The terms were chosen not to exclude usage by the other framework, but because both are common to ethical contexts, and because "respect" seems basically relational and "responsibility" basically agent-centered, befitting the fundamental orientation of each framework. Further, before we get too far along in this discussion, it should be noted that our use of the phrase "ethics of responsibility" bears no connection to Max Weber's use of it in discussing politics. Our use has to do with ethical theorizing.

From the foregoing, it is apparent that by a framework, we mean a pre-theoretical orientation that one adopts or utilizes when one begins to reflect more systematically upon the nature and meaning of ethical norms or conduct. This orientation may in turn influence one's understanding of the very nature, meaning, and relative importance of the ethical norms and conduct themselves. The template of respect and the template of responsibility as frameworks are not two theories of ethics, but approaches within which theorizing will take place. As such, not only do these frameworks not generate particular norms, but they do not even generate the principles from which those norms are derived. This is not to say, however, that the frameworks lack the power to constrain or generate implications. If they were totally vacuous, they would be of no service. What they do is provide the central or orienting characteristics of the problem, and thereby guide one in reaching the kinds of answers likely to be acceptable. Moreover, frameworks help to provide boundary conditions for what is within the scope of a topic or area—in this case, ethics. In addition, frameworks can provide a basis for weighting some values over others. They do all of these things because they may arguably refer to certain existential conditions that render the frameworks themselves plausible.

Both the frameworks here, for example, might have within them a norm to the effect that stealing is ethically defective. The reasons for that defectiveness, however, might be put in different terms, such as its showing a lack of respect for others or reflecting an unwillingness to be responsible for what one does. Language may even cross over the frameworks, with someone working within the template of responsibility framing principles in terms of respecting others, and someone from the template of respect talking about the need to take responsibility.[3] The difference would come not merely from the linguistic form of these prescriptions, but from the way they are viewed and how they are networked with other norms within the same framework. Moreover, a given framework may influence patterns of emphasis of value. Toleration, for example, may rank higher and be more consistent with other norms in the framework of the template

---

[3] For example, Mark LeBar, who seems to us to fall under the framework of responsibility, has an extended discussion of respect. See his *The Value of Living Well* (Oxford: Oxford University Press, 2013), pp. 320ff. We examine central features of his views in Chapter 7 and consider the differences between his discussion of respect and ours in the Afterword.

of respect than would, say, courage, which might have more force within the template of responsibility. It is not that each eschews the other value, but rather that the significance of not just either of these two, but *any* given value differs because of the framework in which it appears. In discussing these frameworks, our purpose here is to set out unabashedly the basic nature of the "turn" we are making.

1. Two Framing Perspectives on Ethics

The division between frameworks we are suggesting is not one that is readily apparent in modern understandings of ethics, because the two principal modern ethical approaches of utilitarianism and deontology are, as we see them, both within the template of respect. So-called virtue ethics appears to fall under the rubric of the template of responsibility, but many of the efforts in this direction are, rather, a grafting of virtues into a respect-based ethical framework.[4] So, perhaps it is best to start with some of the characteristics of the template of respect, and then to examine some of the ways in which it contrasts with the template of responsibility. The basic question of a respect-based template of ethics, and its framing perspective, is simply: How should one conduct oneself with regard to persons (including oneself)? A descriptive and phenomenological answer to this question might be to say that our life among persons involves our being directed along some paths and not others by the accepted and enforced norms of society as dictated by social practices, social institutions, and social authorities. Yet, *that* we "should" behave in certain ways as dictated by society does not yet tell us *why* we should. The "why-we-should" in the context of the template of respect has to do with its demands and rules being *worthy* of our allegiance. Our concern at the moment is to discuss not the reason why any norms are worthy, but rather the fact that they are. In various places in the chapters that follow, the why-question will be considered, both as it applies to the template of respect and with regard to norms that fall under the rubric of the template of responsibility. Our purpose at the moment, however, is more paradigmatic than justificatory; that is, we wish here to outline the basic orientations rather than to give either of them a defense.

Ethics in its speculative domain, then, is fundamentally about

---

[4] See Talbot Brewer, *The Retrieval of Ethics* (Oxford: Oxford University Press, 2009), pp. 91ff.

whether the norms or rules are correct, appropriate, or worthy, according to some criteria that will be used to define our obligations and thus direct our conduct. In the case of the template of respect, the subject area of applicable rules is one of defining our relations toward persons. The recommendations or norms which function as conclusions about how conduct ought to proceed are thus the obligations inherent to the framework and the network of norms connected to it. Whatever the recommendations may be for optimal conduct, the basic question in the template of respect remains the same: What obligations do we have to persons?—the answer to which comes in developing or recognizing norms designed to manage or define relations among those persons.

Once one sees relations among persons as the fundamental subject area, one recognizes that the basic source of value in that system is persons themselves. We cannot be centrally concerned about our relations with persons unless we first believe they have some special value or status. It is our relations with persons, among all other things to be found in our environment, that call for the particular kind of consideration that we are taking to be ethics. And it is that same initial valuing—call it, respect—that will help us to judge whether norms we might be asked to follow are "correct." If a given norm seems to ignore or denigrate that initial necessary respecting and foundational priority of persons, we would have grounds to call for a modification or rejection of the norm. Treating someone as a slave, for example, would typically be considered as undermining the priority of respect for persons. It is important to notice, in this regard, that the question of whether persons are deserving of *equal* respect is a derivative question from the sort of respect we are speaking of here. One might say, for instance, that people deserve different forms of respect based upon their accomplishments; but in saying that, one is still showing respect for persons—or, perhaps more clearly, personhood. One is still, in other words, determining the appropriate behavior toward persons by using an initial basic respect toward them, in order to determine what additional levels of respect are appropriate. There is certainly a kind of equality in giving every person respect, though that very equality of respect might also allow for inequality of treatment.

It seems evident why a Kantian-based deontology would fall within the rubric of the template of respect. As Kant notes, the good will has "absolute worth"; and he says of it that "a good will is not good because of what it effects, or accomplishes, nor because of its fitness to attain some intended end, but just because of its willing—that is, in itself."[5] The recognition of what is good in itself ipso facto generates respect. Respect in this context, for Kant, is respect for the moral law, which is what the good will itself comes to advocate. But only certain kinds of beings—namely, persons—can have respect and exercise a good will. Consequently, as Sissela Bok puts it,

> for humans who, alone among living beings, have what [Kant] called the gift of morality—the extraordinary possibility of making moral choices— the fundamental choice is whether or not to choose to be someone of character out of respect not only for other people but for themselves.[6]

In Kant's case, respect is given first to the law rather than persons for, as he tells us, "all respect for a person is actually only respect for the law (of righteousness, etc.) of which he gives us the example."[7] Modern Kantians have reversed the emphasis somewhat and made the respect for persons the reason for respecting the moral law, arguing that the capacity to respect the law is a function of being a person, much as Bok herself is suggesting. The term "personhood" seems to cover both aspects well enough, since the ability to recognize the nature and applicability of law and to promulgate it would be tied to the *meaning* of persons rather than to individuals.[8] In any case, where there are appeals to non-consequentialistic factors such as intention, fairness, incursions of past obligations, and the like, the force of those appeals would result from a conception of the fundamental priority of persons and what that priority implies by way of appropriate conduct. Something is not said to be respected if it is, as

---

[5] Immanuel Kant, *Groundwork of the Metaphysics of Morals*, rev. ed., trans. and ed. Mary Gregor and Jens Timmermann (Cambridge: Cambridge University Press, 2012), 4:394, p. 10. Martha C. Nussbaum notes about respect generally: "respect for persons is not a subjective emotional state, such as a feeling of admiration. It is a way of regarding and treating persons, closely related to the Kantian idea of treating humanity as an end and never as a mere means. Respect is thus closely linked to the idea of dignity, to the idea that humanity has worth and not merely a price. Equal respect would then be respect that appropriately acknowledges the equal dignity and worth that persons have as ends" ("Perfectionist Liberalism and Political Liberalism," *Philosophy & Public Affairs* 39.1 [Winter 2011], pp. 35–6).

[6] Sissela Bok, *Exploring Happiness: From Aristotle to Brain Science* (New Haven, CT: Yale University Press, 2010), p. 32.

[7] Kant, *Groundwork of the Metaphysics of Morals*, 4:402, p. 17n.

[8] We will have more to say about this distinction between persons and individuals shortly.

Kant notes, "a means only."[9] There must be a dimension to it that is promoted because of itself, rather than what it effects.

Under the rubric of the template of respect, then, ethics refers to a pattern of norms derived from and expressive of a respect for persons, the function of which is to orient the actor toward exhibiting such respect by willing or following the norms that define it. Fundamentally, the template of respect is about relations among persons, of which one is usually allowed to include oneself. Hence, we can see that understanding ethics in this way sees persons as associated together under a common set of norms equally applicable to all—and the moral agent, when acting, as seeking to establish relationships in conformity with these norms.[10]

As does the template of respect, the template of responsibility begins by recognizing an existential condition. It sees human beings as being inevitably thrown together and thus in need of norms for guiding their relationships. True as it is that we emerge in the middle of such relations and norms, the first existential condition faced by the template of responsibility is not relations among persons but, rather, the fact that one must make a life for oneself. Whether the relational norms surrounding one in one's social environment are ideal or horrific, one does not escape the task of self-responsibility. One may have that responsibility taken away from one, as in the case of slavery, but one cannot abdicate it. At first blush, this last claim seems false. People appear to abdicate responsibility all the time. Yes, they do, but our point is that *they* are the ones who are attempting to abdicate it, which is another way of saying they are the ones responsible for the attempt at abdication. One can fail to *take* (acknowledge) responsibility, but one cannot fail to *be* responsible and still be a choosing self.

It is important to note at this stage that the issue of being

---

[9] It is important to note that these same factors may be a part of a responsibility-based ethics, as well. For various historical reasons, deontology may be exclusively a respect-based ethics; but some of the concepts normally associated with it might be applicable to both frameworks.

[10] No doubt, this could be put in a number of ways. A good example of this general point, as expressed in the language of duty, is the following by George Kateb: "the first duty, a duty as high as any, is that human agents, whether private or public, must abstain from any action that improperly invades or seizes or destroys or damages or culpably neglects what belongs to a person" (*Human Dignity* [Cambridge, MA: Harvard University Press, 2011], p. 51). Notice that, in this formulation, relations with persons are our first and primary consideration.

responsible for making something of one's life is *not* fundamentally one of discovering what relation one ought to have with oneself. That way of looking at the issue of responsibility is to effectively see oneself as one person among others. That would be exactly what is desired in the template of respect; but here one's existential responsibility places one's own person—and here, we mean oneself as an individual, concrete, flesh-and-blood human being[11]—in the *primary* role for ethical reflection, and thus of more fundamental concern than the role given to persons generally. As just indicated, we may or may not have responsibility for certain persons or things in our environment; but we do not cease to be responsible for ourselves until we cease to be.[12] Our primary concern must, therefore, be ourselves. Putting the point this way in no way implies a lack of concern for others, any more than the respect-for-persons perspective necessarily rejects a concern for oneself. The difference between them lies in what is ultimately the foundational wellspring for ethical action and judgment. In the respect-for-persons framework, one can respect oneself as a person and treat oneself accordingly. In a responsibility template, one is a person whose responsibilities will include interactions with others also similarly responsible for themselves.

In a sense, what we are saying is that in the template of responsibility, one does not end up having a certain kind of relation with oneself. Adam Smith is no doubt correct that we can spectate about ourselves and our own conduct, and that the dialectical self is a common enough factor in ethical reflection.[13] Moreover, relations with oneself have, since antiquity, been a feature of ethical self-development. Still, the notion of responsibility here is not essentially about having a relation with oneself, but rather one of *being* oneself. Consequently, as Aristotle indicates,[14] worrying about the right relationship to have with oneself would be a sign of ethical incompleteness. The object here is not one of constructing the right

---

[11] In the chapters that follow, we will use "person" in this very sense, unless otherwise noted.

[12] As an initial approach to reflections on ethics, the template of responsibility would seem to hold that individuals are prior to persons, whereas the template of respect would hold the opposite.

[13] For a contemporary example in this connection, one need only think of the work of Charles Taylor. See his work, *Sources of the Self: The Making of the Modern Identity* (Cambridge, MA: Harvard University Press, 1989). However, Taylor tends to prefer the term "dialogical."

[14] Aristotle, *Nicomachean Ethics* [hereafter *NE*], II 6.

relations with oneself, but of constructing the self in such a way that there is no division between the acting, willing, and being of the self. Ironically, the final object of the template of responsibility could be to lose the sense of self in favor of unselfconsciously being oneself.[15]

Ironically again, this perspective, and the one taken by us here and in the following chapters, indicates why the template of responsibility (and more particularly, an ethics of individualistic perfectionism that we advocate) is not an egoism. Indeed, the usual way of talking about egoism is to see how a proposed action or good in some way serves the self. But this is no different than making the self something to which one has a relationship; it is just proposed as the *only* relationship that matters. In the template of responsibility, the issue is not how something might benefit the self, but what kind of self one is making by taking on the benefit. The artificiality of egoistic actions is not just the exclusive focus upon self, but the relationalizing of the calculations upon which the actions are based.[16] Put in ontological terms, we are not a mere node in a network of relations, but the ground for such relations. The idea of making the template of responsibility a separate and alternative framework for ethics as against other forms is not exactly original with us. There was, first of all, Alasdair MacIntyre, whose *After Virtue* set itself squarely against contemporary ethical theory in the name of an alternative approach, one grounded in classical ethical thought, especially that of Aristotle and Aquinas.[17] Philippa Foot, in *Natural Goodness*, effectively opens by telling us that she has "in this book the overt aim of setting out a view of moral judgments very different from that of most moral philosophers writing today,"[18] and suggests by her opening chapter title that she may be offering a "fresh start" when it comes to thinking about ethics. And Julia Annas in her important work *The Morality of Happiness* opens by describing something like our ethics of responsibility as being an "entry point for ethical reflection" and notes the following:

---

[15] Sissela Bok (*Exploring Happiness*, p. 57) quotes Iris Murdoch as saying, "Happiness is a matter of one's most ordinary everyday mode of consciousness being busy and lively and unconcerned with self" (*The Nice and the Good* [New York: Penguin, 1978], p. 187).

[16] In this way, it is also like much utilitarian reasoning.

[17] Alasdair MacIntyre, *After Virtue* (Notre Dame, IN: University of Notre Dame Press, 1981).

[18] Philippa Foot, *Natural Goodness* (Oxford: Clarendon Press, 2001), p. 5.

> [T]hought about one's life is no longer seen as central to ethical philoso-phy, at least to ethical theory. At best the question is seen as marginal, to be answered when the main lines of the theory are already established.[19]

After indicating that ancient ethical philosophy did make the fram-ing problem of ethics one of (to put it in our terms) what to make of one's life, Annas goes on to note:

> [I]t is never felt [by ancient ethical philosophers] that the point of ethical theory is to help us to solve hard moral problems or to determine our rules of everyday duty. These are seen as tasks to be fulfilled once the outline structure of ethics has been got right, not as tasks which form that structure itself.[20]

In other words, the movement toward the sorts of issues that pre-dominate within the template of respect would be approached *within* the framework of the template of responsibility, because making something of one's own life is the primary problem and the defining purpose of ethics. Our duties and responses to hard moral questions are to be a function of the kinds of persons we ought to be making of ourselves, rather than the starting point for, and central means to, defining our own ethical nature.

In making the template of responsibility a fundamental alternative orientation for ethics, we are suggesting that this approach is not a relic of the past, but a living and worthy way of understanding ethics. The point is indicated by the title of Talbot Brewer's work, *The Retrieval of Ethics*, which points to the possibility that what is being retrieved is actually ethics itself.[21] The retrieval consists essentially in being unashamed, as Brewer puts it, to put forward the notion that the main focus of ethics is to consider what it means to live a good life, rather than finding a neutral pattern of relations within which to fit one's conception of how to conduct oneself. The quest for neu-

---

[19] Julia Annas, *The Morality of Happiness* (Oxford: Oxford University Press, 1993), p. 27.

[20] Ibid., p. 28. See also Julia Annas, *Intelligent Virtue* (Oxford: Oxford University Press, 2011).

[21] See note 4. Among other books trying to recapture ethics of the sort involved in what we are calling the template of responsibility, one might consider Philippa Foot's *Natural Goodness* or George W. Harris, *Agent-Centered Morality: An Aristotelian Alternative to Kantian Internalism* (Berkeley: University of California Press, 1999). For a history of many of the schools of thought likely to fit under this rubric, see Terence Irwin, *The Development of Ethics: A Historical and Critical Study*, Vols. 1 and 2 (Oxford: Oxford University Press, 2007).

trality may stem from the inclination to see ethics as a tool for social management, where rules must apply equally to all in the same way. That aspiration is itself made possible by the theoretical separation of the good from the right. No doubt as a result of the Sidgwickean opposition between self-interest and duty, what concerns one's own well-being generally (the good) has been relegated to one ethical paradigm and one's duties (the right) to another. So far as it goes, this separation may have some appeal to common sense; but it does not match our division of templates here, since an ethics within the template of respect will tend to relegate matters of self-fulfillment to a secondary or alternative status. That tendency is the result of the inherently other-oriented character of respect, which blends the self into others, issuing in a tendency toward universalism. By contrast, the paradigm of responsibility, while giving priority to self-perfection, recognizes the self as a social animal, and thus does not tend to separate the right from the good.

We have argued elsewhere that the division between the good and the right, here placed within the template of respect, tends to trivialize the good.[22] The good, in other words, tends to take a back seat to the search for universal norms of right, usually of justice, that can regulate what it means to give respect. So, although on the surface it looks as though one is equally free to discuss the right (relations among persons) and the good (the values, aspirations, and virtues one should have), the right turns out to be all that really matters when the template of respect's framework is employed. To say that the template of responsibility has the same problem of finding room in its framework for a discussion of right is, as Brewer notes,[23] to fail to understand the problem. For finding a place for one or the other is already to have adopted the framework of the template of respect, where the two are separate concerns, as noted above. The good and the right remain united in the template of responsibility, and understanding why that is so is to understand the problem (to which we address most of what follows in this book). We do not, therefore, in the end,

---

[22] Douglas B. Rasmussen and Douglas J. Den Uyl, *Norms of Liberty: A Perfectionist Basis for Non-Perfectionist Politics* [hereafter, *NOL*] (University Park: Pennsylvania State University Press, 2005), chap. 2.

[23] As previously noted, we deal with the separation between the good and the right in *NOL* chap. 2, but Brewer gives it a more substantial treatment in "Against Modern Dualism about the Good," in *The Retrieval of Ethics*, chap. 6, pp. 192–235.

have the convenience of "reconciling" the two fundamental ethical frameworks of respect and responsibility by allowing one to be used when we want to emphasize the right and the other when we want to emphasize the good. Thus, the template of responsibility, in which the good and the right are not understandable apart from each other, is a *primary alternative*, and not just another "perspective" on something called "ethics," in which the emphasis is placed on the good.

Needless to say, if there really are two fundamental and opposed approaches to understanding the meaning and nature of ethics, the obvious question is: How does one decide between them? A possible answer might be that one does not, in the end, have to choose between them, but could instead somehow embrace both. Such an answer seems to be, for example, that of Robert Nozick, in his division between moral pushes and moral pulls. Roughly, moral pulls for Nozick look like our template of respect, with pushes resembling the template of responsibility. One will recall that moral pushes concern "what behavior should flow from me," while moral pulls are "which behavior should flow toward you" (or others).[24] Nozick explicitly ties moral pushes to ancient moral philosophers and concludes that it is defective as the sole understanding of ethics, because "to center ethics mainly on moral push (as the Greek theorists did) leaves ethical behavior as, at best, fortunate fallout from living the best life."[25] Nozick concludes, partly as a consequence of this, that the ideal condition would be one where moral pushes and pulls have roughly equal sway, with neither commanding more (or less) of our understanding of ethics than the other.

---

[24] Robert Nozick, *Philosophical Explanations* (Cambridge, MA: Belknap Press of Harvard University Press, 1983), p. 401. In *The Examined Life: Philosophical Meditations* (New York: Simon and Schuster, 1989), Nozick's ethical views become more involved. He claims that ethics has four layers: respect, responsiveness, caring, and light (pp. 212–15); and in his last work, *Invariances: The Structure of the Objective World* (Cambridge, MA: Belknap Press of Harvard University Press, 2001), he notes that an ethics of respect "corresponds to an (extended) ethics mandating cooperation to mutual benefit. Here there are rules and principles mandating respecting another (adult) person's life and autonomy . . . issuing in a more general set of (what has been termed as negative) rights" (p. 280). He asserts that an ethics of respect is the ground for the other ethical layers (ibid., p. 280). Nozick sees ethics "as something rooted in the governance of opportunities for cooperation to mutual benefit, but which grows (slowly) outward from there, eventually reaching, in some cases, the loftiest heights of the ethical and spiritual imagination" (ibid., p. 284).

[25] Nozick, *Philosophical Explanations*, p. 402.

This equilibrium solution is certainly an attractive answer to the framework problem, because it would seem to allow for all our intuitions to be simultaneously captured. The solution does also, however, raise the question of why there are dual cores to ethics. That is a much harder problem to solve, and we shall speak of it more, both directly and indirectly, in what follows. Here we can only note our view: the equilibrium solution is not ultimately viable, because it contains an inherent tendency to drift to one side or the other, not just in specific cases, but generally. Indeed, we believe that Nozick actually looks at ethics within the template of respect, for two main reasons. First, the sentence just quoted indicates that so-called ethical behavior is not primarily about what one makes of one's life, but about how one presents oneself to others (either in the way we push ourselves or are pulled by them). Our relations are thus the fundamental problem. By contrast, in the template of responsibility, as we see it, the issue of how to present oneself to others is part of the deeper matter of what one is to make of one's life. Second, Nozick seems to embrace the division between the good and the right, whereas we have suggested we do not.[26] Accepting this division goes some distance in buttressing the needed duality of moral pushes and pulls; but it also signals a deontological drift toward the right, which is a turn away from the sort of perfectionism we will advocate. If so, duality is inherently unstable, leading one to end up pretty much where we are now, with paradigmatic templates for approaching ethics. In our view, then, one must choose one of the paradigms, and not hope for some imagined equilibrium between them.[27]

A full answer, however, to whether or not reconciliation is possible would, of course, involve an exploration of a number of other philosophical commitments one might have to make, including whether there is a need to adopt a comprehensive philosophical framework (as opposed to trying to solve the issue without reference to anything outside of ethics). Though we do have some things to say about comprehensive philosophy in Chapters 3 and 4, our discussion there is really limited to analyzing and criticizing the claim that political

[26] Ibid., pp. 494ff. Nozick in this section also admits an "obvious leaning toward deontology" (ibid., p. 498).

[27] In this respect, it seems that Rawls can be understood as regarding what we have called "frameworks" as intuitions, and not pre-theoretical framing orientations for ethical reflection itself. Thus, he sees the ethicists' task as finding equilibrium between them, rather than arguing for what in reality is most basic.

theory can be undertaken without any comprehensive commitments. To do more would take us well beyond what we can accomplish here. As our title suggests, we endeavor to say some things in favor of making a certain kind of "turn." As already implied, the perfectionist turn is, for us, a turn toward the template of responsibility and a turn away from the template of respect. We do not pretend that we will have sufficiently covered all the possible reasons for making the turn. We hope only to have indicated why making the turn is not implausible.

2. Responsibility versus Respect

It should be clear from the above that each of the two basic frameworks includes a family of implications as a consequence of its adoption.[28] Each template may thus include a large range of ethical theories. For the template of responsibility, we would allow much of ancient ethics, as well as medieval forms that continue that tradition. These might include the standard doctrines of Plato, Aristotle, the Stoics, Aquinas, and the like. It is quite conceivable that certain eighteenth-century ethicists such as Hume or Smith might fit here, as well, since their focus often tends to revolve around the well-being of the agent. Or, to put it another way, their focus is arguably to evaluate relations among persons in light of their contribution to well-being. We have indicated as well that most modern doctrines, whether Kantian deontology or utilitarianism or egoism or altruism or certain forms of sentimentalism, all fall under an ethics of respect.[29] We have noted above that, given what the nature of a "framework" is—namely, that frameworks are inherently archetypical—particular theories may possess some characteristics of an opposing archetype, while yet remaining within a given framework overall. At this level of abstraction, then, the question is whether there are some charac-

---

[28] "Implication" is not used here in a strictly logical sense. The concept is best thought of in terms of the phrase "family of implications," indicating a set of likely implications, rather than strictly logically entailed ones. This is because frameworks provide the scaffolding for a theory without its details. What is thus "implied" appears to cohere well with other dimensions of the scaffolding.

[29] Since our templates are paradigmatic, it is prudent to note that individual thinkers may not fit neatly into one template or another. This is partly a function of interpretation, which can differ widely with respect to any given thinker. Our purpose here is not to box in or categorize individuals, but rather to describe orientations as a means of helping to clarify and understand the nature of ethics.

teristics common to both archetypes. In our view, there is at least one thing both frameworks have in common, and that is a recognition that ethics requires a conception of worthiness. A concern and search for what is choice-worthy is the underlying unifying feature of both pre-theoretical orientations.

It is not uncommon these days, most especially among those outside of moral theory who speak about ethics, to confuse normatively guided behavior with ethical conduct. A person may follow norms because they are customary, handed down by authorities or tradition. Norms may be arbitrary, selected at random, chosen to maintain someone's position of power, a response to incentives, or biologically programmed. The conduct exhibited in following norms according to these prescriptive inducements may reflect actions *capable* of being thought worthy within a framework; but in the absence of worthiness, there is an absence of ethics. For there to be ethical conduct, an action must be recognized by an actor as conforming to or exemplifying a standard thought to be valuable because it represents some principle worthy of exemplification in action. The ethical framework, along with the details of an ethical theory, will describe the nature of any principle of worthiness; but agents can act on such principles without knowing, or even being able to articulate, all the dimensions of the standard of worthiness itself. It is enough that agents see their actions as not simply conforming to or exemplifying a norm, but as being justifiable because the norm it exemplifies is itself justifiable—that is, worthy. Thus, for example, one could follow a norm because "everyone else does." Yet, unless the agent has some sense of why what everyone is doing is worthy of being done, the conduct is not ethical. The point is the same if we are moved by our biological dispositions to be altruistic or egoistic. Without a recognition of worthiness, a behavior induced by any natural tendencies has all the outward signs of moral action, without actually being such.[30]

One might wish to claim that worthiness is epiphenomenal, and that it is the action itself that determines the ethical character of a given situation. Yet, actions devoid of any conception of their

---

[30] We are, of course, raising the issue of the so-called naturalistic fallacy, and we will discuss this and related issues in Chapters 5 and 6. We are also in accord with the general sensibilities of Stephen Darwall, whose emphasis on worthiness we would second, but whose particular understanding of it we put within the framework of respect and discuss in Chapter 7.

worthiness would lack the basis for attributing levels of merit to the agent. There may be some theories where individuals are not regarded, after all, as the basic unit of ethical action. But even if some other unit, such as the family or group, were considered primitive, it is still likely that ethical actions by these units need to have some conception of worthiness. Without the added dimension of worthiness, one has, no doubt, actions—even "beneficial" or "good" ones—but not yet a way to separate ethical from non-ethical conduct. It is important here to note, as well, that we should not confuse having an ethical framework for grasping the nature of worthiness with having a basis for making prescriptive recommendations. One can prescribe a course of action for all sorts of reasons, including unethical ones, that would allow one to say one *ought* to do X. A *moral* "ought" presents us with some sense of the worthiness of an action. Hence, the presence of an "ought" is not sufficient in itself to tag a proposition as a moral one. Moral philosophers, for this reason, speak of "moral oughts." The standards of worthiness may differ or receive different emphases from ethical theorists, but the need for a standard of worthiness applies to all cases.[31] That standard comes from there being something that must be regarded as an end in itself.

Aristotle noted long ago that for an action to be ethical, it must be chosen, chosen for the right reason, and chosen out of a fixed disposition.[32] One sees in Aristotle's claim that worthiness gets its meaning from both the notion of worthiness as well as the need for a framework. We have admitted that both of the frameworks under consideration here are consistent with the requirement for worthiness. The template of respect, however, insofar as it is concerned with defining relations among persons, has a special task of finding a way to distinguish worthy from unworthy relations among persons, since people can be organized in all sorts of ways that may have little to do with ethical norms. Because relations-among-persons is the defining issue of the template of respect, this framework cannot countenance any norm simply because that norm is interpersonal in nature, or

---

[31] The more interesting question here is not whether one's standard of worthiness is defensible, but whether one even has a conception of worthiness. For example, doing something because everyone else is doing it is to act in the absence of worthiness. But one might claim that a good, worthy reason for doing something is because everyone else does it—that being one's standard of worthiness. If we assume this is an indefensible standard of worthiness, does regarding an action to be worthy in light of it still put it in the category of "ethical" conduct?

[32] Aristotle, *NE*, 1105a 31–3.

because it defines relations among persons. Instead, there must be a standard which can serve as a basis for calling some relations worthy, and others not. But since actual empirical relations among persons are typically insufficient to serve as the basis for a standard of worthiness—since those may be wrongly motivated or structurally defective—there has been a tendency to rely upon meta-persons, such as noumenal selves, impartial spectators, social utility calculators, appeals to "public reason," and "views from nowhere" in order to keep within the framework, while still providing a basis for distinguishing the worthy from the unworthy relations. In the template of respect, then, the phenomenal characteristics of the agent and the agent's relationships are thought to be either irrelevant or insufficient as a basis for determining standards of worthiness. This move is needed precisely in order to subject ordinary human relations to some sort of test of worthiness, which obviously calls for a standard beyond those relations themselves. The basic standard used today to determine worthiness under this template is the degree to which an action impersonally conforms to the dictates of inherent human dignity.[33]

By contrast, the template of responsibility, when looking for standards of worthiness, proceeds from the agent's own actual actions, character, and circumstances, which are grasped empirically. Its central problem is one of deriving norms grounded in our nature, amidst the realities of our circumstances that can serve as independent measures of the actions themselves. We shall take up this issue more completely later, especially in Part II, when we discuss the teleological character of the good. For the moment, we can say—somewhat ironically, given the common notion that teleological arguments impose standards *upon* the agent—that worthiness is predicated endogenously upon the individual agent him- or herself in the template of responsibility. For the template of responsibility, it is the agent's actions or purposes—or, more metaphysically stated, the nature of the agent understood in terms of what and who and where the agent is as an individual—that is the ultimate ground

---

[33] Some, such as George Kateb, say that dignity is existential in a person and not fundamentally attributional, noumenal, or otherwise metaphysical. See *Human Dignity*, sec. 1, especially pp. 1–27. While we remain unconvinced by the argument there, it is interesting to note that Kateb feels compelled to give our species dignity, and not just leave dignity with individuals. This is because Kateb worries about the "egocentrism" of rights, if only individuals possess dignity (see sec. 2, pp. 28ff.); and leaving the matter there will not, it would seem, be enough to be relationship-focused.

for determining standards of worthiness. By "empirical" above, we mean being based on an awareness of the actual character and actions of individuals, as opposed to the application of some rational construct to those actions or character. In essence, then, the template of responsibility is, we believe, quite amenable to an individualistic perspective. In sum, both templates, though quite different in various ways, are alike in positing conditions of worthiness.

It might be argued that reason is also a common characteristic of both frameworks. Only beings with reason can respect one another; and only a being with reason can understand what it means to take responsibility for an action, as opposed to simply following a desire and acting. Indeed, only beings with reason can have a concept of worthiness! So far as it goes, we can say that both these frameworks share in giving reason, in this sense, a central place. However, as we shall see later, reason is not like worthiness in its level of funda-mentality, if we look to more than what we have just posited. In the template of respect, the relevant properties of reason that tend to get emphasized—for example, universality and neutrality—are not the ones central to the template of responsibility. In the latter case, reason as a cognitive tool for understanding the nature or properties of things is more critical than its formal properties. This more or less realist conception of reason will be employed throughout the discussions to follow, and its role will be considered in various ways. As such, we need not delay ourselves with it here.

We do not mean to conclude, however, that worthiness is the only dimension on which the two templates might find common ground. There may be other dimensions, or perhaps other ways of noting a commonality, that do not appear to be generated by one of the templates alone. Nozick's "being an I," where having a "special mode of reflexive consciousness which only an I, only a self, has,"[34] might be an example of a neutral formulation acceptable to both templates. Here, the deontological associations carried by the term "dignity" are not necessarily directly implied; nor is there a prejudice against forms of naturalism; so both templates might be able to work with Nozick's formulation. That is to say, "dignity," so commonly referenced in much of contemporary ethics, could be easily derived from the foregoing formulation of Nozick's, as could the teleological naturalism we would advance. Hence, "being an I" could be neutral with respect to both templates.

[34] Nozick, *Philosophical Explanations*, p. 453.

Perhaps we are best served, then, by looking for a couple of salient differences between the templates as a means to their further clarification. We can begin by considering what is likely to be the ultimate value in each system, and why that would be the case. As we have already noted concerning the template of respect, the foundation for determining worthiness is dignity. If dignity is the basis for worthiness in the template of respect, then its ultimate value is what we shall call "consideration." To respect dignity, we must give consideration to all those who possess it. A failure to give consideration is the fundamental type of moral failing in the template of respect. We see this reflected today in calls for inclusiveness found in doctrines from Nussbaum and Sen to Rawls and Gaus. Perhaps there is no better and more complete account of consideration, and possibly of the nature of the template of respect, than Stephen Darwall's second-person perspective and his distinction between appraisal and recognition respect. We shall have a few things to say about this theory in Chapter 7. Here we need only note that the template of respect allows for the possibility that the mere presence of another person is sufficient in itself to give rise to certain fundamental sorts of moral considerations with a corresponding set of obligations.

But we need not exclude utilitarian theories from this claim about the primacy of consideration. The members of the set of beings for whom our calculations are to maximize value belong to that set because they possess certain qualities that give the appropriate actions their worthiness. A failure of consideration—that is, a failure to consider an agent or factor about the agent relevant to the calculation—would render the calculation itself a failure and thus of no moral worth. Saying that we must be careful about consideration in this utilitarian context is another way of saying that the members of the defined class are dignified within this theory. The basis for dignity could be the possession of certain qualities, such as the ability to feel pleasure and pain; but whatever the basis, consideration must be given to beings which possess the appropriate qualities. Obviously, if pleasure and pain are alone the basis, the question arises as to whether the class of beings to whom one is required to give consideration would include animals, as well. The point is not to argue, one way or the other, over the inclusion of animals in the class of qualified beings, but rather to notice that the utilitarian enterprise must give primacy to the value of consideration in order to even begin to function.

If the fundamental value of the template of respect is

consideration, its fundamental virtue is tolerance or openness. Tolerance, in this sense, encompasses classic willingness to tolerate as well as inclusiveness. To give consideration is to be open to all that must be considered, which is at least a minimal way of understanding what it means to be inclusive. One is continually on guard not to miss considering a qualified candidate for inclusion. And although tolerating doctrines one may disapprove of is not quite complete openness, it is a recognition that the relation is of more importance than the substance of a given doctrine itself. This does not mean tolerance and openness cannot be virtues within the framework of the template of responsibility. It only means that these virtues will tend to be given special emphasis or priority within the template of respect.

For the template of responsibility, the basis for determining worthiness is human flourishing or well-being of some sort. Its ultimate value is integrity. Integrity expresses itself interpersonally in honor; but when applied to the agent herself, the term "integrity" signifies a coherent, integral whole of virtues and values, allowing for consistency between word and deed and for reliability in action. Integrity is probably still the best term to use and represents the central virtue of this framework.[35] For if the fundamental problem of ethics is taking responsibility for figuring out how to fashion one's life, then a certain coherent picture of what one wants to be immediately reveals the object of the enterprise. Perhaps "honor" is too old-fashioned a term for today's usage, but it does capture the sense of what it means to greet the world with integrity. Thus, in relationships with others, a person of honor is someone one can count upon to be consistent with her own mode of being, because there is an integrated self that endeavors to maintain the nexus of principles and dispositions with actions that support and express them. Unlike the framework of the template of respect, where what is shared in interpersonal relationships is the common rule or normative command that defines the ethical relationship, what one finds in the template of responsibility is that the ethical relationship cannot be defined prior to the intersec-

---

[35] For an extended discussion of integrity, see Greg Scherkoske, *Integrity and the Virtues of Reason* (Cambridge: Cambridge University Press, 2013). Although Scherkoske's epistemic understanding of integrity is not our own, our emphasis on practical reason does make his discussion one of value. See also Harris, *Agent-Centered Morality*, particularly as it pertains to the attempt by some neo-Kantians to combine impersonalism with an Aristotelian ethics' concern for integrity.

tion of agents which compose it, since those agents are the basis for defining what the relationship should be.[36]

In speaking in terms of integrity as a coherency of self, one imagines immediately the objection that someone might decide to live a spontaneous, disjointed, and incoherent life, having thereby addressed the fundamental problem of what kind of life to fashion, but not in a way that results in integrity. The problem with this objection (and with a number of similar objections we shall deal with in the chapters that follow) is that one may accomplish this incoherent life in one of two ways: either by planning for it, or by abdicating the responsibility to work on figuring one's life out. In the first case, planning well for incoherency is itself a kind of integrity with its own internal logic.[37] In the second case, one does not have an objection, but rather an example of ethical failing, for the point is not that an incoherent life is not possible or not a life, but rather that such is not an *ethical* life. To *be* responsible for one's life has normative implications for *taking* responsibility—at least in the sense that whatever one does, there are effects upon what one becomes. That fact alone compels us to consider measures of success and failure. Thus, to fail to take responsibility does not lessen one's being responsible, but only the degree of success ascribed to it.

Besides having different orientations toward their basic values and virtues, our two frameworks also have rather different understandings of the role reason plays in determining the structure of moral norms. We have already examined one role for reason in helping formulate a notion of worthiness. Here we are referring instead to what could be called reason as it affects the structure of a moral judgment. Obviously, such an issue is a complicated business; and we shall have a number of things to say about moral judgments and reason in various chapters to follow. Here it is enough to note that, contrary to assumptions held by the majority of contemporary ethicists, reason's structural output in ethics does not cash itself out in only one form. In one way or another, the rational structure of a

---

36 It is not that we cannot describe certain general principles of a relationship as a friendship or one of keeping a promise or the like, but rather that such descriptions are abstractions in the template of responsibility and a pre-existing bundle of obligations in the template of respect.

37 At a radical level it cannot be done because coherency and incoherency contradict each other. But what people usually mean here is a concerted effort to not fall into regularized patterns of indifference action. To avoid this systematically requires a good deal of integrated action! Consider Henry David Thoreau.

judgment within the template of respect is caught up in the problem of securing universality. Besides guiding the search for principles that could be universalized according to some standard of formal supervenience (for example, treat similar cases similarly), universality in the template of respect endeavors to secure judgments that would substantively command the respect of every rational being. There are subtle variations ranging from what every rational being would not reject, to what all would positively command. The object of universality here, however, supposes a substantive like-mindedness on any moral conclusion that qualifies as rational.[38] That is to say, assuming no biases or defectiveness in reasoning, if P_1 draws a rational conclusion about the morality of doing action A, then P_2–P_n would also need to draw the same conclusion about A. This is as true for the utilitarian as for the traditional deontologist. For if P rationally concludes that A maximizes overall social utility—and we assume for the sake of argument that the rationality and feasibility of the way that is determined has itself met the test of rationality— then P_2–P_n would be drawing exactly the same conclusion about A. Obviously for the deontologist, if A is a duty that reason commands, then anyone else under similar circumstances and conditions must also accede to A. Even the modern consequentialist, who might not otherwise be a classical utilitarian, would claim that if effects E stemming from A are the best according to some rationally accepted standard, then A would be recommended equally to all under like conditions.

In the template of responsibility, by contrast, if P_1 draws a rational conclusion about the morality of doing action A, it does not follow that P_2–P_n would likewise have to draw the same conclusion under the same circumstances. Hence, an action A which is correct for P_1 may not be correct for P_2–P_n, even under similar conditions. This result is the case because, under this template, P_1 is not substantively interchangeable with P_2–P_n, for their particular form of agency is the basis for structuring the moral judgment, rather than serving as an instantiation of one. Moreover, it is also conceivable that judgments made about the correctness of A for P_1 might legitimately be different between P_2 and P_3, and P_1 herself. Though it would not be correct to hold that the variation of rational assessments of A is unlimited, the template of responsibility is open to the possibility that there could

---

[38] See, for example, Derek Parfit, *On What Matters: Volume One* (Oxford: Oxford University Press, 2011), pp. 338ff.

be a plurality of plausible ethical choices, no one of which is necessarily decisive over others.[39] Though perhaps looking like relativism or situationalism at this stage, such conclusions, as we shall see later, are not implications of our position. Indeed, we think of ourselves largely as objectivists in ethics. In general, the agent-centered focus of the template of responsibility opens the door to the possibility that the right course of action might differ from one agent to the next, even with respect to their conduct toward others. In addition, that focus also opens the door to the possibility of alternative weightings of principles and actions between agents. Thus, the structure of moral judgments in the template of responsibility is ultimately different in character from that of those in the template of respect, in which actions are typically constrained by some inherent standard of rationality. In the template of responsibility, by contrast, standards of rationality are developed in terms of the agent's nature, dispositions, circumstances, and abilities, rather than the formal properties of rationality itself.[40]

It is, no doubt, the agent-centered nature of the template of responsibility that gives pause to many who reflect on ethics, and precisely because of its being so focused upon the agent. We saw earlier, for example, Nozick's worries that we would not somehow get to ethics if we stuck only with ethical pushes. Nozick further worries that even conceptions of Kantian autonomy—what he calls "Kantian structuring"—produce too much ethical push and not enough ethical

---

[39] It should be noted, too, that it does not follow from this that there are no normative judgments that are essentially decisive for all, only that the universe may not be (and is not, according to our conception of ethics) populated solely by the universally decisive ones. This is not a version of the perfect/imperfect duty distinction, or of the distinction between supererogatory and necessary obligations. In the template of responsibility, any candidates for a universally decisive moral judgment would not thereby have a higher level of moral significance or centrality than judgments which do not bear all the marks of a universalized proposition. Indeed, while what we call "metanorms" (which is the concept we develop in Rasmussen and Den Uyl, *NOL*, to explain the exact character of individual rights) might be candidates for such norms, they are to our minds of lesser moral significance than conclusions which are not so decisively universal. Still, we do not wish to exclude from the template of responsibility a theory which holds that P_1-P_n would have to draw the same conclusion. It is just that, in this template, that conclusion would not be required by the nature of reason itself.

[40] We shall, in various contexts throughout this work, return to the points made in the last two paragraphs. Moreover, the distinctions used here will be defended and further explained.

pull.[41] This worry arises because Kantian autonomy, and the commands of ethics that follow from it, derives too exclusively from the self, leaving one wondering how to incorporate or give equal status to the other. For Nozick, as we saw, we need to give more attention to others who will be generating the requisite (and balancing) ethical pulls; but Nozick is certainly not alone in his concern. For now, it is enough to note that perhaps not all ethical theories under the template of responsibility will be as agent-centered as our own (or perhaps as neutral across agents within the template of respect, as some would have it).[42] Furthermore, we suspect that part of the concern has to do with the rather different roles reason plays in the ethical theorizing in the two templates, than it does with substantive ethics itself. For if the formal properties of rationality are going to be at least partially determinative of the acceptable substantive descriptions of moral conduct, then starting off our theorizing with the self always leaves open the question of how to include the other. Templates of respect want to avoid that problem by making ethics essentially relational. In the template of responsibility, however, assuming the agent is regarded in some essential fashion as a social animal, the presence of the other is already built into the moral landscape. We do not need to "get to" or "derive" the other in order to begin talking about what one should make of one's life. Others are already a part of that life, precisely because one *is* a social animal.[43]

There is another way in which the rationality features of the two templates may affect the degree of satisfaction theorists come to expect from them. If the template of respect is wedded to some of the formal properties of rationality in its structuring of moral judgments, it will be less satisfied with ambiguity and open-endedness than an approach that does not have such strictures. In essence, the template of respect tends to look at the job of moral theory as being one of providing answers to the question of what we morally must do. In

---

[41] Nozick, *Philosophical Explanations*, pp. 550ff.

[42] For example, someone like J. L. A. Garcia, who would put the virtues themselves at the center of ethics, and who would seem to fall within the template of responsibility, would not seem to put as much weight upon the agent-centered character of the good as we do. See, for example, his essay "The Virtues of the Natural Moral Law," in *Natural Moral Law in Contemporary Society*, ed. Holger Zaborowski (Washington, DC: Catholic University of America Press, 2010), pp. 99–140.

[43] See Chapter 1. Also, we argue in Rasmussen and Den Uyl, *NOL*, pp. 141–3 that individualism is not atomism.

the template of responsibility, however, it is possible to hold that the job of moral theory is not to provide answers about what must be done, but rather to provide aid in the form of principles and insights, on the basis of which individuals can fashion conclusions for themselves according to their circumstances. Although we would not want to claim that the template of responsibility requires this degree of openness to ambiguity and radical pluralism, it is instructive of the nature of this approach to ethics that the responsibility template can be comfortable with such openness. In this respect, the template of responsibility is significantly less "rationalistic" than is the template of respect. Its judgments are meant to fit patterns of actual practice, rather than to encourage a formal structure, as would be the tendency under the template of respect. As such, its form of rationality would be along the lines of the realism hinted at above, rather than a more formal rationalism. In this respect, as we have also suggested, ethical norms of universal applicability are not necessarily of a superior or more fundamental status in the template of responsibility, as they would be within the template of respect.

The rationalism of the template of respect no doubt dominates the modalities of ethical theorizing today in ways that obscure possible alternative modes of understanding the functionality of ethics in social life. The tendency toward universalism and law-like pronouncements in the template of respect encourages the view that ethics is a tool of social control and one that trumps all other candidates in cases of conflict. "A is wrong" is sufficient in itself to disallow consideration of any alternative reason for doing A; and "A is right" is sufficient in itself to require doing A. On this model, ethics is both a necessary and sufficient reason for taking or avoiding any action; and if it is not the sole regulator of action, all other candidates are at least in need of permission from ethics for doing so. Consequently, ethics within the template of respect organizes patterns of consistent behavior among diverse actors along the lines dictated by the normative rules derived from the ethical theory. In short, ethics becomes the principal vehicle by which to command or create social order.[44] In the template of responsibility, however, one would expect the socially organizing norms of ethics as universally applied to be few and functionally limited. Social coordination would be predicated more upon cooperation than upon conformity

---

[44] See our discussion of this issue in section 2, "Ethics versus Politics and Law: The Importance of Liberal Political Order," of Chapter 2.

to a standard; and such normative standards as do exist would as likely be descriptions of modes of cooperation or practices, as they would be the basis for imposing such order. Consequently, the template of responsibility sees ethics not so much as the means of defining relations among persons, but more as a tool for guiding and regulating the interests and purposes of agents as they search for shared reasons to interact. Cooperation is more the epigraph for the template of responsibility, which holds accommodation and mutual interest as the basis of social relations. For the template of respect, by contrast, obligation is more the epigraph and duty the basis for cementing social unity.

In subsequent chapters, we develop further the role of norms within the template of responsibility along the lines just suggested. To reiterate, it is not our contention that all ethical theories within the template of responsibility need be as accommodating toward interest-based social connections as we find acceptable. One would not be inclined to think, for example, of the classical natural law position as being as loose in its understanding of permissible social relations; yet, we would put that tradition largely within the template of responsibility. The template of responsibility, then, can accommodate the sort of open-endedness that we mentioned earlier, even if it is not the only approach within it. This is because an ethics within the template of responsibility is more interested in living well than in living rightly. And as Kant ably illustrated, there is less certainty in seeking to live well than in seeking to live rightly.[45] From our perspective, then, we would say that the template of respect issues forth ethical doctrines that wield the sword of righteousness, whereas the template of responsibility yields doctrines more dependent upon the exercise of discipline. If so, the social outlook of the template of responsibility will be one of finding ways to enhance the forms of cooperation that have been created whereas, under the template of respect, the prospect is one of either defining the forms of social interaction themselves, or reforming the ones that exist, in order to meet the required standards of conduct.

---

[45] Standard utilitarianism does nothing to change this. It, too, is only interested in living rightly—that is, in organizing conduct so it meets the rule of maximized overall social utility.

3. Individualistic Perfectionism: An Ethics of Responsibility

It is clear, from all that we have said to this point, that the turn we wish to make is toward the template of responsibility and some sort of perfectionist theory falling under its rubric. In this regard, we offer four structural pillars for our particular approach within the template of responsibility. These pillars follow the four structural characteristics Julia Annas uses to describe ancient ethics.[46] The first of these is that the object of ethics and the standard for measuring ethical conduct center around the agent having a final end that is a good for that agent. Second, that final end is not a good like other goods, even those pursued for their own sake, but a way of organizing the other goods. Third, the final good is concerned with one's life as a whole, and not simply with parts of one's life. And finally, the final good does have objective properties and some formal constraints.[47] These propositions guide us throughout what follows in the chapters to come, in explicating and defending a version of a neo-Aristotelian, eudaimonistic, naturalistic ethics. We regard such an ethics as being "perfectionist" because its norms are grounded in a developmental (teleological) process dictated by the nature of the agent. These norms serve to orient the agent toward the agent's own flourishing or "perfection." We seek to explain in what the agent's flourishing consists and to argue that such flourishing is integrally tied to the agent's own particular circumstances, nature, and dispositions—all of which must factor into an integrated set of relations determined by practical wisdom. Hence, we refer to this understanding of ethics as individualistic perfectionism (IP).

Part I begins with an account of the basic characteristics of IP, so as to help both to define it and to contrast it with alternative ethical and political perspectives throughout the chapters that follow. But recognizing even the viability of IP is significantly impeded by the general tendency to see ethics and politics as having essentially similar, if not identical, structural characteristics. These similarities include universality, agent-neutrality, and a legislative propensity when considering one's obligations. In light of this, we follow our

---

[46] Annas, *The Morality of Happiness*, pp. 34–45.

[47] Annas notes that in Aristotle, two of the formal constraints were completeness and self-sufficiency, the latter often being dropped by later philosophers (ibid., pp. 40–3). Our account of the formal constraints appears mostly in Chapters 1, 5, and 6.

statement of the characteristics of IP with an examination of the difficulties involved in searching for universal ethical and political principles. We give particular attention to liberalism, both because we hold to liberalism as a political doctrine and, more importantly, because liberalism is particularly disposed to the problems standing in the way of IP. Our argument is that the basic characteristics of IP imply certain conclusions about how to see liberalism—most notably, that liberalism should not be regarded as an ethical philosophy, because to do so would involve the wrong understanding of the kind of universalism that must be given in an ethical justification of a political/legal order.

The tendency to give structural similarity to ethics and politics is especially aggravated in liberal political theory in two ways. First, fueled by the belief that consent alone matters, there is the desire to avoid comprehensive philosophizing. The second impetus for structural similarity in ethics and politics is the tendency to see liberal political values as the primary moral values. Since we ourselves defend political liberalism, we believe the most efficient way both to indicate that there is an alternative foundation for liberalism, and to clarify the distinctive nature of our ethical theory, is to devote some attention to the relation between ethics and politics as discussed by some prominent liberal thinkers. We use our discussion of the characteristics of IP and the issues we raise about universality as a basis for criticizing certain liberal theories. Because of the two tendencies just mentioned, this use of IP and its associated doctrines becomes necessary if ethics is to be divested of its political structure. The result of these discussions, we hope, is not only the general liberation of ethics from politics, but also the restoration of ethics to a superior level of prominence.

Having distinguished the nature and uniqueness of IP from liberal politics and alternative conceptions of ethics, and having identified the basic properties of IP, we have now made "the perfectionist turn." It thus becomes necessary to give a defense and account of the properties of IP we have identified earlier, and to say something about how they might function, which is the purpose of Part II.

Having freed ethics from political theory, we change our focus to the basic questions of ethics and metaethics. Our aim now is to explain and defend the foundational principles upon which IP rests. We argue that IP, which is grounded in a life-based, non-reductionist account of natural teleology, does not commit the so-called naturalistic fallacy—which involves not one issue, but many—and that it can meet J. L. Mackie's challenge as to what in reality provides the basis for moral evaluation. *It is the life-form of a being, not its mere existence, that provides the basis of our understanding its good*; and for living beings such as ourselves, that can choose and reason, it is the basis for any obligations we might have. As a result, a large measure of this part of the book involves our championing the idea that ethical knowledge exists because "a moral evaluation does not stand over against the statement of a matter of fact, but rather has to do with facts about a particular subject matter" and because life is at the center of this subject matter.[48]

In order to better appreciate all that IP involves, we also in many places compare IP with various forms of constructivism. Constructivism holds that evaluative or normative claims are true or false because they are based on principles that are constructions of moral thought, and not because they are discovered, detected, or grounded in anything real apart from such thought. We argue that, contrary to the constructivist approach, "human flourishing" needs to be understood in a perfectionist manner—that is, as a naturalism where moral truths are ultimately more realized and discovered than constructed. We maintain that IP has the resources to provide a controlling vision for a perfectionist account of human flourishing, and thus one need not resort to constructivism either for foundational purposes or to give ethics subtlety or depth. Particularly, we show that human good can be fundamentally self-directed in character, without requiring that it be determined in a constructivist manner. In addition, constructivism faces a problem of its own—namely, lacking a basic standard for judging practical reasoning which, in our account, is provided by teleology. In keeping with our rejection of constructivism and our acceptance of the individualist understanding of human flourishing, we conclude by introducing a powerful analogy between the practitioner of practical wisdom and the entrepreneur, an analogy which we hope will indicate how practical ethical action does not function like the legislative directives so common in other ethical theories.

In the Afterword, we take up the question of whether, even granting all we want to hold about IP, the conception of morality it endorses is but a middling sort of morality, incapable of accounting for great forms of good or evil. In contrast to the view that we

---

[48] Foot, *Natural Goodness*, pp. 5 and 24.

can only account for such extremes when we move away from self-responsibility in some way and directly consider the other, we argue that it is precisely the focus on self-responsibility that best accounts for the extremes of evil or goodness.

Part I

Making the Turn

1

An Overview of Individualistic Perfectionism

Everybody, however, must resolutely hold fast to his own peculiar gifts, in so far as they are peculiar only and not vicious, in order that propriety, which is the object of our inquiry, may the more easily be secured. For we must so act as not to oppose the universal laws of human nature, but, while safeguarding those, to follow the bent of our own particular nature, and even if other careers should be better and nobler, we may still regulate our own pursuits by the standard of our own nature.

Cicero, *De Officiis*

Perfectionism is a normative theory that treats the actualization of human nature as pivotal to an account of human good and moral obligation. Particularly for the Aristotelian perfectionist tradition, *eudaimonia*—happiness, or human flourishing—is the ultimate good or *telos* (end) for human beings; and living in a practically wise and virtuous manner is the primary obligation dictated by that end. Succinctly stated, human flourishing is understood by us to mean "the exercise of one's own practical wisdom." Though there are some, as we shall see in "The Perfectionist Turn" chapter of Part II, who think that human flourishing and the goods and virtues that constitute it can be adequately understood apart from the actualization of human nature, we do not. As we shall argue there, we do not think that there is an ontological gap between what is a good human being and what is good for a human being. Indeed, we believe holding that human flourishing is the ultimate end and good for human beings is compatible with there being many diverse forms of human flourishing[1] and with self-direction being vital to the very actuality of human flourishing, and we emphasize both in what follows.

---

[1] See Douglas B. Rasmussen and Douglas J. Den Uyl, *Norms of Liberty: A Perfectionist Basis for Non-Perfectionist Politics* [hereafter, *NOL*] (University Park: Pennsylvania State University Press, 2005), pp. 173–83 for a refutation of John Gray's claim (which is inspired in part by Joseph Raz's discussion of incommensurability in *The Morality of Freedom* [Oxford: Clarendon Press, 1986], pp. 321–66) that value pluralism is destructive of the very idea of perfectionism.

Finally, we further believe that acknowledging the self-directed and individualized character of human flourishing is compatible with its being both real and socially achieved. We thus seek to advance a neo-Aristotelian account of human flourishing, in which human good is characterized by these interrelated and interpenetrating features: (1) objectivity, (2) inclusivity, (3) individuality, (4) agent-relativity, (5) self-directedness, and (6) sociality.

1. Features of Human Flourishing

In what follows,[2] we shall indicate why we regard each of these features as potentially compatible with the others, and how they might combine to provide a conception of perfectionism that is different from more traditional accounts. We will also provide reasons why such a conception is plausible for characterizing human good, though our argument will be more fully developed in the ensuing chapters. We shall begin with what is arguably one of the more distinctive features of our account, relative to traditional eudaimonic theories: agent-relativity.

AGENT-RELATIVITY

Crucial to our account of perfectionism is the distinction between an agent-neutral and agent-relative understanding of any value, ranking, or reason V. According to an agent-neutral understanding: if a person P_1 is justified in holding V, then P_2–P_n under appropriately similar conditions *must* hold V as well. Morally speaking, individuals or persons are interchangeable. Hence, it is impossible to weight V more heavily, or at all, simply because it is one's own V. Such an understanding of V is sometimes called "impersonalism" and is often said to be definitive of the so-called moral point of view.[3] According to an agent-relative understanding, by contrast, there are no V's that are not the V's for some person or other. V's necessarily involve a reference to some person. Hence, the distinctive presence of V_1 in world W_1 is a basis or reason for P_1 ranking W_1 over W_2, even though V_1

---

[2] Some of the paragraphs below have been taken, others adapted, from Rasmussen and Den Uyl, *NOL*, pp. 129–32, 136–7, 159–60, and 172–3.

[3] This point of view calls on one to be impartial not only in the sense of objective, but also in the sense of impersonal. For a valuable discussion of moral-point-of-view theories, see Kai Nielsen, "Moral Point of View Theories," *Crítica: Revista Hispanoamericana de Filosofía* 31.93 (Diciembre 1999): pp. 105–16.

may not be a basis or reason for any other person ranking W_1 over W_2. Thus, it is possible for G_1 to be the good for P_1 and what P_1 ought to pursue, without either being the case for P_2–P_n.

According to our individualistic perfectionist account, human good is agent-relative. It is always and necessarily the good for some person or other. There is thus no human good-at-large. Human good is not merely an occurrence in, a happening to, or a possession of some person, as if the person were a mere placeholder for human good.[4] Rather, human good arises, obtains, and exists in relationship to a person's life itself and expresses itself through the immanent activities that constitute the perfecting or actualizing of that individual human being. Human good is *essentially* the good-for-some-person-or-other.[5]

As a result, it is not the case that ethical reasoning will require one to be indifferent to whose good is being achieved.[6] Contrary to an agent-neutral view, it is legitimate to give more weight to a good because it is one's own, even though it is not necessarily anyone else's. By contrast, Thomas Nagel has famously argued against the agent-relativity of V's. He has contended that if V's were agent-relative, then one would not seek some end today for the sake of attaining some end in the future. In effect, one would disassociate one's present self from one's future self. However, since we are persisting individuals, Nagel claims, V's must be outside of time, and so one must have equal concern for all moments of time.[7] Moreover,

---

[4] Though we share different views about the nature of agent-relativity and ethics in general, we think that Connie S. Rosati's "Objectivism and Relational Good," *Social Philosophy & Policy* 25.1 (Winter 2008): pp. 314–49 does an excellent job in countering Moorean and neo-Moorean attempts to explain agent-relative good as merely the possession of agent-neutral good.

[5] What is right (in the sense of that which is appropriate) is agent-relative, too, according to individualistic perfectionism. (See our discussion of practical wisdom in section 2 of this chapter.) But, as we argue in Rasmussen and Den Uyl, *NOL*, a right (in the sense of a basic ethical claim on how the political/legal order should regulate human conduct) is not agent-relative, but rather is a metanormative principle that determines the context for the practice of the ethical or moral life. We explain this idea in section 2 of Chapter 2. Though a right in this latter sense is an ethical principle, its fundamental function is political and legal.

[6] As we will argue in Chapter 2, the principle of universalizability does not require the adoption of impersonalism or the rejection of an agent-relative account of human good or moral obligation.

[7] Thomas Nagel, *The Possibility of Altruism* (Princeton: Princeton University Press, 1970), pp. 58–62.

Nagel has insisted that just as V's are timeless, so, too, they are not restricted to specific individuals. V's of others give one as much a reason to act as do V's pertaining to one's own future.[8] Hence, it is false that V's are agent-relative.

We find Nagel's arguments unpersuasive. First, there is nothing about holding that V's are agent-relative that prevents differentiating a V-for-P_1-now from a V-for-P_1-tomorrow, and hence nothing that makes P_1 incapable of seeing herself as a persisting individual, or of doing something today for the sake of achieving something tomorrow. Moreover, there is nothing in Nagel's arguments that prevents a person from holding a value *over* time. Granted, V's are not limited to any particular time for some person. But while they can be sought or exercised *any* time, that seeking or exercising must happen *some* time. Yet, this is not the same as claiming that V's are timeless, and certainly no grounds for saying that equal concern for each moment of time is required. Indeed, if equal concern for each moment of time were required, then there would be no basis for rationally preferring, *ceteris paribus*, a good now to a good later. And, ironically, if there is an equal concern for a good at all moments, then there is really no basis for preferring any good at all, since preferences occur in time. Second, though V's can be V's for *any* person, they must be V's for *some* person. There are no agent-less V's, and definitely no basis for saying that the V's of others must be of equal worth to one's own V's.[9]

At this point, it is important to note that agent-relativity should not be confused with so-called ethical egoism. Such weighting can be found in what is generally understood as altruistic conduct, because it is perfectly possible for P_1's V's to be for the sake of others, while the V's of P_2–P_n are not. It is just as much an example of agent-relativity for it to be only valuable for you to sacrifice excellence in your career for the sake of having full concern for your family and friends, as it is only valuable for you to pursue excellence in your career at the cost of a less than full concern for your family and friends. Both are examples of agent-relativity. Moreover, it should be emphasized that this possibility does not show that such professedly altruistic V's are agent-neutral, because benefiting others must still be a value, reason, or ranking *for* P_1, even though it need not be so for P_2–P_n. Finally,

---

[8] Ibid., pp. 87–8 and 104–7.

[9] See also Eric Mack, "Against Agent-Neutral Values," *Reason Papers* 14 (Spring 1989): pp. 76–86.

the fact that P_1–P_{10} sacrifice career for family, while P_{11}–P_{20} do not, does not show that the value V in any given set of choices is thereby neutral between agents, since something's *being* (or not being) V is dependent upon *each* agent's particular valuation.

We need to further note that just because something is only valuable relative to some person, its value is not necessarily a mere matter of that person's attitude toward it or, indeed, of its being desired, wanted, or chosen. Nor is it merely a matter of a person's point of view or beliefs.[10] The question "Relative to what?" is important here. Human good is agent-relative in the sense that it is essentially related to some person or other, but this does not mean that any given V must be rendered as essentially related to what a person merely desires, wants, or chooses. Our neo-Aristotelian theory assumes that a human being is more than a bundle of passions and desires, and that there are real potentialities, needs, and circumstances that characterize both what and who a person is. That one is interested in, or has a desire for, something does not necessarily mean that it is *good* for one.

What is even more important, however, is that agent-relativity is compatible with human flourishing's being the ultimate good or telos for human beings. As already implied, since we hold that there is no flourishing-at-large, flourishing is essentially the flourishing-for-some-person. The human telos just is, then, the flourishing of each individual. Its valuable character lies in the immanent activities that comprise the fulfillment of individual human beings. As such, human flourishing is not something that competes with the good of individual human beings—a view we consider in Chapter 5—but instead is the very flourishing of their lives. Thus, it is perfectly consistent for the flourishing of individual human beings to be valuable in its own right *and* essentially related to individual persons.[11] Indeed, this is fundamental to our ethical ideal.

---

[10] Thus, it is possible on our account of agent-relativity for someone to falsely believe that X-ing is good for them. The sheer fact of their believing X-ing is good for them would not make it "true for them." Thus, our view avoids one of the main reasons for rejecting agent-relative accounts of human good. For example, see Thomas Hurka, "'Good' and 'Good For,'" *Mind* 96.381 (1987): pp. 71–3. Also, see Talbot Brewer's critique of person-relative goodness in his work, *The Retrieval of Ethics* (Oxford: Oxford University Press, 2009), p. 219.

[11] See Richard Kraut, *Against Absolute Goodness* (Oxford: Oxford University Press, 2011). Kraut argues in favor of the idea that good is always the good *for* or *of* something and against the idea of non-relational good and, more particularly, against the "impersonally good." If one identifies the adjectives "absolute" or

INCLUSIVITY

In our understanding of individualistic perfectionism (IP), we hold that human flourishing is an activity that is the ultimate end or good of human life, but it is not the only activity of inherent worth. It is not a "dominant" end that instrumentalizes the value of everything else. Rather, it is "the *most* final end and is never sought for the sake of anything else, because it includes all final ends."[12] Human flourishing is thus an "inclusive" end. It comprises basic or "generic" goods and virtues—for example, such goods as knowledge, health, friendship, creative achievement, beauty, and pleasure; and such virtues (or rational dispositions) as integrity, temperance, courage, and justice.[13] They are valuable not as mere means to human flourishing, but as expressions or realizations of it—at least partially, if not completely so. As such, these goods and virtues are final[14] ends and valuable in

---

"*simpliciter*" with the non-relational, then we, too, have no problem in arguing against absolute good or good *simpliciter*. But for us, the more basic point is that the relational character of good flows from the very essence of good. As we argue in Chapter 2, it is perfectly possible to abstractly *consider* good without regard to its precise relation to someone or something, and thus to speak of good *simpliciter*, yet nonetheless to hold that it must *be* related in *some* manner to someone or something.

[12] J. L. Ackrill, "Aristotle on *Eudaimonia*," in *Essays on Aristotle's Ethics*, ed. Amelie O. Rorty (Berkeley: University of California Press, 1980), p. 23.

[13] This list of generic goods and virtues is inspired by Aristotle, *Rhetoric*, 1362b 10–28; Aquinas, *Summa Theologiae* [hereafter *ST*], I-II, 94.2, trans. Fathers of English Dominican Province (Benziger Bros. ed., 1947, available at <http://dhspriory.org/thomas/summa/FP.html>, last accessed October 2, 2015); and John Finnis, *The Fundamentals of Ethics* (Washington, DC: Georgetown University Press, 1983), p. 75. For an account of the various lists of basic drives and inclinations from psychological and anthropological literature that is still helpful, see Thomas Davitt, S. J., *The Basic Values in Law: A Study of the Ethico-legal Implications of Psychology and Anthropology* (*Transactions of the American Philosophical Society*, New Series, Vol. 58, Pt. 5, Philadelphia: American Philosophical Society, 1968). These lists express an initial but well-established understanding of the general potentialities whose actualizations make up the overall character of human flourishing and the self-perfecting process.

[14] "A is more final than B if, though B is sought for its own sake (and hence is indeed a final and not merely intermediate goal), it is also sought for the sake of A" (Ackrill, "Aristotle on *Eudaimonia*," p. 21). Richard Kraut observes: "There is no incompatibility, in Aristotle's ethics, between choosing virtuous acts for themselves and choosing them only on condition that they are principal ingredients of happiness" ("Aristotle on Choosing Virtue for Itself," *Archiv für Geschichte Der Philosophie* 58.3 [1976]: p. 238).

their own right. Not only is their inherent worth compatible with their being essentially related to what is good *for* some person or other, but more: their inherent worth is grounded in such a relation.

To understand this idea better, we should consider two different ways in which activities are subordinated to some end: (a) on the one hand, there are activities that are purely means or instruments to that end—the dominant-end perspective; and (b) on the other, there are activities that are ingredients in or constituents of that end—the inclusive-end perspective. For example, consider the difference between the relationship of obtaining golf clubs to playing golf and the relationship of putting to playing golf. While both activities are "for the sake of" playing golf, obtaining clubs is only a necessary preliminary to golfing, while putting is one of the activities that makes golfing what it is. Furthermore, the actions taken to obtain golf clubs produce an outcome separate from that activity—namely, the possession of golf clubs that can be used—but putting has no end or result apart from itself. The value of putting is not that of a mere means. Its value lies in its being an expression or realization of the activity of which it is a constituent. As Ackrill states, "One does not putt *in order to* play golf . . . Putting *is* playing golf (though not all that playing golf is)."[15]

Another point that is crucial to appreciating what it means for human flourishing to be an "inclusive" end is that there is yet a third form of subordination, namely, (c) activities that are done for their own sake, and yet also for the sake of something else. (C) is possible, since flourishing is not the *result* of the efforts of a lifetime; it is not something that one looks forward to enjoying in the future. Rather, it is a continuous process of living in a certain manner. Thus, the constituents of such living are more than merely means for bringing about what is to follow; they are also worthwhile in themselves. It is perfectly possible for something to be pursued for its own sake and still be a constituent of human flourishing. Indeed, as Aristotle states:

> What is always chosen as an end in itself and never as a means to something else is called final in an unqualified sense. This description seems to apply to *eudaimonia* above all else; for we always choose *eudaimonia* as an end in itself and never for the sake of something else. Honor, pleasure,

---

[15] Ackrill, "Aristotle on *Eudaimonia*," p. 19. See Scott MacDonald, "Ultimate Ends in Practical Reasoning: Aquinas's Aristotelian Moral Psychology and Anscombe's Fallacy," *The Philosophical Review* 100 (January 1991): pp. 31–66 for a thorough defense of the idea that human good is an inclusive end.

intelligence, and all virtue we choose partly for themselves—for we would choose each of them even if no further advantage would accrue from them—but we also choose them partly for the sake of *eudaimonia*. . . .[16]

The theory of obligation generated by this inclusive view of human flourishing is one in which it is not necessary to calculate what the expected consequences of every proposed course of conduct might be in order to determine what is good and ought to be done. Nor is it even necessary to be always open to the possibility of such calculation. Though calculation of consequences would be appropriate for dealing with matters that are entirely instrumental to human flourishing, this is not so for the components of human flourishing itself. The first principle of practical reason is, as Aquinas noted: "Good is to be done and pursued; and evil is to be avoided."[17] Once one discerns what is good or virtuous, one knows what ought to be done; but the major concern is determining what in the particular and contingent is really good or virtuous. It is in this respect that IP is not a consequentialistic normative theory. Some virtues and goods are seen as activities that characterize our human flourishing itself, because they exist through their exercise and not merely as external means.

This is not to say, however, that there might not be other senses (for example, a personal or a non-maximizing sense) in which this view can be termed "consequentialistic." The problem with consequentialism as it is commonly understood is not that consequences have no role to play within morality,[18] but that it is seen as foundational in determining obligations. Indeed, once the constituent goods and virtues of human flourishing that ought to be pursued and practiced are determined, reflection on consequences is then necessary in order to integrate the conduct that expresses these goods and virtues into a flourishing life for that individual. An individual needs to consider, for example, whether the consequences of the pursuit of one good are compatible with the pursuit of another. Determining how to incorporate such conduct into an integrated whole is the central task faced by practical wisdom. Thus, it is only consequentialism

---

[16] Aristotle, *Nicomachean Ethics*, trans. Martin Ostwald (Upper Saddle River, NJ: Prentice Hall, 1999), 1097a 34–1097b. We have replaced "happiness" in the translation with "*eudaimonia*."

[17] Aquinas, *ST*, I-II, 94.2.

[18] See Philippa Foot, *Natural Goodness* (Oxford: Clarendon Press, 2001), pp. 48–50.

considered as a theory for determining the nature of moral obligations and their foundational character that IP rejects. It does not deny that consequences have a role—albeit, a derivative and bounded one—to play in an individual's determining what actions to take. We shall explore this issue further when we consider, both here and in the following chapters, the central role practical wisdom plays in IP.

Finally, this inclusive view of human flourishing admits the possibility that there may *not* be a preset weighting or evaluative pattern for the basic or generic goods and virtues that constitute it. Even if all the aforementioned goods and virtues are in fact necessary to flourishing, an abstract analysis of human nature does not show us what their evaluative ranking should be. Such an analysis does not tell us how much time and effort should be spent in the pursuit of one necessary good or virtue as opposed to another. As we shall see next, the individual is necessary for any actual evaluative ranking, and the role of the individual in the ranking process provides a basis for a conception of human flourishing that is different in many respects from that usually associated with traditional perfectionist theories.

INDIVIDUALITY

Closely related to the agent-relativity of human flourishing is its individualized character. Rather than looking at the way values are operating within human flourishing, individuality refers to the notion of flourishing as a whole. Human flourishing is not some abstract universal, but is individualized. However, it is essential to grasp that individuals do more than provide spatial differentiation. Contrary to what John Finnis and Robert George seem to hold,[19] individuals are not mere loci for the attainment of human flourishing. Human flourishing achieves determinacy and reality only when the generic goods and virtues find expression through the individual's unique talents, potentialities, and circumstances (which we call his or her "nexus" and develop in greater detail in section 2 of this chapter). Thus, the concrete character of human flourishing is dependent on *who* one is as well as *what* one is, and it is thus not identical across persons, but unique to each one. Yet, this account of human flourishing offers a

---

[19] John Finnis states that "every human being is a locus of human flourishing" (*Natural Law and Natural Rights* [Oxford: Clarendon Press, 1980], p. 22). Robert George describes persons "as loci of human goods" (*Making Men Moral* [Oxford: Clarendon Press, 1993], p. 39).

version of moral individualism that is not simply subjectivism. Just as we take human flourishing to be both agent-relative and objective, so, too, do we take it to be individualized and objective.[20]

Naturally, to say that human flourishing is unique for each concrete individual human being is not to say that one cannot through abstraction discover some factors common to all the various forms of flourishing and thus develop an account of "generic" goods and virtues. Instead, it is to say that one should not presume that the ability to consider the constitutive goods and virtues of human flourishing without regard to their particular determination requires either that they exist in such a generic manner, or that they can be properly understood without those particular determinations. We can speak of what is common to the various forms of human flourishing without having to posit the existence of some abstract universal good of human flourishing, or having to adopt an ethical rationalism that supposes such abstract knowledge of human flourishing to suffice for determining moral obligation. We shall have more to say on this last point shortly.

The difference, then, between IP and how perfectionism has been often understood can be stated as follows: Though we may abstractly speak of a *summum bonum*, there are in reality only many *summa bona*. There are only many *summa bona*, because each individual's flourishing is the *summum bonum* for him- or herself, and because there is no single *summum bonum* without unique form or apart from the lives of individual human beings.[21]

OBJECTIVITY

For IP, the character of human good—specifically, human flourishing—is agent-relative, inclusive, and individualized. Contrary

---

[20] See Paul Bloomfield's discussion of individuality in *The Virtues of Happiness: A Theory of the Good Life* (Oxford: Oxford University Press, 2014), pp. 163–5.

[21] For how this view pertains to the common good and the political community, see the following works by Rasmussen and Den Uyl: *NOL*, pp. 197–205; "*Norms of Liberty*: Challenges and Prospects," in *Reading Rasmussen and Den Uyl: Critical Essays on* Norms of Liberty, ed. Aeon J. Skoble (Lanham, MD: Lexington Books, 2008), pp. 186–99; and "The Myth of Atomism," *The Review of Metaphysics* 59 (June 2006): pp. 843–70. Finally, see Douglas B. Rasmussen and Douglas J. Den Uyl, *Liberty and Nature: An Aristotelian Defense of Liberal Order* (La Salle, IL: Open Court, 1991), pp. 131–71.

to what L. W. Sumner contends,[22] however, human flourishing in our agent-relative, individualized, and inclusive sense does not reduce to simply a matter of one's attitudes or feelings. That is to say, it is not something subjective. Thinking or feeling does not make it so. Rather, human flourishing is objective.[23] And by this, we mean (in terms similar to those used by Socrates in interrogating Euthyphro) that though human flourishing is indeed an object of desire, its desirability and choice-worthiness do not stem simply from its being an object of desire (or of choice or commitment or attitude). Rather, the desirability and choice-worthiness of human flourishing stems from what it *is*, from its very constitution. Human flourishing is a way of being. It is ontological and not merely a feeling or experience. Thus, Robert Nozick and Henry B. Veatch[24] were on target to claim that human flourishing cannot be simply having experiences, feelings, or satisfaction of desires, but must also be something active and actual. To choose a life on Nozick's "experience machine," in which one only has pleasant experiences and all desires are satisfied by the machine, is to choose not "to live (an active verb) . . . in contact with reality."[25] It is for one to fail to engage in the activity of being real or actualized. And though we might all imagine circumstances in which one might be tempted by such a choice, it is not something anyone would seriously say is the aim of his or her life. Indeed, as Nozick states, it is "a kind of suicide."[26]

Perhaps it could be argued that the experience machine example does not really refute a desire-based understanding of human flourishing, where to flourish is to satisfy one's desires, because satisfaction of one's desires requires direct, efficacious interaction with reality and not merely having an experience or mental state. If so, then a desire-based theory need not say that one should plug in to the experience

---

[22] L. W. Sumner, *Welfare, Happiness, and Ethics* (Oxford: Clarendon Press, 1996), p. 43.

[23] For an incisive critique of the attempt to identify objective good with an idealized version of subjective good—be it in terms of intersubjective theories or of individualized ones—see Robert C. Koons, *Realism Regained: An Exact Theory of Causation, Teleology, and the Mind* (Oxford: Oxford University Press, 2000), pp. 257–60; and for a defense of objective good, see pp. 138–9.

[24] Robert Nozick, *Anarchy, State, and Utopia* (New York: Basic Books, 1974), pp. 42–5; Henry B. Veatch, *Rational Man: A Modern Interpretation of Aristotelian Ethics* (Indianapolis: Liberty Fund, 2003), p. 32.

[25] Nozick, *Anarchy, State, and Utopia*, p. 45.

[26] Ibid., p. 43.

machine,[27] for it is not mental states alone that can be desired: objects of desire instead require actual changes in oneself and/or in the world in order to obtain them. In other words, explaining human flourishing in terms of desire may not mean or require that human flourishing is simply an experience understood as a mental state, and Nozick's thought-experiment thus would miss its mark. But if this is so, then it can be countered that an objectivist understanding of human flourishing does not preclude human flourishing's being inherently bound up with being desired. Desire is part of the traditional understanding of human flourishing. The issue is whether desire alone is sufficient to make something good or desirable. We believe it is not, and that desire must be based in something that is not itself desire. We will discuss this matter in some detail in Chapter 6. It is enough to say here that an objective account of human flourishing is one that can be characterized as a life of *right* desire, and that what *makes* a desire right is not simply that someone *has* that desire.

The crucial ontological feature of the individualistic perfectionist account of human good is that human flourishing is a particular mode of living, and this means that human good cannot be understood for what it is apart from a biocentric context. This account does not suppose that value, meaning, or purpose is provided to life by some transcendent source. Rather, the significance of life is simply that without life, there would be no significance. Life is the context in which value, meaning, or purpose occur—as Jonathan Haidt has observed, "purpose *within* life."[28] As we shall see in the forthcoming chapters of Part II—"The Perfectionist Turn" and "Because"—life makes human flourishing more than a mere description of an actualized or perfected human being; it makes human flourishing desirable and choice-worthy. But since human flourishing is a *way* of living, there is also more to being an actualized or perfected human being than self-preservation or survival. Life of a certain type is at the very center of this account of human good; and who and what we are as living things provides a foundation for our discovering what our particular purposes need to be, and thus to what our particular forms of human flourishing amount.

---

[27] Katarzyna de Lazari-Radek and Peter Singer, *The Point of View of the Universe: Sidgwick and Contemporary Ethics* (Oxford: Oxford University Press, 2014), p. 255.

[28] Jonathan Haidt, *The Happiness Hypothesis: Finding Modern Truth in Ancient Wisdom* (New York: Basic Books, 2006), p. 218.

Ontologically considered, *human* flourishing is an activity, an actuality, and an end that is realized (or a function that is performed) through the self-directed exercise of an individual's rational capacity. We shall have more to say about self-direction and reason below. As an actuality, human flourishing consists of activities that both produce and express in a human being an actualization of potentialities that are specific to the kind of living thing a human being is and that are unique to each human being as an individual. *Omne ens perficitur in actu.*[29] Such actualization involves attaining, maintaining, and enjoying generic goods (as well as exercising virtues) in a manner that is appropriate for each individual human being. Moreover, as an end (*telos*) or function (*ergon*), human flourishing is that to which human beings are naturally attracted. Human beings are not *driven* to the actualization of these potentialities. Instead, the actualization is dependent on the self-directed exercise of our rational capacities. Nonetheless, human beings do have an inherent and irreducible potentiality *for* their mature state; and as we will see in subsequent chapters, this is the touchstone for how human life can naturally have a direction without being directed. Human flourishing is not only, then, the actualization of the aforementioned potentialities, but also the attainment of a human being's natural end or the performance of a human being's natural function. Human conduct is ultimately for the sake of human flourishing.

It is, then, the teleological character of human flourishing that gets the perfectionist ethical enterprise off the ground, so to speak. It is by consideration of a human being's natural end or function that a description of a human being can also be an evaluation, and that a basis for determining what is choice-worthy and ought to be done can be provided. Yet, it is just on this point of natural teleology that many contemporary philosophers hesitate.[30] Katarzyna de Lazari-Radek and Peter Singer express this hesitation in an archetypal fashion.

> Aristotle's view makes sense within the framework of a teleological vision of the universe, but without that framework the idea that human beings have a function collapses, and with it Aristotle's foundation for the view that we ought to perfect traits that are essential to us. Without the idea

---

[29] The meaning of this statement is that perfection is found in actuality, but the usual sense of it is that perfection is found in action. Both are, of course, the very points we are making.

[30] Thomas Hurka, for example, expresses such hesitation in *Perfectionism* (New York: Oxford University Press, 1993), p. 24.

that we were put on Earth for some purpose, attempts to retain the view that it is good for us to perfect our human nature run the risk of skating over the gap between "is" and "ought."[31]

Though we will have much to say in Part II about what natural teleology involves, as well as the alleged gap between "is" and "ought," a brief response to this account of teleology needs to be made. Simply put, this account fails to distinguish between what might be called a "Platonic" model and an "Aristotelian" model of teleology.[32] The former requires the actions of a rational agent or mind whose intentions apply to the entire cosmos, and whose intentions are those in terms of which processes in the natural world are judged good or bad. For this model, the telos of an entity is "external" to it and is in principle no different from that of an artifact—for example, a chair's proper function and standard for goodness is the purpose for which it was created. In contrast, an "Aristotelian" model does not require a rational agent or mind whose intentions apply to the entire cosmos. Rather, teleology is based on the character of living things and is "immanent" or "internal" to the organism. The telos of a living thing results from an internal directive principle that is an irreducible feature of the developmental process of the living organism itself. Additionally, the process does not require an immaterial, separable force, an *élan vital*, within an organism. Rather, the process is irreducible: the movement from potentiality to actuality is intrinsic to the constitution of the organism in such a way that other kinds of accounts (for example, mechanical or chemical) are insufficient explanations of this movement.

The issue of natural teleology is not only a critical juncture for any naturalistic perfectionist account of human good, but is also decisive for how moral objectivity in general is understood. If it is supposed that natural teleology is not credible, then there will be no basis in the natural[33] order for determining what human good is; for indeed,

---

[31] De Lazari-Radek and Singer, *The Point of View of the Universe*, pp. 233–4.

[32] James G. Lennox, "Teleology," in *Keywords in Evolutionary Biology*, ed. Evelyn Fox Keller and Elisabeth A. Lloyd (Cambridge, MA: Harvard University Press, 1992), pp. 324–33; and Denis Walsh, "Teleology," in *Oxford Handbook of Evolutionary Biology*, ed. Michael Ruse (Oxford: Oxford University Press, 2008), pp. 113–37. See also Koons, *Realism Regained*, pp. 141–53.

[33] We note in Chapter 6 that "natural" or "nature" can be quite ambiguous, and we strive there to explain the exact sense in which IP is a naturalistic theory. Suffice here to say, it is a view of natural or nature that is neither *defined* by what the sciences report, nor reductionist in character.

there will be an ontological gap between what is fact and what is valuable.[34] For many contemporary ethicists, the rejection of natural teleology has meant either adopting the view that human good refers to a moral reality that transcends the natural order,[35] or taking the perspective that human good is based on our beliefs about morality and virtue—that is to say, by taking a constructivist view of morality. We will argue in Chapters 3 and 4 (and again later in Part II) against the adequacy of such a constructivist approach to moral objectivity.

Yet, such metaphysical and metaethical concerns may not be the only issue confronting teleology. Rather, it simply may be that the entire idea of a natural end is repugnant to a human world in which there are many paths to worthwhile living. If, as teleology seems to suppose, our ends are fixed, then it would seem that we have very little choice about how we should live our lives. Choices, then, would concern means only, giving no scope to the idea of multiple, legitimate ways of living. For if the good is a single end we all need to achieve as human beings in order to live the life of an ethical flourisher, then change itself would seem to be a sign one has not yet found the required path. Indeed, such a worry is not confined to philosophers, as the following remark by Nobel Laureate economist James Buchanan attests:

> If I may resort to philosophical terms, what I am objecting to in modern economic theory is its *teleological* foundations, its tendency to force all analyzable behavior into the straitjacket of "maximizing a utility or objective function under constraint." In one way, I am suggesting that the utilitarian origins of nineteenth-century political economy may have come to haunt us and to do us great damage.[36]

Buchanan is arguing against the idea in economics that all behavior is a function of maximizing utility under certain constraints within

---

[34] See de Lazari-Radek and Singer, *The Point of View of the Universe*, pp. 235–8 for a critique of Thomas Hurka's attempt (in his work, *Perfectionism*) to develop a viable form of perfectionism without natural teleology.

[35] An excellent example of this gambit is Russ Shafer-Landau's *Moral Realism: A Defense* (Oxford: Clarendon Press, 2003). Shafer-Landau's account of goodness is a quite nuanced interpretation of G. E. Moore's non-naturalism and is similar to our interpretation of Moore in Chapter 6. Shafer-Landau claims that moral properties are supervenient on natural ones but are, nonetheless, in no sense descriptive of the natural order (ibid., p. 77). We challenge claims of this sort in Chapter 6 as well.

[36] James Buchanan, "Natural and Artifactual Man," in *The Collected Works of James M. Buchanan*, Vol. 1 (Indianapolis: Liberty Fund, 2001), p. 250.

a fixed set of preferences. In this picture, the preferences are given, and the constraints act to channel our choices toward maximizing the satisfaction of our preferences. Constraints may vary and thus alter behavior, but preference sets remain pretty much constant. The diversity of behavior that we observe gives the appearance of a diversity of preference sets, but it is the variety of constraints that actually produces the array of behaviors, not a variety of preference sets. To put this in more ordinary language: Buchanan is against the idea implied in the maximization model that persons cannot become something other than they are now—for example, by imagining themselves as a different type of person, and as a result trying to improve themselves by adopting a different set of preferences than those they now possess. As Buchanan puts it:

> Once all of the possible constraints are accounted for (historical, geographic, cultural, physical, genetic, sexual), there still remains a large set of possible persons that one might imagine himself to be, or might imagine himself capable of becoming. There is room for "improvement," for the construction of what might be. Further, in thinking about realizable prospects, a person is able to rank these in some fashion, to classify members of the set as "better" or "worse."[37]

In light of these truths about human nature, Buchanan wants to describe human beings as being "artifactual." We make ourselves, and we make ourselves over and over again. "Natural man"—if there is such a thing—would be akin to an animal, responding to stimuli and maximizing the chances for attaining a fixed set of preferences. Because we are not like that, teleology is fundamentally false. Indeed,

> nothing teleological can be introduced since man must recognize that even within his own private sphere of action there is no maximand. Individually, man invests in becoming that which he is not . . . *not even* individuals have well-defined and well-articulated objects that exist independently of choices themselves.[38]

Buchanan's points raise important questions about the meaning of teleology. They do, however, miss the mark as criticisms of the sort of teleology IP involves. First of all, as we have already explained, IP does not hold to a dominant-end theory of human nature and teleology, as have some historical interpretations of Aristotle. We adopt a so-called inclusive-end position, in which there are multiple final

---

[37] Buchanan, "Natural and Artifactual Man," p. 258.
[38] Ibid., p. 258.

ends that have to be managed in a complex, and individually differentiated, interrelationship we refer to as the individual's "nexus"
(noted earlier). Simply put, there is no single universal maximand.
That should clear up a number of the problems Buchanan is concerned with in his objections, because a plurality of preference sets
secures diversity and the ability to imagine fundamental alternatives.

Second, there is no inconsistency between teleology and becoming
someone different by way of improvement. Indeed, teleology seems
to *rely* upon the idea that we can imagine ourselves to be a different type of person, for acting upon such a mentally projected end
would be the only way for us, as rational beings, to achieve what
we are called upon to achieve by our *telos* (or *teloi*). There is, then,
no difficulty linking teleology and becoming. If there is a problem
here, it would have to be with the person who has failed to attain the
appropriate integration of final ends, not with anyone in *pursuit* of
them. Finally, it is likely that the way an economist looks at a utility
function or a preference set is not the same as the way in which we,
at least, see final ends as used in a neo-Aristotelian ethics. Despite
language by Aristotle and others that appears to be to the contrary, a
final end does not actually function as a maximand. If we *must* speak
in such terms, the sort of maximands which we are considering when
referring to our final ends might be called "procedural maximands,"
as opposed to what might be labeled "accumulative maximands."[39]

An accumulative maximand would be one in which units of
value can be added or subtracted, and in which satiation is conceivable. We can, for example, get more or fewer units of music or fine
wine or prestige; and we might finally have gotten enough of those
units to be satiated by them. The final ends for IP, by contrast, are
exercised, but not used up in the process of their being exercised. In
addition, they order the priority of specific units of value by defining
both their relative merits for the individual who enjoys them and
the way in which they should be consumed. Satiation is essentially
inconceivable here, not simply because the exercise of these procedural maximands tends not to use anything up, but also because
the "maximizing" component of any one of these procedural maximands is not conceived independently of the others. Friendship and

---

[39] The problem here is that "maximand" is essentially a *quantitative* term which
immediately points us in a different direction than we should be going when
thinking of final ends in ethics. However, that sort of gloss has not been absent
from interpretations of the Aristotelian framework in ethics.

health, for example, could serve as two examples of a procedural maximand. While it is certainly possible to say that one may have too many friends or spend too much time in the gym, the notions of friendship and health act more like rules for utilizing goods than as goods themselves. In this respect, these sorts of maximands are meant to be understood in terms of a regulation of the "right amount" of goods, both in terms of what is suggested by the end or maximand itself, and also in terms of the relationship of that end to other ends one ought to pursue. Friendship and health would not be defined in terms of the number of friends one has, but in terms of what it means to be engaging with a friend, and of the qualities that make such engagements possible. Thought of in these terms, one notices that we continually juggle the procedural maximands (final ends) we have in order to meet changing circumstances and opportunities, which in turn affects the relationship one procedural maximand (final end) has with the others. The nexus, in other words, is continually being adjusted. There are, therefore, a number of possible "selves" we can imagine; but all of them will be exercising their procedural maximands (the qualitative dimension of how we treat our friends) in some way that utilizes and gives meaning to the accumulative maximands (the specific individuals or trips to the gym, along the quantitative dimension).

The short point of all this is that achieving final ends does not mean the closing off of options, choices, or possibilities of diverse modes of living or selves. Even a thoroughgoing flourisher *becomes* in important ways. It is true that not everything can count as a flourishing life, but the field is sufficiently wide to not run afoul of Buchanan's worries about teleology.[40] People do define themselves as they choose, at least when we are talking about procedural maximands, because their achievement is expressed through choosing, and not exclusively or necessarily through the consumption of what is chosen. It is, in this regard, quite common, when thinking of final ethical ends, to confuse achievement with completion. The ethical ends that go into composing a flourishing ethical life may be achieved but never completed so long as one lives, because they express the very modes of appropriate living itself. It is only when the maximands are conceived in terms of "how much" rather than "how

---

[40] There are eighty-eight keys on a piano, which also "limit" what one can do musically, but one's musical options are hardly thereby restricted. Having a nature does not necessarily preclude a wide scope of options.

well" that one faces the problems Buchanan legitimately criticizes in his conception of teleology.

SELF-DIRECTEDNESS

Toward the end of *De Anima* II 5, when Aristotle is discussing the difference between intellectual and sensory apprehension, he notes the role of self-direction in human knowing:

> Actual sensation corresponds to the stage of the exercise of knowledge. But between the two cases compared there is a difference; the objects that excite the sensory powers to activity, the seen, the heard, & c., are outside. The ground of this difference is that what actual sensation apprehends is individuals, while what knowledge apprehends is universals, and these are in a sense within the soul itself. That is why *a man can think when he wants to* but his sensation does not depend upon himself—a sensible object must be there.[41]

The intellectual insight necessary for human knowledge depends on the individual human being exercising the effort necessary to initiate and maintain it.

Accordingly, human flourishing—requiring, as it does, intellectual insight[42]—would seem for Aristotle to be a self-directed activity.[43] John Cooper observes: "For Aristotle, *eudaimonia* is necessarily the result of a person's own efforts; success, of whatever kind, could only count as *eudaimonia* if due to one's own efforts."[44] And Veatch argues:

> Is it not evident that not only does a human being not attain his natural end by an automatic process of development and maturity after the manner of a plant or an animal? In addition, no human being ever attains

---

[41] Aristotle, *De Anima*, trans. J. A. Smith in *The Complete Works of Aristotle*, ed. Jonathan Barnes (Princeton: Princeton University Press, 1984), 417b 18–26 (emphasis added). Fred D. Miller, Jr. first directed us to this passage.

[42] This pertains to both speculative and practical wisdom. See Aristotle, *Nicomachean Ethics*, VI 11.

[43] Indeed, Aristotle even notes the importance of self-direction when distinguishing between good fortune and *eudaimonia* for god. "[He] is *eudaimôn* and blessed, but not on account of any external goods *but on account of himself* and because he is by nature of a certain sort—which shows that being fortunate must be different from flourishing. For the goods external to the soul come of themselves by chance, but no one is just or temperate by or through chance" (*Politics*, 1323b 24–9). This translation is John Cooper's in *Reason and Human Good in Aristotle* (Cambridge, MA: Harvard University Press, 1975), p. 123.

[44] Ibid., p. 124.

his natural end or perfection save by his own personal effort and exertion. No one other than the human individual—no agency of society, of family, of friends, or of whatever can make or determine or program an individual to be a good man, or program him to live the life that a human being ought to live. Instead, attaining one's natural end as a human person is nothing if not a "do-it-yourself" job.[45]

Aristotle also claims that if our knowledge and actions are to enable us to *be* good (or virtuous), as opposed to our merely knowing and doing good (or virtue), the three conditions noted in our Introduction must be met. "(1) The agent must act in full consciousness of what he is doing. (2) He must 'will' the action, and will it for its own sake. (3) The act must proceed from a fixed and unchangeable disposition."[46] Only by initiating and maintaining the effort to gain the knowledge, to cultivate the proper habits of character, to exercise correct choices, and to perform the right actions can someone achieve moral excellence.

These statements suggest that Aristotle considers human flourishing as being a fundamentally self-directed activity. Self-direction is thus not merely one of the many conditions necessary for the existence of human flourishing; rather, it is necessary to the very nature of human flourishing—that is, necessary for human flourishing to *be* human flourishing and to be *human* flourishing.

Stated in terms that invoke the inclusive character of human flourishing, we may say that self-direction is the central necessary constituent or ingredient of human flourishing. It is that feature of human flourishing without which no other feature could be a constituent. That is to say, it is both a necessary condition for, and an operating condition of, the pursuit and achievement of any goods or virtues connected to flourishing. Indeed, it is the very activity through which they are made determinate and real. Human flourishing thus consists in exercising rational agency. No matter the level of achievement or specificity, self-direction is a feature of every act of self-perfection.[47]

---

[45] Henry B. Veatch, *Human Rights: Fact or Fancy?* (Baton Rouge: Louisiana State University Press, 1985), p. 84. We have more to say about self-direction in our discussion of practical wisdom below.

[46] Aristotle, *Nicomachean Ethics*, trans. J. A. K. Thomson (Baltimore, MD: Penguin Classics, 2004), rev. ed., 1105a 31–2.

[47] Just as it pertains to the function of a heart for *it*, the heart, to perform the pumping, so it pertains to the function of human beings for each individual to exercise her intelligence in the activity of flourishing. Hence, just as a heart that does not pump on its own is not strictly performing its natural function, so it is with a human being who is not fundamentally directing her own rational agency.

Sociality

Though human flourishing is individualized and self-directed, it is not atomistic. In terms of origins, humans almost always begin their lives in a society or community and then continue to grow and develop in some social context or other. Human lives are intertwined, and cultural environments play a primary role in initial self-conceptions and basic values. Moreover, human beings, to varying degrees and in varying ways, seek the company of others. Indeed, Aristotle observes that only a beast or a god would live outside the polis.[48] Humans are naturally social, and human flourishing is only achieved with or among others.[49] It is thus a fundamental mistake to conceive of human beings achieving maturity or flourishing apart from others and only later taking it upon themselves to join society. Moreover, human flourishing does not require gaining the goods of life exclusively for oneself and never acting for the sake of others. As Scott MacDonald has observed,

> the claim that one seeks the good of others as a part of one's own good does not mean that one does not seek the good of others for its own sake but only for the sake of one's own good. One can seek the constituents of one's own good for their own sakes, and also for the sake of the good of which they are constituents.[50]

To emphasize what was noted earlier, the account of human flourishing that IP embraces is not that of ethical egoism—at least, not as that term is generally used.

Indeed, a significant part of human potentialities is other-oriented. *Philia* (friendship) in all its various forms of relatedness is, for example, one of the basic generic goods identified by Aristotle as an integral feature of the good human life.[51] Furthermore, we would go

---

See Jennifer Whiting, "Aristotle's Function Argument: A Defense," *Ancient Philosophy* 8 (1988): p. 43.

[48] Aristotle, *Politics*, 1253a 27–9.

[49] There is evidence we are hard-wired this way. For example, see Haidt, *The Happiness Hypothesis*, pp. 230ff.

[50] Scott MacDonald, "Egoistic Rationalism: Aquinas's Basis for Christian Morality," in *Christian Theism and the Problems of Philosophy*, ed. Michael D. Beaty (Notre Dame, IN: University of Notre Dame Press, 1990), p. 352 n35. See also Kelly Rogers, "Aristotle on Loving Another for His Own Sake," *Phronēsis* 39.3 (1994): pp. 291–302.

[51] See Rasmussen and Den Uyl, *Liberty and Nature*, pp. 66–8 and 173–206.

so far as to claim, there are no a priori limitations on such relationships. Although relationships with others are based on values that form the basis for a continuum of relations—from close friends to acquaintances to the development of communities and cultures—human sociality is open-ended. Human sociality is not limited, as it seems to be for Aristotle, to the "polis"; it can also exist in a larger, cosmopolitan setting. There is no justification for holding that human beings cannot form relationships with persons with whom no common values have yet been shared. In terms of origin, development, and scope, human flourishing is profoundly social.

To sum up our discussion of all the components of human flourishing, we can note that human flourishing is plural and complex, not monistic and simple, and is attained through involvement with and among others. There is no single generic good or virtue that dominates all others. Each generic good or virtue must be achieved, maintained, exhibited, and enjoyed in a manner that allows it to be coherently integrated with everything else that makes up human flourishing.[52] Moreover, because human flourishing is individualized and agent-relative, the generic goods and virtues must be achieved in concert with the set of circumstances, talents, endowments, interests, beliefs, and histories that descriptively characterize the individual's nexus, as well as in concert with the individual's community and culture. An examination of the human life-form reveals the generic goods and virtues that provide the basic parameters for human flourishing; but such an examination does not make known what the weighting or balancing of these goods and virtues should be. It does not solve the question of how people should conduct their lives. Instead, what is pivotal for this view of human flourishing is practical wisdom, to which we now briefly turn.

2. Flourishing and Practical Wisdom

An examination of human nature in general does not reveal any universal rules that dictate the proper weighting of the goods and virtues of human flourishing. Instead, a proper weighting is only achieved by

---

[52] On this very point, see Kraut's discussion of speaking of "good without qualification" in Aristotle. Kraut notes that when one is so speaking, one is speaking in a general way about the sorts of things that are good for human life. But he points out that Aristotle counsels us to pursue not such abstract or general goodness, but "goodness-for-someone" (*Against Absolute Goodness*, p. 211).

individuals using practical wisdom to discover the proper balance for themselves. Yet, this use of practical wisdom is not mere cleverness or means-end reasoning. Instead, it is the ability of the individual to discern, in particular and contingent circumstances, what is morally required at the time of action. Abstractly considered, there being a plurality of divergent ends that comprise human flourishing does not logically entail that these ends are incompatible. Concretely considered, the exercise of keeping such ends from becoming incompatible by discovering their proper weighting or balance is an individual's central task. Such is the task of practical wisdom.

As noted at the very outset of this chapter, human flourishing is understood by us to mean "the exercise of one's own practical wisdom." Some key terms in this description will be elaborated upon below, but are briefly described here. Consider first, "wisdom," which has three dimensions: (1) the effective and excellent use of practical reason, (2) the development of character, and (3) self-understanding. The last of these involves understanding the world around one, as well as one's own nature, opportunities, and dispositions. Another key term in this description of our telos is "exercise." Our telos is not a state of being, passively understood, but an *exercise* of being; and realizing this helps us understand why the virtues are *both* instrumental *and* ends in themselves. As said earlier, human flourishing is an activity as well as an actuality. Finally, "one's own" is meant to convey that, in the end, it is the individualized character of the good that constitutes the core of ethics and one's telos. In what follows, we offer a brief précis of each of these key terms in our definition of human flourishing, as they particularly apply to the deployment of practical wisdom.

WISDOM

Practical reason is the intellectual faculty employed for guiding conduct. Practical wisdom is the excellent or proper use of this faculty. Practical wisdom as the intellectual virtue for IP is exemplified in Aristotle's definition of virtue: "Virtue ... is a state of character concerned with choice, lying in a mean, i.e., the mean relative to us, this being determined by a rational principle, and by that principle by which the man of practical wisdom would determine it."[53] One can

---

[53] Aristotle, *Nicomachean Ethics*, 1107a 1–3, trans. W. D. Ross, in *The Basic Works of Aristotle*, ed. Richard McKeon (New York: Random House, 1968).

see from this definition the central importance of practical reasoning to Aristotle, and how wisdom is its correct use. Additionally, we see that such wisdom is connected to character development, is active, and is suggestive of a connection directly to individuals.

1. We have noted so far, and will note in what follows, that practical reason concerns the employment of our reason to formulate appropriate goals, as well as to consider the various means to achieve them. It is not done in isolation from the other two components of wisdom, so the nature of practical reason includes reflection on character development and self-understanding. But for our purposes at the moment, we mean by "practical reason" the traditional notion of using reason for purposes of determining and guiding action. Practical reason is often distinguished from theoretical reason and cleverness. But as Aristotle notes, theoretical (or speculative) reason is an activity, so one's pursuit of theoretical reason can factor into one's practical reason. That is, one's decision to engage in theoretical reason, and to do so in varying degrees, is an appropriate object of practical reason. Cleverness constitutes efficient means-end reasoning that pays no attention to the appropriateness of the ends, but only the means to get there. This is the standard Aristotelian distinction; but "appropriateness" of ends introduces the notion of the further distinction between practical reason and practical wisdom. Practical *wisdom's* excellent use of practical reason pays attention not only to effective deployment of practical reason, but also to the nature of the ends or goals being pursued. Practical reason considers the appropriateness of ends; a good choice of ends to be evaluated is evidence of practical wisdom's having been deployed. Hence, insights into the nature of the appropriateness of the ends are what transform reason into wisdom, depending upon the strength and perceptiveness of the insight. We will discuss some of the measures that determine what is and is not appropriate for an IP framework shortly. All such cases involve coherently integrating a nexus of values and goals into a way of living. But certainly one key factor of appropriateness is the degree to which our goals and actions can be organized into a coherent, integral whole, one in which character development and self-understanding operate simultaneously and without conflict.

It is important to note here that one of the central errors we seek to dispel with our account of IP is the idea that ethics is a list of universal duties or claims specifying how persons are to conduct themselves. Rather, as will be argued in the following chapters, ethics should be conceived of as a tool for guiding individual human flourishing by reference to principles and exemplars of conduct. The function for ethics is to assist persons in discovering for themselves how to live. We reject, as a form of ethical rationalism, the entire idea that the task or role of ethics is to provide guidance from an abstract consideration of ethical principles alone. This error stems from two factors: (a) failing to grasp the highly personal and complex character of human flourishing; and (b) taking ethics as primarily a theoretical enterprise, rather than a guide to living well. Erroneous ethical rationalism also reflects various other mistakes: an agent-neutral conception of human good, a conflation of morality with law, and the tendency to identify objectivity with universality. In the remaining chapters of Part I, in an effort to identify and distinguish the distinctive character of ethics, we indicate how these errors are reflected in many contemporary discussions, especially in social/political theorizing. We reject these missteps and seek to leave the ethical life in the hands of the individual human being.

Practical wisdom, as understood in our account, is the central integrating virtue of a good human life. Yet, it might be charged that this account of practical wisdom is myopic, insufficiently appreciative of broader perspectives and points of view, and incapable of empathy—and that in order to achieve the necessary scope and inclusivity, practical wisdom must, contrary to what is being advocated here, call forth again an agent-neutral or impersonal perspective. While we agree, however, that transcending one's own perspective or point of view is vital for moral growth in both its personal and interpersonal dimensions, admitting this does not show that practical wisdom needs to be agent-neutral or impersonal. There are two reasons for this.

First, the charge of myopia or narrowness fails to distinguish between, on the one hand, a procedure (or method) that can be employed by practical reason as an instrument for gaining knowledge and, on the other, the excellent use of practical reason itself. Critically distancing oneself from one's current situation and taking on a perspective other than one's own are valuable means of learning what is possible for oneself as a human being in general, and how to more effectively relate to others in particular. After engaging in such distancing or empathetic acts, one still needs to determine in practice how to utilize one's own potentialities and opportunities compatibly with other necessary goods and virtues. The former is a tool for practical reason; the latter represents the excellent use of practical reason. Taking a neutral perspective does not necessitate a neutral conclusion.

Second, this charge adopts what we later call a "juridical" model of human action. For this model, ethical prescriptions are essentially universal claims or rules that are grounded in a theory of basic values that is in some manner agent-neutral, or that result from a form of Kantian-style universalization. In contrast, our view of practical wisdom stems from an "evaluational" model of human actions; it is grounded in a theory of basic values that is agent-relative and in an essentially Aristotelian conception of self. We will continue to explore the implications of both these errors and corrections as we proceed. Meanwhile, as our earlier discussion of inclusivity suggested, human flourishing pertains to unity or integrity of one's whole life; and this makes a difference to how practical wisdom is conceived. As David L. Norton has observed:

> The eudaimonic individual experiences the whole of this life in every act, and he experiences parts and wholes together as necessary, such that he can will that nothing be changed. But that necessity here introduced is moral necessity, deriving from his choice. Hence, we may say of him interchangeably, "He is where he wants to be, doing what he wants to do," or "He is where he must be, doing what he must do." . . . The whole is present in each of his acts.[54]

To achieve this level of integrity, practical wisdom must direct itself not just to parts of one's life but also, and finally, to the ways in which the goods one pursues relate to each other and affect future chances for integration.

2. Another dimension in which practical wisdom functions is the creation, maintenance, and exercise of dispositions for proper desires and emotional responses. It is in one's development and exercise of the moral virtues—those rational dispositions that reflect one's character—that one lives a flourishing human life. We are in sympathy with the classical notion that one may need to do a large amount of revamping of one's desires, even one's conception of happiness, in order to flourish. Contrary to what is being preached by some moral and evolutionary psychologists these days,[55] we hold that one's appe-

---

[54] David L. Norton, *Personal Destinies: A Philosophy of Ethical Individualism* (Princeton: Princeton University Press, 1976), pp. 222–3.

[55] For an examination of and a response to those contemporary and moral psychologists who disparage the reshaping of our desires into rational desires, see the following: Nancy Snow, "Notes Toward an Empirical Psychology of Virtue: Exploring the Personality Scaffolding of Virtue," in *Aristotelian Ethics in Contemporary Perspective*, ed. Julia Peters (New York: Routledge, 2013),

tites and desires can be influenced and shaped into rational dispositions by one's intelligence, so that what one ought to desire and what one in fact does desire can be in harmony. This is where such moral virtues as integrity, courage, temperance, and honesty assist practical wisdom and reflect its exercise. When considered as a unity, moral virtues are necessary for the coherent achievement and use of multiple basic human goods and, along with practical wisdom, pervade the entire activity of flourishing.

Indeed, the debate as to whether virtues, understood as particular dispositions of character such as honesty or courage, are instrumental or ends in themselves presupposes that such developments of character are part of what morally excellent persons develop. This is so because, given the nature of action over time and in a world of uncertainty, such traits are necessary to ensure that one's actions are not at cross purposes with each other or with one's own dispositions and goals. Because such traits are developed at the behest of practical wisdom, their operation via habitual action can preclude the repeated need for full assessments, and so can serve as a short cut to decision-making. Moreover, such traits are a signal to oneself and others of a certain success in practical reasoning and achievement of practical wisdom. Finally, and perhaps most importantly, these virtues are at least partially the form practical wisdom will take when exercised in action. Consequently, if we take human flourishing to be an activity rather than a passive state, the conflict between an instrumental understanding of virtue and a for-its-own-sake view largely disappears. Virtues are sought for their own sake precisely because they are the form practically wise action will take when carried out. As dispositions appropriate to the situation in which they are expressed, there is nothing other than expressing practical wisdom for the sake of which virtues are deployed. Hence, they are ends in themselves. However, the development of those dispositions, and their habituated character, is for the sake of acting well (eudaimonia)

pp. 130–44; Lorraine Besser-Jones, *Eudaimonic Ethics: The Philosophy and Psychology of Living Well* (New York: Routledge, 2014), pp. 109–27; Neera K. Badhwar, *Well-Being: Happiness in a Worthwhile Life* (Oxford: Oxford University Press, 2014), pp. 118–42; and Owen Flanagan, *Moral Sprouts and Natural Teleologies: 21st Century Moral Psychology Meets Classical Chinese Philosophy* (Milwaukee: Marquette University Press, 2014) who declares himself a supporter of natural teleology and who argues that the empirical work in moral psychology works against the extreme rationalist and a-emotional models of ethics embraced by many ethicists.

and thus is, in this regard, "instrumental." It is, finally, virtually meaningless to speak of virtues independent of practical reason and self-understanding; there is no suggestion we know of in Aristotle that the virtues are to be "blind" to and disassociated from reason and understanding. Habituation does not necessitate mindlessness.

3. From the individualist perfectionist standpoint, perhaps no dimension of wisdom is more important than self-understanding. If our telos and the good it represents are individuated, then self-understanding is critical not only to its realization, but also to the form in which it is realized. Yet, nothing has pulled us away from such understanding more completely than modern ethics. For if ethics is agent-neutral and universalistic, then one's own agency matters little; and the goals and directions of one's life can be determined in an impersonalist fashion by the prevalent norms of society, reason, or other common norm generators. By contrast, for IP, there is a push toward the notion that the central ethical problem is one of distinguishing oneself from those common norms. This process does not require a rejection of such norms (though it may well permit or encourage rejection), but instead typically involves making those norms one's own. Making those norms one's own involves more than accepting them and choosing them. It is primarily a realization of their place and value, given one's own particular circumstances and the dispositions and connections of values one has already realized. Thus, while moral philosophers of all stripes want autonomy (understood as the self-acceptance of guiding norms), we further demand self-realization. It is one thing to see norms of conduct as one's own; it is quite another to see norms of conduct as one's own *because* they contribute to or express one's self-perfection. It is the latter that constitutes self-understanding. In addition, self-understanding as a form of wisdom sees the self as engaged with both the "external" world and the "internal" world. Externally, we have society, opportunities, physical circumstances and condition, and tools of action that all require attention. Internally, we have our dispositions, propensities, talents, tastes, and heritage to consider. As we work within both dimensions, we come to realize that they become integrated through us and are thus not necessarily as distinct as their initial descriptions might suggest. We are, for example, internally shaped by our sociality as much as we confront it externally. And many of our external relations with others are a function of choices, habits, and influences others have had upon us in the past. Moreover, situations, things, and dispositions all have natures that require our attention to the

ways their natures may or may not allow them to be integrated with our goals and aspirations. Understanding ourselves is very much a result of the successful understanding of these things, as well. In sum, self-understanding is at the center of practical wisdom because one's self is, finally, the object of ethical reflection; and to reflect well is what it means to perfect oneself. As we noted at the very beginning of this work, the central problem of ethics is how *I* should live *my* life, not how life should be lived.

One's Own

In discussing self-understanding, we have gone some distance toward explaining that self-direction is essential to moral development and success. It is, as we argued in *NOL*, the central good which a political/legal order is set up to protect. In ethics, self-perfection is a function of self-direction because any attained "perfection" that is not a function of one's self-direction is not a perfection of the self, but a gift, an accident, or a happening-to-one. Because our telos is individualized, and because our reasoning and actions are iterated over time, we must continually strive for integration and selfhood. It is not a given. Ours is not an ethics of mere individualism, but an ethics of individualistic *perfectionism*: the "self" with which one begins calls for development and deployment in a manner that will ultimately shape the self one becomes. For us, the self one becomes is more significant ethically than the self with which one starts. Such a view is in marked contrast to that of an "ethics of respect." In an ethics of respect, talk of what one might or should become is ignored completely in favor of descriptions of and inferences upon what one is. Needless to say, that is a markedly different perspective from our own.

Another point to note in this connection is that in advocating the importance of one's good, norms of conduct, etc., being "one's own," we are not thereby advocating a form of atomism. As noted above, we are social animals; but our sociality is itself open to choice, reflection, and individualized orientations. We reject socialized ethics, which sees ethics as primarily a form of social management. Norms do, indeed, become socialized and can have a tremendous impact on governing our lives. But at the margin, we still do (and should) process those norms as individuals; and that processing is what constitutes the core of ethics. The fact that a norm is general, forceful, cohesive, authoritative, and socially binding is not sufficient to render it a moral norm in an individualistic perfectionist framework. Such norms must also be one's own both in the sense that they are adopted by us as individuals, and in the sense that they appropriately conform to our own individual natures, circumstances, and dispositions which, if not always exactly peculiar to ourselves, are not necessarily identical to any other either.

Perhaps another way to bring this point home is to consider what would result if we were to ignore "one's own" in the above formulation. While it might be possible to possess practical wisdom—that is, a wisdom that could be used to suggest to others how to behave— such wisdom would not be ethical, in our view, because it would lack the appropriate ontological grounding. No doubt, we can use our wisdom to advise others and even point out errors in their own pursuit of self-perfection. What we cannot do for these others, however, is to transform that advice into self-direction *for them*. Only each individual can do that and thus make it "one's own." Because ethics is about action, ethical advice can never be a sufficient description of ethical action. Ethical action is, finally, the province of individuals, even when they are acting as members of a group.

EXERCISE

Adam Smith once noted that "man is made for action,"[56] and nowhere is this more evident, yet more forgotten, than in the case of eudaimonia. We are tempted to confuse eudaimonia and fulfillment with contentment, but they are not the same. Flourishing, perhaps, expresses that difference better than the other two terms, because there seems to be something inherently active about it, and that is the key point here. The achievement of our telos is a form of activity, not a state of being content, feeling fulfilled, or reflecting on a litany of accomplishments or an achievement. In psychological terms, the "flow" literature[57] expresses the idea of eudaimonia or flourishing best, both because flow only occurs when one is doing something and because, ironically, one is not self-conscious about what one is doing. One just does it. The particular doing one does, however, in fulfilling one's telos is the exercising of practical wisdom itself. We can speak

---

[56] Adam Smith, *The Theory of Moral Sentiments*, ed. D. D. Raphael and A. L. Macfie (Indianapolis: Liberty Fund, 1984), II.iii.3.3, p. 106.

[57] See, for example, Mihaly Csikszentmihalyi, *Flow: The Psychology of Optimal Experience* (New York: Harper and Row, 1990).

of the various dispositions we possess (innately or otherwise), of the social circumstances we find ourselves in, of the objective opportunities we face, and of our accomplishments therein; but what our telos calls for is the *making* of ourselves, according to our best understanding of how to integrate the plethora of factors in ourselves and in the environment which we confront.

We may take pride in our accomplishments, satisfaction in the respect we are given by others, contentment in the realization of our goals, and relief in the satisfaction of all the psychological "triggers" nature has urged us to satisfy; but all these results have their point for us only because they are products of our practical wisdom actually having been put to use. Practical wisdom may, indeed, tell us to occasionally enjoy these states of being; but that, too, is itself an exercise of practical wisdom! And it is no accident that Aristotle thought it necessary to point out that the contemplative life is also a life of activity—albeit, activity of an unusual sort, because he understood, as well, that our telos was not a state of passivity, but a state of activity. Once one takes this seriously, one realizes that problems, disappointments, weaknesses, and failings are not a problem for perfectionist ethics, because none of them is an ipso facto threat to the exercise of practical wisdom. All of them are the stuff upon which practical wisdom exercises and displays itself. Indeed, even the propensity we might have to fail to exercise practical wisdom can itself become a factor in its exercise, as when we adopt measures to control for those very failures.[58]

Finally, we should note why we did not formulate this description of our telos as "the exercise of practical wisdom *for* oneself." Such a formulation might have kept all the components we have described above; but it also would have suggested some abstracted process of practical wisdom that an individual might latch on to, but which ultimately remains distinct from that individual. And while we would be the first to admit that there can be general truths and experiences that any exercise of practical wisdom would need to consider, practical wisdom must, in the end, reflect its ontology—that is, it must be

---

[58] For an insightful response to those social psychologists who claim that the empirical evidence for the existence of behavioral dispositions is very poor, see Daniel C. Russell, "Aristotelian Virtue Theory: After the Person–Situation Debate," *Revue internationale de philosophie* 1/2014 (No. 267): pp. 37–63, available at <http://www.cairn.info/revue-revue-internationale-de-philosophie-2014-1-page-37.htm>, last accessed October 2, 2015.

tied directly to the various teloi that operate in the world around us. Hence, practical wisdom is itself individualized. It is not perfectionism *for* oneself, but perfection *by* oneself.

3. Conclusion

We have in this chapter described the general features of IP and indicated how it might operate. The final ends that constitute human flourishing as teloi are not ineluctable forces that can only be exhibited through one form of life or behavior. Rather, these ends are dispositional propensities whose "completion" is defined and shaped by judgments of practical wisdom. Practical wisdom is itself an individual affair, in which these dispositional propensities are integrated with others and one's environment in a way that is both coherent and suited to the individual. As a consequence, it is unlikely that normative judgments in this framework will issue in commands, legislative pronouncements, duties, rules, or "answers." Instead, one is likely to find the development of virtues, the use of exemplars, and the considering of alternatively plausible models of choice that are specific to any given situation. The rather open-ended character of the normative landscape of individualistic perfectionism would thus stand in contrast to that of theories which view ethics as primarily a tool for managing and defining social interaction. The latter approach needs definitive answers in order to direct conduct. By contrast, the perfectionist approach we endorse uses norms as guides to clarifying and exhibiting an appropriate range of choices.

Overall, IP holds that the nature of human good or human flourishing is an objective, inclusive, self-directed, socially achieved, and highly personal telos. It is not an abstract, dominant end that is collectively determined, atomistic, or impersonal. The term "*self-perfection*" most aptly describes the nature of human good or flourishing, because the individual human being is not only the *object* of perfection, but also the *agent* of perfection. The individual human being is the foundation for the relata that make human good essentially agent-relative.

2

The Search for Universal Principles in Ethics and Politics

Practical wisdom is concerned with the ultimate particular, which is not the object of scientific knowledge but of perception—not the perception of qualities peculiar to one sense but a perception akin to that by which we perceive that the particular figure before us is a triangle.

Aristotle, *Nicomachean Ethics*, 1142a 26–9, trans. W. D. Ross

In *Norms of Liberty* (NOL),[1] while in the process of arguing for the moral necessity of a political/legal order whose fundamental structural principles are individual basic negative rights,[2] we discovered that there is much confusion about the role and function of universality in ethics and political philosophy. Moreover, we discovered that the role and function of universality varied greatly, depending on how one conceived not only the nature of what is good and obligatory, but also deeper issues in philosophy. We were thus drawn to questions about the nature of ethics and the difference between practical and epistemic universals—matters applicable to both politics and ethics.

1. Avoiding Modernity's Pitfalls: The Four Constraints

It is our contention that we need to free ourselves from certain epistemological and metaethical assumptions of Modernity—to wit,

---

[1] Douglas B. Rasmussen and Douglas J. Den Uyl, *Norms of Liberty: A Perfectionist Basis for Non-Perfectionist Politics* [hereafter *NOL*] (University Park: Pennsylvania State University Press, 2005).

[2] Very briefly stated, these rights are the ethical basis for a political/legal order that requires that the lives and resources, as well as conduct of individuals, may *not* be used or directed to purposes to which they have not consented and, accordingly, that persons are prohibited from initiating, or threatening to initiate, physical force in any or all of its forms against other persons. See Rasmussen and Den Uyl, *NOL*, chaps. 4, 5, 11, and 12 for a full account and defense. Some further elaboration is provided below in section 2.

the following interrelated claims (to be referred to as "the Four Constraints"): (1) in order for moral or ethical claims to qualify as knowledge, they must have the same form as those of theoretical or speculative science; (2) universality is necessary for objectivity; (3) universality can replace objectivity; and (4) the ethical is essentially legislative. As we shall see, both in this chapter and in the ones to follow, our conclusions with respect to the Four Constraints will affect our arguments in both the political and the ethical realms. Moreover, by indicating how we may not actually be bound by these constraints, we will be taking some necessary steps toward our goal of liberating ethics from modalities more appropriate to politics.

In order to bring about this philosophical liberation from the Four Constraints, it is necessary first to consider the proper use of abstractions. Our starting principle is that although abstractions are tools for knowing reality, they are not the realities themselves; and thus we should be careful not to ascribe their form or mode to the realities they disclose. As Aquinas states,

> For although it is necessary for the truth of a cognition that the cognition answer to the thing known, still it is not necessary that the mode of being of the thing known be the same as the mode of being of its cognition.[3]

This view of abstraction will stand behind our analysis as we examine each of the Four Constraints.

ETHICAL KNOWLEDGE DISTINGUISHED FROM THEORETICAL OR SPECULATIVE KNOWLEDGE

Though comprehending moral or ethical claims certainly presupposes, and indeed requires, a theoretical foundation for those claims, it is nonetheless a great confusion to treat such claims as having the same form or modality as those found in the theoretical or speculative sciences. What fundamentally differentiates moral or ethical claims from those of the theoretical or speculative sciences is two-fold: (1) morality or ethics is concerned not merely with the truth, but with what is inherently worthwhile and obligatory; and (2) morality or ethics is concerned not simply with knowledge, but with action. That is, ethics is a *practical* science whose aim is the achievement for a human being of what is inherently worthwhile or appropriate.

Our primary concern in this subsection, then, is that ethical

---

[3] Aquinas, *Summa Contra Gentiles*, II, 75 (our translation).

knowledge be understood as being practical. Ethical knowledge is concerned with guiding the conduct of an individual human being in situations that change and are not the same from individual to individual—which is to say, it is concerned with what is contingent and particular. Theoretical or speculative knowledge, on the other hand, is concerned with what does not change and with what is the same from instance to instance—that is, with what is necessary and universal. Thus, since moral or ethical propositions deal with the contingent and particular, they consider the unique features of every situation and the differences among the individuals confronting them. Our position is that, despite appearances to the contrary, ethical propositions are not essentially guides to conduct that can be invariably replicated across diverse individuals. Indeed, though this is often thought to be the ultimate achievement for theoretical or speculative knowledge, it is in fact a failure for morals or ethics, for it gives consideration neither to the reality of the situation and circumstances, nor to the individuality of the persons involved.

The point of this observation is not, however, to contend that there is no theoretical or speculative insight to be found in moral or ethical claims. Rather, the point is that there is a certain modality to one's theoretical understanding of the plausible candidates for the basic generic goods and virtues that constitute the worthwhile or flourishing life for individual human beings. This theoretical understanding has to be recognized as reflecting in a certain fashion what is good for human beings—namely, as an abstract consideration, and not as a reality—and thus, for understanding human flourishing as a reality, this theoretical approach is incomplete.

Yet, the issue here is not merely that such basic generic goods as knowledge, friendship, health, and pleasure or such basic generic virtues as temperance, honesty, integrity, and justice need to find a place in space and time in which they are instantiated. Rather, the issue is more profound: such generic goods and virtues do not actually have form and reality until they are, as noted in Chapter 1, individualized in light of the circumstances, talents, endowments, interests, beliefs, and histories that descriptively characterize the individual—what we call a person's "nexus." Further, such individualization is an exercise of the virtue of practical wisdom; and this virtue only occurs at the time of action, and never apart from the agency of the individual.[4] So, it is always with an eye toward the agenthood of the individual

---

[4] See Rasmussen and Den Uyl, *NOL*, pp. 143–52.

that any abstract consideration of the human good or flourishing must be formed, and it should never be assumed that one has found the reality that is the human good until the individual has acted.

There is still another facet to this account, however. Human good or flourishing does not just *allow* for there to be different concrete forms; rather, it *requires* that there be different concrete forms of flourishing. There can be no such thing as an abstract understanding of the human good unless there are first many concrete forms of it. Before one can ever obtain an abstract account of the human good, one must first come in contact with many of its various forms. Thus, while one can, indeed, form an abstract account of human flourishing, one cannot assume that one initially *starts* with an abstract account, and then treat it as if its concrete manifestations were merely ancillary to its reality or simply examples of its more perfected form. Instead, the situation is ontologically, and should be epistemologically, the reverse: one first encounters various concrete forms of flourishing, and only then develops a theoretical account.[5] However, our point is not simply that we should begin with the concrete forms of human flourishing and then develop a theoretical account that applies to *every* human being. It is even more fundamental, because our point concerns the very process by which *any* particular human being comes to have an understanding of his or her own human flourishing that applies across different situations, circumstances, and times. How does such theoretical knowledge come about, and why are ethical universals necessary?

The answer to these questions is found by considering the situation of any given individual. One discovers in what one's good consists in a particular concrete situation; and then by a process of abstraction (which we will describe in the next subsection), one is able to discern the general, or what we call "generic," features of one's good—features that apply to other situations, circumstances, and times. Such abstraction is necessary because human beings are limited; and each individual human being needs to find a way cognitively, and ultimately practically, to deal with the diversity and complexity that each situation presents. An individual needs to develop a manner or mode of cognition that will provide a general guide to the kinds of activities his or her flourishing comprises. In this way, each

---

[5] See Christopher Gill, "In What Sense Are Ancient Ethical Norms Universal?" in *Virtue, Norms, and Objectivity: Issues in Ancient and Modern Ethics*, ed. Christopher Gill (Oxford: Clarendon Press, 2005), pp. 15–40.

time that a new situation is confronted, one does not have to begin all over again and go through the same discovery process, but instead has, so to speak, a template or model by which to guide one's conduct. This is why ethical principles or universals are necessary for the individual, regardless of whether the conduct in question is entirely personal or, as is most often the case, social. Moreover, it is through this abstraction of generic goods and virtues, which practical wisdom sees at the time of action to be manifested in the particular and contingent situation, that one comes to know why a particular action ought to be taken. In the practical syllogism, to put it in Aristotelian terms, the generic goods or virtues function as the universals that provide the middle term that helps us reason about the appropriate action. But it must be understood that the "right action" is a function of *both* the applicable universal(s) *and* insight into the particular situation through acts of recognition, evaluation, and judgment. While various "situational" responses emphasize the particular, such "particulars" never occur in isolation, but only within a context of at least potentially relevant additional particulars. Our point is neither to emphasize the particular over the universal nor vice versa.[6] Both are necessary; because at the same time that we are deciding what to do, we are also integrating that action into a pattern of other actions. Modern academic ethics tends to regard only the universals as being relevant to ethical conduct, with the particulars merely being instances of the applicable universals.

Because, in the first instance, the function of ethics is to guide the *individual* in leading a good human life,[7] it might seem, at least theoretically, that the social character of ethics has only a secondary status. But of course, as Aristotle noted and we emphasized earlier, we are profoundly social animals, so it is impossible to understand what it means for each of us to live a good human life apart from social considerations. Nonetheless, those social considerations can, and ought to, be adapted to individual endeavors toward flourishing as well. Some social situations are changeable, while others—such as

---

[6] So, even though we describe human flourishing and the moral obligations that arise from it as individualized and agent-relative (or agent-specific) in character, we are not claiming that there is no place for ethical principles, as, for example, Jonathan Dancy seems to argue in *Ethics Without Principles* (Oxford: Clarendon Press, 2004).

[7] Much of this book, as indicated in the Introduction, is devoted to demonstrating the validity of this claim.

customs, cultural practices, and laws—are relatively inflexible; and the individual must work with it all. The paradox is that the more increasingly acute one becomes at ethical reasoning and conduct, the *less* is transferable from oneself to others—that is, the less universal the principle upon which one may be acting becomes. By contrast, we would argue, the better one gets at *political* reasoning, the *more* universal the principles must be. Liberalism, as we argued in *NOL*, is the best "solution" to this paradox, because it effectively tends toward increasing universality in politics and increasing particularity in ethics, in ways appropriate to both. For now, however, our point is that universal principles are necessary instruments for ethical conduct, rather than its final cause or defining property.

What should be equally obvious from all of this, however, is that there is nothing automatic about the process of ethical action. It is always to each individual's nexus *and* agenthood that the theoretical account of the human good must be related.[8] Thus, any example of ethical knowledge that is beyond merely abstract statements must bring into focus the individual and his or her choices. Yet, once this is done, it must be realized that unless one treats individuals as interchangeable, such concrete ethical knowledge is not necessarily applicable across individuals or situations. So, the speculative or theoretical ideal of knowledge as something universal and necessary is especially inappropriate to ethical knowledge and is by no means the standard by which to judge it.

OBJECTIVITY VERSUS UNIVERSALITY

Implicit in the preceding discussion is the idea that the human good or flourishing can be something objective and real, and yet at the same time *not* something universal. Being universal applies either to what we predicate of something or to how we quantify a proposition. We can, for example, say "Socrates is flourishing," "Aristotle is flourishing," or "Every human being should pursue his or her flourishing." But all such statements involve how we conceptually grasp or understand human flourishing, and do not require that universality pertain to human flourishing itself. As our earlier quotation from Aquinas indicated, there is a difference between the mode of existence that something has when cognized and the mode of existence that something has when it exists independently and apart from

---

[8] We shall take up the discussion of agent-relativity in a later subsection.

cognition. What is grasped or understood universally need not *exist* in such a manner.

Yet, the terms "human flourishing itself" or "human good" or "human goodness" have often been seen as requiring that they signify a universal reality. And here the point is not so much that the use of such terms requires the existence of some universal Platonic reality, but rather it is that the use of these terms requires that human flourishing or human good bears no necessary relation to individual human beings and their situations. Accordingly, even if human good or flourishing is always found instantiated in the conduct and lives of some individuals, it is still thought to be, in its very character, something that is universal and that stands apart from the individuals involved. In the end, the argument seems to be: if we can talk about what human flourishing or human good is without regard to whose flourishing or good it is, then that means or implies that this is a reality which, in its very essence, carries no necessary connection to particular persons or situations; and so universality[9] does lie at the very heart of ethics or morality after all.

This argument is flawed, however. Our ability to think of human flourishing without thinking of its having a particular determination or its being someone's flourishing no more implies that it can so exist than does our ability to think of Henry VIII without thinking of his weight imply that he can exist without some weight or other.[10] Even though our thought must answer to reality if we are to find truth, there is nonetheless a difference between *thinking* something is thus-and-so and its *being* thus-and-so. Our knowledge must be *of* reality, but that does not mean that our knowledge *is* reality.

Yet, to understand how it is possible to predicate flourishing of

---

9 We hasten to note here that there is a difference between universality and universalizability, and that we will discuss the latter shortly.

10 Anthony Kenny puts this point as follows: "To think a thing to *be* otherwise than it is is certainly to think falsely. But if all that is meant by 'thinking a thing other than it is' is that the way it is with our thinking is different from the way it is with the thing we are thinking about, in its own existence, then there need be no falsehood involved. To think that Henry the VIII had no weight is to think a false thought; but there is no falsehood in thinking of Henry the VIII without thinking of his weight. Henry the VIII could never exist without having some weight or other, but a thought of Henry the VIII can certainly exist without any thought at all about his weight" (*The Metaphysics of Mind* [Oxford: Clarendon Press, 1989], p. 134). We will revisit this argument, example, and related points in Chapter 5.

both Socrates and Aristotle or to regard it as the end of human conduct, without flourishing itself being something universal, depends on how one understands abstraction. It is here that we avail ourselves of an account of abstraction that was seldom considered, much less understood, in Modernity.[11] This account is called moderate realism, and it comes from Aquinas.[12] It holds that abstraction is a tool of cognition and that it can be used in a variety of ways and serve different functions. We need not go into a complete discussion of this view of abstraction, but a distinction between two basic kinds of abstraction is useful for dealing with the issue we are here considering.

Aquinas distinguishes between two ways of abstracting the form or character of an existent. The first way, which is called "non-precisive" abstraction (that is, abstraction without precision), considers the form or character of an existent as a whole and thus makes it possible to affirm an identity between an individual and its form or character. For example, we say that Socrates is a human being, that Socrates is an animal, and that Socrates is a living thing. Each of these predicates characterizes Socrates in a distinctive way, but each applies to Socrates taken as a whole, in his entirety, and not as some part. Further, each of these propositions asserts an identity[13] between these respective forms or characters and Socrates.

The second way of abstracting the form or character of an existent, which is called "precisive" abstraction (that is, abstraction with precision), is not concerned with making possible the identification of an individual with its form or character. This type of abstraction occurs when we seek instead to focus on the form itself, rather than the form as fully embodied and individualized. Humanity is, for example, a form of Socrates' nature, but it is not Socrates' very form or nature. It is by means of precisive abstraction that such abstract

---

[11] Modern philosophers generally treat abstraction as only a "partial conception" of the form of an existent. See, for example, John Locke, *An Essay Concerning Human Understanding*, Vol. 2, ed. A. C. Fraser (New York: Dover, 1959), p. 84. Yet, abstraction can and often should be understood as bearing primarily on the entire form of an existent, and not on the traits that are "taken away." See Aquinas, *Summa Contra Gentiles*, II, 75 and 77.

[12] Aquinas, *On Being and Essence*, 2nd rev. ed., trans. Armand Mauer, C. S. B. (Toronto: The Pontifical Institute of Mediaeval Studies, 1968), pp. 42–3 and 47. See also translator's note 15, p. 39.

[13] See Henry B. Veatch, *Intentional Logic: A Logic Based on Philosophical Realism* (New Haven, CT: Yale University Press, 1954; Hamden, CT: Archon Books, 1970).

notions as animality and corporeality are fashioned as well. They, too, respectively refer to forms that are constituents of Socrates' nature. Each is considered as something just in itself.[14]

Precisive abstraction occurs when we focus on the form or character of an existent *as not* related to its individual differences and manner of existence—that is to say, we consider the form or character as excluded or "cut off" from its individual differences and manner of existence. The form so considered is but a logical or conceptual "part" of the whole reality from which it is abstracted. As a result, one properly speaking could not predicate a form so abstracted of the subject in which it exists. One should not predicate, for example, humanity to Socrates. It is false to affirm that Socrates is humanity. Precisive abstraction is not of use in attempting to truly predicate something of something else.

Similarly, when human flourishing is so abstracted—that is, when we consider human flourishing as not fully embodied and individualized by some human agent's activity—it refers to the form of human flourishing just in itself (that is, its constituent goods and virtues) but excludes the individual differences and manner of existence within some subject. Human flourishing so considered is but a logical or conceptual "part" and thus cannot be truly predicated of the entire individual. So, just as one could not truly say that "Socrates is humanity," neither could one truly say, for example, "Socrates is human flourishing" or "Aristotle is human flourishing" *in the sense that each is the very form of human flourishing.* In spite of this, precisive abstraction of human flourishing can be an important tool for understanding the very form or character of human flourishing. Precisive abstraction allows us to examine what human flourishing comprises. It allows us to analyze the generic goods and virtues as such, considered apart from any embodiment. But this does not

---

[14] See Joseph Owens, *Cognition: An Epistemological Inquiry* (Houston, TX: Center for Thomistic Studies, 1992), p. 149. Parts of this discussion of non-precisive and precisive abstraction are taken, with minor changes, from Douglas B. Rasmussen, "Grounding Necessary Truth in the Nature of Things: A Redux," in *Shifting the Paradigm: Alternative Perspectives on Induction*, ed. Paolo C. Biondi and Louis F. Groarke (Berlin: De Gruyter, 2014), pp. 323–58. Finally, the abstract nouns noted in this paragraph do not refer to any physical distinction between the form and the subject in which they inhere. This distinction is made within cognition. Moreover, this distinction does not even show that a material thing is composed of two physical principles, namely, form and matter. That claim must come from an investigation of things, not merely from our ability to abstract.

mean, of course, that human flourishing or its generic goods and virtues, or any form so considered, actually exists in such a manner.

Non-precisive abstraction, as opposed to precisive abstraction, occurs when we focus on the form or character of an existent *not* as related to its individual differences and manner of existence (rather than as *not* related to them). That is, rather than cutting off or positively excluding the relationship, we are simply not considering it. Instead, we are treating the individual differences and manner of existence as implicit by not expressing them. Such a consideration is made possible by focusing on the entire form in an indeterminate manner, so that its individual differences are not specified, but are nonetheless regarded as requiring specific determination. The form *must*—within a range—be specified or determined. Thus, when we consider the form or character of a human being abstractly, but without precision, we are considering the form or character as a logical or conceptual "whole," without regard to its specification; but we know, nonetheless, that it must have *some* specification. This allows us to form, for example, the concept of a "human being," and thus to properly predicate being a human being not only of Socrates in his entirety, but of Aristotle and any other individual human being, as well.

Likewise, when we consider the activity of human flourishing abstractly, but without precision, we focus on its form as a logical or conceptual "whole" or "unit," without regard to its specification or determination (or manner of existence). Yet, at the same time, this "whole" or "unit" is treated as requiring that it take some specific determination (and manner of existence) for some individual human being or other. Human flourishing so abstracted must exist in some determinate manner or form for *some* individual human being, but it can so exist in *any*. We can thus predicate human flourishing of various individuals—that is, we can truly say "Socrates is flourishing" or "Aristotle is flourishing"—but what is predicated of each is human flourishing, considered in this indeterminate manner. That is to say, what is predicated of Socrates and Aristotle are *not* generic goods and virtues understood apart from their specific manner of determination, but these goods and virtues as *requiring* some specific determination and unique manner of existence.

The cognitive signification of "human flourishing" involves, then, the individual differences in the sense that this manner of abstraction allows these differences to be different in each instance when they are made explicit. It is human flourishing treated as an indeterminate "whole" or "unit" (which includes potentially all its manifestations in the lives of unique individuals) that determines the signification of "human flourishing." This is what allows human flourishing to be truly predicated of Aristotle and Socrates and any human being who engages in self-perfection. It allows human flourishing to be a predicate and thus logically (or cognitively) a universal, without requiring that in reality it be a universal. This is the basis for our saying that human good or flourishing is always and necessarily related to each individual's nexus and agenthood.

Yet, it is important to understand that for this moderate realist view, our concepts cannot do all the work. Indeed, moderate realism rejects the assumptions of concept rationalism—namely, that concepts are the immediate and direct objects of cognition and that the implicit individual differences that are not expressed in our abstractions can be discerned or made explicit by a process of *inspectio mentis*. Or, stated in a more contemporary vein, this moderate realist view rejects conceptual analysis as a guide to knowledge in general and especially to ethics. Rather, when discovering how the contingent and particular give determination and reality to the form of human flourishing that is abstractly, but non-precisely, considered, there is a crucial role for looking outside the act of cognition to the reality confronted by sense perception generally, as well as to the deployment of practical wisdom in human conduct specifically. Neither concept rationalism nor ethical rationalism will do.

The specified form of a characteristic or attribute is not necessarily merely an instance of the general characteristic or attribute—indeed, it seldom is; and in the case of human flourishing, it is never merely so. To illustrate this point, we can consider the generic good of friendship. Friendship may be applicable to all forms of human flourishing; and yet, not only are the friends different from one case to the next, but the relevant balance and modes of connectivity of friendship to the other characteristics of human flourishing are so, as well. Moreover, it is only through practical wisdom that this and other generic goods and virtues become determinate and real. Thus, our ability to think of human flourishing without regard to its specific determination or whose flourishing not only does not imply that human flourishing exists universally and unrelated to particular persons, their situations, and agency, but in fact requires that flourishing exist in a determinate manner through the agency of some particular person or other.

Universality is not a necessary condition for the human good or flourishing to be objective and real. Some thing or activity can be good for someone, even if it is not good for everyone. Universality thus refers to predicability or scope, while objectivity refers to applicability; and they should not be confused. However, to say that the human good or flourishing is something that is objective and real, but not universal, does not mean that it cannot be universalized. Yet again, one must be careful not to confuse or conflate the mode of cognition with reality. Even if the human good or flourishing is something knowable, and thus can be universalized, that still does not make it universal. To demonstrate: let us say that F_1 is the flourishing of P_1, and that since F_1 is P_1's good, then P_1 ought to pursue F_1. Now, if it is true that F_1 being P_1's good justifies P_1 pursuing F_1, then F_2 being P_2's good justifies P_2 pursuing F_2, and so on for P_n pursuing F_n. *The knowledge that something is one's good and legitimates one's conduct is what is universalized (this is our mode of cognition), but none of this requires that the character of the human good or flourishing (which is the content of our cognition) be something universal, not individualized, or not necessarily related to individuals.* Nor does this reasoning require that what P_1 ought to do in a certain situation ought to be done also by P_2 in the very same situation.[15] Further, this reasoning does not show that P_1 ought to pursue the mode of flourishing that is F_2, or that P_2 ought to pursue the mode of flourishing that is F_1; and lastly, it does not provide a way of resolving any conflict that might occur between their pursuits of their respective goods. Individuality ethically matters, and there is no justification for ignoring it.

So, the human good or flourishing can be objective, real, and thoroughly individualized—and thus not universal; but since it is real and knowable, it is universalizable. Yet, the ability to universalize or abstractly consider the human good or flourishing provides very little guidance to human conduct, because the major problem for ethics is to determine what an individual, who is not interchangeable with another individual, ought to do in a given situation, which is contingent and particular. Furthermore, and as we shall see later, universalizability does not handle the central problems of political philosophy either. If these problems are to be handled, then, it is important to

---

[15] Paul Bloomfield also makes this point: "At the level of individuals, we should not assume that what one individual ought to do in a particular situation is what every individual ought to do in that situation" (*Moral Reality* [Oxford: Oxford University Press, 2001], p. 39).

remember that abstractions are neither alternative modes of existence, nor shortcuts to knowing what is real or good. Rather, they are tools of cognition that we must learn how to use properly; and this is true not only for knowledge in general, but for ethical knowledge in particular.

UNIVERSALITY CANNOT REPLACE OBJECTIVITY

Kant argued that the paramount principle of morality must be categorical—namely, an imperative that is not conditional on achieving any end or purpose[16]—and that this imperative requires that one make universalizability the centerpiece for the moral use of practical reason. This principle requires that one "*act only according to that maxim through which you can at the same time will that it become a universal law.*"[17] There are five major problems with using this principle as a guide to practical reason.

First, is this principle necessary and sufficient to determine what actions ought to be done? Consider, for example, the question of whether one should gossip. Obviously, to attempt to universalize either (a) "I may gossip about others but they may not gossip about me," or (b) "I may not gossip about others but they may gossip about me," is inconsistent. Yet, there is no inconsistency with universalizing either (c) "I may gossip about others and they may gossip about me," or (d) "I may not gossip about others and they may not gossip about me." Either rule (c) or (d) can be universalized without inconsistency, so universalizability is not sufficient to determine which course of conduct one should follow in these cases.[18]

Of course, Kant notoriously switches the test from whether a proposed maxim is internally consistent when universalized to whether one can wish this maxim to be universalized. Suppose, for example, that we were to consider whether one should follow, on the one hand,

---

[16] "An action from duty has its moral worth *not in the purpose* to be attained by it, but in the maxim according to which it is resolved upon. . . . That the purposes that we may have when we act, and their effects, as ends and incentives of the will, can bestow on actions no unconditional and moral worth . . . " (Immanuel Kant, *Groundwork of the Metaphysics of Morals*, rev. ed., trans. and ed. Mary Gregor and Jens Timmermann [Cambridge: Cambridge University Press, 2012], 4:399–400, p. 15).

[17] Ibid., 4:421, p. 34.

[18] John Hospers, *Human Conduct: Problems of Ethics*, 2nd ed. (New York: Harcourt Brace Jovanovich, 1982), p. 187.

the maxim "Always develop one's talents to their fullest—forgo the easy pleasure of today and plan as much as you can for what tomorrow may bring," or, on the other hand, the maxim "Always be easygoing—gather pleasure and happiness while one may with the least amount of effort and never worry very much about tomorrow." Kant would claim that a person should follow the former maxim, and that one cannot wish to universalize the latter, "for as a rational being, he necessarily wills that all capacities in him be developed, because they serve him and are given to him for all sorts of possible purposes."[19] Yet, *why* can one not will the latter? What is it that guides practical reason? Here we find the second major problem for Kant's approach to ethics. If it is merely one's desire or wish that determines what should become by one's will a universal law, then Kant will have abandoned the categorical imperative for a hypothetical one. In this case, it would be a hypothetical imperative of the *problematic* sort: *if* you seek this end, then you must take the following steps. Or, if the guide to practical reason is an end that is desired or chosen because it is *desirable* or *choice-worthy*—that is, something that desire and choice are *for*, something that *is* their end or purpose—then he will have again abandoned the categorical imperative for a hypothetical imperative. In this case, however, the hypothetical would be *assertoric* in character: *since* you seek this end, then you must take the following steps. In either instance, however, he will have abandoned his claim that ethics or morality must provide guidance in a categorical manner, because moral imperatives will be, in some manner or other, conditional on achieving an end or purpose. Lastly, if Kant seeks to avoid this consequence by claiming that the only thing that is ultimately desirable or choice-worthy in itself is a good will, and a good will is one that wills in accordance with the categorical imperative, then he will have argued in a circle in attempting to provide guidance to practical reason. Further, he will have not explained what to choose when confronted by two equally universalizable maxims.

Possibly, the best way to understand Kant's use of universalizability is not to regard this principle as a necessary and sufficient test, but simply as a necessary one. Yet, is even this true? When the character of Thomas More in Robert Bolt's play *A Man for All Seasons* refuses to swear to the Act of Succession, or when Martin Luther declares before the Diet of Worms, "Here I stand, I can do no other," each is speaking for himself and not claiming that others in

---

[19] Kant, *Groundwork of the Metaphysics of Morals*, 4:423, p. 35.

the same situation should do as he does. But more generally, even in matters that might not be considered as involving basic questions of personal conscience, it is by no means obvious that what Mary ought to do in a certain set of circumstances, Bill ought, in those very same circumstances, to do as well. Mary and Bill are individuals, and *who* they are matters in determining what they should do. Indeed, as long as we are considering the conduct of flesh-and-blood individuals, it is most implausible to assume that practical reason must be governed by a rule for conduct that is equally applicable across individuals. As noted earlier, the nexus of each individual should not be ignored. Yet, this is what Kant's principle requires, and so it does not seem that universalizability is even a necessary test for guiding human conduct. This is the third problem for Kant's use of universalizability.

It is important to realize that this problem stems from confusing or conflating abstractions with realities.[20] In all their concrete particularity, actions, like individuals, are different from one another. Each is unique. Unless there is some goal or end for which they are directed, or some principle they are supposed to follow, there is nothing about them upon which to base the charge of an inconsistency between them. For example, if one moves north at one time and then south at another, one is certainly taking different actions; but they only become inconsistent, *as opposed to being merely different*, if one has the goal of going either north or south, but not both. Strictly speaking, an individual's concrete actions are not themselves either consistent or inconsistent. Rather, they become so only when they are, via abstraction, considered as manifesting a choice—for example, choosing to pursue generic goods or virtues or choosing to follow maxims, rules, or propositions. It is the choice to pursue some goal or follow some rule that is tested, not the concrete actions themselves. Put a little differently, actions only become consistent or inconsistent when they become a matter of human conduct. It is only human conduct that is consistent or inconsistent, not concrete actions.

Yet, since individuals, as well as their circumstances, are not the same, there will always be some difference between the conduct of one person and that of another, and hence always a basis for differentiating among the choices and actions of individuals. This applies to the choices and actions of a single individual, as well, for there

---

[20] We take this confusion or conflation to be the basic source of constructivism, which we will discuss in later chapters.

will always be differences due to circumstance and time, even for that individual. Thus, a fundamental question is: What determines what maxim is exemplified by a particular concrete choice and action in a specific set of circumstances at a certain time? Consider the following observation by John Hospers:

> Just as a mink can be classified as a mammal, a fur bearer, or a quadruped, depending on what features of the animal we are taking as the basis of classification, so lies also can be classified as those told out of spite, those told with the intent to deceive, those told to save lives, those told out of mercy, and so on. Moreover, lies themselves can be classified more generally as statements, as emissions from human vocal cords, and so on. For example, of a given lie which somebody tells, we can say of it that it is (1) a lie told to save a life, (2) a deliberate falsehood (a lie, plain and simple), and (3) a statement. The second is more specific (less general) than the third, and the first is more specific than the second. At which level of generality should the act be placed? Kant chose to place it at the second by calling it a lie, and he concluded that all telling of lies is wrong. Why can't we make it more general, calling it a statement, and say perhaps that it is right to make a statement? Or why can't we place it as a less general level, calling it a lie told to save a life, and then say that lies told under such a condition are right?[21]

Of course, one may argue that some of these differences are trivial or morally irrelevant to the issue at hand; but this in turn raises the further question: What determines what is morally relevant or irrelevant? Here, on the one hand, an appeal to an account of human flourishing that requires the virtue of practical wisdom might be extremely helpful; but that would, of course, move us away from the idea that universality is the sine qua non of ethics. If, on the other hand, one attempts to answer this question by appealing to the principle of universalizability alone, then it must be explained why some features of individuals, their choices, and their actions (for example, personhood) are chosen as the basis for a universal maxim. What determines which features are ethically relevant and irrelevant?

Kant's solution to this problem was metaphysical and epistemological. He argued that human beings were ultimately noumenal selves—that is, purely rational beings, whose reason or will is autonomous because it is moved not by any desire or appetite (even supposing that those desires are for the sake of some human *telos*), but only by the principle of reason itself. Such a will is autonomous

---

[21] Hospers, *Human Conduct*, p. 196.

only insofar as it wills in accordance with the categorical imperative. Thus, consideration of individual differences and circumstances, as well as the desires and inclinations that flow from them, is irrelevant to a purely rational and free being; only exceptionlessness or universality matters. To let individual differences, circumstances, and desires enter into one's moral considerations is to make the human will heteronomous, not autonomous. Human autonomy consists in making oneself an instance of this categorical imperative—that is, one becomes a universal legislator. Kant regarded such autonomy as the condition for the possibility of moral conduct, and he understood that the noumenal order is needed in order to make this type of rationality dominant. Moreover, he thought that trying to determine through abstraction what is morally relevant or irrelevant is utterly beside the basic point and hopeless.

For Kant, the foundations for all of human knowledge, and moral knowledge especially, cannot be found by abstracting from experience. Rather, there are a priori conditions that are presupposed by the very possibility of knowledge; and unless one makes this critical turn and accepts this approach, there would be no way to avoid skepticism regarding knowledge in general and morality in particular. (Here is the source of constructivism in both its epistemological and moral modes.) Indeed, it is vital to note that Kant's entire critical philosophy is based on the supposition that the *mode* of intellectual knowledge, which we have been discussing here in terms of universality, actually enters into the *content* of such knowledge, so that it is both impossible for any object of human knowledge not to have this form, and, at the same time, impossible for that form to be indicative of what reality actually is in itself. In one move, cognition of the forms or natures of beings that exist and are what they are apart from cognition is replaced by awareness of objects whose forms or natures are the product of the very organizing categories and schema of the human intellect. So, given Kant's view of the nature of human cognition, what we have suggested above as problems for the universalizability test are not really problems for him.

The Kantian critical or transcendental turn is, of course, the central gambit in Modernity's story of human knowledge; and though it is regarded in some places as a brilliant and profound switching of fundamental cognitive paradigms, it is for us, as neo-Aristotelians, the very embodiment of the central fallacy that characterizes so much of Modern thought—namely, confusing or confounding the mode and form of cognition with the mode and form of reality. The assumption behind this fallacy—Kant's implicit premise—is this: If human cognition is to disclose the nature of things, then it cannot do so by a particular process or in a certain manner; and if human cognition does have a mode or manner of cognition, then the content of what is known is thereby conditioned by this mode or manner of cognition.[22] Yet, from the fact that some means of cognition must be employed for knowledge to exist, it does not follow that those means must structure the content of what is known and prevent one from having knowledge of the nature of things.[23] Furthermore, if one does not accept what Thomas Reid called "the way of ideas" or assume that all abstraction must operate in an exclusionary manner or treat sensory knowledge as providing nothing more than data that are "entirely loose and separate" from each other, then the need to accept Kant's critical turn is reduced considerably. Finally, when one considers the implausibility of Kant's account of human beings as noumenal selves, untouched and unmoved by desires or inclinations, then, indeed, the critical turn becomes most dubious for dealing with questions of ethics or morality.

This is, then, the fourth major problem: Why should one accept Kant's implicit premise regarding human cognition—or the assumptions of Modernity regarding human knowledge—or the implausible philosophical anthropology? Especially for the concerns of this chapter, we can ask: Are we really purely rational beings who exist beyond space and time, and who are capable of reasoning independently and apart from all desire, inclination, and cultural influence? Are we ultimately only thinking things? Furthermore, is it even meaningful to talk of practical rationality purged of all associations with the pursuit of ends? And even if so, why is such a sort of practical rationality, as advocated by Kant, superior to the sort found in the acts of endeavoring that constitute the lives of flesh-and-blood human beings? Finally, given Kant's critical philosophy, how are we to account for this knowledge of the noumenal order?

Of course, perhaps with these last comments, we are not being

---

[22] Douglas B. Rasmussen, "The Significance for Cognitive Realism of the Thought of John Poinsot," *American Catholic Philosophical Quarterly* 68 (Summer 1994): pp. 409–24.

[23] For a critique of this claim, see Douglas B. Rasmussen, "The Importance of Metaphysical Realism for Ethical Knowledge," *Social Philosophy & Policy* 25.1 (Winter 2008): pp. 56–99, especially pp. 90–8.

fully fair to Kant. Could not one interpret Kant[24] as claiming that such a model of human reason and freedom was not an account of knowledge of the noumenal order, but rather merely a regulative ideal for morality? And is this not what is often called the "moral point of view"? According to this view (which we described in Chapter 1), one should approach all moral judgment and conduct in an impersonal fashion. This means that all morally salient values, reasons, and rankings are construed as "agent-neutral"; and what makes them so is that they do *not* involve as part of their description an essential reference to the person for whom the value or reason exists, or for whom the ranking is correct.

> For any value, reason or ranking V, if a person P_1 is justified in holding V, then so are P_2–P_n under appropriately similar conditions. . . . On an agent-neutral conception it is impossible to weight more heavily or at all, V, simply because it is one's own value.[25]

One person can, in effect, be substituted for any other in determining what ought to be done. The individual is merely a locus around which rules and abstract principles revolve. In describing a value, reason, or ranking, it does not ethically matter *whose* value, reason, or ranking it is. According to this so-called regulative ideal, any consideration that cannot be applied in an impersonal fashion is not morally relevant.

In contrast to this view of morality, there is the view (which we also described in Chapter 1 and will expand upon here) that treats morally salient values, reasons, and rankings as fundamentally personal. What makes them so is that they are ultimately "agent-relative"; and they are agent-relative if and only if their distinctive presence in world W_1 is a basis for some person P ranking W_1 over world W_2, even though they may not be the basis for *any other* persons ranking W_1 over W_2. Simply put, there are no morally salient values, reasons,

---

[24] We have been considering here what we regard as the received view of Kant's moral philosophy, which is a deontological interpretation of his ethics. For a discussion of the various interpretations and a marshaling of some crucial passages in Kant that support the received view of Kant, see Mark Johnson, "Kant's Moral Philosophy," *Stanford Encyclopedia of Philosophy* (summer 2014 ed.), ed. Edward N. Zalta, available at <http://plato.stanford.edu/archives/sum2014/entries/kant-moral/>, last accessed October 2, 2015.

[25] Douglas J. Den Uyl, *The Virtue of Prudence* (New York: Peter Lang, 1991), p. 27. See especially Eric Mack, "Moral Individualism: Agent Relativity and Deontic Restraints," *Social Philosophy & Policy* 7 (Autumn 1989): pp. 81–111.

or rankings *full stop*. Rather, they are always and necessarily values, reasons, and rankings *for* some person or other. Accordingly, there is no justification for regarding considerations that apply to only one person as morally irrelevant. This is, of course, not to say that what one ought to do is merely conventionally or subjectively determined. There can be a basis for objectively determining what is the appropriate course of conduct for oneself, and we shall take it up shortly. Instead, this is to say that one can most certainly determine what the appropriate course of conduct is for oneself, without having to suppose that this conduct *must* apply to others.

Indeed, just as the individualized character of human flourishing does not prevent it from being capable of universalization, so the same can be said *mutatis mutandis* regarding morally salient values, reasons, and rankings that are agent-relative—namely, they, too, can be universalized. Universalizability as a logical matter does not mean or require impersonalism. To demonstrate: let us say that values, reasons, and rankings, V_1, for a person, P_1, are agent-relative; and let us further say that the same holds true, respectively, for values, reasons, and rankings V_2–V_n for persons P_2–P_n. Conduct based on such agent-relative values, reasons, and rankings can be universalized as follows: if V_1 provides a basis for P_1 to act, so does V_2 provide a basis for P_2 to act, and so as well for any V_n and P_n. One cannot claim that V_1 provides P_1 with a legitimate reason to act without acknowledging that V_2 provides P_2 with a legitimate reason to act, and so on. What is universalized here is the knowledge that something's having some value, reason, or ranking for some person is what provides a basis for that person's conduct. Yet, there is nothing about this universalization that requires that what is a value, reason, or ranking for one person must be so for another.[26] There is, of course, the question of just what it is that makes the basis for conduct V desirable or choice-worthy for someone; but that is a question which for us, as neo-Aristotelians, is answered by appealing to the nature of the human good or flourishing and its own agent-relative or agent-

---

[26] That you can understand or appreciate why V_1 provides P_1 with a reason to act, without that implying that V_1 provides you with a reason to act, is often not grasped by contemporary ethicists. Even so careful a thinker as Connie S. Rosati misses this point when she claims: "Good-for value . . . is objective in that it gives anyone reason for action . . ." ("Objectivism and Relational Good," *Social Philosophy & Policy* 25.1 [Winter 2008], p. 344). Clearly, she conflates universality with objectivity. We will see other examples of this error in later chapters.

centered character. Ultimately, our values, reasons, and rankings are grounded in personal flourishing, and there is nothing about agent-relativity that precludes it from functioning in practical reasoning.

If this is so, however, then the impersonalist rendering of universalizability creates the fifth major problem for trying to make universalizability the guide for practical reason. The problem is simply this: Why should one ever agree to follow the so-called moral point of view? What can be said in reply to those who ask why they ought to be moral *in an impersonal sense*? There is nothing incoherent in asking why one ought to adopt an impersonal moral theory—that is, why it would be good, worthy, or appropriate *for me* to do so.[27] And since there is, *by definition*, no way that an impersonal moral theory can give a reason that is not agent-neutral, it cannot provide an agent-relative reason to the person who asks why he should be moral in an impersonal sense. If, in response to this difficulty, it is claimed that moral reasoning just is impersonal and agent-neutral, and that it is not necessary to provide agent-relative reasons, then it is, to say the least, very difficult to see what significance moral injunctions could have for our conduct. What develops, then, from this argumentative ploy is the most fundamental expression of this fifth problem: morality becomes irrelevant to our lives, with no basis for explaining why we should be moral.[28]

ETHICS IS NOT ESSENTIALLY LEGISLATIVE

Most recently, while discussing universality and objectivity in ancient ethics, Christopher Gill noted what we take to be the central point for a proper understanding of ethics per se—namely, that "objectivity in

---

[27] For an in-depth analysis and critique of the claim that it is either pointless or illegitimate to ask "Why be moral?" (where "moral" is interpreted in an impersonal sense), see Irfan A. Khawaja, *Foundationalism and the Foundations of Ethics* (Ann Arbor: University Microfilms, 2008), chaps 4 and 5, pp. 116–209.

[28] Interestingly enough, this problem applies to utilitarianism, too, as well as to any approach to ethics that would seek to explain the good or the obligatory in an impersonalist fashion. In this regard, Richard Kraut argues against the idea of non-relational good—what he calls "absolute goodness"—not because it is conceptual nonsense, but because it fails to be a reason-giving property (*Against Absolute Goodness* [Oxford: Oxford University Press, 2011], p. 27). Also, though we are not sure he would see it this way, see Larry S. Temkin, *Rethinking the Good* (Oxford: Oxford University Press, 2012) for an exhaustive analysis of the difficulties for practical reasoning that result from an impersonalist view of human good.

ethics as in other areas is defined, not by reference to universality, but to knowledge of the truth."[29] This involves many factors: knowledge of what kind of living thing a human being is; knowledge of what Philippa Foot calls "a natural-history story" of how human beings achieve their goods; knowledge of how what we have called generic goods and virtues are expressed in the normative paradigms and illustrative narratives of one's society and culture; knowledge of who one is—that is, of one's nexus; and knowledge of the concrete situation in which one's conduct takes place. All of these factors enter into the truth that defines objectivity in ethics. Yet, knowledge of these factors is also a process, and not something static. One is learning all the while; so, it may be more accurate to say that in these matters, we work in a continuum. We often start with established opinions and slowly see these opinions become knowledge after successfully meeting challenges from contrary accounts and beliefs. Yet, what is most important to notice here is that the kind of knowledge that especially matters is not the theoretical or universal, but the practical—that is to say, the type of knowledge that we described earlier as being provided by practical wisdom. Trying to put all of the foregoing considerations together into a coherent whole in order to determine the appropriate course of action for a person in a concrete situation is crucial and is why practical wisdom is the primary intellectual virtue.

It is, at this point, important to differentiate the tools needed to obtain the knowledge of the factors mentioned in the previous paragraph from how this knowledge is applied to direct conduct. For example, as noted in the previous chapter, taking a perspective other than one's own—whether it is that of an ideal or a friend or *any* human being—is a valuable instrument for acquiring knowledge. The moral growth of individuals, in both its personal and interpersonal dimensions, requires that individuals critically distance themselves from, or put themselves outside, their current situation in order to consider abstractly the best that is possible for themselves as human beings or to relate to others. Such procedures are necessary for learning about one's potentialities and understanding others.

However, it is a mistake to equate the value of taking such perspectives with the idea that values and reasons for conduct should or must be equally applicable to all individuals—that is, agent-neutral in character. Indeed, abstraction, imagination, empathy, and interpersonal perspectives—speculative reason in general—are tools

[29] Gill, "In What Sense Are Ancient Ethical Norms Universal?" p. 28.

for practical reason, but not determinate of the essential nature of practical reason. They should not be confused with the reality of the human being as an individual who acts in different situations and who is a participant in various levels of sociality and community. Rather, they are tools that the individual who is in those particular situations might use to negotiate those same situations.[30]

Quite simply put, we need to know when our concern is with knowing what is true and good and when, instead, it is with achieving what is good. We should not confuse speculative with practical reason. We need to distinguish between, on the one hand, the speculative activity of determining, for example, what are the generic goods and virtues of human flourishing as they might be ordered apart from their relation to any particular person and, on the other hand, the practical activity of determining their proper weighting and balance—that is, their value relative to some individual. The former abstract analysis is necessary for a general understanding of human flourishing; but, after engaging in such abstract considerations, we need to return to our own cases in order to determine in practice what ought to be done.

As was implied in our discussion of universalizability in the immediately preceding subsection, it is important to determine at what level of generality or universality one needs to operate. What is the morally relevant level of abstraction? The answer, however, is not built into the nature of ethical reasoning itself, but is simply a function of the problems to be solved. If one is looking for truth about the nature of the human good, then one is working at a level of universality that is quite different from that involved in the "rules of thumb" one develops in order to know the truth about the specific form of flourishing that is appropriate for oneself. And, of course, this knowledge is different yet from what is needed to achieve that proper form for oneself in contingent and particular situations. What is vital to see here, however, is that there is nothing about the use of abstraction that demands that one always operate at the highest level

---

[30] In an important way, we may here be diverging slightly from Aristotle. Practical reason, for him, is often characterized as the employment of some sort of practical syllogism—a process whereby a universal is stated in the major premise, a particular of some sort in the minor, and a conclusion drawn about how the two relate in the inference. Matters of sympathy or empathy, imagination, conformity, inertia, custom, and the like are all a part of circumstances that can factor legitimately into one's nexus, but which are not in themselves essentially "rational."

of universality. Nor is such universality sufficient for determining what is to be done. Perhaps any level of universality could generate a rule and thus provide some guidance, but there is nothing in *any* level of universality per se that speaks to the appropriateness of that level of universality. The appropriateness of a level of universality is a function of the problem posed by reality itself, plus the recognition of the extent to which any answer put in general terms actually provides guidance. There is, in other words, *always* the question of whether something less (or possibly more) general could be formulated as a principle for guiding action. That question cannot be answered by universality itself.

For example, devising policies as a member of an ethics board at a hospital obviously calls for a different level of abstraction and universality than that required for deciding what portion of one's income to devote to charitable causes. Though the telos is the same (human flourishing), the first situation is one where formulating rules of some universality is the actual object of ethical exercise. In the latter case, the conclusion at which one arrives may apply to no one other than oneself, even if that conclusion could be *stated* in general, universalistic terms. Indeed, it would be more surprising than not, if the conclusion *did* apply to more than one person!

As noted, the rule-governed approach to ethics seeks to treat the two cases just mentioned as being essentially identical. The goal is to find a universal rule that applies to the situation, so that any agent who is substituted for any other can know what to do in that situation (for example, "Ten percent of one's income should go to charity"). This might be thought of as a full-determination approach to ethics, in which the goal for any proposed moral action A, is, in principle, a full description of all relevant normative and circumstantial considerations, such that a rule can be formulated applicable to, and directive of, any agent in a like case at any time past, present, or future. We have argued elsewhere,[31] by contrast, that ethics is fundamentally *under*determined; and by that, we mean not only that universal rules do not cover every case, but that they should not. Full determination is a commitment within, not a requirement of, ethics. Underdetermination is not only a recognition of a plurality of forms of flourishing, but also a recognition of a certain ontological disposition. The force of an ethical proposition should come from reality itself, not the formal structure of the rule.

---

[31] Den Uyl, *The Virtue of Prudence*, pp. 176–81.

In the end, therefore, the main thing that recognizing the moderate realist view of abstraction does is to liberate us from the legislative model of ethics so prevalent in the nature and attitudes of modern ethics and ethicists. Instead of seeking to organize people through ethical norms according to common patterns of behavior, we would think of principled inducements to flourishing. That two people face similar situations dissimilarly would be less our worry than whether the reasons for the dissimilarity are grounded in the respective contributions made to flourishing for the individuals in question. It is not, therefore, ethics as a tool of social control to which we must be wedded, but ethics as a tool of successful living. This latter conception, we might add, because of its inherent openness to diversity and the critical need for practical wisdom on the part of the agent, makes respect for others a *consequence* of the approach. Because, on the other hand, the legislative approach sees agents as undifferentiated and interchangeable, it must (à la Kant) build respect into the structure of the doctrine itself in order to find it at all. While that may initially have good rhetorical appeal, the effect in practice (as we see) is the need for continual calls to respect each other and to tolerate diversity. What is primarily respected under the legislative model is the authority of the rule rather than the person. Consequently, what one tends to be concerned about is conformity of behavior toward a rule rather than toward the person herself. Those tendencies make ethics essentially legislative. The personalism of the Aristotelian model, by contrast, gives respect to the person because agency is prior to principle. Moral principles, like the abstractions upon which they are based, grow out of actual actions and ways of living rather than formal rules. Ethics thus tends not toward legislation but toward pluralism.

2. Ethics versus Politics and Law: The Importance of Liberal Political Order

If we can free ourselves from the Four Constraints, then it becomes possible to see what is unique about a liberal political order that holds individual negative rights as universal political principles. This order, as we have characterized it in *NOL*, seeks to distinguish the political from the ethical by rejecting an assumption about politics that has been operative since Plato—namely, that politics is the institutionalization of the ethical, that statecraft is soulcraft.

It certainly should not be assumed at the outset that there is a direct or isomorphic relationship between ethics and politics, much less an identity.[32] To say that some activity X is morally right or good and ought to be done does not, by itself, imply that doing X ought to be politically/legally required. Further, to say that doing X is morally wrong and ought not to be done does not, by itself, imply that doing X ought to be politically/legally prohibited.[33] Or, as Aquinas suggests,[34] there is a difference between demands of justice that are morally binding and demands of justice that are morally *and* legally binding. It thus cannot be taken for granted that politics is simply ethics writ large.

Determining the nature of the connection between the ethical order and the political/legal order is a question that has had different answers throughout the history of political philosophy. Broadly speaking, there have been two traditions of answers: an ancient and a modern one. The ancient tradition, working with the idea of a "polis" and a more or less monistic understanding of the human good, does not distinguish significantly between the ethical order and the political/legal one. Statecraft is primarily a version of soulcraft—that is to say, the function of the political is "to make men moral."[35] The modern tradition, working with the idea of a society that extends far beyond that of a "polis," as well as offering a more pluralistic view of the human good, rejects the idea that the state should make people good. Instead, securing peace and liberty is the primary aim of the modern political/legal order. Liberalism belongs

---

[32] The following pages are largely taken with some modifications from various parts of Rasmussen and Den Uyl, *NOL*. For a full presentation and defense of the argument presented here, see *NOL*.

[33] In addition, it does not follow from the fact that R is a political regime whose legitimacy is grounded in a moral principle that, therefore, all moral principles, or even moral principles generally, are under the purview of R. See Douglas J. Den Uyl, "Response to 'On Communitarian and Global Sources of Legitimacy,'" *The Review of Politics* 73.1 (Winter 2011): pp. 135–43. Finally, see our extended discussion of this issue: Douglas B. Rasmussen and Douglas J. Den Uyl, "*Norms of Liberty*: Challenges and Prospects," in *Reading Rasmussen and Den Uyl: Critical Essays on* Norms of Liberty, ed. Aeon J. Skoble (Lanham, MD: Lexington Books, 2008), pp. 179–86.

[34] Aquinas, *Summa Theologiae*, II-II, 23.3, Reply to Objection 1, and 80.1, trans. Fathers of English Dominican Province (Benziger Bros. ed., 1947, available at <http://dhspriory.org/thomas/summa/FP.html>, last accessed October 2, 2015).

[35] In Aquinas, there is a distinction between the two orders. Ultimately, however, this is not based on some principled difference between them, but simply on the practical difficulties in achieving the common good of the political community.

to the modern tradition of political philosophy. But if the defense of liberalism is not to collapse back into the classical view, it cannot regard peace (cooperation) and liberty as equivalent to the morally best life. If it does, then it, too, is simply exerting political authority to make men good, as the classical model holds—albeit according to a different form of ethical goodness. Hence, what both the critics and proponents of liberalism do not often realize is that the essential uniqueness of liberalism as a political theory is its *divestment* of substantive morality from the politics. It is not simply substituting its new good (liberty and cooperation) for the old one(s) touted by the ancients. Liberalism stands, by contrast, in direct opposition to how politics has been conceived, since Plato, as the effective institutionalization of the ethical. Liberalism's true uniqueness is its endeavor to *distinguish* politics from morality in the same way it is generally recognized to have done with respect to religion.

A good way to get an accurate understanding of liberalism is to reflect upon a problem that has seldom been considered by any other political tradition. Put abstractly, it is the political problem of integrated diversity. But we have called it "liberalism's problem" (LP), because liberalism has been, by and large, the only political tradition to appreciate its fundamentality and importance. It is not a problem *for* liberalism, but rather one that liberalism recognizes, takes on as its task, and tries to solve. The central issue is the relationship of ethics to a certain sort of social or political order. We have expressed LP as follows:

> How . . . is the appropriate political/legal *order—the order that provides the overall structure to the social/political context*—to be determined? What is its ethical basis? Since the structure provided by the political/legal order will rule over all equally, how can the universalism of *political/legal* structural principles square with the pluralism and self-direction required by human flourishing? Hence, how is it possible to have an ethical basis for an overall or general social/political context—a context that is open-ended or cosmopolitan—that will not require, as a matter of principle, that one form of human flourishing be preferred to another? How, in other words, can the possibility that various forms of human flourishing will not be in structural conflict be achieved?[36]

LP does not arise from any antecedent commitment to liberalism, but from the very character of human flourishing. That is to say, it

---

[36] Rasmussen and Den Uyl, *NOL*, p. 271 (emphasis added and slightly reworded).

arises from the agent-relative, inclusive, individualized, objective, self-directed, and social[37] character of human flourishing.

We now come to what we believe is the crucial realization in the search for universal political principles. It should be recognized that one is *not* trying to find principles that will conform to some normative ideal, as that is generally understood. That is to say, one is *not* trying, for example, to make it possible for human beings to flourish, or to achieve the greatest good for the greatest number, or to keep fundamental social agreements, or to improve moral character or the quality of life—or indeed to operate in accord with the dictates of impersonal duty. Rather, one is trying to find a solution to LP. This is the central issue of political philosophy, and this is what distinguishes[38] politics from ethics. This is the problem to be solved.

So, to get a handle on LP, we need to devise a political/legal order which

1. does not *structurally* prejudice the overall social context more toward some forms of human flourishing than others;
2. is universal or equally applicable to all forms of human flourishing—that is, social in the open-ended or cosmopolitan sense;
3. is grounded in what is *concretely* present in any and every form of human flourishing—that is, grounded in some common critical element that runs through any and all forms of human flourishing (or its pursuit); and
4. appeals to some aspect of human flourishing in which every person has a necessary stake.

Granted, the foregoing criteria are a tall order (especially 3 and 4), but reflection upon this list suggests why ethics proper must be distinguished from the political, and that the connection between the two cannot be a matter of just instantiating what we regard as moral into some sort of political system. Further, and most importantly, one notices that the principles just enumerated do *not* constitute the

---

[37] Moreover, human sociality qua sociality is not limited to life in the "polis"; it is open-ended and thus, as a matter of principle, not limited to a select pool or group. In fact, for human sociality to be achieved, it needs to be possible for humans to live in the company of strangers. Ultimately, then, there is a cosmopolitan character to human sociality.

[38] To distinguish politics from ethics is not to deny that there is a connection. Yet, it is determining the nature of that connection—if, indeed, there is one—that is the *datum explanandum* of political philosophy.

basis for ethical norms that offer guidance to individuals in seeking human flourishing or in fulfilling obligations to others. *Rather, they constitute the basis for ethical principles that regulate conduct so as to establish conditions that secure and maintain the* **possibility** *of individuals pursuing their own forms of human flourishing and engaging in moral activity among others.* The principles that secure the conditions for the possibility of pursuing human flourishing do not necessarily consider the particular situation, culture, or nexus of persons—be they of a person's self, others, or any interrelationships. Rather, they establish a structural framework (or backdrop) that provides *the* general social context for the *pursuit* of one's moral well-being. An ethical principle like this we have called a "metanorm."

Simply put, then, liberalism is a political philosophy of what we term "metanorms"—not a moral program or philosophy of living—and herein lies much of what goes unrecognized in thinking about norms. It is generally granted that norms describing the possible forms of cooperation—as determined, say, by social science—need some further sanctioning to qualify as ethical norms. But it is critical to recognize that ethical norms themselves are not, in fact, all of one type.[39] It may be that some ethical norms regulate the conditions under which moral conduct may take place, while others are more directly prescriptive of moral conduct itself. In light of this possibility, it is not appropriate to say that liberalism is a "normative political philosophy" in the usual sense. Liberalism seeks not to guide individual conduct in moral activity, but rather to regulate conduct so that conditions might be obtained where moral action can take place.[40] To contrast liberalism directly with alternative ethical systems or values is, therefore, something of a category mistake.

Liberalism (as we conceive and argue for it) does not link ethics and politics by making moral goodness or rightness the object of political action, but it also does not put itself outside the realm of ethics altogether. The link between ethics and politics is the link

---

[39] The view that all ethical norms are of one type we call "equinormativity," and regard it as a mistaken conception of ethical norms. See *NOL*, pp. 34–41.

[40] "For to say that one obeys the rules of a baseball game while playing is quite different from saying one is a good player or even that one really understands what it takes to play well. Consequently, while it can be said that one who respects the rights of others is a morally 'better' person than one who does not, this is a sign that one is a player in the moral universe within a social context, not that one is yet a good player, or even that doing so is an instance of good playing" (Rasmussen and Den Uyl, *NOL*, p. 288).

between norms and metanorms—namely, self-directedness.[41] What is needed, in other words, is a principle that is necessary for any moral act to qualify as moral, while at the same time not ruling out any possible forms of flourishing which, we might recall, can be highly diverse and individuated. Self-directedness is the key because it must be present for moral responsibility to occur, and yet does not in itself define any particular form of flourishing. Self-directedness, then, is the critical dimension in need of protection if morality is to have any viability. Metanorms are essentially rules for the protection of the possibility of self-direction, and liberalism is the political expression of that. Liberalism is thus deeply concerned with the ethical, without being in any way ethically directive. *It is the profound recognition of the centrality of self-directedness to morality, and thus a recognition of the need to protect it, that gives rise to liberalism's championing of individual rights.*[42] *Moreover, this recognition should be the standard for judging the legitimacy of a liberal order that holds individual negative rights as universal political principles.*

3. Conclusion

By having overcome the Four Constraints, we are now able to proceed to a discussion in the next two chapters of the importance of tethering political principles to comprehensive philosophical views. There we shall see how the connection between ethics and politics is affected by certain models of abstraction, universality, and knowledge, even though they may be only tacitly identified. In showing these connections and their implications, we shall simultaneously be indicating how ethics need not be bound to the conditions that constrain it in these models, and thus why the alternative we advocate is a viable one. In effect, by indicating how the views discussed here inform and direct the political projects elsewhere, we not only identify the forms and effects of the tetherings employed by others, but also, in the process, make it possible for an ethic of individualistic perfectionism (IP) to be a plausible alternative to the more dominant

---

[41] Self-direction should not be confused with autonomy in either the Kantian or Millean sense. For us, self-direction is simply "the act of using one's reason and judgment upon the world in an effort to understand one's surroundings, to make plans to act, and to act within or upon those surroundings" (Rasmussen and Den Uyl, *NOL*, p. 89).

[42] See note 2 above.

connections of ethics and politics. Having used the elements of IP discussed here and in the previous chapter to wrest ethics from the clutches of these alternative models, we are now able to take up the task of offering a further account and defense of IP in Part II. There, when we present our account of the character of human good, we shall continue to see the importance of overcoming the Four Constraints.

3

Tethering I

A constitutional regime does not require an agreement on a comprehensive doctrine: the basis of its social unity lies elsewhere.

John Rawls, *Political Liberalism*

This chapter is about the need for tethering, and more specifically about the practice of political philosophers over the last few decades, of *untethering* political philosophy in particular from the rest of philosophy generally. Following John Rawls, the current practice often involves a rejection of what is called "comprehensive philosophy," in favor of a self-contained domain of political theorizing. It is this untethering of political theory from philosophy generally to which we object and which we reject. The effort to avoid comprehensive philosophy has given political theory a false sense of independence and a false sense of practicability. There are a number of causes for these problems, but the two in particular that seem most important are: (1) the belief that doctrines or principles are separated or separable if there is not a direct and immediate implication among them; and (2) the apparent belief that consensus constitutes both justification and rationality. In the end, we shall see that certain sorts of comprehensiveness are not avoided, but simply taken for granted by political theorists—as for example, not only in the case of Rawls, but also Martha Nussbaum and, to a lesser degree, Amartya Sen. Another way of stating the last point is to say that political theories are in fact tethered, and the issues are whether a theorist recognizes these deeper ties and takes some responsibility for what is involved in recognizing them. In what follows, we shall try to indicate some of the reasons why we believe that "tethering" and some form of comprehensiveness is unavoidable, and that the current trend in political theorizing does not actually establish its own self-sufficiency.[1] In the

---

[1] It is important to understand here that our chief complaint is about the theoretical and practical insinuation, if not direct claim and argument, that political theory is a self-contained and self-sufficient area of inquiry and quite independent of more comprehensive philosophical frameworks. It is not our contention that what is

broadest sense, mainstream political theory is tethered to the framework of an ethics of respect and thus does not avoid its own bête noire of a controversial comprehensive framework. Perfectionism, as we present it here, has at least the advantage of keeping its tethered aspects out in the open for all to see, as will hopefully become evident as we move along.

1. Nussbaum

We shall discuss aspects of Rawls's untethering project in the next section, but we shall begin with Martha Nussbaum's somewhat surprising defense of "political liberalism" against "perfectionist liberalism."[2] Following Charles Larmore, Nussbaum defines perfectionist liberalism as a "family of views that base political principles on 'ideals claiming to shape our overall conception of the good life, and not just our role as citizens.'"[3] Perfectionist liberalism is a form of comprehensive liberalism and is contrasted to "political liberalism." All perfectionist liberalisms are comprehensive liberalisms, but not all comprehensive liberalisms are perfectionist. Nussbaum mentions Ronald Dworkin as one who holds a comprehensive liberalism without being perfectionist because, although he does not limit himself to discussing "just our role as citizens," he does not endorse any conception of the good life either. Consequently, political liberalism wants to separate itself from what Nussbaum calls "comprehensive normative ethical doctrines"[4] (such as utilitarianism), in favor of a focus upon the political alone. Given Nussbaum's earlier endeavors to ground political conclusions in "human capabilities,"[5] which to us seems not only a comprehensive doctrine but a perfectionist one

---

done under the "untethered" rubric of separated political theorizing is without value. To the contrary, such theorizing is important, interesting, and insightful. It is rather what is missing from such an approach and the hubristic posturing of self-sufficiency that concerns us here—not so much the theorizing itself.

[2] Martha C. Nussbaum, "Perfectionist Liberalism and Political Liberalism," *Philosophy & Public Affairs* 39.1 (Winter 2011): pp. 3–45.

[3] Ibid., p. 5.

[4] Ibid., p. 7.

[5] See the following works by Martha C. Nussbaum: *Women and Human Development: The Capability Approach* (Cambridge: Cambridge University Press, 2000); and "Non-Relative Virtues: An Aristotelian Approach," in *The Quality of Life*, ed. Martha C. Nussbaum and Amartya Sen (Oxford: Clarendon Press, 1993), pp. 242–69.

as well, her move here in defense of political liberalism is surprising. Nevertheless, our concern is with the rejection of comprehensiveness itself, not with whether Nussbaum's own doctrines are consistent.

Nussbaum's discussion of perfectionist liberalism centers on the views of Isaiah Berlin and Joseph Raz, both of whom argue for pluralism. In each case, that pluralism turns out to be perfectionist in nature, because although each of them argues for this view in somewhat different ways, toleration inherent in pluralism is the right kind of life for all. Indeed, it is because pluralism is true that one needs to live tolerantly. As a consequence, the doctrine is both "comprehensive" and perfectionist. It is comprehensive because it addresses more than just the political, and it is perfectionist because it offers an ideal of how to live (the life of tolerance). In contrast to the approach taken by Berlin and Raz is the recognition that not everyone agrees that pluralism is good or the best life. There is, consequently, a fundamental disagreement about values. Because of this *fundamental* disagreement about values, Nussbaum, following Larmore, posits the need for a "thin core morality"[6] to ground political principles—a morality that can be shared by monists and pluralists alike. Its main point is to avoid controversial ideas and arrive at a minimalist set of principles all parties can accept.[7] Where there is a consensus about social organization, acceptance by citizens of these "freestanding" principles as a means for endorsing a liberal order is the motivating force behind political liberalism.[8]

---

[6] Nussbaum, "Perfectionist Liberalism and Political Liberalism," p. 15.

[7] Larmore, Nussbaum, and Rawls all imagine these disagreements coming under "conditions of political freedom" and take this as an indication of the disagreement being genuine and fundamental. First of all, being in conditions of freedom does not imply that a doctrine being advocated is any more genuine than one advocated without those conditions. Conditions of freedom only imply that the doctrine advocated is consonant with one's desires. Being consonant with one's desires can only matter if one is trying to establish a consensus. However, consensus does not establish truth, even in politics; and neither has any justification been given for holding consensus as the ultimate good.

[8] Virtually the whole of political philosophy, as we see here, adopts what could be called a "norm/obedience" approach to thinking about social issues and organizations. The idea is that once political theorists find and articulate the right (ethical) norms, they can then expect people to obey them. If people do not follow those norms, that is a practical, not a theoretical matter. This approach assumes that all norms function the same way—namely, to define patterns of appropriate, legitimate, and desirable forms of interpersonal conduct—and that the propagation of norms of conduct is either the sole basis upon which society

In this connection, the operating normative value is one of respect for persons.[9] Indeed, this may be the only value needed in Nussbaum's view, since "one can get to political liberalism through respect alone."[10] Yet, getting to political liberalism through respect alone only works if Nussbaum is right that "equal respect is a political, not a comprehensive, value";[11] for if equal respect is comprehensive, chances are good it might be perfectionist as well. In any case, if equal respect is in any way comprehensive, a pure political liberalism is undermined. It is our position that equal respect is both comprehensive and perfectionist. A purely political "equal respect" assumes that consensus building and equal respect are coterminous—that is to say, that equal respect is required for building a consensus. This seems not only unlikely, but false. As a practical matter, human history suggests that politics is neither exclusively about consensus building nor about equal respect. In any case, equal respect is not necessary for a consensus to be reached. All that is necessary is that all parties find a basis for an agreement, and that basis may have nothing at all to do with respect or propriety in general. If equal respect is to be taken as a *normative* ideal for politics, it begs all the questions we are here trying to answer. It would be advocating a particular kind of politics done in a particular sort of way—presumably, the liberal way, in which equal respect is paramount—without having dealt with all the incumbent questions about the derivation of those norms.

It is thus certain that any notions of equal respect would depend heavily on other normative principles and would thus be very likely, in the end, to go well beyond the political. This last point holds because equal respect is completely bound up in its expression. Until one determines what is going to count as giving others equal respect, one cannot know when it is present and thus of service for consensus building. But if that is true, equal respect is likely to be comprehensive and perfectionist as well, because one would, at the outset, have to regard giving others equal respect as being the generally right way to treat people, in order to then establish any framework for living

---

can be organized, or is a basis that trumps any other (for example, interest). We call this assumption "equinormativity." We challenge these assumptions in our work, *Norms of Liberty* (see note 14 below).

[9] Nussbaum, "Perfectionist Liberalism and Political Liberalism," p. 18.

[10] Ibid., p. 20. She adopts this approach, positing a specific value in a positive way, rather than the "burden of judgments" approach, which points to difficulties in coming to agreement on values.

[11] Ibid., p. 18.

together politically.[12] Thus, the dangers here for the untethered, political approach are circularity (respect is only manifest when consensus is reached) and comprehensive perfectionism (showing equal respect is the right way for us all to treat others, as demonstrated by its consensus-building qualities). We are thus highly skeptical that equal respect will get one very far, but more on all these points in a moment.[13]

In fairness to Nussbaum, she is in search of what we call in *Norms of Liberty* (hereafter *NOL*)[14] "structurally neutral" norms that can serve to define the rules under which people in a political/legal order will operate, without structurally biasing that order in favor of one form of life over another. She notes in this connection, for example, that governments should not be issuing edicts based upon a Christian (or other) perspective on how to live one's life. Thus, her hope is that she can limit equal respect in such a way that only its neutral political dimensions remain. Yet, as we have just indicated, the bases for justifying and determining the nature of such limitations are themselves dependent upon a perspective on how one actually effects equal respect; and that process is inherently normative. If nothing else is evident, it is that political norms require justification; and our claim is that such justification cannot remain within the realm of the political alone.

Our task here is not, however, to re-argue our own case for struc-

---

[12] Nussbaum actually speaks in terms of "worth" and "human dignity," but then says that equal respect can be adopted for "political purposes," without having to endorse a Kantian framework or its equivalent (ibid., p. 18). But if this is so, it is not at all clear what "equal respect" means, or even why it is needed. It is much clearer, and we would suggest probably more accurate, to start as James Buchanan does with purely self-interested agents who do not give a hoot about "equal respect," and then to imagine the likely outcomes in terms of norm development and consensus building.

[13] Nussbaum believes that a "confident monist" will be deterred by equal respect from coercing her "fellow citizens into salvation" (ibid., p. 18). To us, this indicates how much liberal baggage is already being carried by Nussbaum and others. It could be precisely *because* of equal respect that the confident monist would coerce another into salvation, since that might show true concern for the well-being of another in her eyes. One fears that the meaning of "equal respect," in these cases, will be defined by outcomes favorable to the theorist positing its centrality.

[14] Douglas B. Rasmussen and Douglas J. Den Uyl, *Norms of Liberty: A Perfectionist Basis for Non-Perfectionist Politics* [hereafter, *NOL*] (University Park: Pennsylvania State University Press, 2005).

tural neutrality as presented in *NOL* (and summarized briefly in section 2, "Ethics versus Politics and Law: The Importance of Liberal Political Order," of the previous chapter), but to make an entirely different point. By indicating that such notions as "equal respect" often come loaded with normative content that is often tacitly smuggled into an account, we help establish our position that political principles are indeed unavoidably tethered to broader, more comprehensive ones. Such smuggling is thus actually a form of *tethering*, albeit one achieved by stealth and under cover of presumed untethering. It is characterized by some principle or doctrine being presented as unconnected to and separable from a more comprehensive framework or set of principles, but which nevertheless is informed by them.[15] By leaving such grounding commitments unstated, they are thereby regarded as not present.[16] A "purely political equal respect" seems to us an example of a principle that smuggles in other, more comprehensive ones. It assumes that the political can be justified without reaching outside of itself, even as it attempts to reach outside uncontroversially.

Smuggling need not always occur in the form of grounding theory on the illusion of a "thin" normative principle disconnected from a comprehensive doctrine. The placing of contractors behind the "veil of ignorance" under certain ideal constraints, for example, might be thought a way of purging political theory of disputes based on comprehensive normative frameworks, analogous to removing bias from a given person's perspective on their social roles.[17] For ostensibly, if we cannot know our particular positions in society, comprehensive doctrines become mere abstractions with little value for informing

---

[15] The modern rationalist presumption that what is distinct is also separable no doubt pervades this whole discussion. As an epistemological and ontological point, this is a doctrine we as neo-Aristotelians reject. This presumption—that the rational is the world, such that if there is not a logical connection, there is thereby no ontological or other connection to be had—seems central to the process of untethering political theory from ethical foundations particularly and broader metaphysical frameworks generally. Even Nussbaum's efforts to avoid these "burdens of judgment" problems supposes that by distinguishing the "purely political," one has thereby separated the political from a comprehensive moral doctrine. Such an act may obscure the connection, as we see below, but it does not thereby remove it.

[16] As we noted in Chapter 2, this move has a good deal to do with one's view of abstractions.

[17] We should note that comprehensive frameworks are not the same as general facts and theories which the contractors are allowed to know.

any contractual moves. Consequently, we can avoid debating the merits of comprehensive doctrines and look instead to the behavioral propensities of the ideal observers behind the veil of ignorance. There would appear to be no smuggling in such a procedure, but rather simply a claim to be using a different starting point than one which utilizes some form of a normative principle(s) or theory such as equal respect, open access, or even reasonable dialogue.[18] Yet, there must be a basis for the constraints under which, and propensities from which, the contractors operate, and which undoubtedly nudge them toward certain likely conclusions; so that is where the smuggling is likely to occur, since those constraints and propensities define the very value structure presupposed by the contractors. One suspects those values are almost certainly tethered. We say some things about these moves below, but they do not seem to be Nussbaum's.

Rather, to avoid tying "equal respect" to any comprehensive doctrine when attempting to determine who will have a say about when there is consensus, Nussbaum must face the issue of distinguishing the "reasonable" from the "unreasonable"; for a quest for complete unanimity, or even for a general consensus, among all possible citizens is hopeless, given the diversity of values both rational and irrational. Yet, in drawing such a distinction, the impending circularity of an argument that makes consensus dependent upon "reasonableness" seems palpable, since to be reasonable just "is to endorse a liberal political conception" or to "respect other citizens as equals."[19] Hence, the fact of consensus tells us we are in the presence of the right kind of people (those who are "reasonable"), and only those who are reasonable will qualify as candidates to form a consensus.

In addition, setting aside comprehensive doctrines would seem here to be a manifest case of the *Meno* problem of supposing that knowledge can be ignored for the sake of true opinion. For even if consensus could be achieved by dismissing the comprehensive frameworks that likely inform any particular value(s) V upon which a real consensus is built, it does not yet follow that one has established a

---

[18] As Nussbaum presents him ("Perfectionist Liberalism and Political Liberalism," pp. 22ff.), Rawls smuggles, too, through his concept of "reasonableness," which already includes some acceptance of "democratic freedoms" (ibid., p. 24). Nussbaum admits that Rawls uses reasonableness in an "ethical" sense; but she wants to push, with Samuel Freeman, for a reading of "reasonable" in Rawls that is purely epistemic. Even if successful, however, the unaddressed issue of whether the epistemic can be separated from the ethical looms over this tactic.

[19] Ibid., pp. 26 and 33.

case for the acceptance of V by characterizing it as the basis for a consensus—unless, of course, one is willing to say V's worthiness is simply a function of its serviceability for a consensus—unless, that is, one is willing to acknowledge that answering the question of why one should accept V as worthy or appropriate as a basis for generating a consensus is not equivalent to justifying the value of the consensus itself. Indeed, we would contend that even if V is an expression of a worthy or appropriate value, to leave out the reasons *why* one holds V or is justified in holding it beyond its utility for building a consensus actually opens one up to the possibility of very illiberal outcomes. Consider, for example, a more common area in which one's comprehensive doctrines seem irrelevant, yet consensus is arrived at—namely, trade. It matters not what your religious or other views are, or why you hold them, so long as you have something another wants, and the other gives something to you in return. All that matters in this case is the perceived mutual advantage which allows the parties to form a consensus about at least this particular transaction and then to trade or not. But this sort of consensus works because of self-interest. What exactly is the basis for consensus in the order desired by Nussbaum?

In Nussbaum's conception, the basis for consensus can only be one of agreement with what Nussbaum takes to be a "liberal political conception" or giving "respect to other citizens as equal." Unlike the case of trade, where the cement of the consensus is self-interest, here, ironically, the cement is a commonality of outlook, presumably incorporating a whole body of "liberal" moral and political principles. Should one fall outside of the way in which Nussbaum wants to interpret holding a "liberal political conception," one must be either ignored or forced to participate as a proper liberal. Either prospect is itself "illiberal" in nature. Even if we ignore the foregoing issue of conflating consensus with justification, consensus as a function of a common outlook may suppress its comprehensive connections, but it does not avoid its own sort of perfectionism. By suppressing the comprehensive connections that one might employ when approaching a situation of consensus building, and by eschewing self-interest altogether, one is left largely with the exertion of power by those controlling what is to count as the appropriate common outlook of any value V such as "equal respect." That is, if the *particular* way in which one chooses to interact with others does not meet the standards of "reasonableness," then one is either ostracized as "unreasonable" or made to conform. This is unlike the case of trade, in which there is no *additional* element of trade required upon which to forge a common commitment. In Nussbaum's conception, the typical foundations for building a consensus—namely, self-interest or the prospect of enjoying living in one's world view—are absent.

One should not misunderstand us here. We are not opposed to the true opinion that one should treat other citizens with equal respect, or that the liberal political conception is the most reasonable. What we are opposed to is the belief that such conclusions either are disconnected from more comprehensive positions, or are of much value to normative political theory when they are so disconnected. Indeed, for us, political philosophy just is the consideration of political matters *within* a more comprehensive framework. Not only is the middle ground of normative theorizing apart from more comprehensive frameworks subject to the same instability as "true opinion" is in Plato's *Meno*; but it is also quite reasonable to conclude that this middle position is unconnected to, and of no use for, the forming of actual political consensus in the "real" world. In a world of thin moralities devoid of comprehensive doctrines, why would anyone think it legitimate, or wish, to follow any of the conclusions drawn about values stripped of a larger context which might give them meaning?[20] The very values Nussbaum touts, such as "nonsubordination" and "nonendorsement,"[21] which both maintain the equality of every individual under law, were not developed in a climate absent of comprehensive normative frameworks. In the case of the American Founding, for example, to which Nussbaum also refers, a framework of natural rights was held to give meaning to such principles, and was used later on by those with such comprehensive perspectives to advance the abolition of slavery, not to mention other judicial reforms. It is hard to imagine success along those lines with a "thin" moral doctrine acceptable to all major comprehensive perspectives. One would expect an abstracted set of values such as this

---

[20] Again, Nussbaum hopes that, like overlapping Venn diagrams, there will be a "moral content . . . acceptable to all major comprehensive ethical claims" (ibid., p. 36), but which is not itself a function of a particular comprehensive doctrine. But even if such moral content could be found and people were willing to divorce their opinions about its particulars from any broader context, it does not follow that such views are of any use either to building real consensus or to shoring up the comprehensive doctrines with which they might otherwise connect. As Plato noted in the *Meno*, "true opinion" flickers about and does not of its own accord necessarily lead one to knowledge.

[21] Ibid., p. 44.

to engender alienation or indifference from, rather than commitment to, such commonly denominated values. In any case, the endeavor to untether certain values from their comprehensive homes simply replaces comprehensiveness with commonality at some critical juncture; and commonality is both an invitation to suppression and a contrast to the liberal diversity so rhetorically present.

Of course, Nussbaum and others want to suggest that individuals can have whatever comprehensive doctrine they like and still reach consensus. What she is after is that intersection of values which crosses all relevant comprehensive doctrines. It is important to understand at this point that this sort of response is effectively saying that consensus is not arrived at, but *discovered*. The trick, however, is to *find* that set of values which crosses comprehensive doctrines. Analogies to trade and bargaining are thus misleading. We are not talking about a process of consensus building here at all, but rather a state of affairs—a state in which we have shaved away controversial principles and justifications, until a common denominator of values crossing all relevant citizens has been found. It matters not how well-formed the surrounding comprehensive doctrines might be, nor whether any are present at all. Once the common moral content has been found, the political theorist's work is thought to be over.

For the work to be over, however, we must again assume either that the common denominator of values *just is* consensus, or that the common denominator is a plausible basis for arriving at it. The first option, that finding the common denominator of value just is arriving at consensus, simply returns us to our question of why that common denominator should be valued normatively for arranging political order—that is: Why is the "consensual" also prescriptive?[22] To say that we need *some* principles of political order in order to avoid conflict, and that these will avert that conflict, does not help because, as we have already noted, many arrangements will give us political order. Thus, either we again smuggle in a host of principles about what set of common values are going to qualify as acceptable to us—because they have been rightly arrived at or are of the right (for example, liberal) type—or we move to our second option of using the common denominator of values as a basis for *negotiating*

---

[22] This is to ignore the question of why overlapping values is even thought to be a consensus. It would seem rather to be just that, overlapping values. As we note above, for there to be a consensus, there must be agreement, but overlapping values is not equivalent to agreement.

a consensus. Before moving to that second option, we should note that the belief that commonality alone is consensus, without any additional support from broader principles informed by a comprehensive framework, ironically tends toward the highly controversial *comprehensive* view that agreement or commonality is, after all, the standard of truth—where truth, in this case, means legitimacy. Such a position is a version of philosophical pragmatism, and we suspect that much of that view lies in the background here. Needless to say, if that is where one stands, a whole panoply of philosophical questions and doctrines about the nature of truth and its application to moral norms now enters the picture. Moreover, the presence of such philosophical disputes helps support our broader claim that untethered "thin" moralities are philosophical fantasies and potentially dangerous in practice.

To look to our second option of using the common moral denominator as a *means* to consensus, one may either hold to the not-implausible view that commonality of values is a good basis upon which to build a consensus, or that commonality is itself at least a sufficient sign of agreement. Commonality alone, however, cannot constitute a sufficient sign of agreement. Ignoring issues of degree, if you and I both value X, nothing yet follows about what we might be agreeing to, especially in a political context. It might be, for example, that after paring down all the uncommon and distracting values, one discovers that all "citizens" believe calling one's mother at least weekly is an important value. From this, it follows neither that they would be agreeing to making it a norm for structuring the political order, nor that it should serve as such. Instead, it seems more plausible to suggest that such a value might have some prima facie standing as a *basis* for gaining agreement. Yet, however plausible that may seem, we are a long way from having agreement on a *political* principle. For some will want to *require* calls to one's mother with incumbent civil penalties for those failing to comply, while others will want to leave it up to the individual, while still others will want to abandon their commitment to the value altogether, once they witness the dispute about its political manifestations. The only remaining alternative, therefore—short, again, of having elites decide the meaning of these questions—is to abandon the pretext of consensus and simply hold out the common-denominator values as moral ideals. The role of political philosophy, then, is to arrive at moral ideals that can serve as a basis for others finding ways to order political society. In saying this, however, we are back to our old question: Why should we regard this version of moral content as being ideal, justificatory, or worthy of prescription, unless we are already committed to a whole package of comprehensive doctrines on truth, morality, and political desirability?

For now, in raising the possibility that untethering may, in the end, be an illusion, we need to note that tethering takes place in multiple dimensions and directions. A "thin" moral value such as "equal respect" can be tethered to liberalism, which itself might be tethered to more comprehensive doctrines of human dignity. By the same token, "equal respect" can be tethered in the other direction to such things as the promulgation of law and from there further, perhaps, to even more specific values, such as gender and racial equality under law. Our point is twofold. First, we are not against theorizing within frameworks, or against theorizing without making certain background conditions explicit. Rather, we are against the pretense that such conditions are not there, or that they have no relevance to, and need not be considered when theorizing from, one's "starting" principles. Second, we find the quest for the uncontroversial to be hopeless. It is better to embrace one's frameworks and to argue for their superiority in the face of inevitable controversy than to look for the magic bullet of justificatory neutrality. The push toward doctrinal consensus is a form of politicization or democratization of philosophy itself. That is a tendency which not only hampers one from seeing the comprehensive foundations lying in the background, but also constrains one from liberating ethics from politics.

2. Rawls

Whereas Nussbaum gives the impression that expunging comprehensive theories will produce inroads into basic questions of political philosophy and justifications of liberalism, Rawls appears to be much more circumspect. In the first place, Rawls, while seeking to untether political theory from comprehensive doctrines, nevertheless does, in *Political Liberalism*,[23] tether himself to certain broader frameworks such as the social contract tradition and Kantianism, as well as to certain understandings of the meaning of liberalism itself. The rejection of comprehensive doctrines by Rawls could thus be because he holds that certain dimensions of liberalism do not need them, can proceed without them, and will produce a better, more

---

[23] John Rawls, *Political Liberalism* (New York: Columbia University Press, 1993).

stable consensus if they are ignored. It may not, therefore, be the case that Rawls untethers himself from all comprehensive philosophical frameworks, but rather that he believes relevant portions of some of them can be politicized in the service of the problem that seems to occupy him in *Political Liberalism*—namely, consensus building. Nussbaum's approach, in contrast, seems subtly different, though we must admit we are not completely convinced Rawls and Nussbaum are not ultimately in pursuit of the same goal. Nussbaum, on our reading, is not simply saying that we can do without comprehensive doctrines in arriving at basic principles of liberal justice for a political order, but also that because we can, liberalism is not merely a superior political approach for securing justice, but, indeed, the *only* political order able to do so. In this connection, liberalism—or some aspects of it, at least—is a starting point for Rawls; and the arguments that take place within its framework need not *necessarily* be considered as addressing the value of liberalism itself vis-à-vis alternative political orders. For the moment, then, we will assume we are working within an approach that begins with a commitment to some political conception of liberalism and its attendant basic values, and that is working to find a way to arrive at a substantive *liberal* theory of justice within that framework. For convenience, we will generally follow Paul Weithman's reading of Rawls as offering a "conception-based" account rather than a "respect-based" account.[24]

Respect-based accounts take Rawls's "liberal principle of legitimacy"—which holds that

> our exercise of political power is fully proper only when exercised in accordance with a constitution the essentials of which all citizens, as free and equal, may reasonably be expected to endorse in the light of principles and ideals acceptable to their common human reason[25]

—as being more fundamental than the principles of justice themselves and thus as helping to frame the legitimacy of those principles. Yet, if, as Larmore claims, the liberal principle of legitimacy would be selected by those behind the veil of ignorance, and if, therefore, this is an argument for the legitimacy of the basic principles of jus-

---

[24] Paul Weithman, *Why Political Liberalism? On John Rawls's Political Turn* (Oxford: Oxford University Press, 2010). We should note that since Nussbaum claims to follow Larmore, she may conceive herself as offering a conception-based view rather than a respect-based one. But, of course, if that distinction really does not hold, and we believe it does not, then the point becomes moot.

[25] Rawls, *Political Liberalism*, p. 137.

tice, then the relationship between those principles and the liberal principle of legitimacy would be circular. Obviously, then, the exact role of the liberal principle of legitimacy is important with respect to some of the circularity questions we noted above. To avoid such concerns, the conception-based approach takes the liberal principle of legitimacy hypothetically with respect to the principles of justice. That is, *if* one adopts the liberal principle of legitimacy, then we can regard the original position and its products as themselves being legitimate. And we should accept the liberal principle of legitimacy, mainly because we already, in fact, do so, or would be likely to do so.[26] The liberal principle of legitimacy is, in other words, that liberal starting point we just mentioned above. The liberal order is, therefore, not positioned theoretically against other political orders (for example, monarchy), but is one within which one is already working. If it has a claim against other political orders, it would be because others see liberalism at work and want to adopt it for themselves. In any case, the conception-based approach is, as a theoretical posture, more modest in what it claims.

The principle of liberal legitimacy is the spring from which the principles of justice will flow and in terms of which they will be judged.[27] As such, the philosophical question is: What grounds that principle of legitimacy? A conception-based approach has perfectly interesting uses in its own right, but does it escape dependency upon comprehensive doctrines any better than the respect-based view? Given the contents of the principle of liberal legitimacy, are not Kantianism and social contract theory with us under a conception-based approach every bit as much as they are under a respect-based one? Insofar as hypotheticals always seem to be disassociating themselves from any broader framework because they make no explicit connection to one, perhaps, in that respect, the conception-based approach does distance itself from comprehensive doctrines. However, the crucial starting point in this way of looking at things—namely, the principle of political legitimacy—remains unjustified. It is by no means so "thin" and obvious as Weithman seems to suggest. Thus, framing that principle with a hypothetical orientation does not remove some evident connections to broader comprehensive doctrines.

---

[26] We should note as we say below, that accepting something as a fact of one's society is a legitimate beginning point and consonant with the perfectionist perspective we adopt.

[27] There is also the issue of reciprocity here.

We intend to show this connection now—in part, by indicating why, from our neo-Aristotelian perfectionist perspective, the whole approach taken by Rawls and others following him constitutes an alternative comprehensive framework of a "controversial" and, from our perspective, potentially rejectable character. What Rawls and others hope will be the case is that a comprehensive doctrine can be understood as a specific school of thought (for example, utilitarianism), or as an identifiable approach to understanding how to live (for example, Christianity), within which particular values on how to live are generated and contextualized. Rawls himself defines a comprehensive doctrine in the following way:

> [A doctrine] is comprehensive when it includes conceptions of what is of value in human life, and ideals of personal character, as well as ideals of friendship and of familiar and associational relationships, and much else that is to inform our conduct, and in the limit to our life as a whole.[28]

As we have seen, the hope of the social contract would be to leave aside particular prescriptions on how to live, because they are not acceptable to all, and instead to find principles upon which all reasonable people would agree. In this respect, it is not a comprehensive doctrine per se that is being rejected, but what could more specifically be called a comprehensive *moral* doctrine—one that issues in particular values and life orientations. In this respect, some comprehensive philosophical doctrines such as broad understandings of Kantianism and social contract theory seem acceptable. Rawls himself seems to tether his doctrines to precisely these kinds of comprehensive views, for they do not seem to qualify as comprehensive in the way he defines it above. Some understandings of utilitarianism, however, will not work if they are too prescriptive of particular ways to live.

What seems to be the main sticking point regarding the problem with comprehensive doctrines will be mentioned shortly below. In any case, since the history of philosophy, including political philosophy, tends to combine comprehensive doctrines in Rawls's specific sense with broad frameworks such as that connected to Kantianism, the hope of Rawls et al. seems to be to separate the more directive from the procedural dimensions of a philosophical or theoretical doctrine. Social contract theory and Kantianism seem the best candidates for effecting such a separation.[29] We need to ask, however, whether

---

[28] Rawls, *Political Liberalism*, p. 13.
[29] That we can even accomplish such extractions requires a certain epistemological

this whole approach or manner of theorizing is itself dependent on some sort of comprehensive presumptions. It certainly seems to us that the perfectionist approach we adopt is an alternative generalized philosophical framework not likely to be comfortable with such separations.

The Rawlsian approach to the foundations of political order is, by his own admission, a social contract approach. This approach stands in sharp relief from the classical political tradition generally, and from the Aristotelian one in particular. The central and defining difference between social contract theory and these other traditions is that social contract theory begins with individuals completely disassociated from any community or social groupings, and then seeks to produce a set of rules that will come to define the structural and normative properties of a community. In this respect, social contractors either create communities or impose upon them. In this respect, too, social contracting starts with an abstracted or idealized setting, and then seeks to bring its conclusions to the real world of acting agents. By contrast, the Aristotelian tradition regards individuals as already embedded within communities with existing conceptions of justice and norms of conduct. Historically that tradition seeks to move from an understanding of those structures toward principles and forms that will somehow perfect its citizens.[30] In this respect, Aristotelianism moves from the real to the ideal. In any case, there is no basis for consensus here. The doctrines themselves define the nature of the procedural moves within them and determine what sorts of principles can be tethered together. There can be no "consensus" between these two approaches.

The Rawlsian consensus view, however, would contest this last conclusion and claim that there can be certain principles acceptable to one working within the Aristotelian framework that would also be acceptable to the Contractarian, and vice versa. These could then be separated from the doctrines that gave rise to them and be used as a basis for establishing consensual principles covering both doctrines. But, of course, one cannot proceed with such a "consensus," because consensus building itself is getting political philosophy off

frame of reference about the nature of concepts and their connection to reality; we challenged this in Chapter 2. Such attempts are a part of what we call the rationalist, "distinct therefore separable fallacy."

[30] We are contrasting the approaches generally and typically. Our own view is a modified form of Aristotelianism.

on the wrong foot by focusing on the wrong issues. Indeed, whatever the "common principles" are, they would function too differently to be compatible. In the one case (Rawlsian), the project is constructivist. In the Aristotelian case, the project is perfectionist. The former seeks adherence to defined norms. The latter seeks developmental success. Assuming what we elsewhere call equinormativity within each of these approaches—that is, assuming all moral principles within a moral theory are of the same type, even if they have different weights—then even a principle such as "equal status under the law" could not be understood in the same way by the two approaches.[31] If consensus really is the goal, a *theoretical* presentation of principles is not likely to produce it, even among theorists.

We might also, in this connection, wonder whether the acceptance of the liberal principle of legitimacy already qualifies liberalism as expressive of a comprehensive doctrine of some sort. Here the answer is supposed to be "no," because the principle and the liberalism it spawns do not tell us how to live (at least, not until there is agreement about that), but rather offer only a commitment to basic political forms (for example, equal voice, promulgation of rules, democratic basis of power, etc.), which in no way are obviously connected to, or require, a particular comprehensive doctrine to support them. But the view that comprehensive doctrines are thereby excised may be predicated upon a distinction that is itself tethered to a more comprehensive philosophical doctrine—namely, the division between the good and the right. Comprehensive moral doctrines that seem bothersome to Rawls and others are generally doctrines either *of* the good, or which imply an orientation toward a good(s). If one thus removes an orientation toward the good, it would seem that values thereby take on a "procedural," rule-like structure, which in turn suggests that a variety of contexts might be imagined which could support the rule, thus making consensus without comprehensiveness seem possible. In a way, any doctrine which advocates a good is thereby subject to the question of why one should accept that good, and hence inherently open to controversy and lacking in neutrality. The answer to any such "why" question is, therefore, going to have to come in a form that appeals to what an agent will (or should) accept or recognize as good. Those appeals are, in turn, likely to come tethered to a context that provides an answer to the

---

[31] For example, the Aristotelian might opt for proportional equality and the Rawlsian absolute equality.

question of *why* that something is good. There is a close connection, if not identification, between the particular agent and the justification or explanation of the good. The exhortation, for example, to attend church regularly in order to be saved posits a good that calls for an explanation of why it is good, and of why it is good for that agent. Moreover, the explanation is likely, in turn, to call forth some sort of comprehensive doctrine about God and the nature of the soul.

In contrast, although we can also always ask why a rule is "right," the answer would seem to need no appeal to a motivating factor or conception of well-being or human flourishing on the part of the agent, because the rule is thought to be applicable or justifiable independently of anyone's motivation or acceptance, and even irrespective of considerations of his or her well-being. Indeed, the rule can be recommended in the face of contrary motivations and can in turn recommend obligations that may or may not have any bearing on well-being.[32] Should we try to present regular church attendance as a rule for all, for example, we are not likely to get anywhere without having to mention the comprehensive doctrine that explains it. Still, we could imagine a diverse community of believers (Christians, Jews, Muslims) who—provided "church" is interpreted as something like a "place of worship"—could agree that everyone should attend church regularly, without their also having to share the same comprehensive doctrine. The rule-like form appears to shed the contexts in which the "good" is justified or given its meaning. Instead, the good seems to be set aside in favor of the behavior required. Consequently, a rule of "right" seems "impartial," appealing to no particular will or aspiration, thus making a common acceptance dependent only on an agent's recognition of its rightness. This is why Rawls can, without blushing, claim a connection to Kantianism, without believing he is attaching himself to any *comprehensive* doctrine. He has, by doing so, seemingly made no commitment to the sort of comprehensive doctrine that is directive toward a good.

We have elsewhere attacked the division between the good and the right, suggesting that the separation is neither so easy as it appears, nor desirable.[33] We shall not repeat our argument here, except to say

---

[32] In Part II, we are able to consider the nature of the good and its connection to the relationship between motivation, well-being (or human flourishing), and obligation, because the way is being cleared here for their consideration apart from the political.

[33] Rasmussen and Den Uyl, *NOL*, pp. 22–8.

that we are not convinced that even what we have been working with above escapes an appeal to the good. The liberal principle of legitimacy, for example, speaks of what is "proper"; and Rawls is careful to base consensus not upon mutual acceptance alone, but upon "reasonable" acceptance. Moreover, the "Aristotelian principle," which Rawls himself accepts, concerning the desirability of being able to exercise our talents and have a certain degree of autonomy and independence, tethers itself to some version of a comprehensive view of the good life for human beings. These apparent intrusions of some perfectionist concepts could themselves perhaps be justified by other deontic rules, but we believe that one will eventually have to appeal to either a good or a brute fact with good-like value implications (for example, others see it and like it). In short, it seems to us highly improbable that one can present any theory of justice which does not tether itself to—and thereby direct behavior according to—"ideals" represented by a comprehensive theory.

In Rawls's case, "reasonableness" is pegged to do a lot of the work in avoiding any commitment to a comprehensive doctrine. Of course, we are expected to interpret "reasonableness" in a Kantian fashion to mean: compelling to reason without any necessary reference to the agent's good. But even if we accept this and ignore the question of why we should value "reasonableness," it is evident that some good—namely, social peace or cooperation—is driving the entire process. Is it not perhaps the case, then, that social peace and cooperation can and should be explained in terms of something else, something comprehensive? Further, is it not also the case, on Rawls's view, that any doctrine or point of view which does not start with cooperation as the central value (and there have been many in human history holding this to be of secondary value at best) is apparently in the grip of some contestable comprehensive doctrine and thus to be ruled out as unsuitable for consensus building?

Our point here is not to argue for any particular comprehensive doctrine, or to suggest that we are opposed to many of the values Rawls and others would advocate. Rather, our point is to suggest that Rawls may not so fully extricate himself from the grip of a comprehensive doctrine even as he understands it; and to the extent that he fails to do so, the theory will not have much utility for consensus. Thus in response to our question above about whether the comprehensive doctrines could be dropped, the answer is "no." The "right kind of person"—both for engaging in social contracting and for being a citizen of the Rawlsian state—is pretty clearly outlined in Rawls's work. A person with strong convictions about the human good, and who gives those values pride of place over "cooperation," will be every bit as ostracized and demeaned by Rawlsian moralists as Rawlsians are likely to be by that person. At multiple levels, perfectionist approaches to the questions of justice and social order are rejected, and the very acts of rejection are themselves contributions to the detailing of a comprehensive doctrine. Simply put, we have a pretty good idea of how one ought to behave if one is to be a good Rawlsian.[34]

The illusion of comprehensive avoidance comes as a result not only of the separation of the right from the good, but also of the notion that because a given particular value (for example, church attendance) could be adopted by more than one comprehensive view, it, therefore, can serve as a basis for consensus and can be detached from the context that makes it meaningful. With respect to the first, it looks like regular church attendance could only function as a rule of consensus if the Christians, Jews, and Muslims would all drop their comprehensive views; but this is mistaken. It is only *because* they are allowed to *keep* their respective comprehensive views that they agree to the rule about regular church attendance. Should the rule mean only Christian churches, for example, there would be no consensus to be found.

We need to realize that there is a difference between the coincidence of belief and agreement. The former does not guarantee the latter, and the latter is very much dependent upon the retention of one's conception of the good. In other words, if A believes X, and B believes X (for example, both believe in Rawls's "difference principle"), it does not follow that A and B either *accept* X or agree that X is a principle that both are obligated to follow. For agreement to occur, there has to be acceptance, and acceptance is itself dependent upon seeing X in terms of the goods and other principles to which X is tethered. Values do not come to us as discrete atomic particles

---

[34] A somewhat similar idea is expressed by Otfried Hoffe in his criticism of Rawls as failing to distinguish between ethics and law: "Because of this, Rawls runs the danger of distorting the idea of the well-ordered society into an ethical, rather than a juridical-political, ideal. In Kant, a community determined by the laws of virtue, rather than the laws of *Recht*, is called an 'invisible church'" (*Categorical Principles of Law: A Counterpoint to Modernity*, trans. Mark Migotti [University Park: Pennsylvania State University Press, 2002], p. 231). We suspect there is much to the "invisible church" metaphor in regard to adherents to the sort of liberalism being discussed here.

115

to be chosen as such. It is thus not simply and only the *biases* of the agents that stand in the way of making a direct equation between coincidence of belief and agreement. Since principles do not stand alone, but come tethered to other principles, discerning those links is part of what it means to finally accept X. At one level, it is not clear that Rawls and others would deny this distinction. Indeed, the point of liberalism is said to be the flourishing of multiple goods within multiple comprehensive doctrines that exist side by side. But it does not make sense to suppose that one would accept or agree to X, if one would have to give up (or give up knowing) what makes X valuable to oneself. In other words, it does not make sense to suppose that one would be satisfied not knowing what comprehensive doctrine gives X meaning, and whether that doctrine is one's own. As we noted above with Nussbaum, in order to transform coincidence of belief into agreement, an appeal needs to be made to the contractor's good. Ironically, the quest for the neutrality of non-comprehensiveness is a movement away from consensus.[35]

In a way, there is a surreptitious recognition of this fact about consensus. The need for some sort of rules for social organization is the good the contractors seek, and thus the good that motivates their endeavor to make an agreement. Of course, it is not just any rules for social organization they seek, but those rules especially conducive to peace and cooperation. The universe of peace seekers is smaller than the universe of rules seekers, and the universe of peace seekers who operate from "reasonable" comprehensive doctrines is smaller yet. It is perhaps interesting to alter the scope of these various universes; but doing so in no way removes the presence of, or, indeed, the need for, a comprehensive doctrine. The good Rawlsian liberal will for example, in Stephen Pinker's words,[36] eschew communal and hierarchical values in favor of rational and market-like values, and will discourage those who exhibit the former. The comprehensive

---

[35] Comprehensive doctrines function like principles in that they provide a stable context within which to understand and give meaning to particular values and thus keep parties from continually having to renegotiate a consensus. The liberal paradigm, for example, carries with it a host of comprehensive perspectives about the value of persons, the seriousness of conflict, and the value of diversity. If we are not to continually have to renegotiate the consensus, then what these mean, and how they will be cashed out in practice, will have to depend heavily on a comprehensive framework.

[36] Stephen Pinker, *The Better Angels of Our Nature: Why Violence Has Declined* (New York: Viking Penguin, 2011), chap. 10.

doctrine includes not just a particular understanding of what is to count as rational, but also a constructivist approach to justice, a collectivist presumption about resources (they are "ours" to order in some fashion, according to a rule "we" have agreed to), and a contractarian understanding of the most basic social relations. By contrast, if we were to do theoretical work on contracting, the work of James Buchanan would seem the most plausible way of proceeding.[37] Here the presumption is that we start with particular people attached to particular things and projects, and then see what kinds of principles they would likely come to adopt. We suspect that the Rawlsian project generally appeals to, and perhaps means to include only, a certain class of intellectuals for whom attachment to things, traditions, and personal projects does not stand in the way of their recommendations of how to reorder society.

3. Sen

The issue of the nature of reason and reasonableness is now the central one in the conduct of political theory. It is, we believe, one that naturally calls forth more comprehensive ontological and epistemological frameworks within which such concepts can be understood. In coming to appreciate how such concepts are tethered to such broader frameworks and their role in political philosophy, we can perhaps do no better than to consider the work of Amartya Sen and his particular appeal to public reasoning. Unlike Rawls and Nussbaum, Sen at least points to where his political theory is tethered. However, the significance and visibility of those doctrines to which his views are tethered remains mostly tacit. Below we shall make more transparent that to which his views are tethered, as well as some of his deep and controversial premises.

In response to the question of why reason should be accepted as the ultimate arbiter of our ethical (or political) beliefs, Sen responds that the case for using reason to scrutinize such beliefs rests on our

---

[37] For example, James Buchanan, "The Limits of Liberty: Between Anarchy and Leviathan," in *The Collected Works of James M. Buchanan*, Vol. 7 (Indianapolis: Liberty Fund, 2000). Buchanan describes the derivation of moral norms within a framework of self-interested actors, but he is careful not to confuse this work with normative political theory or the justification of the norms themselves. This is, no doubt, why he is of significantly less interest to normative political theorists than is Rawls.

being as objective as we reasonably can be expected to be. It is, consequently, the demand for objectivity that requires the use of reason. Engaging in such rational scrutiny may not always work, but it is the best option we have. Yet, it is here that Sen makes a most fateful and provocative move. He makes it clear that he does not understand objectivity in ethics in terms of how ethical beliefs track ethical objects:

> When we debate the demands of ethical objectivity, we are not crossing swords on the nature and content of some alleged ethical 'object'. . . . Despite some overlap between description and evaluation, ethics cannot be simply a matter of truthful description of specific objects.[38]

His point is thus not merely that a description must somehow involve an evaluation if it is to have any chance for ethical traction but, more importantly, that ontological considerations are insufficient for determining the truth or falsity of ethical beliefs. They do not supply the basis or reason for affirming or denying an ethical belief. To support this claim, Sen cites Hilary Putnam:

> I see the attempt to provide an ontological explanation of the objectivity of mathematics as, in effect, an attempt *to provide reasons which are not part of mathematics for the truth of mathematical statements* and the attempt to provide an ontological explanation of the objectivity of ethics as a similar attempt *to provide reasons which are not part of ethics for the truth of ethical statements*, and I see both as deeply misguided.[39]

For Putnam, trying to determine to what in reality ethical terms refer is no more helpful in providing ethical truth than is determining to what in reality mathematical terms refer in providing mathematical truth. Reference to what actually exists is not necessary for these sorts of truth.[40]

---

[38] Amartya Sen, *The Idea of Justice* (Cambridge, MA: Belknap Press of Harvard University Press, 2009), p. 41.

[39] Ibid. Hilary Putnam, *Ethics Without Ontology* (Cambridge, MA: Harvard University Press, 2004), p. 3.

[40] We would contend that there is a difference between saying there are unique "ethical objects" and saying ethical truths are ultimately grounded in reality. Both Putnam and Sen want not only to avoid "ethical objects" and monistic answers to various ethical questions, but also to avoid attempting to explain how what is valuable, worthy, or obligatory is grounded in what *is*. It is worth to note, in this regard, that Sen observed over thirty years ago that the "full implications" of his line of reasoning regarding objectivity can be worked out only by reexamining the issue of the presumed Cartesian "duality" between the external world and

The irrelevance of ontological considerations for ethical objectivity is, for Putnam, part of a larger view. This view holds that we need more generally to free the notion of objectivity from description, and instead recognize that there are many authentic statements that can be called "correct," "incorrect," "true," "false," "warranted," and "unwarranted," because they "are under rational control, governed by standards appropriate to their particular function and context."[41] Moreover, Putnam rejects the view that there is a world of facts existing in isolation from human conventions, conceptions, and valuings.[42] The concept of a reality that transcends our language or conceptual schemes, conventions, and valuings is unintelligible, because there is a triple entanglement of fact, convention, and value that is interrelating and interpenetrating.

In place of ontology as the ground for ethical truth (or, indeed, truth in general), Putnam defends what he calls "pragmatic pluralism." This view recognizes that not only are there various language games (no single one of which is sufficient for the description of all of reality), but also that there is no need to find

> mysterious and supersensible objects *behind* our language games; the truth can be told in language games we actually play when language is working, and inflations that philosophers have added to those language games are examples, as Wittgenstein said—using a pragmatist turn of phrase—of "the engine idling."[43]

Praxis is, in other words, prior to all attempts to explain what exists in reality and how we cognitively hook on to it. It is only in terms of human practices that we can ultimately explain the meaning of our terms, including those such as "objectivity," "truth," and "reality," that we use in philosophy.[44]

our conceptual powers ("Positional Objectivity," *Philosophy & Public Affairs* 22.2 [Spring 1993]: p. 126 n1). Finally, we would only respond that one does not have to accept a Cartesian view of the cognitive relation to maintain a distinction between what is and what is cognized.

[41] Hilary Putnam, "The Entanglement of Fact and Value," in *The Collapse of the Fact/Value Dichotomy and Other Essays* (Cambridge, MA: Harvard University Press, 2004), chap. 2, p. 33.

[42] Putnam uses the term "valuings" to mean "value judgments of every sort" (*Ethics Without Ontology*, p. 74).

[43] Ibid., p. 22.

[44] For an examination and critique of Putnam's views, see Douglas B. Rasmussen, "The Importance of Metaphysical Realism for Ethical Knowledge," *Social Philosophy & Policy* 25.1 (Winter 2008): pp. 56–99, parts of which have been

We shall see shortly what this sort of pragmatism means for Sen in regard to understanding justice. There are, however, a few initial problems to be noted in regard to Sen's aligning his view of ethical objectivity with Putnam's. First, it is by no means obvious that one can explain mathematical truth without an account of mathematical objects. Second, it certainly does not follow that such an account must be Platonic. In particular, there are non-Platonic varieties of realism upon which to base an account of mathematical objects.[45] Third, one need not assume that ontological claims are mysterious or supersensible and somehow lie behind the world that we perceive, whatever that means. That may apply to some types of ontology, but it certainly need not apply to all.[46] So, claiming that ontological concerns play no part in the truth of mathematical claims is most controversial, as is the particular description of ontology Putnam provides, as well as the pragmatic replacement he tenders for it. Finally, even if ontological concerns are irrelevant to mathematical truth, it still does not follow that they are not vital for the truth of ethical claims. Moral realism—not to mention, versions of ethical naturalism—is most certainly a viable contender for explaining ethical truth.[47] Much more will be said about this issue in Chapter 6. But this much is clear already: Sen's understanding of ethical objectivity has been tethered to a philosophical viewpoint

adapted for use in this section. See also Douglas B. Rasmussen and Douglas J. Den Uyl, "Objectivity or Impartiality? Public Reason and the Relevance of Metaphysics for Political Philosophy," in *Proceedings Metaphysics 2012 5th World Conference*, ed. David G. Murray and Yónatan Melo Pereira (Madrid: Editorial Fundación Fernando Rielo, 2015), pp. 841–65.

[45] See, for example, Ahti-Veikko Pietarinen, "A Realist Modal-Structuralism," December 9, 2011, available at <http://www.helsinki.fi/~pietarin/brpage/A%20 Realist%20Modal-Structuralism.pdf>, last accessed October 2, 2015.

[46] Putnam does not distinguish between those metaphysical views that would overturn or replace our everyday practices and common-sense views, and those metaphysical views that seek to explain more deeply such practices and views. We, for the most part, align ourselves with the latter.

[47] Putnam would contend, however, that "there is no reason to suppose that one cannot be what is called a 'moral realist' in meta-ethics, that is, hold that some 'value judgments' are true as a matter of objective fact, without holding that moral facts are or can be recognition of transcendent facts" ("Are Values Made or Discovered?" in *The Collapse of the Fact/Value Dichotomy and Other Essays*, chap. 6, p. 108). By "transcendent fact," he means a reality whose existence and character are independent of human conceptual schemes, practices, conventions, and valuings. In other words, for Putnam, objectivity in ethics is determined by our conceptual schemes, practices, conventions, and valuings.

that makes deep and contentious claims about the nature of objectivity and truth.

Sen not only explicitly endorses Hilary Putnam's view that ontological considerations are mistaken and unnecessary to an understanding of what it is for an ethical belief to be objective, but also endorses the triple entanglement of fact, convention, and value, as well as Putnam's claim that ethical questions are a type of practical question. This means that the answers to ethical questions are meant to guide action and solve problems; and this in turn involves considerations of valuings,[48] which further in turn involve a complex mixture of philosophical, religious, and factual beliefs. But if this is so, just what is it for an ethical (or a political) belief to be objective?

Putnam answers this question by following what he understands as Dewey's approach to what makes a value objective:

> Dewey's answer to the question, "What makes something valu*able* as opposed to merely being valued"? in a word, is *criticism*. Objective value arises ... from *the criticism of our valuations*. Valuations are incessant and inseparable from all our activities, including our "scientific' ones, but it is by intelligent reflection on our valuations, intelligent reflection of the kind Dewey calls "criticism," that we conclude that some of them are warranted while others are unwarranted. (Philosophy, by the way, is described by Dewey as *criticism of criticism*!)[49]

Putnam is aware, however, that with this approach there is a further question: What are the criteria by which we decide that some valuations are warranted and some are unwarranted? Moreover, he is aware that he must provide criteria in ways that do *not* require him to introduce a view of objectivity that describes, or is based on, metaphysical realities. He does so by what he calls an appeal to the "authority of intelligence." What the authority of intelligence amounts to is what we have learned about inquiry from the conduct of inquiry in general, and which applies to value inquiry in particular.[50] What we have learned is *to make full use of human intelligence*; and this sets the characteristics that inquiry must have if it, in turn, is to determine what valuations are warranted. Thus, one warrants

---

[48] Sen, *The Idea of Justice*, pp. 41 and 119.

[49] Putnam, "Are Values Made or Discovered?" p. 103.

[50] See Putnam, *Ethics Without Ontology*, pp. 89–108; and Putnam, "Pragmatism and Moral Objectivity," in *Words and Life*, ed. James Conant (Cambridge, MA: Harvard University Press, 1994), pp. 170–7.

valuations by engaging in inquiry that meets the criteria that are the precondition for the full application of human intelligence.

According to Putnam, there are four criteria which inquiry must meet, in order to fully employ human intelligence:

1. Inquiry must be a cooperative activity, not one done in isolation. It must involve working with others to actively intervene in and manipulate the environment in order to form and test ideas. This, in turn, involves trying different solutions to problems, or at least considering ways of solving problems others have tried, and then reflecting on the consequences.
2. Inquiry must treat its judgments as fallible—that is, as open to being revised or falsified.
3. Inquiry must respect autonomy and symmetric reciprocity, and must follow principles that are much akin to those of Jürgen Habermas's "discourse ethics." These principles are:
   a. communicating honestly and authentically, trying to win by the force of the better argument, and not by manipulation or involvement in relations of hierarchies of dependence;
   b. not excluding persons affected by any proposed action from participating in the discussion;
   c. not preventing consideration of any proposal or any person's expression of attitudes, wishes, or needs;
   d. neither assuming there will be no disputes over which valuations are warranted, nor trying to eliminate all such disputes; and
   e. keeping the communication going by not allowing coercion or violence or total refusal to discuss.
4. Inquiry must insist on applying the criteria noted in (1)–(3) to more and more institutions and relationships.[51]

For Putnam, as well as for Jürgen Habermas, these criteria provide an account of idealized inquiry or rational acceptability that we have learned from the development of science; and thus they constitute the

---

[51] See Putnam, "Pragmatism and Moral Objectivity"; and Jürgen Habermas, "Discourse Ethics: Notes on a Program of Philosophical Justification," in *Moral Consciousness and Communicative Action*, trans. Christian Lenhardt and Shierry Weber Nicholsen (Cambridge, MA: MIT Press, 1990), pp. 43–115. See Douglas B. Rasmussen, "Political Legitimacy and Discourse Ethics," *International Philosophical Quarterly* 32 (March 1992): pp. 17–34 for an examination and critique of Habermas's theory.

modern conception of rationality. Since facts and values are interdependent and interpenetrating, these criteria show us how to proceed in determining whether our judgments—be they of "fact" or of "value"—are warranted. Nonetheless, they do so without any appeal to metaphysical realities. They are, rather, the norms that we have learned from our practices. Our ability to apply intelligence fully to solving human problems presupposes these norms.[52]

Sen is, of course, primarily concerned with justice, and so he calls on John Rawls—who, he notes, is like Putnam in not being tempted by ontological considerations when determining the objectivity of ethical or political beliefs—in holding that the establishment of a public framework of thought is essential to objectivity.[53] Sen writes:

> We can get considerable guidance from the Rawlsian exposition of objectivity in ethics and political philosophy, particularly from his focus for "a public framework of thought": "we look at our society and our place in it objectively: we share a common standpoint along with others and do not make judgments from a personal slant." Judgments of justice cannot be an entirely private affair—unfathomable to others—and the Rawlsian invoking of "a public framework of thought," which does not in itself demand a "contract," is a critically important move.[54]

Such a framework of public reasoning is to provide conclusions that will be reached on the basis of reasons and evidence. It is to provide objective ethical and political judgments which, for Rawls, is "to say that there are reasons specified by a reasonable and mutually recognizable political conception (satisfying those essentials), sufficient to convince all reasonable persons that it is reasonable."[55]

Whether Rawls's criterion of objectivity matches what will result from public reasoning is, for Sen, a topic open for discussion; but he does not see the differences between Rawls and Habermas (who takes a chiefly procedural approach to objectivity) as being that great on the issue of whether or not there is a procedure-independent identification of what would convince "rational" people. This is due in part to Habermas's exacting requirements on public reasoning, which

---

[52] These last three paragraphs have been taken from Rasmussen, "The Importance of Metaphysical Realism for Ethical Knowledge."

[53] Sen, *The Idea of Justice*, p. 42.

[54] Amartya Sen, "Open and Closed Impartiality," *The Journal of Philosophy* 99.9 (September 2002): pp. 455–6; and John Rawls, *A Theory of Justice* (Cambridge, MA: Harvard University Press, 1971), pp. 516–17.

[55] Rawls, *Political Liberalism*, p. 119.

were noted above; but also it is due to Sen's belief that all human beings can be reasonable. They are all capable of being open-minded, willing to consider information from anyone from anywhere, and capable of deliberating and debating basic issues.

Besides getting considerable guidance from Rawls's and Habermas's accounts of objectivity, Sen sees four respects in which Adam Smith's reasoning involving the idea of an "impartial spectator" provides the overall character of the desired form of public reasoning:[56]

1. *Universalist*: We are "to examine our own conduct as we imagine any other fair and impartial spectator would examine it."[57] This process "requires not only the avoidance of the impact of individual vested interests, but also an exacting scrutiny of parochial moral and social sentiments, which may influence the idea and outcomes in locally separated 'original positions.'"[58] This reasoning must be universalistic and lead to "broadening our viewpoint,"[59] so that our normative demands reflect our membership in the category of human beings. That is to say, we are to be guided by concerns for humanity, and not for just ourselves, our community, our society, or our nation.

2. *Social Realization*: Such public reasoning must involve a consideration of how decisions about the basic structure of our own society might affect the lives of people in other societies. It must take note of social realizations of the conclusions of public reasoning, and not confine itself only to taking note of institutions and rules. This reasoning thus must be sensitive to consequences; but this does not require a single evaluative dimension. Consequential evaluation of proposed ethical and political principles must be made in light of whether they afford people the opportunity to achieve various combinations of valued functionings. Yet, this reasoning must include much more. Evaluations must involve such considerations as (a) the positions from which various evaluations are made; (b) the difference between maximization and optimization of choices; and (c) the role of agent-centered factors, as well the processes of choice, in the proper evaluation of certain states of affairs.[60] The subject matter of

---

[56] Sen, *The Idea of Justice*, p. 70. The order in which these four respects are described here is different from the order in which Sen lists them.

[57] Adam Smith, *The Theory of Moral Sentiments*, ed. D. D. Raphael and A. L. Macfie (Indianapolis: Liberty Fund, 1984), III.I.2.

[58] Sen, *The Idea of Justice*, pp. 124–52; Sen, "Open and Closed Impartiality," p. 459.

[59] Sen, "Open and Closed Impartiality," p. 466.

[60] Amartya Sen, "Consequential Evaluation and Practical Reason," *The Journal of Philosophy* 97.9 (September 2000): pp. 477–502. Sen also contends that the

public reasoning, then, must include considerations (a)–(c) and the development of human capabilities.[61]

3. *Incomplete*: This process of public reasoning does not have to be "total," in the sense that there is agreement on what constitutes perfectly just societal arrangements. In other words, it need not provide what Sen also calls a "transcendental" conception of justice. There may not be one clear winner among theories of justice—that is, only one conception of justice that can withstand public scrutiny. For example, such competing theories of justice as the utilitarian, economic egalitarian, and libertarian all have serious arguments in support of them. "The three arguments each point to a different type of impartial and non-arbitrary reason."[62] It might just be that none of them can be reasonably rejected.

4. *Comparative*: Though incomplete,[63] public reasoning could provide comparative judgments on ranking alternative social arrangements. There still could be shared beliefs among different parties to the process of public reasoning, and these beliefs could allow for a partial ranking of alternatives. As Sen puts it:

> Despite such durable incompleteness, we may still be able to agree readily that there is clear social injustice involved in the persistence of endemic hunger or exclusion from medical access, which calls for a well-specified remedying for the *advancement* of justice (or reduction of injustice), even

---

informational basis of consequential evaluation can accommodate many more considerations than is often thought, and thus need not be subject to the objections that bedevil so-called consequentialistic reasoning. Ibid.

[61] Sen terms the development of human capabilities as the development of "freedom." By concentrating on freedom in terms of the opportunity to use one's capabilities, he is able to blur the distinction between negative and positive freedom. Instead of seeing these as independent and differing conceptions of freedom, he sees them as lying on a conceptual continuum. For example, suffering coercion prevents the utilization of one's capacities, but suffering severe poverty prevents their utilization, as well. They are both forms of "unfreedom," because the opportunity to use one's capabilities is limited in both cases. Therefore, preventing coercion (negative liberty) and alleviating poverty (positive liberty) are both necessary for capabilities to function. Neither has priority, and both need to be balanced. This understanding of freedom is relevant not only for any account of human well-being or flourishing, but also for any analysis of social justice or human development or equality. See Amartya Sen, *Development as Freedom* (Oxford: Oxford University Press, 1999), pp. 13–34.

[62] Sen, *The Idea of Justice*, p. 15.

[63] Amartya Sen, "What Do We Want from a Theory of Justice?" *The Journal of Philosophy* 103.5 (2006): pp. 215–38; and Sen, *The Idea of Justice*, pp. 107–8.

after taking note of the costs involved. Similarly, we may acknowledge the possibility that liberties of different persons may, to some extent, conflict with each other (so that any fine-tuning of the demands of equal liberty may be hard to work out), and yet strongly agree that torturing of accused people would be an unjust violation of liberty and that this injustice calls for an urgent rectification.[64]

The public framework of thought does not become wholly inoperative merely because we cannot reach a total or final decision on what is a just society. Public discourse can agree on some things.

Sen claims that, notwithstanding the differences between the kinds of arguments used by Rawls, Habermas, and Smith, each of them links the objectivity of an ethical or political belief, directly or indirectly, to its ability to endure an informed examination coming from varied places.[65] He also holds that there is "an overarching similarity among them in the shared recognition of the need for reasoned encounter on an impartial basis."[66] Sen endorses their public-reasoning approach to objectivity and declares that he will follow it in determining what justice is, comparatively speaking. Further, he identifies this approach as central to democracy deliberatively understood—that is to say, democracy not as something merely aggregative that works by majority rule, but as the collective engagement in practical reasoning—and argues that it is the deliberative character of democracy that makes it so valuable. Finally, given the crucial role of public reasoning to deliberative democracy, Sen notes that democracy so understood is closely related to justice:

> If the demands of justice can be assessed only with the help of public reasoning, and if public reasoning is constitutively related to the idea of democracy, then there is an intimate connection between justice and democracy, with shared discursive features.[67]

Thus, Sen's approach to objectivity is tied not only to an account of public reasoning, but also to deliberative democracy.

Whether public reasoning is essential to objectivity (and the determination of comparative justice), and to where deliberative democracy fits, if anywhere, in this process, are questions whose

---

[64] Sen, "What Do We Want from a Theory of Justice?" pp. 223–4.

[65] Though Sen does not cite Putnam in this regard, Putnam obviously links objectivity to public scrutiny.

[66] Sen, *The Idea of Justice*, p. 46. Sen notes further that their approaches differ largely on the domain of required impartiality.

[67] Ibid., p. 326.

answers are tied to the link Sen posits between objectivity and impartiality. Thus, what we need to consider now is how Sen understands the relationship between impartiality and objectivity in public reasoning. Certainly, there seems nothing controversial about claiming that impartiality requires of any participants in public reasoning that they not distort any of the V's (that is, values, reasons, and rankings) of someone, or seek to replace them by some set of "favored" V's. The V's of everyone who is affected by the deliberations of public reasoning need to be examined in a straight-forward manner and not ignored. Nor is it unusual, when talking about ethics in general or justice in particular, to forbid the exclusion of some group of human beings from consideration. Assessing the valuations of everyone is required, as well. Moreover, that this moral and political accounting must involve open communication and interpersonal comprehension—every voice is to be heard and understood—does not seem controversial as an ideal. Finally, there seems to be no a priori reason for assuming that any human being is incapable of acting in accord with these procedures. We can thus describe the foregoing as an ordinary or commonplace understanding of impartiality, with no controversial assumptions, because it makes no claim about the nature of V's that are to be used in the public reasoning process. We have no objection to this non-controversial understanding of impartiality.

But it should also be noted that an ordinary or commonplace understanding of impartiality has very little "argumentative punch" when making comparative judgments of justice. To take a real-world example from the United States: should the political/legal order attempt to provide for the health care needs of those at lower income levels by legally mandating that nearly all citizens purchase health care from designated insurance companies? Ordinarily understood, impartiality provides minimal guidance in answering this question. It does not tell us why it is more just to pass such a health care man-date than not. It does not tell us how to choose between conflicting V's. And though there may be other questions of comparative justice whose answers seem obvious and have intuitive appeal, it is not by any means clear that such appeal has anything to do with this ordi-nary understanding of impartiality. Such an understanding of impar-tiality is inadequate as an objective basis for comparative judgments of justice.

There is, however, more to Sen's account of impartiality, and it deals with how Sen grasps the Kantian principle of universalizability—"*act only according to that maxim through which you can at the same time will that it become a universal law*"[68]—and how he understands impartiality in light of a certain interpretation of it. As stated, there is no difficulty with the principle of universalizability, because it is perfectly general.[69] However, let us call upon some conceptual resources developed in Chapters 1 and 2. First, there is the distinction between an approach to morality that is agent-centered and treats all morally salient values, reasons, and rankings (V's) as fundamentally *personal* (or agent-relative), and an approach that is not agent-centered and treats all morally salient values, reasons, and ranking as fundamentally *impersonal* (or agent-neutral). Second, we can recall that nothing about the principle of universalizability as a logical matter precludes a personalist approach to ethics; impersonalism is not required by the principle of universalizability. But if the principle of universalizability does not preclude a personalist approach to morality, then there is a basic problem for Sen's account of public reasoning, because Sen wants to show that "the impartiality of evaluation can provide an understandable and plausible idea of objectivity in moral and political philosophy."[70] But how can this be so, *if* impartiality of evaluation is understood only in terms of what we have called an "ordinary or commonplace" account, *without any hint of impersonalism?* How does one choose between competing V's? Sen needs to show that public reasoning can have some justifiable method for the comparative judgments it issues in regard to differing ethical and political claims.[71] He needs a viable account of objectivity that does not appeal to ethical objects.

What lies behind Sen's belief that impartiality of evaluation can provide a basis for objectivity is his use of Sidgwick's statement of the principle of universalizability: "That whatever is right for me must be right for all persons in similar circumstances."[72] But this

---

[68] Immanuel Kant, *Groundwork of the Metaphysics of Morals*, rev. ed., trans. and ed. Mary Gregor and Jens Timmermann (Cambridge: Cambridge University Press, 2012), 4:421, p. 34.

[69] It might be charged that we are giving much too thin a reading of Kant's principle of universalizability. But if there is to be a thicker understanding of this principle, it must be spelled out and justified; and then there must be an appeal to deeper and more controversial premises.

[70] Sen, *The Idea of Justice*, p. 118.

[71] Could it, to return to our earlier example, justify claiming that passing the health care mandate is comparatively more just than not?

[72] The quotation continues: ". . . which was the form in which I accepted the

statement is not clear. It allows for two understandings of universalizability. If, on the one hand, we interpret "in similar circumstances" in a concrete manner—that is, as pertaining not only to the situation, but also to the respective identities of me and others, so that there are no significant differences among us—then, *ex hypothesi*, there can be no differences between my V's and those of others that result from individual differences. There is nothing particularly problematic about this interpretation of Sidgwick's statement. Indeed, it has the same logical form as Kant's principle of universalizability. Yet, it also contains nothing for Sen to use in developing a viable account of objectivity, because it cannot offer a way for dealing with conflicts between my V's and those of others that may arise from the real differences in our respective identities.

If, on the other hand, we do not concretely interpret "in similar circumstances" and allow for me to be different from other persons and vice versa, then something more than a logical claim about the nature of ethical justifications is being made. Rather, a substantive claim about the nature of ethical or moral V's is being claimed—namely, that they are agent-neutral in character. Thus, in dealing with conflicting V's, the impartial deliberative evaluations of public reasoning are to be understood as proceeding in an impersonal fashion. This is the interpretation that Sen needs for his version of public reasoning to have sufficient "argumentative punch." It allows public reasoning to factor out V's that are grounded in the individuality of persons.

However, this substantive interpretation of Sidgwick's statement of the principle of universalizability raises a host of further questions about proceeding in such an impersonalist manner. Is it evident that what is good for me is necessarily good for you in the same circumstances (or vice versa)? Are we interchangeable? Why should public reasoning preclude from consideration the status of persons as individuals? In particular, why should public reasoning preclude the set of circumstances, talents, endowments, interests, beliefs, and histories that descriptively characterize the individual—what we have called in Chapters 1 and 2 an individual's "nexus"? Is an individual's nexus irrelevant to moral evaluations? Does it play no role in considering the scope and character of the principles that determine justice

Kantian maxim—seemed to me to be certainly fundamental, certainly true, and not without practical importance" (Henry Sidgwick, "Preface," in *The Methods of Ethics*, 7th ed. [Chicago: University of Chicago Press, 1907], p. xvii).

for the political/legal order? Why? Is not the exclusion of personal V's without justification?

One way of trying to get around these concerns is to emphasize that Sen is focusing primarily on justice in an interpersonal sense, and to claim that *inter*personal justice requires *im*personal justice. If this is the gambit, then, in this regard, Sen would be similar to Rawls who admits in *A Theory of Justice* that "we think of the original position as the point of view from which noumenal selves see the world."[73] But does being committed to interpersonal living (even in a most open-ended and universal sense) require that one take on the viewpoint of a noumenal self and/or adopt ethical impersonalism? To say the least, it is highly unlikely that human beings are noumenal selves; and it seems that there are real and legitimate differences among the goods and personal projects of individual human beings. It would thus seem that individuality matters morally, and it matters, as well, for making comparative judgments of justice that are supposed to apply to every human being. Regardless of how inconvenient it may be, individuality cannot be easily ignored by political philosophers. Indeed, among the desiderata of political philosophers is a way to accommodate both the moral propriety of individualism and the profoundly social character of human life.[74] Thus, it is by no means clear how helpful an argumentative ploy it is for Sen to ignore the legitimate differences among goods and personal projects that result from individuality of persons and their lives.

Of course, it might be argued that public reasoning just is impersonal in character, and that such reasoning is the only game in town for objectivity. But why should this be accepted? Why should public reasoning be the chief, if not the only, way by which comparative judgments of justice are made? Sen's answer[75] would seem to be, following a line of argument more or less similar to Putnam's, that public reasoning makes full use of human intelligence. However, this still begs the question. Why might not free and open markets be, as F. A. Hayek argued,[76] the basic social mechanism for using human knowledge to coordinate and deter-

---

[73] Rawls, *A Theory of Justice*, p. 255.

[74] In Rasmussen and Den Uyl, *NOL*, we attempt to find this accommodation and to *not* paper over the real and authentic differences among human beings.

[75] *The Idea of Justice*, pp. 174–93.

[76] F. A. Hayek, "The Use of Knowledge in Society," *American Economic Review* 35.4 (September 1945): pp. 519–30.

mine the best and most useful—indeed, objective—ways to use resources, direct human effort, and solve problems? Could not free and open markets themselves be a most vital expression of human intelligence?[77]

Moreover, despite Sen's criticism of Nozick for having a theory of justice that concentrates only on what justice is for the political/ legal order, and not the problem of comparative judgments of justice,[78] maybe this was just Nozick's point! Maybe the sorts of comparative judgments that so rightly concern Sen can only be handled at the personal level. Maybe the insight of Nozick was to see that the principles of justice for the political/legal order have to be developed in light of, and in appreciation for, the personal character of the moral life. Indeed, it seems that by thinking in impersonalist terms and not allowing individualism a voice in the discourse, Sen actually discounts much of the most important knowledge that we use in seeking human flourishing. Such knowledge is not found in a community of knowers examining a common issue, but is, instead, diversified across many individuals and concerned with only particular and contingent matters. It is significant that there is, for Sen, little or no discussion of the role of how such diversified knowledge is brought to bear on determining what is best and most useful. In short, what is singularly lacking is any discussion of the virtue of practical wisdom.[79] Thus, unlike Hayek, who does not attempt to identify or limit the voices of public reasoning, but sees it as an open-ended process, Sen's impersonalism seeks to identify *ex ante* these voices, and thus close off the open-ended dynamic of the exchange of ideas.

Be this as it may, a possibly more productive line of response to the concerns raised above is to note that Sen admits that the public reasoning process can include personal V's —for example, the value of having the needs of your child met, as opposed to those of any other child. Accordingly, certain values can be given weight not because of the outcomes they tend to produce, but because of the relationship to the person. Therefore, Sen believes that agent-relativity poses no special problem to the consequence-based evaluation of public reasoning. Furthermore, for Sen, there is no problem of objectivity of agent-relative values. Participants in public reasoning can all take the

---

[77] See Mathew Ridley, *The Rational Optimist* (New York: HarperCollins, 2010).

[78] Sen, *The Idea of Justice*, pp. 84 and 96.

[79] See our discussions of practical wisdom in Chapters 1 and 5.

position of the parents and come to understand the evaluation they would make of having their child's needs met, as contrasted to those of some other child.[80] This can all be part of the process of public reasoning for Sen.

Yet, Sen is keen to preserve an impersonalism that does not let the identities of individuals play a role in evaluative considerations. He states that

> evaluator-relativity need not violate any requirement of "impersonality" that may be imposed on the discipline of ethics. Indeed, impersonality must not be confused with what may be called *impositionality*—having to ignore the relevance of a chooser's position or situation vis-à-vis the choices and results. In contrast with impositionality, position-relative impersonality requires, to put it in mildly mathematical terms, that parametric note be taken of the respective *positions* of the different persons, but not to the exact personal *identities* involved.[81]

In other words, the relationship of V to the person is not essential to, or due to the identity or nexus of, the person, but is rather due to the position of the person relative to what is valued. It is the positional relevance of parenthood[82] that is the source of weight accorded one's own children as opposed to those of others. As such, the relationship of that which is valued to the person is strictly external. Indeed, Sen compares it to the relationship between the judgment that, to an observer on earth, the sun and moon look similar in size.[83] He considers such a judgment to be an instance of "positional objectivity," but he also considers this compatible with "objective illusion" or even "false consciousness."[84] Public scrutiny of ethical and political beliefs can acknowledge position-dependent V's, but its goal is assessments that do not vary from person to person.[85] In effect, public reasoning's approach to objectivity is to not allow V's that are essentially related to the identity or nexus of a person.

As should be obvious, however, the preceding response really does not consider agent-relativity as it has been described above or in Chapters 1 and 2. Sen never really considers the possibility that V's

---

[80] Sen, *The Idea of Justice*, p. 160.

[81] Sen, "Consequential Evaluation and Practical Reason," p. 486.

[82] Sen does not say what is the basis for this relevance.

[83] Sen, *The Idea of Justice*, p. 156.

[84] Ibid., pp. 161–7.

[85] See Sen, "Positional Objectivity," p. 145; and Sen, *The Idea of Justice*, p. 161.

are essentially attached to some person or other. Moreover, Sen does not consider how *who* an individual is can provide a basis for V's that are unique. Others can, because of their identities, have bases for V; but they need not. Of course, one can say the following: "If I were you, then I would not choose to take course of action C because of V, and so I can understand the basis for your conduct." Yet, it is also possible to say, "But since I am not you, and we differ in this regard, V is not relevant to me, and I have reason to take action C." Therefore, the ability to understand the V's of other persons or groups does not by itself mean or require that one should make comparative judgments on the basis of their V's. Thus, agent-relative V's place severe limits on the effectiveness of public reasoning in finding agreement.

Additionally, if we permit ourselves to leave, for a moment, the stranglehold that Putnam's view of objectivity has imposed upon this discussion, it might be further noted that even if V were objective in some realistic or naturalistic way, there would still be nothing about its objectivity (that is, its *being* valuable) that required it to be regarded impersonally. Interchangeability with others would not be required. Indeed, objective values could be entirely personal. Thus, based on objective V's, persons may make different (even conflicting) judgments about what course of action to pursue.

Regardless of whether there is a realistic or naturalistic grounding for ethical objectivity in some way or other, V's that are agent-relative do not require interchangeability; and if this is so, the question remains: Why ought public reasoning be conducted in an impersonalist manner? Why, in fact, ought one to adopt such a viewpoint? Even more fundamentally, why must "ought" be construed in an impersonalist manner? These questions are also most ironic, for Sen also allies his use of public reasoning with the advancement and development of human capabilities that constitute human flourishing. But this alignment requires the impersonalist mode of public reasoning (as manifested in a deliberative democracy) to be used in determining not only the relevant set of capabilities that constitute human flourishing, but also their respective weights. As Sen states:

> Even the idea of "needs," including the understanding of "economic needs," requires public discussion and exchange of information, views, and analyses. In this sense, democracy has constructive importance. . . . [O]pen discussion, debate, criticism, and dissent are central to the process of generating informed and considered choices. These processes are

crucial to the formation of values and priorities, and we cannot, in general, take preferences as given independently of public discussion. . . .[86]

But this simply will not work, and it smacks of a conformism that is antithetical to the very character of human flourishing. To recall what was argued in previous chapters, while it is certainly not false to think of human flourishing without thinking of whose flourishing it *is*, it *is* false to think that human flourishing can exist, or provide guidance for conduct, without being the flourishing of some individual or other. Moreover, it is false to regard the individual as simply a placeholder that instantiates the human good or various combinations of human capabilities.[87] Such thinking turns human flourishing into an abstraction and denies it reality, and it forbids the very individuality of persons from entering into an account of human flourishing or playing a role in the judgments of practical reason. Indeed, to hold such a conception is to hold no conception of human flourishing at all.

It seems, then, that the attempt to explain what it is for an ethical or political belief to be objective in terms of its ability to pass the scrutiny of the public reasoning process does not suffice. While impartiality understood in an ordinary or commonplace way is not controversial, it really provides very little basis for determining what to select when making comparative judgments of justice. And if impartiality is understood in an impersonalist sense, there not only appears to be no justification for adopting such a viewpoint, but there also seems to be a conflict between impartiality and the individualistic and personal features of human flourishing.

There is, of course, another alternative for understanding what it is for an ethical or political belief to be objective. This is the realistic—and, for us ultimately, naturalistic—account of ethical objectivity that we champion. Such an approach to ethical objectivity is explicitly tethered to certain metaphysical and epistemological positions. But what must also be realized is that Sen has chosen the route of public reasoning to account for ethical objectivity because he has

---

[86] Amartya Sen, "Democracy as a Universal Value," *Journal of Democracy* 10.3 (1999): p. 10. See also Sen, *The Idea of Justice*, pp. 321–54; and Sen, "Elements of a Theory of Rights," *Philosophy & Public Affairs* 32.4 (2004): p. 333.

[87] See Douglas J. Den Uyl and Douglas B. Rasmussen, "Liberalism in Retreat," *The Review of Metaphysics* 62.4 (June 2009): pp. 875–908 for a critical examination of Sen's and Nussbaum's claim that the individuality of human flourishing is maintained because there can be various combinations of human capabilities.

tethered himself, as well, to some deep philosophical commitments. In accepting Putnam's rejection of the usefulness of ontological considerations in determining the objectivity of ethical and political beliefs, Sen has circumscribed how he is to think about ethical and political terms. This is marked out by the basic tenets of Putnam's "pragmatic pluralism," which precludes understanding objectivity in terms of realities that exist apart from human conceptual schemes, practices, and valuings. As noted earlier, we have critically examined Putnam's views elsewhere,[88] and so it is not necessary to take them up here; but more importantly, we do not need to do so, because it is not germane to our basic point—namely, that accounts of human reason and reasonableness are inherently controversial. And we mean this not in the sense that people may disagree, but in the more radical sense that at least some alternative approaches are rejected rather than assimilated. Such a rejection forces one either to carry on the debate at some level other than the one ostensibly in dispute, or to simply reject out of hand the alternative position(s). Sen seems to recognize, when he links himself to Putnam and others, that his doctrine of public reason is tethered to broader frameworks. What he does not recognize is that the public reasoning approach is not *philosophically* universalist—that is, that it does not incorporate all perspectives. Thus, his public reasoning project either misrepresents the other approaches as being inherently positional, or it begs the question of why we should accept public reasoning as the right way to get at the nature of justice.

4. Conclusion

We have argued in this chapter against the idea that political philosophy can be untethered from more comprehensive frameworks. Such attempts to extract political philosophy from more comprehensive frameworks are based, as we indicated in Chapter 2, on the modern rationalist presumption that what we conceptually consider can be fully analyzed or understood apart from the realities that ground and give rise to the concept itself. But as we showed in that chapter and illustrated further in this one, not much can be accomplished in philosophy, especially political philosophy, without a commitment to a more comprehensive view. Indeed, when untethered political theories

---

[88] See Rasmussen, "The Importance of Metaphysical Realism for Ethical Knowledge."

do appear to offer substantive standards for political philosophy, we find that the seemingly compelling reasons to accept those standards are for the most part illusory. This is so because whatever is accomplished is done only by smuggling into the respective theories undefended assumptions about ethics, human nature, and, indeed, reality. The consequences that flow from where a doctrine is tethered appear in a number of the claims and positions advanced by the authors we have examined. We have been able to challenge those claims both because of the comprehensive context that gives rise to them, and because the comprehensive context to which we ourselves are tethered offers an alternative basis for criticism. Criticism is not establishment; but by having offered criticism, we hope to have at least further described and clarified the nature and implications of our own position, and in Part II, we hope to offer more by way of justification.

4

Tethering II

Civilization is the progress toward a society of privacy. The savage's whole existence is public, ruled by the laws of his tribe. Civilization is the process of setting man free from men.

Ayn Rand, *The Fountainhead*

In this chapter, we will continue for a moment our exploration of tethering by considering two more thinkers who are less reticent about identifying their positions with more comprehensive frameworks—namely, Gerald Gaus and Steven Darwall. We should bear in mind that all the theories in both this and the preceding chapter share the tendency to employ the legislative model of ethics. By combating these positions, we hope we are contributing to our main task of liberating ethics from that particular comprehensive context.

1. Gaus

While we have complained in Chapter 3 of some authors being either unwilling to acknowledge, or in denial about, that to which their doctrines are tethered, Gerald Gaus is not the least bit reticent to tie his views to basic philosophical positions. In his monumental and sophisticated work, *The Order of Public Reason*,[1] Gaus explicitly distances himself from the very roots of the type of position we would defend. His work is about what he calls "social morality," which involves "rules that we are required to act upon and which provide the basis for authoritative demands of one person addressed to another." Or further, Gaus understands social morality as "the set of social-moral rules that require or prohibit actions, and so ground moral imperatives that we direct to each to engage in, or refrain from, certain lines of conduct."[2] The chief and defining problem for

---

[1] Gerald Gaus, *The Order of Public Reason: A Theory of Freedom and Morality in a Diverse and Bounded World* [hereafter OPR] (Cambridge: Cambridge University Press, 2011).
[2] Ibid., pp. 1–2.

social morality is: "How can free and equal moral persons claim authority to prescribe to other free and equal moral persons?" (We shall call this the central concern of social morality.) Hence, social morality is, for Gaus, imperatival in nature, and not concerned with what is good or desirable for a human being—that is, with what is attractive. Its core notions—right, wrong, duty, and obligation—are seen as independent of what is attractive; and these notions Gaus takes to be definitive of Modernity's approach to morality, because its ultimate concern is with what actions and forbearances we can justifiably owe to, or exact from, strangers. In fact, Gaus endorses P. F. Strawson's claim that pursuit of the good or worthwhile life "presupposes an organized social life, and for such a life, there must be a system of shared expectations about what must and must not be done with our interactions with each other."[3]

Social morality is thus immediately contrasted to moralities that include "visions of the good life and conceptions of virtue and vice."[4] These latter ethical theories lie outside of social morality and can be ignored when dealing with the problems Gaus wants to address. Indeed, while, in his Appendix A to this work, Gaus advocates moral pluralism (as against monism), in which there can be different types of moralities, none of which alone covers the universe of moral actions or claims,[5] Gaus has, nonetheless, chosen to focus upon one aspect of that moral universe, with the clear implication that little or nothing from the realm of "virtues and visions" will be of value to his discussion. Indeed, Gaus further claims that "neo-Aristotelian virtue ethics is a rejection of Modernity, rather than a solution to its problems."[6] Yet, while it is certainly true that Alasdair MacIntyre rejects Modernity's approach to ethics and its problems, it is definitely not the case that this is generally true of advocates of

---

[3] Ibid., p. 3.

[4] Ibid., p. 2.

[5] Moralities may concern actions, character, consequences, intentions, social claims, and the like. Gaus eschews the monistic thesis that all moral judgments can be covered under one theory. He does not claim the social morality he discusses in the book is the whole of morality or the "real" or "true morality." He remains agnostic or skeptical about whether the monistic theory can be true (ibid., pp. 551–7). While we have reservations about this conclusion, as discussed below, Gaus does us a favor by reminding us that there is a distinction to be drawn between foundationalism and monism. Gaus avoids the latter, but not the former.

[6] Ibid., p. 8.

a neo-Aristotelian virtue ethics. Such thinkers as Martha Nussbaum[7] and Fred D. Miller, Jr.[8] (as well as ourselves, of course) have sought to apply the insights of such an ethics to modern liberal concerns.[9] In any case, it is far from clear that Gaus's project is not restricted to one type of morality, contrary to what first appearances might suggest. From the opening pages onward, whatever nods to alternative forms or morality there might be from Gaus, his claim to not being limited to social morality alone is muted by indications that he regards social morality as the real stuff of morality.

Gaus's understanding of social morality is, additionally, directly linked to the liberal social and political project, which he describes as primarily concerned with "whether free and equal persons can all endorse a common political order, even though their private judgments about the good and justice are so often opposed."[10] On the surface, the commitment to freedom and equality found from the opening pages onward would seem to be a pre-commitment to some sort of liberalism, which would limit the scope of the realm of social morality, rather than increase it. Despite that appearance, one typically gets the impression that freedom and equality are the values of morality generally, and not just of liberalism. We believe, therefore, that social morality for Gaus is the central type; and while he may deny that it is any more than one among others, the crowding-out effects upon other "types" of moralities are clearly evident here. There is no basis provided by Gaus for any significant push-back against the dictates of social morality by other moralities; and, in any case, if social morality can issue in irrevocable and punishable commands, it would seem to trump any alternative moralities. We shall thus assume that the perspective of social morality is a general one, and not a species of it known as "liberalism."[11]

With that in mind, Gaus's approach once again reminds us of

---

[7] See our discussion of Nussbaum and her works in Chapter 3.

[8] Fred D. Miller, Jr., *Nature, Justice, and Rights in Aristotle's* Politics (Oxford: Clarendon Press, 1995).

[9] Douglas B. Rasmussen and Douglas J. Den Uyl, *Norms of Liberty: A Perfectionist Basis for Non-Perfectionist Politics* [hereafter *NOL*] (University Park: Pennsylvania State University Press, 2005).

[10] Gaus, *OPR*, p. 2.

[11] Nevertheless, a significant part of our motivation in considering Gaus here concerns our worry about the conflation of ethics and politics which, we have argued, must be challenged, in order for the merits of individualistic perfectionism to be appreciated.

the contrast between the framework of respect and the framework of responsibility, with which we opened this work. Gaus self-consciously places himself in the former category by tying himself to Kant, Rousseau, and likeminded others, and by rejecting the virtues-and-visions orientation of the framework of responsibility. To set the contrast, recall that an ethics of respect begins with the proposition that the object of ethics is to discover our duties and to live up to them. In this regard, our duties to others become primary, because this ethic is essentially concerned to be legislative in form by universalizing its propositions.[12] Even duties to self are effectively derivative of our duties to others, because in order to universalize, one's own self must become interchangeable with other selves, or there is no universal. In an ethics of responsibility, by contrast, the first question and object of morality is what one is to make of one's life. As a social being, the answer to that question will depend significantly on one's relations with others; but in the end, the issue comes back to how one is to live *one's own* life. General normative propositions tend to come out of this framework as principles, rather than duties.

One of the main challenges to our position is Gaus's implicit question: If we are concerned with social cooperation and political order, what would the neo-Aristotelian virtues-and-visions approach bring to the table?[13] Obviously, much depends here on what is meant by "neo-Aristotelian virtue ethics" and "liberalism"; and while we have had much to say about both,[14] there is a distinction that also needs to be drawn here, because it works against Gaus's easy dismissal of the relevance of neo-Aristotelian virtue ethics for the concerns of Modernity. As we noted in section 2 of Chapter 2, there are demands of justice that are morally binding, and there are demands of justice that are morally *and* legally binding; and these two considerations

---

[12] In this regard, see Gaus, *OPR*, pp. 298–303.

[13] Gaus seems particularly concerned to avoid the "authoritarian temptation" (ibid., p. 549) of claiming one true morality and dismissing others as false or secondary. "The moral philosopher, impressed by her own rectitude, who proclaims that as we move away from her ideal we move away from a justified true morality, becomes the unwitting enemy of a free moral order" (ibid., p. 549). Although we are given the impression here that Gaus knows that "morality" rejects this attitude, and that the group carries more force or weight, it is by no means clear to us why the prescriptions of the group representing "social morality"—even one to which we have ourselves consented—has more moral authority or standing than the individual moral philosopher mentioned here.

[14] See, for example, Rasmussen and Den Uyl, *NOL*.

should not be conflated. Or to reiterate precisely what we said: it does not follow from "X is good or right" that, therefore, X must be politically or legally enforced; nor does it follow from "Y is bad or wrong" that, therefore, Y should be politically or legally prohibited. Determining the nature of the connection, if any, between the moral and political orders is the central concern of political philosophy; and we cannot simply assume that the connection is direct or isomorphic, or that the obligations of the respective orders are semantically equivalent.

Thus, the ethical and political could be linked, even though their respective tasks are different, and each is not reducible to the other. It is thus quite possible that ethics could be fundamentally attractive in character—as said, concerned with what is good or desirable for a human being—and, nonetheless, still generate principles that are applicable to the question of what justifies interpersonal demands among strangers. The notions of right, wrong, duty, and obligation need not be interpreted as Gaus does—that is, as having meaning and force apart from what is good or desirable for human beings—in order to be relevant to the ethical and political issues of Modernity.

There is, however, another point that follows from the distinction we just made between the ethical and political/legal orders—namely, that the nature of the ethical imperative which social morality seeks to justify needs to be clarified. While Gaus rightly stresses that utilitarianism is as much concerned with duties as is deontology, his account of social morality never provides a principle by which to differentiate those ethical norms that concern the political/legal from those that concern only the moral. When are we dealing with an interpersonal ethical imperative that authorizes both a moral and a political demand, and when are we dealing with an interpersonal ethical imperative that authorizes only a moral demand? Though Gaus does distinguish social morality from political philosophy, and does not assume that their solutions to the central concern for social morality must be the same, he nonetheless sees social morality and political philosophy as addressing the same problem. But there is a difference between the central concern of social morality and the central concern of political philosophy. The question "How can free and equal moral persons claim authority to prescribe to other free and equal moral persons?" is not the same as the question "What is the nature of the connection, if any, between the ethical order and the political/legal order?" It cannot simply be assumed that the concern of social morality is the same as the concern of political philosophy (or vice versa). What one morally "must" do (or not do) in terms of the demands of social morality is not necessarily what one morally must do (or not do) in terms of the demands of political philosophy. Gaus does not keep these sufficiently clear. We can best see the effect of this ambiguity if we put the problem in the form of what we call "the Social Reasoner's Dilemma":[15] Either societies where people are not "free and equal" have "social moralities," or they do not.

Horn A:

1. If a society does have social moralities while being unfree and unequal, then being free and equal is not necessary for there to be a social morality.
2. If the conclusions from assumptions of "freedom and equality" would give different results from those exhibited through alternative social moralities, then there must be a moral theory explaining any priority one has over the other.
3. Therefore, social moralities cannot themselves be the source of their own moral justification, but must appeal to principles beyond themselves.

Horn B:

1. If society does not have a social morality, due to the fact that the society is unfree and unequal, then the society will have to adopt a social morality for one to exist.
2. Some explanation, justification, or reason for adopting both a social morality itself, as well as the specific social morality that accords with freedom and equality, will have to be given.
3. But that explanation, justification, or reason cannot appeal to an existent social morality because, by assumption, one does not yet exist.
4. Therefore, social moralities cannot themselves be the source of their own moral justification, but must draw from principles beyond themselves.

---

[15] We believe this dilemma might have applicability to other forms of social reasoning ethics, such as that found in Rawls and Sen. So, for example, one could substitute "subject to the veil of ignorance" or "impartiality" for "free and equal," or one might substitute "public reason" for "social morality." It shall not be our task here to explore these permutations, but only to suggest that social moralities beg the most fundamental questions about the foundations of moral life.

Either way, the moral dimension of social morality is a function of something that is independent of the social morality itself.[16]

It is important to recognize, at the outset, that the conclusion drawn from this dilemma is precisely the one that Gaus seeks to reject. For him, the point is that if we get our concept of social morality just right, it will *in fact* serve as its own source of justification.[17] This is because a social morality is justified if it reflects, finally, the *actual* values of each and every acting agent in society. A claim on others has "standing" only because others have actually accepted the validity of the claim as reflecting their own values. Thus, those others cannot claim any values or norms have been imposed upon them from outside of the social morality, because those norms or values are actually their own—that is, their own values are internal to the social morality. The incentive for avoiding the foregoing dilemma, then, would seem to be to take on Horn B and claim that once one clears away the "noise" that surrounds moral claims that people typically make for and against each other, eventually one will discover an actual body of values all agree to, at least to the extent that they can demand that others (and themselves) conform to them. That seems to be Gaus's strategy; but taking that strategy would require him to confront Horn A, where one is now speaking about the presence of existing social moralities, rather than about establishing one. The way, therefore, to avoid the impact of Horn A would be to say that there can, in fact, only be *one type* of social morality, finally, so that there is no such thing as an actual social morality that does not exhibit the characteristics of freedom and equality. But, assuming the contents of that morality are at least presently unclear (otherwise, why debate the matter?), that solution would throw us

---

[16] Another way to express this fundamental difficulty is to note that so-called public reason does not provide the justification for the basic claim that it wrongs an individual for her to be subject to coercion (or the action or rule or institution she is being coerced to abide by), absent her having reason to accept that coercion. We thank Eric Mack for this expression of this difficulty. Further, see Chad Van Schoelandt, "Justification, Coercion, and the Place of Public Reason," *Philosophical Studies* 172 (2015): pp. 1031–50 for a further discussion of this fundamental difficulty and an attempt to recast the scope of Gaus's project.

[17] Gaus states that Kant and Rawls understood that "the beginning point of understanding 'true morality' is 'actual morality,'" and that his goal is to develop this insight (*OPR*, pp. 102–3). Further, he notes: "For a society to have a justified social morality, it must possess social rules—rules that are actually followed by its members and so form a basis for an ordered and cooperative social life" (ibid., p. 179).

back to Horn B, where we need at least a basis for separating moral noise from proper social reasoning. But again, unless Gaus would want to claim we already know what that social morality looks like, and that it accords with the requirements of freedom and equality, even the process of clearing the "noise" in the system would presuppose some other "moral" commitments that would justify and bring to light what is being called the true social morality, and to distinguish it from its pretenders. Yet, establishing that there is "noise" in the moral system already suggests both that we do not yet have the process of moral reasoning completely settled, and that we will be appealing to other principles to help us sort through that noise. So, either there can be many social moralities, some of which give pride of place to freedom and equality, or there is only one candidate qualified as a social morality, one that is yet to be fully appreciated and articulated. Either way, we seem to be compelled to come up with a reason outside of the social morality itself for preferring the social morality characterized by that appropriate application and understanding of freedom and equality. No doubt the notion of an "appropriate application and understanding" needs some further elaboration.[18]

What seems to be crucial to Gaus's approach to the interpersonal demands of social morality and its central concern is the need to reconcile two claims: (a) "When you assert your demand as authoritative—something that overrules my views of the matter—our private reason leads us to disagree on what morality requires. Morality does not fax its demands down from above; you are asserting your interpretation of the demands of morality as that which should be followed by me, over my own interpretation";[19] and (b) "A free moral person is one who acts according to her own reasoning about the demands of morality."[20] Gaus's proposed reconciliation of

---

[18] Recently, Gaus has argued in "The Good, the Bad, and the Ugly: Three Agent-Type Challenges to the Order of Public Reason," *Philosophical Studies* 170 (2014): pp. 563–77 that the aim of *OPR* is not to secure moral truth for social morality but, rather, only a social-moral framework that sustains human-cooperative life. He claims that such moral theorizing is not meant to replace the search for moral truth, but to supplement it. The problem, of course, is how we are to understand what does and does not constitute "human-cooperative life," in the absence of some moral standard. Once this question is recognized, we are brought back to "The Social Reasoner's Dilemma" we have presented.

[19] Gaus, *OPR*, p. 11.

[20] Ibid., p. 15.

these two claims is to employ public reason; but before examining that attempted solution, a few comments are necessary about each of these claims.

First, and despite Gaus's claim to be following Locke,[21] (b) is not what Locke holds. As Locke terms it, liberty is not license, but is found when the law of nature is followed. This law entails that "no one ought to harm another in his life, health, liberty or possessions. . . . And that all men may be restrained from invading others' rights, and from doing hurt to one another. . . ."[22] Liberty or freedom is not an amoral condition. Because of this, preventing from doing so those who decide, *by their own reason*, to violate the basic rights of others is not a limit on their freedom or liberty. Unlike for Hobbes, liberty is not, for Locke, doing whatever one decides to do, free of external impediments. It is not simply following one's own reason.[23] Thus, it is by no mean obvious—at least, not in Lockean terms—that (b) is a condition that amounts to liberty or is worthy of protection.

Second, while (a) is true at least in the sense that we understand the demands of morality only through our own cognitive efforts, this does not mean or imply that "moral persons are all equally authoritative interpreters of the demands that morality places on them."[24] Some person's understanding of the demands of morality may be correct, while another's might be wrong. Not all interpretations are equal; and thus the authority of an interpretation rests on the accuracy of the interpreter's understanding of the demands of morality, not on who is making the interpretation. But, of course, Gaus does not claim all interpreters are equally correct, or that one person's judgment is as good as the next. He claims, instead, that another's judgment of the demands of morality lacks authority over one's own judgment.[25] To which we have but one response—namely, it depends. Qua another's judgment of morality's demands, there is,

---

[21] Ibid., p. 14.

[22] John Locke, *Two Treatises of Government*, ed. Peter Laslett (Cambridge: Cambridge University Press, 1988), p. 271, chaps. 6 and 7.

[23] Stated in a more contemporary fashion, liberty exists when basic negative individual rights are protected by means of a political/legal order whose laws are limited to prohibiting the non-consensual use or direction of a person's life, conduct, or resources by others. Such laws ban the initiatory use or threat of physical force (in all its forms) and thus seek to protect the possibility of each individual exercising her own reason when among others. See also note 57 below.

[24] Gaus, *OPR*, p. 15.

[25] Ibid., p. 15.

indeed, no reason to assume that another's judgment is superior to one's own. However, qua another's accurate judgment as compared with one's own inaccurate judgment, then another's judgment is superior to one's own and is authoritative. But it also should be noted that the accuracy of another's judgment over one's own does not by itself require that one be politically or legally required to accept or conform to that judgment. That is an entirely different matter and is the ambiguity highlighted in our dilemma.

Determining the accuracy of one's judgment is, of course, a difficult matter. There are many procedures[26] we have learned about how to determine the accuracy of various judgments, and these are not without moral significance; but they are not the ultimate standards in determining the authority of a given interpretation or judgment. And while it may be useful to have an umpire who renders the final interpretation in matters of conflicting interpretations, this does not mean that the rules of the game, so to speak, are strictly a matter of interpretation. We have some understanding of what, for example, the strike zone is in baseball, independent of the umpire's decisions. Indeed, umpires, whether in baseball or in the context of social morality, can be evaluated regarding the accuracy of their decisions.

Gaus would agree that there are moral demands prior to public justification; but he would, nonetheless, insist that there is no way to access them independent of some interpretation, and thus we are stuck with the conflicting interpretations of morality's demands.[27] We do not think that this conclusion follows, because the fact that one must use one's judgment to know or interpret something does not by itself establish that it is *merely* one's judgment or interpretation. However, we will not pursue this matter any further. What we would like to concentrate on, instead, is whether public justification is itself the ground for moral demands or whether, as our dilemma suggests, it, too, requires something to ground it—and if the latter, just what that ground is.

It should not go unnoticed that in the process of setting up the basis for public reasoning, Gaus observes that the ultimate importance of Hobbes lies not in his account of the clash of self-interest, but in his view of the "problems of rationality and disagreement that arise when individuals rely on their private judgment of what reason

---

[26] Some of these are noted in Putnam's account of idealized inquiry in the section on Sen in the previous chapter.

[27] Gaus, *OPR*, p. 17.

requires."[28] The state of nature is for Hobbes, but not for Locke, amoral, and it cannot ground the demands of morality. There is nowhere else for Hobbes to go than to agreement among contractors; and it is an interesting and basic question as to whether Hobbes sees such agreement as providing justification for the demands of morality[29] or, instead, sees it simply as a description of what human beings do or would do. By the same token, the dilemma continues to raise the question of whether Gaus regards public reasoning as justifying the demands of morality, or merely as describing the practices of human beings.

Be this as it may—at least, for now—Gaus sees the answer to the reconciliation of (a) and (b) in terms of what he calls the dictates of public reason.[30] In other words, when a person makes a moral demand on you regarding what you must do or not do, that person has the standing to make such a demand because she is "calling on you to act according to the rules of your own judgment, and not to behave inconsistently with yourself."[31] The crucial moves here are two: your own judgment or reason is not being considered in terms of how you actually are; and your liberty or freedom is not being understood simply in a negative manner, à la Locke. Gaus quotes Bernard Bosanquet: "The claim to obey only yourself is a claim essential to humanity; and the further significance of it rests upon what you mean by 'yourself.'"[32] To this Gaus adds:

> The insight of positive liberty theorists is that not every action a person chooses is a true expression of her overall aims and values. One sense (it is not the only sense) of a free person is one whose actions and beliefs are

[28] Ibid., p. 9.

[29] See Jeffrey Paul's claim that social contract theories, be they actual or hypothetical, commit the naturalistic fallacy in "Substantive Social Contracts and the Legitimate Basis for Political Authority," *The Monist* 66.4 (1983): pp. 517–28.

[30] It should not go unnoticed here that Gaus endorses Rousseau's view that law is the "salutary organ of the will of all" or "the precepts of public reason" (Jean-Jacques Rousseau, "A Discourse on Political Economy," in *The Social Contract and Discourses*, trans. G. D. H. Cole [London: J. M. Dent, 1973], pp. 256–7; Gaus, *OPR*, p. 25). This is deeply different from Locke's view. Law is, for Locke (who follows Hooker in this regard), the standard or measure for judging human conduct; and this view is based on the nature of human beings and reality in general.

[31] Gaus, *OPR*, p. 29.

[32] Ibid., p. 33. Bernard Bosanquet, *The Philosophical Theory of the State and Related Essays*, ed. Gerald F. Gaus and William Sweet (South Bend, IN: St Augustine Press, 2001), p. 152.

based on her reason. We may think that with more information, a person would appreciate reasons that would cause him to act differently—as in the case of John Stuart Mill's man crossing an unsafe bridge he mistakenly thinks to be sound, his ignorance prevents him from appreciating *his own* reasons. Even Mill did not think stopping this person interfered with his freedom.[33]

Hence, the point of all of this is that when you consider real human beings ideally—that is to say, when you consider them not when they are "sunk in ignorance and passions"[34]—they can be considered Members of the Public who "deliberate well and judge only on the relevant and intelligible values, reasons, and concerns" of real agents they represent and who "seek to legislate impartially for all other Members of the Public."[35] The rules that each and every Member of the Public endorses are good ones; and those who see to their application—those whom Gaus calls "Rule-following Punishers"—will have the standing to do so. This is how (a) and (b) can be reconciled. Public reason turns out to be each person's reason.

Hence, if we return to our dilemma, we see that Gaus would doubtless argue that what is askew in our presentation is the notion that freedom and equality are values to which we should accord our conduct, or to which social reasoning should conform. For Gaus, there is no issue of accordance or conforming here. Instead, freedom and equality are "embedded in our moral practices."[36] This embeddedness is demonstrated by the fact that we can follow or not follow moral advice and recognize its appropriate forms (freedom), while at the same time making claims upon others, and they upon us, of appropriate ways to be treated (equality).[37] But of course, this level of understanding the nature of "freedom and equality" does not offer much help because, if such descriptions are true of all human beings, then humanity has managed, in the process, to give rise to a wide range of practices that would seem to have little regard for freedom or equality. We are thus pushed back to deciding which of those practices are "moral" or not. There is no doubt that within the various "social moralities," people make insistent and irrevocable demands upon the conduct of others, claim to have "standing" in so doing, and feel com-

---

[33] Gaus, *OPR*, p. 33.
[34] Ibid., p. 35.
[35] Ibid., p. 26.
[36] Ibid., p. 22.
[37] Ibid., pp. 15ff.

pelled to obey certain prescriptions that they and others identify as requiring adherence. But merely noting that such demands and claims to standing have been made is some distance from saying that they are thereby justified, as Gaus himself would rightly insist. So, again, either one must find some standard for making such a justification; or one must "abstract away from obvious failures of impartiality and rationality" and stand above the moral noise through "an idealization of some actual individual."[38] In other words, we refine the notion of "actual" so that it exhibits characteristics that lend themselves to the sort of embeddedness we desire.

Gaus is quite aware that this view entails a commitment to Rousseau's notorious claim that persons must be "forced to be free,"[39] by getting them to follow dictates of public reason; but he is willing to roll with this argumentative punch. He claims that "to be free as a rational agent and believer is to act on, and believe on the basis of, one's good reasons."[40] This means, however, that one does *not* accept a person's current set of acknowledged reasons as definitive of the reasons that person has. A person's reasons also include those reasons to which the exercise of a person's rationality could lead.[41] If Mill is correct to say that stopping a man from crossing an unsafe bridge is not an abridgment of his freedom, because he would accept a judgment of the bridge as "being unsafe" as his reason, even if that judgment came from another, then there is a wedge, or so Gaus believes, for using public reason to determine what it means to "obey only yourself." But is Mill correct?

---

[38] Ibid., p. 26. We are told that "social morality comes from all and applies to all, and so it is an expression of moral autonomy" (ibid., p. 29). This is because "morality is 'self-legislated' by all in the sense that, consulting her own (private) reason, each Member of the Public endorses the relevant moral rule as binding on all, and so on herself" (ibid., p. 28). Of course, it would seem from this that it is "moral autonomy" that somehow imbues "social morality" with its moral dimension, suggesting that the justification again lies beyond the realm of social morality per se. Moreover, we might note that the ability to self-legislate does not ipso facto show the presence of "moral autonomy." There is that virtues-and-visions tradition that might locate moral autonomy elsewhere. The point is that a whole string of commitments about the nature of morality are presupposed in such pronouncements. That does not make them wrong or even suspect, but neither does it thereby accord social morality its own standing against competitors.

[39] Ibid., p. 33.

[40] Ibid., p. 35.

[41] Ibid., p. 35.

Stopping a person who does not know that a bridge is unsafe to cross would, in most cases, be something that person would welcome. But suppose a person seeks the thrill of doing something terribly unsafe. In that case, stopping would not be welcomed. Either way, however, this stopping would be an interference with the would-be bridge-crosser's freedom, provided, of course, that crossing this bridge would not involve an interference with the freedom of others—for example, by trespassing on their bridge. The reason that stopping a (non-trespassing) bridge-crosser is usually not considered an abridgement of freedom is that most people "waive their right" to prosecute those who stopped them; and they do so because they appreciate knowing that the action they planned to take would not be good for them. They are quite willing for others to interfere with their freedom in exchange for that knowledge. People want their reasons to be good reasons. As a matter of social morality, it would be a general presumption that most people do not want to do something terribly unsafe. We all can and do act on such presumptions. But it would not follow from this that such a general presumption should be made a rule for the political/legal order—for example, a rule that if actions by others prevent a person from doing something that would be bad for him, then those actions are not to be regarded as an interference with the freedom of that person.[42] The subtle, but vital, line between social morality and the political/ legal order is only made blurry in this case. The example, therefore, upon which Gaus places so much weight really does not provide him with the needed wedge by which to establish public reason as the basis for solving the central concerns of either social morality or political philosophy.

Our problem, then, is the view, on the one hand, that social moralities cannot qualify as social moralities if their actual practices are objectionable by the standards of now-idealized agents of freedom and equality—and, on the other, that idealized versions of persons or rules are themselves sufficient to be called a practice. Such idealized persons or norms *may* be suitable for theoretical reflection, just as certain practices *may* accord with convincing theory. What does not seem to us very compelling is to make claims to moral pluralism, and then to resort to some process of

---

[42] Or even worse: If such actions by others lead to a state of affairs that are or turn out to be good for a person, then those actions are not an interference with the freedom of that person.

idealization to try to wash away the inevitable tensions of moral pluralism.[43]

Just *why* must we wash away those tensions through a process of public reasoning? We can, of course, answer such a question by noting that we are a liberal people with liberal values, so we should proceed from there. In this case, the project would be one of clarifying the nature of those liberal values that we all share. Perhaps this is, after all, simply the extent of Gaus's project. But if it is, we are still in need of a defense of those liberal values. However, we have taken the position here that Gaus is after *any* order that can be endorsed by people with different conceptions of the good and justice, with the degree of liberalness of the order being left open to the result of the public reasoning process. But if that is the project, we must continue on with Horn B of the dilemma, because it is unclear why social reasoning is the required means to solve at least the *political* problem at hand—namely, the endorsement of a "common political order." One way to get everyone to endorse a common political order, despite their different conceptions of the good, is to force them to. Another way is to appeal to authority which, by the way, can have, and has had historically, the unqualified endorsement of those who are subjected to it.[44] Indeed, the undermining of authority has been, and continues to be, the main push-back against the encroachment of liberal orders. Without knowing clearly the connection between the ethical and the political, it is not yet clear, on the one hand, why these solutions do not solve the *political* problem, whatever their ethical consequences—nor, on the other hand, why the ethical should have any bearing upon the political. But since we ourselves are not fans of coercive

[43] This sort of moral proceduralism, adopted in the hope that one can avoid taking any substantive moral position, is every bit as monistic as the substantive theories it hopes to avoid, for a specific body of values is accepted and presumed. To say that such values are standards of rationality rather than morality only begs the obvious questions about the value of standards of rationality in guiding action.

[44] Needless to say, authorities do not need to be coercive to carry weight, only respected. And it is false to say that authorities, in actual societies, have that respect because free and equal persons give it to them. Cultural traditions have ways of thinking that simply reject the notion that the best way to understand our relations to each other is through a supposition of free and equal individuals. The clash of cultures is not solved by declaring even more loudly that liberal values are correct. For an indication of how such assertions can go astray, see Jakob De Roover, Sarah Claerhout, and S. N. Balagangadhara, "Liberal Political Theory and Cultural Migration of Ideas: The Case of Secularism in India," *Political Theory* 39.5 (2011): pp. 571–99.

or authoritarian efforts to secure some set of shared values, we shall leave these approaches aside for the moment. Yet, in doing so, we are certainly not left with only Gaus's solution of public reasoning as the embodiment of freedom and equality. In fact, another way of considering the problem would be to claim that the whole project of public reasoning is unnecessary, because ordinary politics *just is* the endorsement of a common political order by people of diverse values through the various compromises, trades, and deals they cut with each other. This social evolutionary argument is, no doubt, thought to be defective, because it fails to appreciate the supervenient role of morality, as well as because it gives to some an "unfair" advantage over outcomes.[45] But that again raises our old problem of where the lines need to be drawn. It is by no means clear that the "philosophize-and-command" approach taken by Gaus and others in regard to social moralities is, in the end, superior to evolutionary unfolding. Indeed, it might be said that the latter actually produces more enduring, stable, and less divisive forms of commonality, because they are ultimately grounded in actual interest, rather than in idealized agents.

But supposing all these preceding examples to be suffering from a lack of true appreciation of the centrality of freedom and equality, one may still wonder why we do not have both commonality and freedom and equality in following a few simple rules about respect for property rights, securing freedom of trade and association, and strictly limiting governmental intervention to the prevention of the initiatory use of physical force. Would such an arrangement not allow individuals to accommodate themselves to one another according to their actual desires and on the basis of the assets and resources they can bring to bear on any of their cooperative endeavors in a way that is both equal and free? Do we really need to engage in a process of public reasoning to see the qualities of freedom and equality in these

---

[45] It cannot be said that politics cannot be an example of common agreement, because people are still in the process of working out their disagreements, and so they have not yet arrived at that point of commonality. For if the measure of commonality is the cessation of politics or disagreements about values, then surely our standards are utopian. There is a significant difference between saying, on the one hand, that at any given time, T, the various compromises, bargains, arrangements, and the like represent a snapshot of a commonality of values (our point here)—and, on the other hand, that the only states that qualify as common are ones where all agree. The former may have defects of stability, urging us to look for better modes for achieving commonalities; but that does not imply that the latter is the only standard to use when thinking of commonality.

simple rules? The answer to such questions is supposed to be obvious. Either it is pointed out that individuals do not start from equal bargaining positions (thus supposedly undermining the requirement of equality); or it is claimed that these "simple rules" are subject to controversy and thus, at best, a set of *candidates* for an outcome of public reasoning, not assured conclusions. For even if such simple rules were actually in place, they would qualify as a social morality or common political order only when those who do not find justice or value in them could be brought around to seeing that they actually do value these "simple rules" after all, once the noise of their own biases and lapses in reasoning is countered. Our point, of course, is not to argue that public reasoning might not produce something very close to these "simple rules," or that the public reasoning approach is not a good way to understand how such rules might actually underlie our conception of our common political order. On the contrary, these "simple rules" are not too far from those which Gaus imagines public reasoning would produce and which, in actual practice, are more likely to achieve equality of conditions than are alternative positions. No, our problem is with the notion that command-like prescriptions, however refined, are superior in practice to market-like ones in engendering commonality and cooperation, and with the notion that morality—even social morality—is fundamentally captured by thinking in terms of a community of claimants.

The first of these problems is a function of the belief that certain kinds of moral reasoning might really not be very compatible with the modalities of human interaction where *quid pro quo* predominates.[46] Why we should thus begin, or even be particularly concerned, with universalized, commanded moral prescriptions for the bulk of social life is, to us, therefore, an open question. The response to this question of ours would amount to saying that because even our set of "simple rules" takes the form of prescriptive universalized commands, we cannot avoid them ourselves, and thus that is why these types of prescriptions must constitute the very object of the public reasoning project. Fair enough. But in offering this rebuttal, one realizes that our old friend, the elision of the distinction between (if not conflation of) the social and the political that we have spoken about above, is here being undertaken once again. For it can be said—indeed, we have said it—that political rules can take the form of universalized prescriptive

---

[46] For another look at this issue see Ruth W. Grant, *Strings Attached* (Princeton: Princeton University Press, 2012).

commands, but that doing so is not yet to say much of anything about morality and moral rules. It is our position not only that liberalism is fundamentally predicated upon the distinction between ethically informed political rules and moral ones, but also that the "claim-and-command" understanding of morality from Rousseau and Kant onward is fundamentally deficient as a tool of social control and cooperation, as a moral ideal, and even as a social morality.

Perhaps a simple example can help illustrate our point. During the Cultural Revolution in China in the fifties and sixties, it was common twice a day for all to exercise collectively. People were "strongly incentivized" to do so[47]—meaning not only that they could not opt out, but that peer discipline would be exerted upon any slackers. The benefits of a healthy population, both to the society and the individuals involved, are obvious. It is thus hard for us to imagine anything more compelling as a candidate for pure "public reasoning" than this program of public exercise. In the first place, once one filtered away all the noise that sloth, bad habits, ignorance, and various other biases create within our ordinary forms of eating and exercise, one could only conclude that our "actual values" would be significantly more akin to the ones imposed by the Cultural Revolution. Moreover, once we all recognized the validity of these health values, not only would they become our own, but we would have every encouragement to monitor and punish others in their name.[48] Further, those who "monitored" these events would certainly have "standing" in reining in any strays. In this respect, we would have all the basic characteristics of a "social morality." One might be troubled by the aesthetic of collective exercising and want a more individualized approach. That aesthetic qualification would not change the relevance of the example, however, so long as there were some way to ensure that people were doing what social morality dictated with regard to their own health. And although this regimen might appear as the result of the mere dictates of Chairman Mao, it is not clear to us that it matters much how the social morality is articulated, provided all the other criteria for being a social morality are met. In this regard, we find the prospect no more attractive (indeed, less so) were this social morality to be the result of some "democratic" body, rather than a dictator.

We use this example not because we find Gaus endorsing it but,

---

[47] See Michel Kelly-Gagnon, "Jogging with Mao," *Toronto Sun*, April 11, 2012. Kelly-Gagnon notes that this sort of regimen was popular with the Nazis as well.

[48] See in this connection Gaus, *OPR*, pp. 103ff. and 188ff.

rather, because it most clearly indicates how different the claim-and-command approach to morality is from our own. Indeed, even if the claim-and-command approach concluded with the very same "simple rules" we would endorse, the character of those rules would take on a cast quite alien to the appropriate conception of morality, and even to the appropriate conception of politics—not to say, to the one we advocate. That is to say, their meaning would be significantly different from an understanding of the very same norms within the virtues-and-visions conception. Simply stated, the difference comes down to the fact that public reasoning sees claiming and commanding as *itself* being the constituting force of morality. Morality is essentially about people making claims on one another, claims which, when tightened up sufficiently according to certain standards, allow the commands to be issued. By contrast, our view holds that claims and commands, if present at all, must be grounded in something outside of themselves; and it is that in which they are grounded that constitutes the essential character of morality. Morality is not, therefore, the process of meeting certain qualifying conditions for producing the right sort of claims and commands, because morality is not essentially a function of claiming and commanding at all.[49] Whether claims or commands are made is, in other words, not decisive as to whether a moral issue is present, even if the situation is social. Consequently, adopting one of these two ways of understanding morality will certainly affect how one understands any common political order and its authority over one's actions.[50] There is, therefore, a rather significant difference between seeing the aforementioned regimen of exercise as a component of one's self-perfection and seeing that regimen as a

---

[49] Like anything else, morality can, indeed, be conceived in a socialized fashion, giving one the conception that the rules one is asked to follow represent the appropriate distillation of norms society finds worthy of commanding to all. And as for all forms of socialization, the cost is the same diminishing role for, and possibility of, personal responsibility.

[50] Gaus, no doubt, would again want to warn against the specter of monism and say that while he is not necessarily opposed to our way of looking at morality, his approach to social morality is an equally valuable alternative, because monism is false. But apart from all that we have said and will say on this matter, Plato got it right long ago when he suggested that morality could be grounded in convention, authority, tradition, or nature. That public reasoning approaches give us sophisticated forms of conventionalism does not imply a compatibilist moral pluralism. It is not monism that requires one to reject the other three foundations, but rather their a priori removal of the other alternatives as candidates for producers of moral content.

monitored social morality, even if the actual actions were to be the same. We see our issue most acutely by recognizing the inherent blurriness of the line between ethics and politics brought on by socialized morality, with the effect that morality comes off looking *essentially* political (claim-and-command) or legislative. It is the liberation of morality from such constraints that allows individualistic perfectionism to move forward.

Politics, as we have already noted, does, indeed, have something more akin to a claim-and-command structure, since it results in coercion; and it will, at least in liberal orders, be processed through various claims people make about how the system should be structured. Granting that, however, is still a long way from speaking morally, because the fundamentally individualized character of the good is, and must be, largely ignored when shaping political principles. The ethical component to the political, as we have argued more fully elsewhere, enters through the prime directive for establishing a legitimate political order—namely, the protection of the possibility of self-direction.[51] Though the rights that express that protection are indeed claims upon others, those claims are not fundamental, but derivative consequences of securing the very purpose of the political order. That is to say, it is not that rights are the result of sorting through the claims we make upon others and ourselves, but rather that the claims we can make upon others are a function of the rights we possess. This point is significant because, while it is conceivable that one might live in a social situation where one's exercise habits are monitored by one's neighbors, it could never be the case that one's rights could be described in terms of being required to participate in such an exercise regimen. Such could not be the case, because in a true, rights-respecting liberal order, the purpose of the political order has nothing to do with making individuals or society better off, or even necessarily with propagating norms in accord with one's own "values."[52] The sole

[51] We hasten to state again that self-direction need not be understood—and is not, for us, so understood (as we noted in section 2 of Chapter 2 and argue in Rasmussen and Den Uyl, *NOL*, p. 89)—as choosing or reasoning correctly, appropriately, or even with full knowledge. In this regard, our view stands in direct contrast to that of Gaus's. See Gaus, *OPR*, pp. 35–6.

[52] As Gaus rightly points out, social moralities of the type he describes do have social benefits and would be found in any social order. Saying that the political order should be non-perfectionist does not imply much of anything about strategies for social cooperation or the psychology involved in securing it.

purpose of the political order is to protect the possibility that one can be a value pursuer.

Our overall point, then, is that the claim-and-command approach distorts the way one looks at morality by politicizing it. But even politics is not, in the end, for us at least, simply of a claim-and-command form. Though the matter may seem less obvious, it is, nonetheless, the same, if we move away from thinking in terms of the health example and back toward those "simple rules" that we believe do accord with an appropriate understanding of politics. What would be the difference if both public reasoning and "virtues and visions" arrived at the same set of political rules? The difference can best be seen by looking at the ultimate moral value within the respective systems. Unless the ultimate moral value for Gaus is to ensure the presence of a social morality[53] per se, it would seem that autonomy represents the pinnacle of moral accomplishment for Gaus. We are told that "a person acts autonomously when her action is directed by her internalized *nomos* or rule, not by what she most wants or what others expect of her."[54] Such a view is to be contrasted with the classical virtues understanding of ethics, in which the ultimate moral accomplishment is to conform one's desires to the good. In a legislative model of morality, such as the one within which Gaus works, internalization (autonomy) becomes an end in itself because it is necessary for the universalization and socialization of values: "being unable to exercise moral autonomy, they cannot grasp that a demand of social morality is authoritative, that they are required to set aside what they most care for and conform to the rule."[55] In this respect, autonomy is both an expression of the success of a social morality, as well as a means to it. For us, by contrast, the fact that something has been internalized or is autonomous still leaves open the question of whether it is good. It is true that, on our view, all morally perfected persons will be autonomous (in Gaus's sense); but it is not true that all autonomous persons are thereby morally perfected. That would depend on whether they conform to the good. Autonomy thus

---

[53] And we conceive the possibility that this, rather than autonomy, is, after all, the ultimate value for Gaus. In a fundamentally socialized ethics, it would seem that ensuring the presence of a social morality would be the very telos of ethics. For us, however, morality is every bit as present with Robinson Crusoe as it is with Robinson Crusoe plus Friday.

[54] Gaus, *OPR*, p. 204.

[55] Ibid., p. 209.

has value in the virtues-and-visions approach we adopt, but more as a sign of success than of an end sought. Perfected persons will exhibit autonomous behavior, but autonomous behavior per se will be neither the object of their endeavors nor a decisive sign of their completion.

Now, if politics is not about according with or securing perfected moral states, or even encouraging them, but rather about securing their possibility, then the "simple rules" will not be measured by the degree to which people approach perfection or become perfected. Under our framework in other words, very little would be known about the moral health and progress of a society by considering its political rules. By contrast, virtually everything concerning such matters would be known by examining Gaus's political order; and the same statement might be made of Rawls and Sen, as well. So, apart from the fact that authors such as these illegitimately elide the distinction between ethics and politics—which we believe they must do, because they understand morality in terms of public reasoning—the phenomenologies of the two worlds, even with the same rules, are vastly different.

In Gaus's world, given morality's fundamentally social nature, the "simple rules" would express paths through which we monitor each other's conduct. They can be modified if they stand in the way of autonomy for some reason, or otherwise fail to incorporate all the possibilities for a social morality. Life in this world is an endless Facebook page, where privacy becomes difficult and actually signifies a movement away from morality. By contrast again, privacy—in the sense of saying that the nature and degree of one's relations with others is *one's own* responsibility alone—is the very *central* point of the "simple rules." One does not, therefore, look out upon those "simple rules" as descriptions of joint agreements, latent or otherwise, or as rules we can stand upon, to demand their conformity by others. One would look upon them, instead, as a way of giving place to the possibility that one might pursue moral perfection, but that if one does not, or if one should violate one of the "simple rules," any incurred penalties (political or social) are justified not by the authority of others or their social morality, but by the good that is obstructed. In our virtues-and-visions world, moral relations with others are not a matter of claims and commands, but of encouragements and persuasion.

2. Darwall

One of the many interesting features of Darwall's book, *The Second-Person Standpoint* (hereafter *SPS*),[56] is that its index contains no reference to either "liberalism" or "politics." While such an absence might suggest a division between ethics and politics, with Darwall concentrating on the former and thus finally liberating ethics from politics, in this case, the opposite is more likely. The lack of such references is, we believe, highly indicative of how closely aligned ethics and politics are in Darwall. No doubt, Darwall finds some basis for distinguishing the two;[57] but as we shall see, the nature of the theory requires that the ethical translate more or less directly into the political—assuming that the political is largely concerned with our rights. In this regard, the respect-based, second-personal standpoint also comes to define the nature of liberalism itself, which, for Darwall, is, at its core, an ethical doctrine with political implications.[58] That the ethical and political are connected, at root, is described by Darwall early on in the *SPS*:

> Now we are concerned less directly with rights than with *moral obligation*. As Hart himself notes, however, despite the fact that "moral obligation" can sometimes be used as a "general label" for what "morally we ought to do," the concept has a more properly restricted content that is intimately connected with that of rights.... Neither concept can be understood independently of the idea of the (second-personal) authority to claim or demand. Just as a right involves an authority to claim that

---

[56] Stephen Darwall, *The Second-Person Standpoint: Morality, Respect, and Accountability* [hereafter *SPS*] (Cambridge, MA: Harvard University Press, 2006).

[57] Obviously, the term "politics" is a broad one that can carry all sorts of connotations. Neither Darwall nor anyone else would have trouble, for example, distinguishing strategic political maneuvering from morality. But we tend to use politics in these contexts to mean the correct foundation for the political/legal order, and here we would be talking about the nature of the relationship between law and morality (Rasmussen and Den Uyl, *NOL*, p. 271). In this regard, we do not see much distance in Darwall—although, in some respects, he wishes to remain agnostic about the *actual* connection—between law and morality, and their structural relationship is virtually identical. See Stephen Darwall, "Law and the Second-Person Standpoint," in *Morality, Authority, & Law: Essays in Second-Personal Ethics I* (Oxford: Oxford University Press, 2013), p. 172.

[58] As noted above, we do not take Darwall to be operating *within* a pre-defined liberal framework but, rather, to be involved in helping to define the nature of that framework itself.

159

to which one has a right, so also is moral obligation conceptually tied to what the moral community can demand (and what no one has a right not to do). And what I am morally free to do is what no one can justifiably demand that I not do either as a member of the moral community (no conflicting moral obligation) or as an individual (no conflicting right).[59]

That such a connection between ethics (moral obligation) and politics (rights) is itself defining of liberalism, for Darwall, is indicated by the following:

> All in all, therefore, it seems that [Adam] Smith had reasons for genuine ambivalence about honour. Whatever its real attractions for people still in its grip in the middle of the eighteenth century, a culture of honour is deeply at odds with the doctrine of equal human dignity. To be a "respector of persons" in the traditional sense of honouring distinctions of status and rank is decidedly not to respect persons in the sense that Smith would help to bequeath to the tradition of liberal moral and political thought that would follow him.[60]

Furthermore, Darwall argues that the tight connection between rights and moral obligation, as indicated above, goes to the very foundations of modern moral thought.

> I shall argue that what is novel in Grotius is the idea that morality (natural law) creates "obligations" whose binding force cannot be reduced to reasons or "counsels" of any kind. . . . Moreover, central to morality as Grotius understands it, are basic individual "perfect rights" all persons have, *claim rights*, as we would now call them, which entail the standing or "faculty of demanding" rightful treatment from others and others' consequent obligation to provide it. . . . By tying the idea of morality to that of legitimate *demand*, and distinguishing its normative force from

---

[59] Darwall, *SPS*, p. 20. In "Law and the Second-Person Standpoint" (p. 68) Darwall notes: "Although the claims I argue for in my book concern *morality* . . . they would seem also to bear on the *law*. One way of viewing my project, in fact, is as trying to bring out the distinctive character of that part of morality that is modeled on the idea of law. Moral *obligations*, I argue, are not just what there are good (or even compelling) moral reasons for us to do; they are what morality demands of us and what we are accountable for doing, where the latter is understood as what representative persons or members of the moral community have the authority to demand that we do. . . . Similarly, moral *rights* must also be understood in legal or juridical terms."

[60] Stephen Darwall, "Smith's Ambivalence about Honour," in *Essays on the Philosophy of Adam Smith: The Adam Smith Review, Volume 5: Essays Commemorating the 250th Anniversary of the Theory of Moral Sentiments*, ed. Vivienne Brown and Samuel Fleischacker (New York: Routledge, 2010), p. 106.

that of reasons that can but recommend or "counsel" conduct, however strongly, but not yet *require* it, Grotius bequeathed to the modern period the problem of what is nowadays called the "authority of morality," namely, how to understand and account for morality's distinctive normative force.[61]

Needless to say, we hold that the comments made about Smith and Grotius are indicative of Darwall's *own* position, however applicable they may be to the thinkers themselves. Thus, from these passages we see that liberalism, rights, and moral obligation are expected to be closely associated in one theoretical framework. Consequently, we hold the tight connection between rights, moral obligation, and liberalism to be Darwall's.

At this stage, it is probably worthwhile to remind the reader that, in this area of moral and political theory, the contrasts run deep between our own approach and Darwall's. For example, liberalism, in our view, is a political philosophy, not an ethical doctrine; so the tight link Darwall may wish to draw between moral obligation, rights, and liberalism is, at the outset, in direct contrast to our own approach.[62] We do agree that there is, and must be, some connection between liberalism and ethics, or liberalism would not have legitimacy; but liberalism, as expressed through a set of rights, is not about securing or defining our moral obligations, but rather about securing the possibility for any achievement of our moral obligations. In saying this, we are rejecting what seems to be at the heart of Darwall's position as mentioned above—namely, that "moral obligation [is] conceptually tied to what the moral community can demand." Morality, as we view it, is not grounded in the assumption that we begin with a purchase upon others, expressed through a system of claims and demands we may make upon them or they upon us. The claims and demands one might plausibly make are derivative, not foundational, because "moral community" is itself derivative. By "derivative," we mean not that the "moral community" is the standard for determining the legitimacy, authority, or nature of the claims or demands that might be made, but rather that the claims and demands sanctioned by any "moral community" are themselves

---

[61] Stephen Darwall, "Grotius at the Creation of Modern Moral Philosophy," *Archiv für Geschichte Der Philosophie* 94.3 (2012): p. 297.

[62] The argument is fully made in Rasmussen and Den Uyl, *NOL*, where we argue that liberalism is not an ethical philosophy but a limited social/political perspective.

judged according to some other standard—in our case, the principles of individual teleological *eudaimonism*, which we have outlined in the first chapter of this work.

In a responsibility-based system—as opposed to a respect-based one, such as Darwall explicates—the "moral community" is doubly derivative. In other words, moral obligation is not, at root, a communal concept for us, because personal responsibility for one's *own* life is the prime directive out of which, and according to which, any community, moral or otherwise, should be built.[63] Consequently, claiming and demanding are not the primary relational concepts of our moral life, nor the first instances of moral expression; to those places belong, instead, such concepts as self-direction and integrity. And in this respect, noting, as we do, that we are social beings is fundamentally different from saying that ethics itself is *essentially* about our relations with others and, thus, essentially a social or communal phenomenon.[64] There is no logical equivalence between the two. Consequently, in our way of looking at things, rights would be morally sanctioned forms of obligation, but not moral obligation itself, since—given their role in securing the political social order—rights must, by nature, be generic and universal, not individuative and purposeful. As such, ethics and politics, for us, are by no means different dimensions of a single moral universe where all norms have the same function, but instead are functionally different altogether.[65] Such reminders as these are not rebuttals or even arguments; but they do suggest that an alternative understanding exists such that, although a theory like our own can be ignored, it cannot be assumed away.

To say something, however, about *why* we are not committed to Darwall's world of moral community as a defining understanding of the political/legal order, we might do well to begin with his account of Adam Smith's ambivalence about honor, because here we can see that certain distinctions that seem to identify a framework (for example, liberalism) may instead be a function of that

---

[63] See Rasmussen and Den Uyl, *NOL*, chap. 11, pp. 265–83.

[64] Darwall is, no doubt, correct to note that the respect-based approach is likely the predominant one of our times. See his introduction to *Morality, Authority, & Law*, p. xiii.

[65] See our discussion of this point in section 2 of Chapter 2 as well as in *NOL*, pp. 34–41. Also, throughout *NOL*, we argue that since rights are metanorms and have a different function from that of other ethical norms, it is possible for them to be understood as non-consequentialistic ethical norms but, nonetheless, not as ultimately deontological ethical norms.

framework's already having been accepted. To make his case that Smith was ambivalent about honor, Darwall utilizes an important distinction between "appraisal respect" and "recognition respect." As Darwall views it, the respect conferred regarding honor, rank, and social status is a form of "appraisal respect," which "is esteem that is merited or earned by conduct or character."[66] This is to be contrasted with "recognition respect," which is the respect given to dignity and authority, and not to merit or excellence: "recognition respect concerns, not how something is to be evaluated or appraised, but how our relations to it [dignity or authority] are to be regulated or governed."[67] The problem with honor and rank as primary forms of social obligation, for Darwall, is that they represent conventions that have no connection with respecting people on the basis of their inherent dignity; they are said to be dependent on some sort of merit or excellence that the person must possess, rather than personhood itself. A liberal social/political order, by contrast, is rooted in recognition respect, which sees the members of its community as possessors of inherent dignity and a correspondent authority that comes to define certain forms of conduct that exhibit that respect.

In Darwall's parsing of the distinction between appraisal and recognition respect, he seems to suppose that it is the inherent, equal dignity among us that confers the authority to make claims and demands and, thus, to function as a form of recognition respect. We have the authority to make, or expect, certain demands or claims, because those expressions or expectations are a function of our respect for the dignity of other persons, and not simply because they might be good things to do, or are evoked in response to good things that were done. In other words, the authority for, and of, those demands and claims comes from what we owe the other as a result of his or her inherent worthiness of respect. Any actions which fail to accord such respect would, for example, generate the authority to make claims or demands upon the other for some type of rectification of that failure to respect. But what Darwall fails to notice is that in honor societies, in contrast to the "liberal" order he advocates, one's authority comes attached to one's rank or degree of honor; and that authority may or may not be based upon anyone's esteem or estimation of their meritorious actions. It may, instead, be based, for example, upon birth

---

[66] Darwall, *SPS*, p. 122.
[67] Ibid., p. 123.

order, longevity, tradition, or lineage.[68] Yet, even in situations where esteem or recognition of merit *is* the basis for social rank or worthiness of honor, the sort of respect involved must still be fundamentally different—at least, in some ways—from the appraisal respect Darwall accords it. This is because status performs the same structural social purposes as the "rights" of Darwall's liberal social order. In other words, societies need "recognition points" to give themselves a structure; and thus, it is the point of status in honor societies that such status be respected irrespective of the reasons one possesses it.

As a result, in cases of honor or status societies, the "dignity" one possesses may actually issue in a form of appraisal respect, not recognition respect, because that dignity may be a function of how one *uses* the authority connected to one's status, rather than simply being what one possesses. As moderns we may not like the idea that one's dignity is predicated upon authority (rather than the reverse) and is, thus, a function of an appraisal of how one uses that authority; but there is no reason to presume that authority must be a function of dignity, unless liberalism is already made a prior commitment. And if authority need not be a function of dignity, the useful distinction between appraisal respect and recognition respect may cash out in ways other than Darwall suggests they must.[69] Hence, not only are honor societies not devoid of "recognition respect," but there also may be little or no difference between recognition respect behavior when responding to a person's social status in an honor society and when responding to his or her personhood in a liberal order, because, in the former, one is also concerned with how "our relations to [authority] are to be regulated or governed." In both types of society, there is a need for a form of respect that is independent of what one does. Consequently, what does the heavy lifting of justifying a certain type of social order is not the distinction between appraisal respect and recognition respect itself, but might, instead, be what stands behind that distinction.

---

[68] In this connection, it is worth recalling Adam Smith's point that societies may accord status to wealth or position, in contrast to merit and worthiness, and that this is not necessarily a bad thing. See Adam Smith, *The Theory of Moral Sentiments*, ed. D. D. Raphael and A. L. Macfie (Indianapolis: Liberty Fund, 1984), IV.I.9–10.

[69] This is not to say, as Darwall suggests, that Smith was not ambivalent about honor and was, indeed, moving toward a more "liberal" type of ethics. But Smith's ambivalence may also have come from a recognition that authority may have other sources besides dignity.

It might be argued that, in the case of the honor society, one has to do something or become something to gain status; and thus one is inherently speaking of appraisal. In a liberal order, by contrast, one need not do anything to be accorded the authority to command respect; one simply has to exist as a person. But besides the fact that one may not have to do something in the honor society to have the respect attached to social status, it may also be the case, at least in practice, that personhood *does* require one to do something in Darwall's liberal order, in order for one to have the authority to command respect. Presumably, what it means to appropriately receive respect, give respect to, and call for respect from persons will have to be defined in some way—undoubtedly, by the "moral community." That process of definition will elicit certain forms of sanctioned behavior. Failure to act appropriately according to those defined sanctions will result in a lack of conferring "respect." This possibility exists because there is virtually no such thing as a non-acting person. It is thus not completely clear that social status cannot be as underived or basic as personhood in practical social relations. Both will be defined by the moral community and accorded authoritative status because of how they are defined. Both will also come to have socially sanctioned forms of behavior thought to exhibit the appropriate respect for, and violations of, that authority. The point of all this is, of course, to suggest that "second-person" standpoints can be equally found in rather different contexts, thus severing the *necessary* connection between liberal orders and the second-person standpoint.

So, with all that in mind, we can notice once more that, in our account of things, there is a further standard of measurement beyond standpoints and forms of respect, which any moral community must itself either conform to or, at least, not transgress against. That is the advantage of having a naturalistic moral framework, as described throughout our work. No doubt, Kant, in developing his views on dignity and respect, felt the need to make the transcendental turn to noumenal selves for precisely the reason that he did not want moral norms to devolve into conventions. Whether theories like Darwall's, where personhood is grounded in conceptual moral communities, can (or even wish to) finally escape conventionalism cannot be decided here, though we explore this question further in a later chapter, where we again consider Darwall. But in looking into the different forms of respect and the origins of authority, one cannot but wonder anew, with Darwall, whether it is his understanding of "liberalism" that is driving the moral theory, or the moral theory that is driving "liberalism." When they are taken to be so closely conjoined that in doing one, one is doing the other, concerns about conventionalism creeping into the argument become more pressing. For the point of asking whether a given form of respect is the "true" form or "appropriate" form, and not just the "liberal" form, is to ensure that one is not engaged in a sophisticated form of conventionalism—again, assuming one wishes to distance oneself from it. Additionally, we would also want to ensure that what divides us here is not *simply* one of competing understandings of liberalism.

The substantive issue, as we see it, then, is between a view which regards rights as being equivalent to firmly entrenched moral obligations generally and a view (our own) which sees rights as moral obligations of a special type, whose function is to protect the *possibility* of moral conduct in the first place, but not as a way of defining moral obligations generally. Since we have said much about this view of rights elsewhere, we shall devote only a few words to the problem of viewing rights as moral obligations generally. In our view the central problem of doing so is one of over-moralization. For Darwall, our sociable nature must have its correspondent moral obligations conceived in juridical terms, whereby rules are worthy of respect apart from consequences, and their execution comes in the form of claims and demands.[70] The problem he sees with a neo-Aristotelian position like our own is "that it can provide no more than reasonable counsel, however weighty the reasons of the agent's good supporting the counsel might be."[71] One does not get *obligation* out of such counsel or out of the juridical ability to claim and demand, because the grounds of such counsel are always conditional. Perhaps so. But on the other hand, what one does not get from seeing morality as inherently concerned with a juridical sense of obligation is any limit to the juridical.

If morality is essentially juridical in nature, issuing in a world of rules that define appropriate claims and demands that must be either accommodated or rejected, then what is threatened is not only principles which are weighed, balanced, and judged on relevance, but also forms of interaction such as persuasion, influence, bargaining, and creativity. These things are threatened because there is nothing

---

[70] Darwall, "Grotius at the Creation of Modern Moral Philosophy," p. 309. This is a characterization of Grotius's view; but, as noted, these views seem to be Darwall's, as well.

[71] Ibid., p. 313.

in principle that is beyond capture in juridical terms. Darwall wants to suggest that it is only reasoned or reasonable claims and demands that we can make upon one another. And yet, unless a determination of what is reasonable is left to individuals, there is virtually nothing upon which reason may not render consideration and, hence, nothing beyond the grasp of what might potentially become the subject of publicly dictated and sanctioned forms of claiming and demanding. Since human beings interact with all aspects of the world, there are no regions beyond which the pronouncement of what is reasonable or not may not extend—that is to say, for which a rule of appropriate interaction might not be applied. In such a world—and is that world so very far from our own?—counsel may thus come to be seen as a welcome relief from the incessant barrage of demands and claims that such a juridical moral order might produce.

3. Conclusion

Wherein, then, is the source of the problem before us? It is not in pointing to persons, or in the idea of there being obligations. Rather, the problem comes from failing to appreciate that juridical relations are fundamentally closed ones and, more often than not, antagonistic.[72] If so, then the incentive should be to restrict their scope and to reluctantly engage any juridical forms of interaction. Instead of creating points for claiming and demanding, we should be leaving as many points as possible open for persuasion, trading, accommodation, and innovation. As we noted with Gaus and will show again in our last chapter, the market is a better model for moral interaction than the law, precisely because of its openness and cooperative character. If so, there is a need to find a principled limit to where juridical-type obligations reside. The reasonable versus unreasonable, or moral versus non-moral, are not likely to be sufficiently definitive to be of help in this case. Their boundaries are contentious at best; but even if they were clear, the non-moral or unreasonable would have no standing against their opposites, essentially leaving the door open for anything to be moralized or rationalized. In contrast, protecting the possibility for moral conduct versus moral conduct does itself seem to be a clearly demarcating standard, because not everything of value is thereby subject to moralization.

---

[72] Darwall's original guiding example of stepping on someone's toes is a good indication in point.

It may be that Darwall would hold that not all obligations are of the enforceable variety, and that the political versions—the enforceable ones—should not be confused with others. But since Darwall does not seem to allow for the authority to reject authoritative claims and demands, virtually all obligations are enforceable. And while it may sound strange to speak of having the authority to reject authoritative claims and demands, our point is to emphasize that precisely because rights are *different* from moral obligations, one may have the authority to reject authoritative moral claims, provided no one's rights are violated. Rejecting authoritative moral claims may put one in the wrong, incur future negative consequences, or make one a pariah in one's community; but one would still have the "authority" to do so. And this is what we mean by saying that the juridical form "over-moralizes" morality. If that is the essence of modern moral theory, as Darwall suggests, so much the worse for modern moral theory. We need to look, instead, to a vision of moral conduct that is not solely, or even principally, dependent on the juridical form. To that task, we turn in Part II.

Part II

Facing a New Direction

5

The Perfectionist Turn

For to make Brick without Straw or Stubble, is perhaps an easier labour, than to prove Morals without a World, and establish a Conduct of Life without the Supposition of any thing living or extyant besides our immediate Fancy, and World of Imagination.

Shaftesbury, *Miscellaneous Reflections*

Imagine a scenario much like Plato describes at the end of the *Phaedo*, where Socrates, in his jail cell, surrounded by friends, having been condemned to death by the court of Athens, is about to receive the hemlock. Suppose, further, that Socrates, as in Plato's dialogue, drinks the hemlock, but does not die. Instead, a messenger rushes in to announce to those present that Socrates was pardoned from his sentence and that the messenger has an antidote, which he then administers and which will restore Socrates back to his former state of health. The only catch is that Socrates is no longer allowed to practice philosophy in any way or form. Being both obedient to law and opposed to suicide and self-exile, Socrates continues his life without philosophy. He can make love to his wife, play with his children, and chat with people about the weather and politics; but he can do no philosophy—either publicly or in private. We might suppose that Socrates has an immense capacity for philosophy and a compelling disposition toward doing it. But he is equally strong-willed, and each time he is tempted toward philosophy, his *daimon* says no, he must obey the law. It would be commonly said of this Socrates that he now cannot live up to his potential, that he no longer is able to perfect himself. But would we necessarily say he has lost the ability to achieve well-being or human flourishing? Could Socrates not obtain well-being or human flourishing by taking up some other activity with pleasurable and satisfying dimensions, even if they are not philosophical activities? To what degree can one's perfectibility be separated from one's well-being or human flourishing, and how might the latter be dependent upon the former, if it is at all? Is someone's good necessarily good for that person?

Consider another scenario regarding Socrates and the hemlock. In this case, Athens not only pardons Socrates, but completely regrets its decision to keep him from philosophizing. Not only that, Athens wants Socrates, given his great gifts in this area, to actively pursue philosophy as often as and wherever possible. The only problem is that, because of either something in the antidote or the ordeal Socrates had to endure, Socrates no longer has any interest in doing philosophy. He would rather take up gardening. Since he is a law-abiding citizen, however, he continues to philosophize. The same questions we raised above with the first case can be raised again here. Socrates' well-being seems now to lie outside of doing philosophy, but it might still seem that we should say that his perfection consists in his continuing to philosophize.

The issue we are raising with these examples is whether one can plausibly have a "perfectionist" theory of well-being or human flourishing. Or, to put the issue in terms that seem to capture the contemporary debate[1] on these matters: Do the notions of well-being and human flourishing determine how we are to understand self-perfection, or must that which defines self-perfection be the basis for understanding well-being and human flourishing? This question arises, as we shall see, because of a certain sort of naturalism that has traditionally been associated with perfectionism.

"Perfect" is derived from the Latin *perfectus* and its Greek counterpart *teleios*. *Perfectus* entails that a being is completed or finished and involves the idea of a being's having a nature which is its end (*telos*) or function (*ergon*). To "perfect," to "realize," or to "actualize" oneself is thus not to become God-like, immune to degeneration, or incapable of harm, but simply to fulfill those potentialities and capacities that make one human. Accordingly, a good human being has perfected him- or herself—that is to say, being a good human involves actualizing one's basic human potentialities. It involves being

---

[1] See these works: Daniel M. Haybron, *The Pursuit of Unhappiness: The Elusive Psychology of Well-Being* (Oxford: Oxford University Press, 2008); John McDowell, "Two Sorts of Naturalism," in *Virtues and Reasons: Philippa Foot and Moral Theory*, ed. Rosalind Hursthouse, Gavin Lawrence, and Warren Quinn (Oxford: Clarendon Press, 1995), pp. 149–79; Mark LeBar, "Aristotelian Constructivism," *Social Philosophy and Policy* 25.1 (Winter 2008): pp. 182–214; and Daniel C. Russell, *Happiness for Humans* (Oxford: Oxford University Press, 2012). Despite their differences, they all seem, in various ways, to want the *notions* of well-being or human flourishing to wear the trousers when it comes to understanding self-perfection, and not the other way around, as we will argue should be the case.

completed, fulfilled, or actualized—as opposed to being incomplete, unfulfilled, or unactualized, and thus remaining in a state of potentiality with regard to exercising basic human capacities. Perfectionism is thus the view that one's fulfillment as a human being is a function generally of living according to one's nature, usually understood as the realization of one's capacities. What is good for an individual is somehow linked to *being a good human being*, understood as the person's exercising the capacities of his or her nature.

If, however, a person's well-being or flourishing could be understood apart from, or without reference to, his or her capacities or nature, then perhaps we need not understand human good, and thus flourishing or well-being, in terms of perfecting one's nature. Rather, if perfecting our nature is relevant at all to flourishing or well-being, perhaps it is so because such perfection is no longer linked to fulfilling our capacities, and has instead some other meaning. Indeed, the traditional understanding of perfectionism, according to which well-being and flourishing *are* a function of perfecting our nature defined in terms of fulfilling our capacities, has been challenged by Daniel M. Haybron, and by Daniel C. Russell and Mark LeBar. As we shall see soon, Haybron argues that perfectionism is irrelevant for understanding human flourishing. Russell and LeBar argue that Haybron is wrong to think that a neo-Aristotelian account of human flourishing must be perfectionist (at least in the sense that Haybron understands perfectionism); but they nonetheless hold that it is possible to understand human flourishing or well-being by simply appealing to our "deepest convictions," with no particular need for some ontological, naturalistic grounding for these convictions.[2]

Our goal here is to make a start in meeting this challenge. In so doing, we will be taking the side of the classical tradition, according to which well-being and flourishing are a function of perfecting our nature. However, at the same time, we will also suggest that this traditional naturalistic understanding of perfectionism can only meet the challenges to it by adopting a significantly more individualist understanding of human nature than is typical. We can make such a defense, we believe, because human nature has both generic and individuative characteristics. Thus, when the concept of human

---

[2] See Russell, *Happiness for Humans*, pp. 36–64; and Daniel C. Russell and Mark LeBar, "Well-Being and Eudaimonia: A Reply to Haybron," in *Aristotelian Ethics in Contemporary Perspective*, ed. Julia Peters (New York: Routledge, 2013), pp. 52–68.

nature is deployed, neither of these types of characteristics can be utilized to the exclusion of the other, and both must be employed jointly. We call the type of perfectionism we advocate "individualistic perfectionism."

Individualistic perfectionism holds that human good is in its very nature individualized and relative to the agent[3] but is, nonetheless, not simply reducible to either whatever desires one may have, or to the merely conventional or otherwise subjectively determined. Rather, our desires and subjective preferences must be measured against standards that are a function of our human nature. The human life-form consists in a determinate set of potentialities which, when actualized appropriately, amount to what we call human flourishing or the self-perfecting life. This way of life is attained through the exercise of practical wisdom and moral virtue, the aim of which is to determine for an individual the appropriate form (or balance), along with the particular manifestation, of basic or "generic" human goods and virtues (for example, knowledge, health, friendship, pleasure, creativity, integrity, temperance, courage, and justice),[4] as they can be both realized and defined by that individual person. The appropriate form that is expressed in achieving, maintaining, and enjoying these goods and virtues will not issue, then, in either a one-size-fits-all way of life or a set of rules that are to be universally and equally legislated to all agents. Rather, what lies at the heart of ethics is the issue of what is worthy of being valued, which for us is ultimately an individual human being's own self-perfection; and this requires that ethics be primarily concerned with persons determining for themselves in what their individual human good concretely consists. Human good is thus grounded in the individuative and generic features of individual human beings; and it is fully immanent in their self-perfecting choices, actions, and lives. It is this model of individualistic perfectionism that we will use to meet the challenges to perfectionism. Our position seeks to

---

[3] Human good is always and necessarily good for some individual or other. See Chapters 1 and 2 for a discussion of the "agent-relative" and individualized character of human flourishing.

[4] See our account in Chapter 1 of the inclusive character of human good and the role of basic or generic goods and virtues. To repeat what we noted there, these basic or generic goods and virtues express an initial but well-established understanding of the general potentialities whose actualization makes up the overall character of human flourishing and the self-perfecting process.

retain the non-reductive naturalism of the traditional view, while incorporating the need for individualism implied by contemporary criticisms of that view.

We begin, of course, with the general idea that a good human being is one who has actualized his or her human potential; but this idea alone is inadequate to account for human good. We also need to know why one should say that it is worthwhile or valuable to actualize one's own potentialities, for a perfectionist account depends upon making the link between fulfilling potentialities and it being valuable to do so. That link has been challenged, first by P. Glassen, later by L. W. Sumner and Valerie Hardcastle, and more recently, by Haybron.[5] They posit what is claimed to be a fundamental and insoluble difficulty for perfectionist accounts of human good. This difficulty may be stated in different ways. Here are three. Glassen expresses it as follows:

> From the statement that the function of a good lyre-player is to play the lyre well, or in accordance with excellence, what follows is, not that the good of a lyre-player is playing the lyre in accordance with excellence, but rather that the goodness of a lyre-player consists in playing the lyre in accordance with excellence.[6]

Haybron states the difficulty this way;

> I would suggest that the naturalistic perspective, while arguably one source of the Aristotelian view's allures, is not the perspective that gives perfectionism its primary appeal. . . . There is indeed something appealing about the idea that goodness in a lion consists in perfecting its nature *qua* lion. But is it so obvious that lion well-being consists in the exercise of lion excellence? . . . . [I]t is unfortunate when an animal's life is devoid of some major feature of its species—for instance if a lion is never able to hunt. The problem, intuitively, is not lack of perfection—not being a good lion or exercising the virtues proper to lions—but "missing out," failing to enjoy one or more elements of a full life for a lion. Similarly

---

5 See P. Glassen, "A Fallacy in Aristotle's Function Argument about the Good," *Philosophical Quarterly* 7.29 (October 1957): pp. 319–22; L. W. Sumner, *Welfare, Happiness, and Ethics* (Oxford: Clarendon Press, 1996), pp. 78–9; Valerie Gray Hardcastle, "On the Normativity of Functions," in *Functions: New Essays in the Philosophy of Psychology and Biology*, ed. André Ariew, Robert Cummins, and Mark Perlman (Oxford: Oxford University Press, 2002), pp. 143–56; and Haybron, *The Pursuit of Unhappiness*, pp. 155–75. This problem may go as far back as Sidgwick; see Talbot Brewer, *The Retrieval of Ethics* (Oxford: Oxford University Press, 2009), pp. 194ff.

6 Glassen, "A Fallacy in Aristotle's Function Argument," p. 320.

when a person is born blind, retarded, etc. . . . . What I do deny is that well-being fundamentally concerns perfection.[7]

Finally, as Russell succinctly frames the matter: "Well-being must be a good *for the agent* in question, and being a good specimen (say) just is not that kind of good."[8]

We can summarize these concerns as follows: Even if performing one's natural function makes someone a good human being, it does not seem to follow from this alone that such a performance is good for one. It does not even seem to follow that it is valuable to be actualized, or that an individual human being has any necessary stake in being actualized. There thus seems to be a difference between the human good understood in terms of perfecting our nature and a view that sees human good in terms of what might contribute to one's flourishing or well-being. In other words, one might say that a wedge has been driven between what is human good *simpliciter* and what is good *for* a particular human being insofar as it might contribute to that person's well-being or flourishing.[9] Accordingly, these challenges for any perfectionist view of human good can be framed in terms of a fundamental question (call it the "G" question): What is the connection between being a good human being and such a state of affairs being good for a human being?

We regard this question as important not only because failing to resolve it threatens the viability of a *perfectionist* account of the human good having any connection to value, but also because resolving it offers the chance of seeing perfectionism in a new light—that

[7] Haybron, *The Pursuit of Unhappiness*, pp. 174–5. In making this claim, Haybron is also expressing Thomas Hurka's claim that, for perfectionism, there is a disconnect between being a good human being and what is good for a human being: "Perfectionism should never be expressed in terms of well-being. It gives an account of the good human life, or of what is good in a human being, but not of what is 'good for' a human being in the sense tied to well-being" (*Perfectionism* [Oxford: Oxford University Press, 1993], pp. 17–18).

[8] Russell, *Happiness for Humans*, p. 47. Russell is summarizing Haybron here in this statement of the problem. But he, too, sees this problem as real or legitimate *when perfectionism is understood as Haybron describes it*. Russell calls Haybron's account of perfectionism: "'Perfectionism' (with a capital P)" (ibid., p. 46; see below).

[9] For other discussions of this distinction, or more generally the distinction between "good" and "good for," see Talbot Brewer, "Against Modern Dualism about the Good," in *The Retrieval of Ethics*, chap. 6, pp. 192–235; and Toni Ronow-Rasmussen, "Mo(o)re Objections," in *Personal Value* (Oxford: Oxford University Press, 2011), chap. 7, pp. 95–108.

is, in a way that is different from most traditional accounts. If individualistic perfectionism can serve as a model for helping to resolve the issue here, then we believe it offers a chance to see perfectionism without transcendence—whether such transcendence is expressed in terms of some deity or Platonic Form, or in terms of society, culture, biology, gender, or history—by making the nature of the individual human being the ultimate standard for perfection. Indeed, in endeavoring to meet this challenge, we suggest that the solution lies in following up on Philippa Foot's claim that "*life* will be at the centre,"[10] because life is both the link between being good and being good for, and the basis for showing why it is worthwhile to be actualized. Life as it is actually lived by human beings is a process expressive of both individuative and generic characteristics of human nature. With the life-based approach, the problems the "G" question presents can become mostly "dissolved," rather than solved.

1. Distinct, but Not Separable

One factor that seems to be behind the problems that the "G" question presents is the claim that if one holds that human good is always and necessarily good *for* some individual human being, then one is disallowed from speaking of generic human goods or human good itself—that is, of human good *simpliciter*—because such expressions seem to require human good to be universal in nature and independent of the agent (agent-neutral). This apparent incompatibility is based on an error, however.[11] It assumes that an abstract consideration of human good requires denying both its individuality and its essential relatedness. But, to return to a basic point we developed in

[10] Philippa Foot, *Natural Goodness* (Oxford: Clarendon Press, 2001), p. 5. She also states: "'Natural' goodness, as I define it, which is attributable only to living things themselves and to their parts, characteristics, and operations, is intrinsic or 'autonomous' goodness in that it depends directly on the relation of an individual to the 'life-form' of its species" (ibid., pp. 26–7). However, Foot is not concerned with "the good of a species, as if a species were itself a gradually developing, one-off organism, whose life might stretch for millions of years," but rather with the goodness that can be attributed to individual living things (as well as to their parts, characteristics, and operations) "that belong to a species at a certain time" (ibid., p. 32 n10).

[11] Some of what is presented in this section is adapted from Douglas B. Rasmussen and Douglas J. Den Uyl, *Norms of Liberty: A Perfectionist Basis for Non-Perfectionist Politics* [hereafter *NOL*] (University Park: Pennsylvania State University Press, 2005), pp. 153–8.

Chapter 2, this does not follow. To think of human good without thinking of whose good it is or what concrete form it takes is not the same as denying that human good is individualized or essentially related in its very nature. The mode and manner of *thinking* something thus-and-so need not determine its manner of *being* thus-and-so. To assume that it does is to confuse the mode of our cognition with the manner of existence of what is cognized. Abstraction need not entail separating what is unified in reality. Accordingly, it is possible (and, we shall argue, correct) to speak of the activities that are the generic goods and virtues that constitute human good, and to note that everyone needs to engage in these activities, without thereby making the human good a universal independent of the individual agent. Appreciating this point is necessary for appreciating what we regard as being the correct understanding of human nature and thus human good.

When we say that Socrates and Aristotle are perfecting themselves, what are predicated of Socrates and Aristotle are not generic goods and virtues understood as universals, *but these goods and virtues as requiring some specific determination and unique manner of existence*. To illustrate this point, we can recall our example from Chapter 2 of the generic good of friendship. Friendship may be involved in any understanding of human good; and yet, not only are the friends different from one situation to the next, but the relevant balance and modes of connectivity of friendship to any of the other constituents of human good are so, as well. There is thus no reason to *assume* that a perfectionist understanding of human good requires it to be a universal reality. We can predicate human good of different individuals, but that only makes human good universalizable. It does not make it universal. As Henry B. Veatch noted:

> If the good of X is indeed but the actuality of X's potentialities, then this is a fact that not just X needs to recognize, but anyone and everyone else as well. And yet given the mere fact that a certain good needs to be recognized, and recognized universally, to be the good of X, it by no means follows that X's good must be taken to be Y's good as well, any more than the actuality or perfection or fulfillment of X needs to be recognized as being the actuality or perfection of Y as well.[12]

---

[12] Henry B. Veatch, "Ethical Egoism, New Style: Should Its Trademark Be Aristotelian or Libertarian?" in *Swimming Against the Current in Contemporary Philosophy* (Washington, DC: The Catholic University of America Press, 1990), p. 194.

Though our perfectionist understanding of the human good is not about universals, our understanding of that good as individualized is universaliz*able*. What is universalized here is the knowledge that a value, reason, or ranking for some person is what provides a basis for a person's conduct. Yet, there is nothing about this universalization that requires a value, reason, or ranking for one person to be such for another. As we argued in Chapter 2, universalizability does not mean or require either universality or agent-neutrality of human good—that is, it does not require that the value of human good have standing in its own right, apart from individuals whose good it actually is.

There is, of course, the question of just what it is that makes value V desirable or choice-worthy for someone; but for us as neo-Aristotelians, that is a question answered by appealing to the nature of individual human beings. Ultimately, our values, reasons, and rankings are grounded in both what and who we are; and this is an involved and complex story for each of us—about which we will have something more to say later. Nonetheless, what should be clear already is that, for us, what lies at the heart of ethics is not the universalizable, but the goods that can be realized for individuals themselves.

In short, then, distinguishing (a) what is a good human being from (b) what is good for a human being does not require one to hold that there are correspondingly two types of human good: a universal human good and an individualized human good. That we can speak sensibly of human good without referring to individuals, and can also speak sensibly of good for particular individuals without noticing what the person might have in common with others, does not signify that we have thereby identified two different forms of good. This is so not because a reality is determined by a conceptual distinction itself but because, if anything, the reverse holds: such distinctions are tools used in grasping what a reality is, not in determining it. But the point that distinctions do not determine reality is, of course, only a logical point when applied to an ethical context like this one; so we need to consider these matters more deeply. Particularly, we need to consider our suggestion that it may not even make sense to attempt to understand either (a) or (b) without the other. To that problem we now turn.

2. Problems with Separating "Good" from "Good for"

Haybron argues that "perfectionism . . . bears no necessary connection to anything that can plausibly be viewed as an organism's goals:

179

for one can achieve perfection, at least to some degree, merely by ful-filling a capacity. . . ."[13] Accordingly, he believes that perfectionism cannot adequately answer what we call the "G" question, because perfectionism provides only the type of value that is concerned with doing things excellently, not the type of value that is concerned with "succeeding in one's goals."[14] Perfectionism offers *performance* value, where what is needed to explain human flourishing or well-being, he says, is *success* value. "The perfectionist's fundamental mistake lies in not recognizing that well-being is what we might call a *success* value: it concerns the success of an organism in achieving its goals."[15] Thus, he claims the following:

> To conceive of well-being or flourishing in terms of perfection, then, is to engage in an inescapably Procrustean enterprise: we will invariably be able to imagine cases in which excellence meets nothing that could be considered among the individual's goals, or where the degree of excel-lence attained outstrips the degree of goal-attainment.[16]

Perfectionism, for Haybron, is clearly a non-starter for understand-ing human flourishing or well-being.

Haybron makes his complaint against perfectionism on two levels. The first level is concerned with what performance value or excellent activity has to do concretely with an individual's own goals and life. That is, how does being excellent at something help one determine what choices to make here and now? How does it help one deter-mine in what one's own well-being or human flourishing concretely consists? The second level is concerned with what performance value or excellent activity, understood as the fulfillment of basic human capacities, has to do generally with the goal of human flourishing or well-being. Why think that fulfilling basic human capacities has anything at all to do with the goal of human flourishing? We will consider the second level of complaint first.

---

[13] Haybron, *The Pursuit of Unhappiness*, p. 169.

[14] Ibid., p. 169.

[15] Ibid., p. 169. It might be suggested that Haybron's point could be made another way: The type of well-being that one finds in performance value is not the type of well-being that one finds in success value. This point is fine so far as it goes; but we choose not to frame the issue in these terms, because we are dubious of how far one can really get with a merely intuitive understanding of well-being or human flourishing. Our concern is more basic—namely, we are interested in what shapes our understanding of well-being or human flourishing in the first place.

[16] Ibid., p. 169.

Performance value or excellent activity considered apart from success value—or, more generally speaking, fulfilling basic human capacities considered apart from the goal of human flourishing—is, to say the least, very difficult to understand. Haybron rightly asks why one should care about such activities *if* they are separated from standards of success or human flourishing; but he does not recognize that this very separation is what makes his attack on, and understanding of, perfectionism so wrong-headed. The separation of performance from success value leaves open the questions: What is the context that gives rise to performance value or excellent activity? and: Why would people engage in fulfilling basic human capacities if there were not something to be achieved? The issue here is not what the best account of human good is, but simply whether it makes sense to conceive of performance value or excellent activity, or fulfilling basic human capacities, apart from a context that gives rise to the need to do so—keeping in mind, all the while, that to ignore a context is not to eliminate it. Without there being something these activities are for—namely, well-being or flourishing itself—and without a reason for choosing to engage in such activities, why would they be an object of concern or value? Regardless of how one cashes out "being a good human being," there needs to be something achieved, accomplished, done, or fulfilled to make sense of these activities. The question of "Why care?" still matters. To talk of performance value apart from a context that explains these activities—that is, to think of capacities as abstracted from context—is to render them valueless.

Similarly, what would it mean to flourish as a human being or to attain *well*-being, if the standard or measure for determining human flourishing or wellness of being is not based on what a human being is—that is, upon the central dispositions and capacities involved in human living? What is the point of the adjective "human"? It is important to consider briefly how Haybron frames his answer to this question. Haybron explicitly rejects subjectivist approaches to human well-being[17] and states that "'authentic happiness' . . . has intrinsic prudential value as an aspect of self-fulfillment."[18] However, this self-fulfillment is "non-perfectionist and internalist, grounding nature-fulfillment in the arbitrarily idiosyncratic make-up of the individual."[19] Putting aside the question of why the idiosyncratic

---

[17] Ibid., pp. 177–9.
[18] Ibid., p. 178.
[19] Ibid., p. 193.

make-up of individuals might be called "arbitrary," as well as doubts about the adequacy of his account of the so-called self, it is, nonetheless, clear that Haybron not only wants to emphasize the *individualized* character of human flourishing against merely fulfilling generic human capacities, but also to make it exhaustive. But there is no justification for taking such an extreme position, especially if one has doubts about Haybron's account of perfectionism in the first place. Our point here is, of course, not to deny the importance of individualized flourishing, but only to note that none of this denies that individualized flourishing has a general shape or contour, in virtue of which it is *a* version of *human* flourishing. Indeed, there would not be much sense in telling someone who pursues no friendships, or cares nothing for knowledge, or disdains any concern for how to use and control her emotions, that she is living an unfulfilled or undeveloped life and is, therefore, not "authentically happy," *if* there were not something about her being human that supported this admonition.[20] Colloquially, we would say that such a person is a "miserable human being"; and the point of this expression would be just to note this person's failure to pursue the goods that she needs in order to be a good *human* being.

It seems that Haybron assumes that letting the generic character of human beings play a role in an account of human flourishing is incompatible with its individualized and thus pluralistic character. But this is by no means necessary. As Isaiah Berlin has noted, our ends and values might be many, but not infinitely so. "They must come within the human horizon," because "the nature of men, however various and subject to change, must possess some generic character if it is to be called human at all."[21] At this general level, then, we can simply note that nothing about emphasizing individuality requires rejecting that one is a human being as well, and that this fact plays an important role in determining in what individualized human flourishing consists. What remains to be considered, however, is Haybron's first level of complaint—that is: What do performance value or excellent activity (that is, being a good human being) have

---

[20] We take this to be the basic point of Russell's excellent argument in his use of the "Crumb" example in Chapter 2 of *Happiness for Humans*.

[21] Isaiah Berlin, "The Pursuit of the Ideal" and "Alleged Relativism in Eighteenth-Century European Thought," in *The Crooked Timber of Humanity: Chapters in the History of Ideas* (New York: Alfred A. Knopf, 1991), pp. 11 and 80, respectively.

to do concretely with an individual's own goals and life (that is, being good for a human being)?

Haybron complains that it is during the making of concrete decisions on how to conduct one's life that we can see the basic weakness of tying human flourishing to perfectionism. He offers concrete examples. We find most interesting and revealing his example of Angela, who faces a choice between retiring and continuing as a career diplomat. Haybron offers a highly detailed description of Angela and her situation;[22] and he nicely shows that, for Angela, neither of the alternatives is obviously better than the other: there are pros and cons to both, and the choice depends on many personal factors, as well as time and context. Haybron has Angela choose the path of the career diplomat over retirement, because it exercises more of her capacities as a human being; but he also indicates that her well-being would more likely consist in her choosing retirement. The example is used to show that to speak of a good human being is not to speak of what is good for a human being.

Thus, Angela's decision to accept the new assignment and continue as a diplomat gives Haybron the opportunity to claim that a perfectionist (specifically, an Aristotelian) would hold that the diplomatic assignment involves greater perfection: "She more fully exercises her capacities, functioning more fully *qua* human being than she would as a retiree."[23] The life of a diplomat is more excellent than the life of a retiree, because it involves a greater use of what is uniquely human—that is, a greater use of human intelligence. But Haybron thinks, as well, that "she would clearly have been better off taking the early retirement":[24]

> In taking the job, Angela chose the path of greater excellence and virtue, a life that more fully exercised her capacities as a human being. But she was not securing or promoting her happiness or well-being. She was *sacrificing* it.[25]

We think otherwise: (1) We do not think that continuing on as a diplomat would necessarily involve greater excellence or perfection than retirement; and (2) we do not think that, in making that choice, she was sacrificing her well-being or human flourishing. Our ability to

---

[22] Haybron, *The Pursuit of Unhappiness*, pp. 161–2.
[23] Ibid., pp. 162–3.
[24] Ibid., p. 162.
[25] Ibid., p. 163.

make both of these points is what gives our theory of individualized perfectionism its distinctive shape.

Regarding (1): Haybron construes "qua human being" far too narrowly. We hold that perfection is not confined to simply the formal character of our nature—that is, to our humanity—but must be found in our nature as a whole.[26] Hence, when one speaks of functioning qua human being, one must consider not just what is uniquely human, but all that is involved in being the sort of living thing a human is. So, just as "it is towards intelligent living that all our powers and capacities are ultimately directed, including our powers of knowledge, and . . . it is man himself that counts more than all his knowledge . . .,"[27] so, too, it is the *application* of intelligence to the activities of human living that matters most, and not just the *exercise* of intelligence. As was mentioned earlier, such is the role of practical wisdom in our model of individualistic perfectionism. Consequently, regardless of what Aristotle may have thought (and this is by no means clear or settled), much of Haybron's worry about perfectionism would be alleviated if he were to recognize that *human* virtue or excellence (that is, human perfection) is found first and foremost in the life of practical wisdom, and not in the life of *theoria* or in any other single capacity. The excellence of any capacity must be understood within a larger context of excellence for individual human living as mediated by practical wisdom. An individual's talents and dispositions and circumstances must be jointly considered as they pertain to the particular individual through the use of his or her practical wisdom.

In this regard, as Kathryn V. Wilkes notes: "the *ergon* of man is indeed 'activity of *psuche* in accordance with rational principle,' the rational principle in question is, broadly, intelligence in general: intelligence that may be applied to art, craft, science, politics, philosophy, or any other domain."[28] The central task is to find the balance or "mean," but this is no mere average. It is the balance of basic goods at a given time that is found to be appropriate for the

---

[26] Dale Dorsey in his critique of perfectionism—"Three Arguments for Perfectionism," *Noûs* 44.1 (2010): pp. 59–79—also fails to consider the nature of a human being as a whole and thus suffers from an inadequate view of a human being's function.

[27] Henry B. Veatch, *Rational Man: A Modern Interpretation of Aristotelian Ethics* (Indianapolis: Liberty Fund, 2003), p. 40.

[28] Kathryn V. Wilkes, "The Good Man and the Good for Man," *Mind* 87 (October 1978): p. 568.

individual—that is to say, it is a balance of basic goods which is determined in light of "a consideration of the set of circumstances, talents, endowments, interests, and beliefs that descriptively characterize the individual,"[29] which, as noted in previous chapters, we call his or her "nexus." The excellent use of practical reason applies as much to the choice of friends and leisure as it does to the choice of career and work. One can function as much qua human in fashioning a life in retirement as in making decisions as a diplomat. Human excellence or perfection is confined neither to one particular form of life (for example, the philosophical life), nor more generally to those forms of human life that require more (or less) theoretical or abstract reasoning. Practical wisdom is an individualized affair. It is expressed in the choices and conduct of an individual engaged in the task of human living.[30]

The difficulty for some, but the virtue for us, with our position here, is that it would not likely issue, except in rather extreme cases, in definitive, law-like pronouncements about how one is to conduct one's life. For some, perhaps, the goal of ethics is to arrive at decisive claims about what should concretely be done in a given set of circumstances. On their view, the chief object of any reflections on what to do is to arrive at some kind of normative commandment. By contrast, we hold that normative reflection has the purpose of refining our capacity for judgment, all the while knowing that judgments are often open-ended and may not be the same for different individuals in the same circumstances. Angela's generic capacities, though not to be ignored, are not the only things to be considered; none of them excludes, or eliminates the importance of considering, her other generic capacities and her particular propensities and circumstances. To say that remaining a diplomat will, on balance, exercise more of Angela's intellectual excellences might be correct, and might be considered in isolation the single most powerful argument for her continuing as a diplomat. But that single most powerful argument may be outweighed by the confluence of other factors that, if taken by themselves, are less compelling but, if taken jointly, result in flourishing through retirement. On the other hand, perhaps that same intellectual thrust is, after all, sufficient to override other considerations, or to induce innovative ways to integrate remaining a diplomat with other factors with which that disposition is now in tension. Such

---

[29] Rasmussen and Den Uyl, *NOL*, p. 144.
[30] See ibid., pp. 143–52.

is the role and nature of judgment. It cannot be exhausted from the philosopher's armchair, nor can it be rendered formulaic.

Hence, regarding (2), we do not think Angela was necessarily sacrificing her well-being: because of the individualized nature of human excellence or perfection, the weight of any basic (or generic) good[31] of human flourishing, such as intellectual activity, can vary in prominence for different persons. Thus, Angela's decision at that time to take the assignment and to continue on in her diplomatic career could certainly be understood in terms that reflected her deepest interests, talents, endowments, and concerns. The more we know about Angela, or the more we presume Angela to know about herself, the more plausible our conjectures become about what was the most suitable path for her to follow. We have no difficulty seeing, given the information we have, that the choice she made to continue her diplomatic career represented her understanding of herself, of who she is, of her very individuality. "In doing what she does best" (as Haybron describes it), she would find the pleasure, the joy, the satisfaction of the central form of excellence for her life. This is her form of self-perfection, her form of human flourishing; and it is by no means clear or obvious that she would have been better off if she had chosen instead to retire. Indeed, from everything we know about Angela from Haybron's description, the opposite *seems* to be the case. However, if she had made the choice to continue as a diplomat for reasons that did not employ her intelligence toward the appropriate mix of her talents and circumstances, then we would, indeed, expect a lack of well-being and flourishing.

Russell agrees with Haybron that we can and should avoid perfectionism in the way Haybron understands it, and which Russell calls perfectionism with a capital "P."[32] Two of the problems of capital "P" Perfectionism are the "under-specification problem" and the "agent-neutrality problem."[33] The first problem concerns the issue of saying that happiness consists in achieving some kind of "perfection," and then being unable to specify clearly the sorts of perfection that lead to happiness, because there are so many candidates for happy lives and so many paths for achieving them. This particular issue arises precisely because individuals can be so different, and are in such different circumstances, that the tendency is for one's

---

[31] See note 4.
[32] See note 8.
[33] Russell, *Happiness for Humans*, pp. 46–7.

recommendations to remain on too general a prescriptive plane to be useful. The problem of agent-neutrality is virtually the opposite problem and involves holding that by fulfilling certain generic human capacities, one is thereby eudaimonic as an individual. In our discussion of Haybron and his two levels concerning excellence and success, we dealt with both of these issues. But here, we now see them as the same issue—namely, one of failing to consider the alternative, the view that human nature has both individuative and generic capacities, and that talking of one without tying it back to the other is, of course, going to pose problems.

The issue of the generic and its relationship to the individuative is, however, carried over, to some degree, in Russell's and Haybron's discussion of "welfare internalism" versus "welfare externalism"; and what follows here is meant to underscore our earlier comments regarding Haybron's separation of individuative from generic considerations (and vice versa). Welfare internalism is the view that happiness is solely a function of the individual's make-up as an individual. Welfare externalism is the view that the happiness of an individual is not wholly dependent on the individual's make-up, but also upon other factors outside of the individual. In this connection, Russell wants to introduce the notion of a person's "humanity," to help avoid having to consider solely an individual's particular existing goals and values. This is the idea that there are some things about just being a human being that can help contribute to happiness, even if one individually fails to see their relevance and thus fails to act for them. Russell gives the example of a man without love in his life, who also fails to see how his humanity indicates that love really would make a contribution to his happiness, even if there is nothing in him now pointing in that direction. Of course, if our human nature includes both individuative and generic human capacities, this argument is more than plausible, because both would be factors in any final assessment of well-being, and both would be applicable to a full understanding of one's humanity. To argue otherwise would be to suppose that generic and individuative characteristics of human nature are separated in the individual, such that human nature refers to a kind of holding receptacle of shared capacities, and that one's unique capacities are not part of one's nature as a human being. If a given agent is somehow not now exhibiting one of the shared capacities (for example, love), we need to draw that one from "human nature" and add it to the agent's personal profile. But either a disposition like loving is connected to human nature, or it is not.

If not, how would speaking of "humanity" get us any closer to the importance of loving for this agent?

It is conceivable that any given characteristic could be accounted for by another more general source, such as an "ethical context" or our moral convictions, which we then could use to infuse the desired characteristics into human nature. We find that to be mysterious, however, since presumably the point of all the "human nature" talk is to help conceptualize the nature of an ethical context in the first place. But more on this issue shortly. For now, we just want to note that "human nature," in our scheme of things, may end up doing quite similar work to Russell's "humanity," though we prefer the former concept because (as noted in our discussion of Angela) it is more integrative, in that it refers to human nature as a whole, not just to an abstract part of it. Moreover, the term "human nature" more directly links our view to a naturalism than would a term like "humanity."

Thus, welfare internalism, like welfare externalism, is, at best, a tool for helping one to figure out the nature of happiness. By narrowing the focus, one can reflect more deeply on individual dispositions; but that must always be done with an eye toward the broader perspective, and vice versa. Indeed, we are willing to go even further and consider social and cultural circumstances when reflecting upon "external" contributions to happiness. We extend consideration to these circumstances on the grounds that "man is a social animal," making one's well-being, in some degree, a function of how one is regarded by others. Russell's conclusion, consequently, is one which we would endorse, because he wants to include consideration of humanity in order to help broaden the narrowness of welfare internalism and, thus, to argue that humanity should be a part of any consideration of happiness or, in our case, perfection.

Like Haybron, Russell mentions certain characteristics such as autonomy and emotional fulfillment as factors in happiness, well-being, or human flourishing. Our dispute, then, does not seem to come down to substantive differences about goods to consider when thinking about these matters. The dispute instead seems to be about how to frame the context for consideration of how happiness, well-being, or human flourishing should be understood. What determines our deepest convictions about the character of well-being or human flourishing? What makes it worthwhile to exercise, for example, the capacities to love or to know? Surely, nearly no one would think a human life worthwhile without love or knowledge; but why is this?

What grounds these convictions? It seems that there is a reluctance to face these sorts of questions. Indeed, it is our view that this is due to a desire to avoid precisely what we want to embrace—namely, teleology—and to thus bring the evaluative dimension in from somewhere else. To wit:

> One way of thinking about human nature aims at deriving ethical facts from ethically neutral facts about our nature (call this our "first nature").... By contrast, one might hold instead that ethical facts can be ascertained only within an ethical outlook as a whole, and that such an outlook must include certain normative views about what it means to be human (call this "second nature").[34]

Russell seems to accept the above distinction, originally posited by McDowell,[35] and adds: "My own view is that we need a conception of human happiness in terms of *second* nature as opposed to first nature (even if some eudaimonists have thought in terms of first nature)."[36] Russell thinks it is a mistake to see ethics as a function of "first nature," where norms are adopted because they make possible the realization of some natural capacity we might have. Instead, ethics must concern itself only with second natures that occur within the context of "an ethical outlook as a whole." Presumably, this means we do not derive norms directly from "bald" facts about human nature but, rather, recognize a context for normative reflection itself, and then derive the particular norms within that context. The problem with perfectionism as a "first nature" idea is that it supposes that by providing norms connected to fulfilling a capacity of some sort, we have thereby given a reason to fulfill that capacity as a way of contributing to the agent's well-being or flourishing. But that seems an entirely separate step, not necessarily related at all.

However, the effort to shove perfectionism into the category of "first nature" and to talk about ethics only with respect to "second

---

[34] Ibid., p. 42.

[35] McDowell, "Two Sorts of Naturalism," pp. 149–79. Understanding McDowell's position may be a more complicated matter, however, for he does say that "the innate endowment of human nature must put some limits on the shapings of second nature that are possible for them" (ibid., p. 171). But he does not, to our knowledge, claim that these endowments of first nature, even if understood teleologically, could be directive for the human will and intellect. In fact, he seems to imply the *opposite*. In this regard, see John Hacker-Wright, *Philippa Foot's Moral Thought* (London: Bloomsbury, 2013), p. 125.

[36] Russell, *Happiness for Humans*, p. 43.

nature" would suggest that an individual's capacities have nothing to do with understanding the context in which ethical norms are considered. Indeed, our point would be that there is a unity between first and second natures. Capacities are *meant* to be exercised and can only be understood as the sorts of capacities they are through their exercise, such that the very context of ethical reasoning is a function of both together and neither alone.[37] Now, Russell believes we can make the separation because, for example, a Nietzschean conception of fulfilling capacities for greatness is to be pursued irrespective of whether such pursuit promotes the agent's happiness, while the Aristotelian wants capacities to be fulfilled so as to realize the happiness of the agent. Deciding between these two positions is a matter of normative judgment that Russell claims stands outside, and is imported into, any factual description of human nature.[38]

One problem with this argument is that, according to Aristotle, and in our view as well, a correct description of the nature of a human being is *inherently* value-laden. Thus, there cannot be any neutral or "bald" facts about human nature that are devoid of value implications. This means that one cannot consider capacity fulfillment without considering the role of such fulfillment generally and in a person's life in particular. Because capacities are things to be realized, they come packed with value-laden elements such as when, where, and why the capacity is to be exercised. We are thus not *deriving* ethical norms *from* "first nature" facts, so much as we are *discovering* the normative dimensions *within* those "facts." Moreover,

---

[37] It might be objected that this move is too quick. One may have the capacity to ride a unicycle, for instance; if one tried, one could learn to do it. Yet, does one have a reason to exercise that capacity? Maybe—but if one does, it is not in virtue of the sheer logical structure of that capacity. That is to say, it is true that one can understand one's capacity only in terms of a certain kind of exercise of it; but one can still ask whether focusing on developing that capacity is a good way of working toward one's well-being. However, this objection misses the point and ignores the teleological context of this discussion. We are talking about certain kinds of capacities here—namely, generic human dispositions. Riding a unicycle is not one of them. Generic human dispositions are capacities that define the life-form of the being in question. They would tend to be present (which is not to say: utilized) across virtually all contexts of activities and independent of any artifacts they might employ in their exercise. As such, they are inherently reason-giving, because they are part of what defines what is valuable for that kind of thing. Pleasure and maintaining one's balance might be such generic human capacities; riding a unicycle is not, though it may be a function of these other two.

[38] Russell, *Happiness for Humans*, p. 43.

the point of considering human nature in the first place just is to give us a standard for measuring normative claims, such that any appeal to a normative context to decide between the Nietzschean and the Aristotelian would either be using that very human nature or appealing to some other standard. If the latter, we are always confronted with having to justify that other standard. In the former case, we might simply say that there's something wrong with Nietzsche's conception of human nature—as, indeed, there is, precisely because that very human nature tells us something about how to judge the Nietzschean conception of it.

The general mistake, of course, is to suppose that capacities are things bearing no relation to the agent's well-being. Because they are inherently normative, pointing to standards of success and fulfillment, the key is to figure out how they are so related. Discovering that mistake allows us to speak of the misuse of the concept of capacities by Nietzsche and others. Properly doing all this requires using the actual capacity the individual possesses, in conjunction with other capacities the agent may possess—not to mention the agent's circumstances and social connections—in order to determine the ways in which that capacity can contribute to the agent's living well. The agent's living well is his or her normative context for making judgments between different normative postures.[39] The fact that someone can fulfill one capacity without paying attention to other capacities does not constitute an argument for the claim that one is properly conceiving the capacity by considering it in isolation. We can say that this way of looking at a capacity is mistaken precisely because we deny that there is such a thing as a "first nature" capacity, devoid of normative dimensions that contribute to some sort of fulfillment through its exercise with other such capacities. That is the whole nature and value that teleology brings to this discussion, and is perhaps why the distinction between first and second natures only makes sense if teleology is ignored. We might say, then, that it is the absence of teleology that makes possible the entire discussion of "bald facts" or McDowell's understanding of "first nature."

---

[39] It should be noted that we take normative judgments to be more "open-ended" than might suit some moral theories. That is, the training in reflecting upon choices, the development of virtues, and the assessment of circumstances disinclines us to suppose that there must always be a "right answer" or particularized rule that should define the solution to any given ethical situation, or that it is the philosopher's job to find such "answers."

Russell, following McDowell, wants to argue that we cannot derive norms from bald facts, because any given bald fact requires reflection, which moves it to a "second nature" status.[40] In other words, although one has the capacity to eat meat because of the presence of incisors in one's mouth, it is only upon reflection about whether one has a reason to eat meat or not that the capacity can be exercised in any relevant way. But that very reflection moves the "first nature" to a "second nature," and thus supports the claim that we cannot derive values directly from facts about human nature. The only problem with this argument is that reflection is itself a capacity, so either one has not moved off of the "first nature" position after all, or one is bringing to bear an "ethical context" that will help in deciding how to use the capacity. The latter option seems to be where Russell and McDowell want to go, but doing so would give "ethics" a categorizing property completely independent of human nature, though capable of being applied to it. In other words, "ethics" or "ethical context" is being used to understand human nature, rather than human nature informing and determining the content of ethics. Perhaps this remnant of Kantianism is plausible, but it does not explain why human nature matters at all. We might try to solve the problem by employing a concept such as "humanity," which is somehow inherently ethical because of certain other features it possesses, such as choice and dignity. But such a move, in the end, reduces to "this is what 'ethics' means"; and since we have another paradigm to offer, we are not convinced at all that this is what ethics *has* to mean.

In making our point here, we have also gone some distance toward understanding how the "G" question, with which we began, must be handled. A "natural" reading of the question presents us with an ambiguity, and even a propensity to move in the wrong direction. The question asks: "What is the connection between being a good human being and such a state of affairs being good for a human being?" Stated in this form, there is a tendency to read the first phrase—"being a good human being"—in a general and generic way only. Thus, the ambiguity is in whether we are to read "being a good human being" in this strictly generic sense, or in the full sense which includes both individuative and generic characteristics. Read in the strictly generic sense, the question asks how those generic characteristics help in thinking about what is necessary for flourishing or perfection. Since those are not the only considerations, there would, in

[40] Russell, *Happiness for Humans*, p. 44.

192

the end, be some distance between those sorts of reflections and any remaining issues of what is good for human beings, since the individuative dimensions have yet to be considered. In a sense, Haybron, Russell and others rely upon this "natural" reading to make their points.[41] If, by contrast, we read "being a good human being" in the full sense of including both dimensions, then the "being good" and the "good for" become interpenetrating notions. Consequently, the ostensible divide between "being good" and the "good for" is another example of a distinction without a separation. The result is that the "G" question ultimately dissolves as a question about the *nature* of the human good under perfectionism. It is, at most, a question about the relationship between two aspects of a distinction.

3. Natural Teleology and the Self-Perfecting Life

What, then, is required in order for there to be in "first nature," no separation of "being good" from "good for," so that perfectionism can get off the ground? Though we will, in the next chapter, answer this question in greater detail when dealing with the so-called naturalistic fallacy, we can now respond as follows: What is required is a type of entity whose very existence as the kind[42] of thing it is calls for actualizing certain potentialities. The need for this process of actualization gives rise to the very notion of what will or will not benefit the thing in question, because its very existence, qua the kind of thing it is, *is* its ultimate[43] end. It is here, as we noted in the introduction of this chapter, that Philippa Foot's claim that "*life* will be at the centre" is most instructive. By noting the centrality of life to any form of natural goodness, Foot proposes to expand upon the general idea of goodness as the actualization of X's potentialities with the additional notion of X needing (or benefiting from) their actualization.

---

[41] As our discussion of Angela revealed, our view of perfectionism rejects the idea that developing talents is ipso facto the same thing as self-perfection, and that such perfection can develop apart from the life of practical wisdom.

[42] For a defense of the claim that individual beings have a nature and can be classified in terms of natural kinds, see David S. Oderberg, *Real Essentialism* (New York: Routledge, 2007). See also Douglas B. Rasmussen, "Quine and Aristotelian Essentialism," *The New Scholasticism* 58 (Summer 1984): pp. 316–35.

[43] "Ultimate" refers to that end which gives rise to and explains the need for the actualization of certain potentialities by a thing. Such an end is only ultimate in relation to the thing in question. Its ultimacy is not based on some alleged hierarchy (or structure) of existence or some chronological ordering.

Life is a process for which the question of benefit or lack thereof is primary and ever-present, because the forms of existence of living things are the very aim of their activities. All the various senses of benefit (or harm) arise from and develop within this life-form context. Let us examine this claim a bit further.

The actualization of the potentialities that make a living thing what it is *is* the actualization of potentialities that constitute its life. But by the very same token, it also requires that life not be defined as simply not being dead. As Foot has observed, "the teleological story goes beyond survival itself."[44] There is no such thing as life that is not this or that *form* of life. Being alive must involve living in a certain manner. Living as a certain kind or sort of thing provides, then, the basis for determining what potentialities are the relevant ones for actualization and why their actualization is valuable.[45] The centrality of *life-form* is the crucial insight here. The form of a living thing determines what potentialities are to be actualized if it is to be a good instance of its kind, and its life provides the need for their actualization. The life-form provides direction to the process of actualizing potentialities; in a word, it provides the telos—the end or goal of the process. Regardless of what their life-forms may be, the actions of living things ultimately make a difference to their forms of existence—specifically, to their living as the kinds of things they are. A living thing's actions can succeed or fail in this regard and, accordingly, can be judged on that basis as beneficial or harmful, good or bad.

To appreciate this insight, it is crucial not to treat what can be *conceptually* distinguished—namely, an entity's life and its form—as *ontologically* separable features that can be fully analyzed and understood apart from one another. For beings such as ourselves, whose life-form is essentially characterized by the ability to reflect on the features that make up our life-form and to consider explicitly, not only what we are, but also our very individuality, the issue of actualizing our nature as living things is a complicated matter. But there

---

[44] Foot, *Natural Goodness*, p. 43.

[45] However, it would be wrong to assume from this that one could determine the good of any kind of living thing or the good of any individual living thing of a certain kind merely from understanding that the processes by which living things actualize themselves must involve activities that are good for them. There is a difference between explaining the basis in "first nature" for why it is valuable for living things to actualize their basic potentialities, and giving an account of what such actualization involves for a certain individual or kind of living thing.

is, nonetheless, a common conceptual structure involved in how human good is determined and how good is determined for any other living thing. This common conceptual structure is what Julia Annas describes as "continuities between our ways of evaluating ourselves and the evaluative patterns to be found in the lives of animals and plants."[46] And as Philippa Foot has noted:

> For there is a "natural-history story" about how human beings achieve this good as there is about how plants and animals achieve theirs. There are truths such as "Humans make clothes and build houses" that are to be compared with "Birds grow feathers and build nests"; but also propositions such as "Humans establish rules of conduct and recognize rights". To determine what is goodness and what defect of character, disposition, and choice, we must consider what human good is and how human beings live: in other words, *what kind of a living thing a human being is.*[47]

Though there is more to this story than can be discussed here, we can summarize our basic point: Regardless of differences in particular life-forms, *it is the life-form of the being in question, not its mere existence, that will provide the basis of our understanding its good.* It is the life-form exemplified in and by each individual that unifies the good and the good-for, because the centrality of that life-form ensures that there are no goods that can be understood apart from being goods for some agent. This way of putting the matter is another way of stating the essence of teleology.

Natural teleology does not suppose that there is some divine craftsman whose intentions determine the functions of living things.[48] Nor does it suppose that even if there were such intentions, they would be relevant to a natural-teleological account of living things. Such accounts are, as Michael Thompson notes:

> as far as can be possibly imagined from the category of intention or psychical teleology . . . [n]atural-teleological judgments . . . organize the

---

[46] Julia Annas, "Virtue Ethics: What Kind of Naturalism?" in *Virtue Ethics Old and New*, ed. Stephen M. Gardiner (Ithaca, NY: Cornell University Press, 2005), p. 17.

[47] Foot, *Natural Goodness*, p. 51 (emphasis added).

[48] See André Ariew, "Platonic and Aristotelian Roots of Teleological Arguments," in *Functions*, pp. 7–32; James G. Lennox, "Teleology," in *Keywords in Evolutionary Biology*, ed. Evelyn Fox Keller and Elisabeth A. Lloyd (Cambridge, MA: Harvard University Press, 1992), pp. 324–33, and Denis Walsh, "Teleology," in *Oxford Handbook of Evolutionary Biology*, ed. Michael Ruse (Oxford: Oxford University Press, 2008), pp. 113–37.

elements of a natural history: they articulate the relations of dependence among the various elements and aspects and phases of a given kind of life. . . . Even if the Divine Mind *were* to bring a certain life-form into being "with a view to" securing an abundance of pink fur along the shores of the Monongahela, this "purpose" would have no effect on the inner natural-teleological description of that form of life. . . .[49]

Just as life-form is crucial to understanding the unity of good and good-for in living things, so, too, it is crucial to understanding natural teleology.

Despite Thompson's well-founded point, natural teleology is still often associated with dubious metaphysical views—namely, that there is some grand telos for the cosmos, or that there is a *scala naturae* ascending from simple elements to an unmoved mover. Moreover, natural teleology is thought to entail such suspect positions as vitalism or a providential conception of nature and to involve its advocates in the fallacy of anthropomorphism. Finally, it is often thought that natural teleology holds that species are fixed and do not evolve. It is not necessary, however, for advocates of natural teleology to hold such questionable metaphysical views, adopt such controversial positions, or commit such an elementary fallacy.[50] Rather, all that is necessary for the natural teleologist to hold is that there is an internal directive principle in living organisms that is an irreducible feature of their developmental processes. The process is irreducible, in the sense that the movement from potentiality to actuality is inherent in the structure of the organism in such a way that other forms of explanation (for instance, mechanical or chemical) are insufficient to account for the phenomenon. In other words, the capacity that living things have for the development to maturity cannot be accounted for merely by appealing to the potentialities of the material elements that compose their structures. Thus, natural teleology holds that living things have causal powers that are the result of properties that are

---

[49] Michael Thompson, *Life and Action: Elementary Structures of Practice and Practical Thought* (Cambridge, MA: Harvard University Press, 2008), pp. 78–9.

[50] See the following: Allan Gotthelf, "Aristotle's Conception of Final Causality" and "Postscript 1986," in *Teleology, First Principles, and Scientific Method in Aristotle's Biology* (Oxford: Oxford University Press, 2012), pp. 3–44; Fred D. Miller, Jr., *Nature, Justice, and Rights in Aristotle's* Politics (Oxford: Clarendon Press, 1995), pp. 336–46; Paul Bloomfield, *The Virtues of Happiness: A Theory of the Good Life* (Oxford: Oxford University Press, 2014), pp. 160–1 n9; and Bloomfield, *Moral Reality* (Oxford: Oxford University Press, 2001), pp. 25–55. See also note 49.

not reductively identifiable with the properties of the material elements that compose them. These non-reductive properties[51] augment the ontology of the world and provide a mode of causation that is rooted in the very natures of living things.[52] What living things are and how they operate can only be adequately understood insofar as they are functioning for the sake of their mature state.[53] These teleological considerations reveal, then, part of the ontological basis that would support an individualistic, life-centered, perfectionist account of human good.

A reductionist or eliminationist approach to ontology, as well as to the sciences, would reject this account of natural teleology; but it is by no means obvious that either ontology or science requires such an approach.[54] Indeed, trying to define the natural order in terms of the methodologies of the so-called hard sciences is ultimately Procrustean. It lets method determine the "natures" of things. Moreover, it leaves the methodology of these sciences vulnerable to challenge. If these methods are the ultimate determiners of what is natural and real, then what justifies these methods if they are challenged—for example, by their coming in conflict with some religious or political values one holds more dearly? Is science just another faith or ideology? Or, is science entirely instrumental and not concerned in telling us what things are? Such a situation, not

---

[51] "[E]ven if one holds that final *aitia* [causes] are ontologically irreducible to material causes, it does not follow that these irreducible properties are forward-'looking,' intentional 'vital forces.' A 'vital force' is a force that drives a causal process. Picking one out would be to pick out a source of motion or developmental change. However, in Aristotle's account of explanation, to attribute this role to final *aitia* would be to collapse the distinction between final *aitia* and *efficient causes*.... " (Ariew, "Platonic and Aristotelian Roots of Teleological Arguments," p. 18). See also D. M. Balme, "Teleology and Necessity," in *Philosophical Issues in Aristotle's Biology*, ed. Allan Gotthelf and James Lennox (Cambridge: Cambridge University Press, 1987), pp. 275–85.

[52] Richard Cameron, "How to Be a Realist about *Sui Generis* Teleology Yet Feel at Home in the 21st Century," *The Monist* 87.1 (2004): pp. 72–95.

[53] On the idea that the principle behind Aristotle's teleology can be defended without accepting his account of the physical processes involved, see Michael Bradie and Fred D. Miller, Jr., "Teleology and Natural Necessity in Aristotle," *History of Philosophy Quarterly* 1 (April 1984): pp. 133–46.

[54] Sandra D. Mitchell gives a masterful account of where reductionism both does and does not have a point in her recent work, *Unsimple Truths: Science, Complexity, and Policy* (Chicago: University of Chicago Press, 2009). She makes an important case for emergent properties. See also Sandra D. Mitchell, *Biological Complexity and Integrative Pluralism* (Cambridge: Cambridge University Press, 2003).

surprisingly, is what results from getting the epistemological cart in front of the metaphysical horse. Thus, we agree with Mark Bedau in rejecting what he calls "narrow naturalism" for not only failing to provide us with an adequate understanding of the natures of things, but also for failing to accommodate the reality of natural teleology.[55]

To be sure, there remains more to say on behalf of natural teleology and much more to say about the basis for values in nature (as we shall see in the next chapter); but it is clear that natural teleology of the type outlined here is neither implausible nor subject to those sorts of a priori objections.

Though it has been argued that the theoretical core of natural teleology is vindicated by modern biology,[56] it is not necessary here to take up a discussion of its role in genetics or in an evolutionary account of the species. It is only necessary to hold that individual living things have natural ends. Nonetheless, to many it appears that if, as teleology seems to suppose, we have ends by nature, then we have very little choice about how we should live our lives; and that, in turn, seems to run contrary to pluralism. Choices, then, would concern means only, giving no scope to multiple legitimate modes of living or to improving oneself by becoming someone different.

This conclusion, however, neither follows nor is true. To revisit three points from Chapter 1:

1. Our neo-Aristotelian perspective does not embrace a dominant-end view of human good. Rather, we have adopted a so-called inclusive-end view of human good, according to which there are multiple constitutive, final ends (also called basic or generic goods) that must be managed in a complex interrelationship, individually differentiated in light of the individual's "nexus." Simply put, human good is not a single universal maximand.

2. There is no contradiction between teleology and the choice to become, by way of improvement, someone different from the way one is now. Obviously, teleology allows for change, in the sense that one can move toward or away from one's telos. But the worry here is that teleology would prevent one from aspiring to remake oneself in

---

[55] Mark Bedau, "Naturalism and Teleology," in *Naturalism: A Critical Appraisal*, ed. Steven J. Wagner and Richard Warner (Notre Dame, IN: Notre Dame University Press, 1993), p. 47.

[56] See Max Delbrück, "Aristotle-totle-totle," in *Of Microbes and Life*, ed. Jacques Monad and Ernest Borek (New York: Columbia University Press, 1971), pp. 54–5.

different ways, since there would only be "one path" available within a teleological context of self-improvement. But does teleology lay down tracks upon which we must either proceed or be derailed, with nothing in between? Perhaps that is true for some life-forms. For us humans, however, the perfected state is an actuality that is an *active*, not a passive, state and, thus, one that exhibits itself through action of some type. Since human rationality (as expressed in both speculative and practical wisdom) is the mode in which human potentialities are actualized, it is the exercise of this form of rationality that constitutes the perfection, not some final resting place or quantity of good achieved.[57] Thus, we cannot understand the good *for* a living thing as being finally different from the good *of* that living thing. In this regard, the first example of Socrates, with which we opened this chapter, is applicable here. The prevention of philosophizing cripples and deforms Socrates in a way contrary to his life-form and, thus, to his well-being. And the second case, that of the philosophy-averse Socrates, might be regarded as a situation of a life-form in transition or altered, requiring new standards for measuring success.

3. Achieving one's natural end, which comprises many constituent final ends, does not mean the closing off of options, choices, or possibilities of diverse modes of living or selves. Even a thoroughgoing flourisher *becomes* in important ways. It is true that not everything can count as a flourishing life, but the field is sufficiently wide to not preclude pluralism.[58] People do define themselves as they

[57] Our view is no doubt within the camp of what Julia Annas calls the "stronger relation between our rationality and our human nature" ("Virtue Ethics," pp. 22ff.), where human nature is the "material" with which rationality works. It is not clear from her own discussion of this stronger relation, however, whether human nature puts any constraints upon our rationality, whether rationality is limited to working only on human nature or also on what human nature confronts, and whether rationality is treated like a "second nature" that brings norms to the "first nature materials." In this regard, we would tend to speak of virtues not as ways of achieving or providing flourishing, as Annas seems willing to do, but rather as generalized descriptions of flourishing activities themselves, thus indicating more directly the unity between flourishing and virtue, while avoiding the temptation to speak of first and second natures. Finally, it is likely that our understanding of the life-form is more individualistic than Annas's account of the stronger relation. Nevertheless, Annas certainly provides one of the more useful analyses of what needs to be considered when tying ethical value to human nature.

[58] To reiterate a useful analogy from Chapter 1: There are eighty-eight keys on a piano, which also "limit" what one can do; but one's musical options are hardly

choose, because their achievement is expressed through choosing, and not exclusively or necessarily through the consumption of what is chosen. It is, in this regard, quite common, when thinking of final ethical ends, to confuse achievement with completion. The ethical ends that go into composing a self-perfecting life may be achieved, but the process never stops so long as one lives, because those ends express the very modes of appropriate living itself. It is only when the maximands are conceived in terms of "how much," rather than "how well," that one faces the problems of reconciling pluralism and choice with teleology.

4. Conclusion

"What is the basic standard of value?" is a question that has occupied ethicists for millennia; and the answers have been fundamentally: custom, authority, reason, or nature. The Aristotelian tradition, to which we attach ourselves, primarily answers the question with "nature." The other categories are not thereby excluded, but this ethical tradition ultimately measures what is reasonable and what is valuable in custom and authority by looking to what we are by nature. That naturalistic standard, as we have tried to show above, not only does not exclude, but actually presupposes, choice, purposefulness, or self-direction. Thus reason, custom, and authority are the modes or tools through which our nature is realized; but these modes would not themselves be the ultimate grounding for value in the neo-Aristotelian framework we adopt. That is to say, what counts as reasonable, authoritative, or appropriate socially would have to be measured, in the end, against a naturalistic standard of value. In the next chapter, we will consider and defend our account of a naturalistic standard of value.

thereby restricted. The type of essentialism with which we wish to associate ourselves holds, in the broadest terms, that things have natures. Hence, what qualifies as a good human life has limits as a result of the structure of an ontology that says there is a human nature. But exactly how "limiting" those ontological commitments are seems to us a very open question.

6

Because[1]

What is the connection between the natural fact that an action is a piece of deliberate cruelty—say, causing pain just for fun—and the moral fact that it is wrong? It cannot be an entailment, a logical or semantic necessity. Yet it is not merely that two features occur together. The wrongness must somehow be "consequential" or "supervenient"; it is wrong because it is a piece of deliberate cruelty. But just what in the world is signified by this "because"?

J. L. Mackie, *Ethics: Inventing Right and Wrong*

It might seem that Mackie's wonder as to what it is that provides the basis or "because"[2] for the moral evaluation of wanton cruelty as wrong is nothing more than the continuation of a line of reasoning often attributed to Hume: since there is a logical gap between statements of what is and what ought to be (the reasoning goes), there is an ontological gap between what is and what is valuable or choiceworthy. But does the existence of an ontological gap even follow from the existence of a logical gap? As Hume observed:

In *every system* of *morality*, which I have hitherto met with, I have always remarked, that the author proceeds for some time in the ordinary way of reasoning, and establishes the being of a God, or makes observations concerning human affairs; when of a sudden I am surprised to find, that instead of the usual copulations of propositions, *is*, and *is not*, I meet with no proposition that is not connected with an *ought*, or an *ought not*. This change is imperceptible; but is, however, of the last consequence. For as this *ought*, or *ought not*, expresses some new relation or affirmation, it is necessary that it should be observed and explained; and at the same time that a reason should be given, for what seems altogether inconceivable, how this new relation can be a deduction from others, which are entirely different from it. But as authors do not commonly use this precaution,

---

[1] We would like to thank Jonathan Jacobs for suggesting this title.

[2] J. L. Mackie, *Ethics: Inventing Right and Wrong* (New York: Penguin, 1977), p. 41. See also Nick Zangwill, "Moral Epistemology and the Because Constraint," in *Contemporary Debates in Moral Theory*, ed. James Dreier (Oxford: Blackwell, 2006), pp. 263–81.

I shall presume to recommend it to the readers; and am persuaded, that this small attention would subvert all the vulgar *systems* of *morality*, and let us see, that the distinction of vice and virtue is not founded merely on the relations of objects, nor is perceived by reason.[3]

It may be that Hume intends only to note that there is a difference and, hence, a distinction, between statements that are speculative and statements that are practical—that is, between statements that seek to tell us what is true and statements that try to guide our conduct. Even so, there is still the matter of whether this distinction establishes some unbridgeable gap between knowing what something is and our taking an action on the basis of such knowledge, as well as whether this shows that reason cannot grasp the distinction between vice and virtue. These questions will be examined later in this chapter. Yet, Hume may be making an even larger claim. That is to say, he may be claiming that since (a) what ought to be done cannot be derived from premises that do not involve an "ought"—or, *mutatis mutandis*, what is good, virtuous, desirable, or choice-worthy cannot be derived from premises that do not involve in some way an expression of what is worthy of valuing—then, (b) there is an ontological chasm between what is and what ought to be done (or is valuable), and thus moral or ethical conclusions (or conclusions about what is in general valuable) cannot be based on what things are.

However, Charles Pigden[4] has pointed out that though (a) is obviously true, (b) does not follow from it. The logical gap noted by (a) does not imply anything about the nature of the relationship between what is and what is valuable. Rather, it has to do with the character of deductive logic: one cannot get a conclusion about some subject-matter for which there is no mention made of it in the premises. He argues that just as one cannot get conclusions about hedgehogs from premises that make no mention of hedgehogs, so one cannot get conclusions about what is valuable from premises that make no mention of what is valuable. But just as the difference between non-hedgehog premises and hedgehog conclusions does not show that there is a fact/hedgehog gap, neither does the difference between premises that make no mention of what is valuable and conclusions that do make mention of what is valuable show that there is a gap between what

---

[3] David Hume, *A Treatise of Human Nature*, ed. L. A. Selby-Bigge (Oxford: Clarendon Press, 1973), III.I.I, pp. 469–70.

[4] Charles R. Pigden, "Naturalism," in *A Companion to Ethics*, ed. Peter Singer (Oxford: Basil Blackwell, 1991), pp. 421–30.

is and what is valuable.[5] Thus, if Hume claims (a), he is making a perfectly legitimate point; but this does not show that what ought to be done or what is valuable cannot be based on what things are.[6] It does not show that there cannot be factual statements that are also statements of what is valuable.

Of course, neither does saying all this show that there is a way in which what ought to be (or ought not to be) done can be based on what something *is*. Mackie's question remains to be answered. But Pigden's point should warn anyone beginning an inquiry about the "because" to be careful about ontological assumptions. Though there certainly seems to be a difference between saying that something is and saying that something is valuable, is this difference indicative of a difference between what is factual and what is not factual, or is it indicative only of a difference in kinds or types of facts? Put slightly differently, it surely can be admitted that there is a difference between a descriptive claim and an evaluative one,[7] but is that sufficient to show that there is an ontological gap between what justifies the truth or falsity of these respective claims? Does it show that truth or falsity of an evaluative claim cannot be based on what is?[8]

Needless to say, it can be argued, as Mackie does, that evaluative claims are the result of a massive error, because there is no such

---

[5] Ibid., pp. 423–4. See also Max Black, "The Gap Between 'Is' and 'Should'," *The Philosophical Review* 73.2 (April 1964), p. 166.

[6] We make no claim as to whether Hume actually intended to establish (b). See Horacio Spector, "Hume's Theory of Justice," *Revista de Instituciones, Ideas y Mercados* 25 (2014): pp. 47–63. Our point is simply that the existence of a logical gap does not establish an ontological one.

[7] We will have more to say about whether the distinction between descriptive and evaluative claims constitutes an ontological gap, when we deal with so-called thick evaluative concepts in our discussion of the epistemological gap.

[8] Certainly G. E. Moore thought there were different kinds of facts—non-natural ones—that justified evaluative claims. See *Principia Ethica* (Cambridge: Cambridge University Press, 1971), sec. 13, pp. 15–17. So, there can be different kinds of facts in that sense; but also a naturalistic approach need not be a reductive one, and so might allow for different kinds of facts that might be relevant in justifying an evaluative claim. To make this point, however, is to raise such questions as: "What is meant by 'natural'?"; "Is *what is* exhausted by the natural?"; and "To what kind of naturalism is perfectionism, particularly individualistic perfectionism, committed?" These questions are basic and complex; but as should be clear from our discussion of perfectionism and natural teleology in the previous chapter, we seek to defend only a non-reductive naturalism for the grounding of evaluative claims. We will have more to say about these matters later in this chapter.

property as "objective prescriptivity"[9] and, thus, that they are false. Or, it can be argued that evaluative claims are neither true nor false, because their truth or falsity is internal or relative to conventions, mores, belief systems, or commitments that are not themselves either true or false. Further, evaluative claims might be considered expressions of feelings, attitudes, or stances,[10] or the expression of principles that prescribe, proscribe, or permit some activity,[11] but again are not themselves either true or false. Finally, evaluative claims might be seen as true or false because they are based on principles that are constructions of moral thought, and not discovered, detected, or grounded in anything real apart from such thought.[12] Hence, it can be argued that there is, at the foundational level, an ontological gap between what is valuable and what is. *But this certainly seems to represent a conclusion and not a premise.* Thus, one cannot, at the beginning of an investigation of the 'because," simply assume that there is an ontological gap. To do so is clearly to beg the question. There may indeed be such an ontological gap; but that must be shown, not assumed. Finally, to say this is, of course, not to show that evaluative claims are factual claims; that needs to be shown, as well. Both possibilities are viable at the start.

It might be replied, however, that we are moving too quickly here. The point is not so much that there is an ontological gap indicated by the two statements "Jones is six-feet tall" and "Jones is a good human being," but rather that both statements are reactions to descriptive properties of Jones. The second reaction projects our positive evaluation of Jones, whereas the first does not. But in either case, there is only the same kind of facts—descriptive properties—and our reactions to them. This reply misses the basic point at issue, however. The

---

[9] Mackie, *Ethics*, pp. 38–42.

[10] Simon Blackburn, "How to Be an Ethical Antirealist," in *Moral Discourse and Practice: Some Philosophical Approaches*, ed. Stephen Darwall, Allan Gibbard, and Peter Railton (Oxford: Oxford University Press, 1996): pp. 167–78.

[11] See R. M. Hare, *Freedom and Reason* (Oxford: Oxford University Press, 1963), chap. 2. See also Allan Gibbard, *Wise Choices, Apt Feelings* (Cambridge: Cambridge University Press, 1990), chap. 3; and Gibbard, *Thinking How to Live* (Cambridge, MA: Harvard University Press, 2003). For a clearly written account of more recent developments in non-cognitivism, see Mark Schroeder, *Noncognitivism in Ethics* (London: Routledge, 2010).

[12] John Rawls, "Kantian Constructivism in Moral Theory: The Dewey Lectures 1980," *Journal of Philosophy* 77 (1980): pp. 515–72; Christine Korsgaard, *The Sources of Normativity* (Cambridge: Cambridge University Press, 1996), pp. 19, 34–48, and 246–7.

truth or falsity of "Jones is six-feet tall" is warranted by character-istics, features, and relationships of Jones; but is the truth or falsity of "Jones is a good human being" so warranted?[13] Is there anything about Jones that merits our positive evaluation of him? There are, of course, conflicting answers to these questions. However, if it is claimed that the characteristics, features, and relationships of Jones (or whatever else is involved in the set of descriptive properties of Jones) cannot justify our evaluation of Jones, or if it is claimed that that this evaluation is merely an expression of an attitude and is neither true nor false, then reasons for these claims are needed. Now, there are arguments to be made on behalf of these claims; but whatever the argument may be, it cannot rest on the additional claim that descriptive properties cannot provide the basis for the truth or falsity of "Jones is a good human being." Again, that would suppose that there is an ontological gap between what determines the truth or falsity of "Jones is six-feet tall" and what would do so for "Jones is a good human being"; and that is, as said, the point at issue. An ontological gap cannot be merely assumed.

Following Mackie, then, we would say that the problem we have in explaining the "because" is how to address the so-called natu-ralistic fallacy. The naturalistic fallacy purports to show that there is a gap between what something is and what is valuable (usually called a fact–value gap) and, hence, that it is erroneous to attempt to determine what ought to be done by an appeal to the nature of something. Since perfectionism generally bases itself on what human beings *are*, it is often claimed to be a primary example of this fallacy. Accordingly, as a normative theory, perfectionism is considered by many to be a non-starter. Thus, since we are proposing a form of perfectionist theory, we must consider this supposed fallacy as well.

At the outset, however, there is the interesting problem that what the naturalistic fallacy explicitly amounts to is not always clear[14] and

---

[13] There is another possibility here—namely, that of Hilary Putnam—which rejects this way of warranting truth claims. Facts are, for Putnam, laden with values, because facts are a function of conceptual systems that express our values. Yet, see our discussion of this view in Chapter 3; and for a full account and critique, see Douglas B. Rasmussen, "The Importance of Metaphysical Realism for Ethical Knowledge," *Social Philosophy & Policy* 25.1 (Winter 2008): pp. 56–99.

[14] This is due not only to a lack of clarity regarding just what the naturalistic fallacy is, but also an ambiguity regarding just what ethical naturalism is. See Robert B. Scott, Jr., "Five Types of Ethical Naturalism," *American Philosophical Quarterly* 17 (1980): pp. 261–70. See also John McDowell, "Two Sorts of Naturalism," in

that there is indeed more than one way of understanding what is meant by this putative fallacy. It has been pointed out that there are, in fact, at least five ways of understanding the supposed gap between facts and values—that is, as being a gap that is ontological, logical, semantic, epistemological, or motivational.[15] We have already discussed the logical gap and shown that the existence of such a gap does not imply an ontological one. Further, we have noted that one cannot simply assume that there is an ontological gap. It must be established. Thus, although we will not now spend more time on this issue, we will, as we examine other alleged gaps, comment on the purported ontological gap when it seems to reappear.

Before we consider the remaining gaps, however, it should be acknowledged that even if we show that individualistic perfectionism is not subject to some supposed naturalistic fallacy, this does not by itself show that we have answered Mackie's question as to "what exactly in the world" is signified by "because." Thus, following our discussion of the alleged motivational gap, we intend to respond directly to Mackie's challenge in section 4, called "Because." We will present the implicit structure of the reasoning by which our version of perfectionism moves from what is to what is valuable, and thus to what one ought to do.

1. A Semantic Gap: Values Are Not Definable in Terms of Some Fact of Nature

This supposed gap is pivotal to the success or failure of nearly any form of perfectionism. Our examination of this issue is involved and has a number of twists and turns, which will be indicated by subsections. It will also differentiate our approach to the foundations of perfectionism from more traditional ones. Not surprisingly, G. E. Moore will serve as the starting point.

Moore held that how we define good is the most fundamental question in ethics; and he made it clear that this is not merely some

Virtues and Reasons: Philippa Foot and Moral Theory, ed. Rosalind Hursthouse, Gavin Lawrence, and Warren Quinn (Oxford: Clarendon Press, 1995), pp. 149–79. He discusses some of the problems for ethical naturalism when one's understanding of naturalism is confined to what the modern sciences reveal. But as we suggested in Chapter 5, we are not convinced McDowell's solution works.

[15] We owe delineation of these gaps to Stephen R. Brown, Moral Virtue and Nature: A Defense of Ethical Naturalism (London: Continuum, 2008), pp. 75–6.

verbal or linguistic question—that is, a question about how the term "good" is used. Rather, defining good is concerned with the "nature of that object" which "good" is used to stand for.[16] What is good in itself, what is the nature of goodness? Moore claimed that "the good is definable, and . . . that good itself is indefinable."[17] There could be true propositions of the form "Intelligence is good" or "Intelligence alone is good"; but when we say something is good, what we attribute is indefinable. Goodness is, for Moore, not only an indefinable (and simple), non-natural property, but also *sui generis*. Thus, there is, for Moore, only one answer to our question—namely, "that good is good."[18] Any other attempted answer confuses goodness with something else and, hence, is erroneous. He labeled this alleged error the "naturalistic fallacy." Though Bernard Williams was surely correct to note that "it is hard to think of any other widely used phrase in the history of philosophy that is such a spectacular misnomer,"[19] the label is still frequently used in philosophical discourse.

There are two features of Moore's account of the naturalistic fallacy that will be considered. The first deals with his so-called open-question argument (OQA), and the second deals with his view of the kind of reality he takes goodness to be. We are, in the end, more concerned with his account of goodness than with his OQA. We are so because this account ultimately helps to raise the issue of whether perfectionism—particularly, in Aristotelian–Thomistic form—might not face a most threatening version of the naturalistic fallacy in the form of a semantic gap, despite (as we shall see) there being similarities between the Aristotelian–Thomistic view of goodness and Moore's apparent view. This issue will, in turn, afford the opportunity to suggest that there is, nonetheless, a type of perfectionism (advocated by Philippa Foot, among others, and described in Chapters 1 and 5) that can avoid this version of the supposed naturalistic fallacy. However, in order to provide a context for our account of a naturalistic grounding of goodness, it is necessary to state the reasons—some fairly well-established—as to why the OQA

---

[16] Moore, *Principia Ethica*, p. 6. Moore also states that he is asking for "definitions that describe the real nature of the object" (ibid., p. 7). Thus, for Moore the issue of a semantic gap is never merely a verbal or linguistic matter, *but an ontological one as well.*

[17] Ibid., p. 9.

[18] Ibid., p. 6.

[19] Bernard Williams, *Ethics and the Limits of Philosophy* (Cambridge, MA: Harvard University Press, 1985), p. 121.

(at least, in terms of making a semantic point) is not as devastating as once thought[20] to defining the real nature of the object to which "good" refers.

MOORE'S "OPEN-QUESTION ARGUMENT"

The OQA employs the following technique: If, in regard to any purported definition, it can be significantly asked regarding the *definiens* whether it is really good, and if we can understand what it means to doubt it, then the *definiens* is open to question. Moore claimed that this shows "clearly that we have two different notions before our minds"[21] and, thus, that our definition fails. Such definitions provide an account of goodness in terms of something other than itself.

It must be emphasized that Moore was not concerned with a mere nominal definition of "good," but with the "the nature of that object" for which "good" stands—that is to say, with what is more or less traditionally called a "real definition." Yet, since a real definition purports to tell us what something really is, it is the nature of the reality and not some criterion in mind (or mere set of practices or conventions) that we are trying to grasp. A real definition seeks to advance our knowledge. Yet, if this is so, then the ability in principle to ask significantly whether the definition is correct, or to raise a doubt, is not some disqualifying feature. Rather, it is a core feature of genuine inquiry.[22] It is reality that determines whether our

---

[20] There have been attempts to revise the OQA. Most concern the so-called motivational gap. For example, Stephen Darwall, Allan Gibbard, and Peter Railton argue that despite its numerous difficulties, a revised form of the OQA still makes a valid point. This is because "attributions of goodness appear to have a conceptual link with guidance of action," and this link is tested "whenever we gloss the open question 'Is P really good?' as 'Is it clear that, other things equal, we really ought to, or must, devote ourselves to bringing about P?'" ("Toward *Fin de siècle* Ethics: Some Trends," in *Moral Discourse and Practice*, p. 4). In other words, they hold that the ability to ask intelligibly whether a fully informed, clear-headed person who knows the description P is good would be motivated to act (or have a reason to act) for P is an indication of a motivational gap. We will consider this issue when we discuss the alleged motivational gap.

[21] Moore, *Principia Ethica*, p. 16.

[22] See Paul Bloomfield, *Moral Reality* (Oxford: Oxford University Press, 2001), pp. 127–8; Henry B. Veatch, *For an Ontology of Morals: A Critique of Contemporary Ethical Theory* (Evanston, IL: Northwestern University Press, 1971), pp. 104–5; and Douglas B. Rasmussen and Douglas J. Den Uyl, *Liberty and Nature: An*

definition is true, not our theories, practices, or conventions; and as long as we can distinguish[23] what is real from what is believed to be real, then it is in principle significant to ask whether what we take to be so is indeed the case. It is just as incoherent to say one wants to know what goodness *is*, and at the same time claim that any definition of it must in principle not be open to question, as it is to say this of hydrogen or any other reality whose nature we want to know.

Of course, part of Moore's reason for thinking that the OQA is decisive is that a definition is supposed to tell us what something necessarily is, and Moore seemed to assume that all necessary truths are analytic.[24] In other words, he assumed that statements only are necessarily true when the predicate P means the very same thing[25] as the subject S. This assumption is most problematic;[26] and there are other problems with this approach to necessary truth, as well. Here are three that reveal the deeply flawed character of the OQA:[27]

1. The OQA assumes that being a substitution-instance of the principle of identity is sufficient to explain a statement's necessary truth. Yet, what is it about a statement having the A-is-A form that makes it a necessary truth? To ask this is not to question that having such a form (or its *denial* having the A-is-not-A form) is the test for determining if a statement is a necessary truth; nor is it to question that the principle of identity (or non-contradiction) is a self-evident truth. Instead, it is to ask what it is that grounds or explains its necessary truth. If one responds that being a necessary truth just is to have the A-is-A form, then nothing is explained, and the circle is only

---

Aristotelian Defense of Liberal Order (La Salle, IL: Open Court, 1991): pp. 51–5.

[23] This is not to say that because we can distinguish (a) some statement being true from (b) our thinking it is so, we can say that the attempt to identify (a) with (b) is known a priori to be wrong; rather, it is only to say that such a claim must be shown to be correct.

[24] Moore, *Principia Ethica*, pp. 7–8.

[25] In other words, to say S is P is no different than saying S is S. The predicate must repeat the very same meaning as the subject.

[26] For an important but underappreciated critique of analyticity, see Henry B. Veatch, *Two Logics: The Conflict between Classical and Neo-Analytic Philosophy* (Evanston, IL: Northwestern University Press, 1968), chaps. 3–5, pp. 63–125; and especially as this notion relates to the alleged dichotomy between facts and values, see chap. 12, pp. 242–53.

[27] For basic and important criticisms of the OQA, see William K. Frankena, "The Naturalistic Fallacy," *Mind* 48 (1939): pp. 464–77; and Israel Scheffler, "Anti-Naturalist Restrictions in Ethics," *Journal of Philosophy* 50 (1953): pp. 457–66.

enlarged.[28] Thus, even if difficulties[29] about determining the meaning of the subject and predicate are left aside, it is by no means clear that an appeal to analyticity is sufficient to explain a statement's necessary truth. Hence, analyticity is not crucial in assessing the viability of a definition.

2. The OQA mixes a question of the meaning of a mark or sound with a question of what something necessarily is. To answer the former is not to answer the latter. In other words, an account of the meaning of "good" is not a statement about what goodness necessarily is. There is thus a failure to appreciate what might be called the difference between meaning and essence.[30] Moreover, if we take Moore to have been serious about wanting a real definition, then the determination of the meaning of "good" should not be reduced to some criterion in mind. That is to say, the meaning of "good" is not to be determined merely by some process of *inspectio mentis*. Rather, it must be the nature of the object meant[31] that determines whether one has a necessary truth or not. To make this point in a more contemporary way, but without necessarily endorsing a causal theory of reference, it seems that David O. Brink has it right when he notes, regarding a referential view of meaning, that "the meaning of our terms is fixed by the nature of the world and can be known only through substantive investigation."[32] Clearly then, we might have statements that are necessarily true, but whose necessity is not determined in an immediate or obvious manner.[33] Appealing

---

[28] See Arthur Pap, *Semantics and Necessary Truth* (New Haven, CT: Yale University Press, 1958), p. 8; and Panayot Butchvarov, *The Concept of Knowledge* (Evanston, IL: Northwestern University Press, 1970), pp. 105–52.

[29] W. V. O. Quine, "Two Dogmas of Empiricism," *The Philosophical Review* 60 (1951): pp. 20–43; and Morton G. White, "The Analytic and the Synthetic: An Untenable Dualism," in *John Dewey: Philosopher of Science and Freedom*, ed. Sidney Hook (New York: Dial Press, 1950), pp. 316–30 are the *loci classicus* for a discussion of such difficulties.

[30] See Douglas B. Rasmussen, "Quine and Aristotelian Essentialism," *The New Scholasticism* 58 (Summer 1984): pp. 316–35.

[31] Ibid., pp. 316–35. See also Veatch, *Two Logics*. Also, as we have argued in Chapter 2, to speak of the nature of something is not to speak of a universal.

[32] David O. Brink, "Realism, Naturalism, and Moral Semantics," *Social Philosophy & Policy* 18.2 (Summer 2001): p. 161.

[33] For a critique of the claim that the conceivability or imaginability of a statement's opposite is the criterion for determining whether or not that statement is a necessary truth, see Douglas B. Rasmussen, "Grounding Necessary Truth in the Nature of Things: A Redux," in *Shifting the Paradigm: Alternative Perspectives*

to some criterion in mind is not a legitimate technique for assessing whether a putative real definition states what something necessarily is.

3. The OQA ultimately makes a mockery of any attempt to define what something really is. We do not attempt to define some subject, S, if we already know what S fundamentally is, but only because we need information about it in some form or other. On Moore's approach, however, if we attempt to provide any sort of information whatever about S, then, we are told, such a definition does not count, because we have attempted to define S by something other than S. Only a definition that defines S by S will be acceptable. But if this is so, then there is no point in trying to find a real definition of S. Indeed, on such an account of definition, there is no way to determine what something is. We are stuck with a seemingly paradoxical situation[34] of definitional statements being empty tautologies—as for example, "Good is good."

MOORE AND PERFECTIONISM

Moore was not only upfront about the disappointing character of his answer to the question of what is goodness, but also committed to his answer. It is clear that he thought that goodness is a simple property—that is, that it has no parts; and given his view that a real definition is an assay of a complex object (including its parts, as well as their arrangement), this means that goodness must be indefinable. Further, for Moore, a non-natural property does not exist in time.[35] Thus, goodness does not exist in time. Though he said that good is simple, just as yellow is, this is not so helpful, because yellow is a natural and phenomenal property, and goodness is supposed to be neither. Indeed, exactly what Moore's account of goodness amounts to is ambiguous and unconvincing, and thus a matter of dispute. It is often thought to prepare

---

on Induction, ed. Paolo C. Biondi and Louis F. Groarke (Berlin: De Gruyter, 2014), pp. 323–58.

[34] This complaint has been registered by many, but see Max Black, "The Paradox of Analysis," Mind 53 (1944): pp. 263–7. Finally, it should be noted that Moore himself observed that all of his supposed proofs in Principia Ethica that goodness is indefinable "were certainly fallacious" ("Is Goodness a Quality?" Proceedings of the Aristotelian Society, Supplementary Volume 11 [1932]: p. 127).

[35] Moore, Principia Ethica, p. 41.

the way toward a position he clearly did not espouse—namely, non-cognitivism.[36]

From the standpoint of perfectionism, however, what is most important about Moore's view of goodness is his claim that it is *sui generis*. This is particularly so in light of his so-called Admission of Supervenience passage:

> I should never have thought of suggesting that goodness was "non-natural," unless I had supposed that it was "derivative" in the sense that, whenever a thing is good (in the sense in question) its goodness . . . "depends on the presence of certain non-ethical characteristics" possessed by the thing in question: I have always supposed that it did so "depend," in the sense that, if a thing is good (in my sense), then that it is so *follows* from the fact that it possesses certain natural intrinsic properties, which are such that from the fact that it is good it does *not follow* conversely that it has those properties.[37]

Moore certainly wanted to block the strict identification of a thing's goodness with its natural properties and to claim that goodness is "indefinable" or *sui generis* in this sense. Yet, it is not the case that he wanted to hold that natural properties do not fix or determine how goodness applies to something. Indeed, since a thing's natural properties constitute grounds for its being good, two things cannot differ in respect to their goodness without differing in respect to their natural properties. Thus, for Moore, goodness strongly supervenes (or goes "piggy-back") on natural properties. As Panayot Butchvarov observes:

> Moore . . . held that ethics involves reference to the world as a whole. . . . Such a view of ethics was not novel. For Plato the philosophic life culminated in a glimpse of the Form of the Good, which he held to be indescribable. Aquinas placed Good in the company of Being, One, Truth, and Beauty, the so-called transcendentals, which were said to range across the categories, that is, the highest genera, and thus to lack

---

[36] See, for example, Philippa Foot, ed., *Theories of Ethics* (New York: Oxford University Press, 1967), p. 5.

[37] G. E. Moore, "A Reply to My Critics," in *The Philosophy of G. E. Moore*, ed. Paul Arthur Schilpp (La Salle, IL: Open Court, 1942), p. 588. Jamie Dreier calls this passage a "hermeneutic disaster," but thinks that, for Moore, "the goodness of a thing follows with *some* kind of necessity from its natural intrinsic properties even though it does not follow deductively *that* a thing is good, just from the propositions about its natural qualities" ("Was Moore a Moorean?" in *Metaethics after Moore*, ed. Terry Horgan and Mark Timmons [Oxford: Clarendon Press, 2006], pp. 203–4).

even the status of categories of things in the world, much less the status of things.[38]

In other words, something's goodness can be dependent on its being a, b, and c, without that goodness being identical with being a, b, and c. Goodness is derived from these properties, but is not reducible without remainder to them.[39]

Simon Blackburn has argued that supervenience actually provides a basis for rejecting moral facts.[40] He thinks that a moral realist (naturalistic or non-naturalistic) cannot explain how goodness follows from, or supervenes upon, some natural intrinsic properties; and he thinks *this* because he assumes that, since it is possible to conceive of a world in which the natural intrinsic properties that subserve goodness do not do so, there need be no ontological necessity between these base natural properties and goodness. However, it seems that much of his argument is based on rejecting the distinction between meaning and essence that was noted in the previous discussion of the OQA.[41] Moreover, as Russ Shafer-Landau notes, "People can conceive many things that are not metaphysically possible. If certain base properties *metaphysically* necessitate the presence of specified moral properties, the *conceptual* possibility that they fail to do so reveals only a limitation on our appreciation of the relevant metaphysical relations."[42] So, it certainly does not seem obvious, as Moore seems to suggest, that supervenience cannot be based on, and necessarily related to, natural properties in some way.

Nonetheless, the vital questions for Moore remain: "What are the natural properties that fix or determine how goodness applies

---

[38] Panayot Butchvarov, "Ethics Dehumanized," in *Metaethics after Moore*, p. 382.

[39] Richard Kraut in *Against Absolute Goodness* (Oxford: Oxford University Press, 2011) takes Moore as the paradigm case of an advocate of a non-relational conception of goodness, which Kraut calls "absolute goodness." It is by no means clear, however, that such a view of goodness is compatible with Moore's admission of supervenience.

[40] See Simon Blackburn, "Supervenience Revisited," in *Essays in Quasi-Realism* (New York: Oxford University Press, 1993), pp. 130–48.

[41] For a reply to Blackburn on this particular issue, see James Dreier, "The Supervenience Argument against Moral Realism," *The Southern Journal of Philosophy* 30.3 (1992): pp. 13–38.

[42] Russ Shafer-Landau, *Moral Realism: A Defense* (Oxford: Clarendon Press, 2003), p. 86; see also pp. 88–9 for a most effective challenge to Blackburn's expressivist account of supervenience. See also Bloomfield, *Moral Reality*, pp. 48–55.

213

to something?" "How are they determined?" "How is goodness derived from these properties?" "How or why should goodness supervene on these properties and not others?" and "What is the nature of this dependence?"[43] Moreover, it is not clear that Moore was ever able answer these questions. Be this as it may, it is not our purpose to untangle Moore's position or offer an interpretation of his views regarding these questions.[44] Rather, our purpose is to note that Moore's admission of supervenience opens the door to another way of understanding the indefinability of goodness and to a possible accommodation with a non-reductive naturalistic account of goodness.[45] Particularly, there is a possible accommodation with an Aristotelian–Thomistic account of goodness that was offered by Henry B. Veatch in his *For an Ontology of Morals*.

Veatch's explanation of goodness will be examined in the remainder of this subsection. His account bears lengthy quotation:

> To use some stock examples from the literature, a strawberry is said to be a good one, because it is sweet, red, juicy, etc., or a man is a good man, because he has good judgment, has the courage of his convictions, is fair-minded, etc. And why should being sweet, red, and juicy constitute grounds for calling a strawberry good, or having good judgment, the courage of convictions, etc. be grounds for calling a man good? The answer is that it is precisely the fully developed, perfect strawberry that has such properties; or, analogously, it is only the man of reason and judgment, of courage and justice, who approximates to what a human being might be or could be, and who in this sense has really actualized the full potentialities of being human. In other words, the logic of the consequential or supervenient character of goodness or value becomes clear. Thus a thing is said to be good because it has properties *a*, *b*, and *c*. And

---

[43] Moore's inability to show what in reality can provide answers to these questions has led to seemingly endless accounts of supervenience in the current literature that attempt to substitute a "logical" or "linguistic" or even constructivist account of the dependence of goodness on subvening properties for an ontological one. See our discussion of Mark LeBar's constructivist view of supervenience in Chapter 7.

[44] But see Panayot Butchvarov, *Skepticism in Ethics* (Bloomington: Indiana University Press, 1989) for a most helpful account, as well as development, of Moore's views.

[45] Susana Nuccetelli and Gary Seay, in their attempt to revise the OQA in "What's Right with the Open Question Argument," note that "no such argument could have force against *non-reductive* naturalism in ethics" (in *Themes from G. E. Moore: New Essays in Epistemology and Ethics*, ed. Susana Nuccetelli and Gary Seay [Oxford: Oxford University Press, 2007], p. 263 [emphasis added]).

why should *a*, *b*, and *c* make such a thing good? It is simply because *a*, *b*, and *c* are characteristics of that thing in its full actuality or perfection, and to be good means to be actual as over against being merely potential. And so it is that our definition of goodness not only takes cognizance of the fact that goodness is anything but a simple property of the ordinary kind, but also makes it intelligible just why and in what sense goodness is a supervenient property.[46]

Veatch held that goodness is not a property in the usual or ordinary sense. The goodness of a strawberry, for example, is not merely one of a cluster of properties belonging to it. Rather, it is a result of those properties in virtue of which the strawberry is said to be mature or complete—that is, actual as compared with just potential. Thus, to say that a strawberry is good is not to say that it just *is* red, juicy, and sweet. Rather, it is good *because* it is red, juicy, and sweet—that is, because these properties reveal its maturity, completion, or actuality. Goodness is the actual as compared with the potential. Goodness is, for Veatch, an ontological and relational property, and as such is found throughout all of reality in the relation of the actual to the potential. It is, hence, not subsumable under any single category or genus and can only be "defined" in a broad, analogical manner. Strictly speaking, goodness is impossible to define. That is to say, it cannot be defined *per genus et differentiam*.[47] Thus, there is a sense in which a perfectionist approach to goodness could agree with

---

[46] Veatch, *For an Ontology of Morals*, pp. 109–10. Of course, strawberries, like many other things in nature, can be changed and developed by humans for their own purposes and thus, in turn, can be judged good or bad in those terms. But there remains, nonetheless, a difference between what is a good strawberry for humans and what is good for a strawberry as such. Further, if the analogy between a strawberry and a human being is to work, then it must be emphasized—as was noted in the previous chapter—that human rationality is the mode in which human potentialities are actualized. There is nothing passive about human self-actualization. These considerations are developed in our discussion of the supposed epistemological gap in the following section. Finally, it might be argued that the analogy is better understood as between a strawberry *plant* and a human. Yet, since the example of a strawberry is long established and, indeed, venerable (see, for example, R. M. Hare, *The Language of Morals* [Oxford: Oxford University Press, 1969], p. 85), we shall continue in its use.

[47] Indeed, Veatch admits this very point. See *For an Ontology of Morals*, p. 106 n8. This is also the sense of indefinability that Butchvarov attributes to Moore and develops in *Skepticism in Ethics*, pp. 61 and 115–22. See also Panayot Butchvarov, "That Simple, Indefinable, Nonnatural Property Good," *The Review of Metaphysics* 36 (1982): pp. 51–75.

Moore regarding goodness being indefinable; and it seems also that Moore's non-naturalism, at least as expressed in the Admission of Supervenience passage cited from his "Reply to My Critics," would not be opposed in principle to a naturalistic *grounding* for goodness and thus to an account (even if not a formal definition) of what goodness is. Indeed, such grounding would explain quite well how supervenience could be objective for Moore. And if this is so, then it would seem that such a perfectionist account of goodness would avoid the naturalistic fallacy in the sense that Moore conceives it, and thus could explain what "because" signifies.

ANOTHER VERSION OF THE SEMANTIC GAP FOR PERFECTIONISM— AND ITS SOLUTION

Despite a possible accommodation between this understanding of Moore's account of goodness and that of the Aristotelian–Thomistic tradition (as advanced by Veatch), it is by no means clear that such a perfectionist approach to goodness avoids the supposed naturalistic fallacy. It might be claimed that there is still a semantic (and, indeed, an ontological) gap. First, why are red, juicy, and sweet, but not green, dry, and bitter, chosen as the properties upon which goodness supervenes? And if it is replied that the latter trio of properties are examples of privations or defects, while the former are not, then the question is: What justifies this claim? Are not greenness, dryness, and bitterness as much actualities as sweetness, juiciness, and redness?[48] Second, it is one thing to discuss what it is to be a good strawberry (or a good human being), but it is quite another to discuss what is good for a strawberry (or good for a human being). Put more generally, and to renew our considerations of the "G" question of the previous chapter, there may be natural goodness—that is to say, a good entity, one which actualizes (or conforms to) its nature—but this does not show that natural goodness is the good *for* that entity (or the good *of* that entity). Moreover, although conformity to its nature is supposed to be an entity's ultimate and comprehensive (or

---

[48] Another way to put this objection is that Veatch's account of supervenience is not really akin to Moore's, because Veatch has goodness supervening on evaluative properties—the sweetness, juiciness, redness of the strawberry (and good judgment, courage, fair-mindedness of a man)—whereas, for Moore, goodness supervenes on "non-ethical characteristics." It seems, then, that Veatch is illicitly smuggling evaluative properties into his supposedly naturalistic account.

inclusive) good, it has not also been shown to be the good for that entity. There remains a gap.

These are important objections, and it brings this account of natural goodness to a critical juncture: (1) How is one to determine what are the actualities that give rise to goodness as opposed to those that do not? and (2) How is one to understand the "for" when one speaks of "the ultimate good for an entity"? There is a sense in which every potentiality is a potentiality *for* some actuality; but this does not suffice as a response to these questions, because it explains neither what actualities are relevant to something's being a good entity, nor why actuality is valuable for that entity in the first place. Put fundamentally, why is it good for that entity to be actualized?[49] Why is it desirable?

Aquinas's answer to this last question is based on the claim that a thing's goodness consists not only in its actuality, but also in this actuality being what is desirable and, thus, the object of desire for that thing.[50] The notion of desire ultimately employed here is not merely psychological, but metaphysical. It is an expression of final causality—that is, an expression of a potentiality for an actuality that is its end. The terminus of thing's potentiality is to be understood, then, not only in terms of attaining something actual, but also in terms of attaining something desirable and, as such, is something at which a thing naturally aims. Goodness is, then, not only the actual as compared with the potential, but the desirable as compared with the activity of desiring. In other words, in the very idea of a thing's potentiality being ordered to its actuality, we find the "ontological pull" of both the actual and the desirable.

But the question remains: What places actuality under the aspect

---

[49] We take this question to express a concern that is similar to that of Mark Schroeder who, in *Slave of the Passions* (Oxford: Oxford University Press, 2007), p. 70, wants to know why normative properties supervene on certain subvenient natural properties.

[50] Aquinas states: "The essence of goodness consists in this that it is in some way desirable. Hence the Philosopher says: '*Goodness is what all desire*.' Now it is clear that a thing is desirable only in so far as it is perfect; for all desire their own perfection. But everything is perfect so far as it is actual. Therefore it is clear that a thing is perfect so far as it exists; for it is existence that makes all things actual. . . . Hence it is clear that goodness and being are the same really. But goodness presents the aspect of desirableness, which being does not present" (*Summa Theologiae* [hereafter *ST*], I, 5.1, trans. Fathers of English Dominican Province [Benziger Bros. ed., 1947, available at <http://dhspriory.org/thomas/summa/FP.html>, last accessed October 2, 2015]).

of desirability? Aquinas sees the desire for actuality, and thus for the desirable, as pertaining to changes in every existing thing. This is dubious, however, because it seems too sweeping. For example, the respective potentialities of water to boil, of a rock to roll downhill, of an acid to react to a base, or even of a body to stay in motion or rest, do not seem to be the kinds of potentialities best described, even analogically, in terms of desire for the desirable. First, they are "passive," not "active" potentialities. That is, they are not powers to do or be something.[51] Second, they are not "for the sake of" the forms of existence of water, rocks, acids, or bodies—that is to say, their actualization is not needed in order for them to be what they are. If we are to understand how the relation of potentiality for actuality is also a relation of desire for the desirable, then the relation of potentiality for actuality must involve active and irreducible potentialities *for* the actualization of those characteristics and features *that are distinctive and proper to a thing being what it is.* Yet, these are just the sort of potentialities that one finds with living things. Living things are the sorts of things for which their forms of existence are also the very aim of their activities. Hence, the claim that there is a desire or appetite for actuality and, hence, for the desirable has plausibility only if it is limited to the domain of living beings. Being alive is the source of active potentiality and directedness toward an end.

Of course, it might be replied that this criticism of Aquinas misses what is fundamental about his account of ontological goodness—namely, that it involves not only Aristotle's relation of potentiality to actuality in individual beings, but also the actuality that God's creative act of existence provides through divine ideas that are the standards of perfection for all beings. Yet, this gambit not only (a) makes what is to be a good entity dependent on something other than the concrete nature of an individual entity—namely, the divine ideas, which are the eternal law and are identical with the divine essence—but also (b) locates the source of desirability in something other than an individual being's nature. Teleology here is no longer immanent.[52] The "for" is provided by an external source. Hence, it is by no means

---

[51] See Aristotle, *Metaphysics*, Bk. IX, chap. 1, 1046a 20–9.

[52] See Douglas B. Rasmussen and Douglas J. Den Uyl, "Agent Centeredness and Natural Law: Perfectionism, Immanence, and Transcendence," in *Reason, Religion, and Natural Law: From Plato to Spinoza*, ed. Jonathan Jacobs (Oxford: Oxford University Press, 2012), pp. 222–58.

clear that the difference between being a good entity and being good for that entity can be negotiated by Aquinas.

Indeed, if we are to answer questions (1) and (2) and provide an explanation for why actuality is valuable (and here we expand upon what we have said in Chapter 5 regarding the "G" question), what is required is an entity for which being actual in the relevant sense (as opposed to being merely potential) is worthwhile. In other words, what is required is a type of entity that needs to take certain actions in order for it to exist as the kind of thing it is—an entity for which its existence as the kind of thing it is gives rise to and explains the necessity[53] for actualizing certain potentialities. As stated in Chapter 5, it must be an entity for which its very existence qua kind of thing it *is* is its ultimate end, and it is here that Philippa Foot's claim that "*life* will be at the centre"[54] is crucial. This points to the metaphysical importance of life in rounding out any account of natural goodness and allows the notion of need or benefit to complete the traditional perfectionist understanding of goodness as the actual (as compared with the potential). Something cannot be completed, perfected, or actualized as the kind of living thing it is, without the actions of that thing meeting certain needs of, or providing certain benefits for, its life. For a living thing to be a good instance of its kind, it must attain certain actualities that enable it to be a good *living* thing. Actuality for a living thing must involve being living.

However, none of this is to say that, due to circumstances that are beyond its control, there are never occasions where the activities of a living thing that would normally make it a good instance of its kind nevertheless have results that are not beneficial, perhaps even disastrous. Chance and circumstances always play a role and can never be ignored in any of these considerations. Indeed, there are many factors that determine what is actually good for a living thing in the concrete case, and the importance of the individualistic character of natural goodness can never be ignored. This is especially important in regard to human good, because it is sometimes mistakenly claimed that a commitment to natural goodness for human beings implies that what one ought to do in the concrete case is simply read off human nature in a rule-like fashion. This claim by no means follows, as has been argued in the last chapter. The basic point remains, however,

---

[53] That is to say, a "necessity" in the sense that something is required to attain an end.

[54] Philippa Foot, *Natural Goodness* (Oxford: Clarendon Press, 2001), p. 5.

and bears repeating: being of benefit is necessarily part of the natural goodness of a living thing. For living things, there is no ontological separation between what is a good entity and what is good for that entity. For living things, being a good entity involves activities that are in principle good for it.

Without a doubt, actuality for a living thing must involve being alive, but this realization also requires that life not be understood as simply not being dead. There is no such thing as life that is not this or that form of life. As previously noted, the teleological story goes beyond survival itself. Put more generally, actuality is more than mere existence. Goodness only enters the picture because existence has to be some form. Mere existence is not a sufficient condition for goodness, precisely because it cannot identify anything. To be anything is to have some form. Being alive therefore must involve living in a certain manner.

Living as a certain kind or sort of thing provides, then, the basis for determining what actualities are relevant and why they are valuable. *Life-form* is the decisive factor here. It explains the desirability of actuality. As observed in the previous chapter, the form of a living thing determines what potentialities are to be actualized if it is to be good, and it is its life that provides the need for their actualization. Life-form provides direction to the process; in a word, it provides the *telos*. Regardless of what their life-forms may be, the actions of living things, in the last analysis, make a difference to their living as the kinds of things they are. They are, accordingly, judged good or bad in terms of whether they succeed or fail in this regard.[55]

We should pause here to note that we are following a line of thinking about teleology, suggested by Foot and others, arguing that natural teleology is fundamentally grounded in the nature of living things; and so, teleology is no longer cosmic, but instead of more limited scope. Yet, there is another possibility that is worthy of mention. David S. Oderberg suggests that we understand natural teleology or natural function broadly—that is, as being applicable to anything that has a natural specific activity (usually in the context of larger events or processes)—but then to also note that the kind of teleology

---

[55] As Foot states: "On barren Mars there is no natural goodness, and even secondary goodness can be attributed to things on that planet only by relating them to our own lives, or to living things existing elsewhere" (*Natural Goodness*, p. 27). For Foot's discussion of "secondary goodness," see ibid., pp. 26–7. See also Ayn Rand, *Atlas Shrugged* (New York: Random House, 1957), pp. 1012–13.

or function that has value-significance is one that is due to causes and effects within one and the same being (immanent causation), not resulting from causes and effects belonging to different beings (transient causation). Hence, it is only to living things that teleology has value or significance:

> Stones and electrons might have functions but they cannot flourish, or behave better or worse, rightly or wrongly, or be harmed, satisfied, or possess any of the fundamental normative states belonging to subjects of immanent causation, that is living things. There is no mere continuum here, but a point at which nature is carved at the joints. Yet the normative functions of living things are as real as the nonnormative functions of everything else in the cosmos. Natural goodness is as real as natural viscosity, natural harm as natural radioactivity.[56]

Regardless of what we take the scope of teleology to be, if the importance of life-form is to be understood, then it is vital not to treat an entity's life and form as ontologically separable features that can be analyzed and understood apart from one another. As we have stressed throughout this work, what can be conceptually distinguished need not be ontologically separable. Thus, it is quite consistent with what is being claimed here that the life-form of a living entity might require actions on its part that lead to its death, in order to continue the existence of future members of its species. We commonly see this in the plant and insect world and, indeed, among some animals. A good living thing, in such cases, would be a living thing whose actions are good for the continued existence of other members of its kind. For beings, however, whose life-form is essentially characterized by the ability to reflect on the features that make up their life-form, and who can consider explicitly not only what they are, but also their very individuality and mortality, and ultimately make choices in light of these reflections and considerations, the issue of actualizing their nature as a living thing is a vastly more complicated matter. There is, nonetheless, an analogy here. There are instances in which the human life-form of individuals involves considerations— for example, of friends, family, or personal integrity—that can call for conduct that puts their continued existence at great risk or,

---

[56] David S. Oderberg, "The Metaphysical Foundations of Natural Law," in *Natural Moral Law in Contemporary Society*, ed. Holger Zaborowski (Washington, DC: Catholic University of America Press, 2010), pp. 44–75. See also David S. Oderberg, "Teleology: Inorganic or Organic," in *Contemporary Perspectives on Natural Law*, ed. A. M. González (Aldershot: Ashgate, 2008), pp. 259–79.

indeed, leads to their death. To repeat our fundamental point regarding our answer to questions (1) and (2): *it is not the mere existence of the being in question but its life-form that will provide the basis of our understanding of what is good for it.* We shall discuss what the human life-form involves, and how our understanding of it applies to morality, in our consideration of the so-called epistemological gap in the next section. But what goodness is, in its most general sense, can be stated: it is the conformity of a living thing to its nature.

Finally, there is another issue regarding an entity's life-form in determining what is good for that living thing. Though it is an error to suppose that the good for a living thing is merely to exist, as opposed to living as the kind of thing it is, one might still want to hold that there is a difference between what is good for a *particular* living thing and what is good for the *kind* of thing it is. For example, consider the legendary account of the male praying mantis submitting to being devoured by the female in order for mating to be completed.[57] If for some reason the female praying mantis dies after mating, but does so before she can devour the male (or is for some other reason prevented from devouring him), then the male praying mantis not only continues to exist, but continues to exist as a male praying mantis. It would then seem that the actions of this male praying mantis will neither help propagate the species to continue, nor live up to the kind of behavior appropriate to a male praying mantis. Yet, so long as this male struggles to continue to exist in its own right, it would seem that it benefited by the demise of the female praying mantis. Thus, her demise (and his not being devoured) is good for *this particular* male praying mantis, but not good for the *kind* of thing it is.

In fact, however, the premature death of the female is *not* a benefit to this particular male. It only seems so, because we import an illicitly abstracted notion of good and ignore the life-form in question. It is not the case that "survival is always good" is simply true. It might seem to be true because, generally, being alive is better than not being alive. But as we have noted, that ignores that the good for a living

---

[57] The example being used here is designed to illustrate a general point and not to represent actual biology. We are aware that recent research has shown that more often than not the female does not eat the male and that when she does so it is mainly to advance or secure the reproductive process itself. However, our somewhat counterfactual way of putting the issue does serve the purpose of highlighting what we mean by acting in accord with a life-form and the relationship between final and efficient causality.

thing must be being alive as the *kind* of thing it is. Having been left alive would be no more beneficial to this male praying mantis than having its legs cut off or being subjected to some other deforming act. One might think the situation is different if one considers the efficient cause separable from the final cause; so if the male praying mantis is not contributing to the continued existence of members of its species (final cause), it can nevertheless take actions to continue living as a male praying mantis (efficient cause) and thus have the benefit of living on. In other words, it may seem that failing to achieve a final cause does not alter the character of the actions needed to continue as the efficient cause of continuing to live on (for example, eating). *In fact, however, this is false.* Failing to die *does* alter the character of the actions. Under the celebrated account with which we have been working, the male praying mantis's conative propensities would be thwarted by remaining alive and must be understood in a new light—namely, as a deficiency of this praying mantis. This deformity may merely express itself in disorientation or frustration of basic tendencies; but it means that if given the chance to mate again, it will do so, and it will then submit to its demise, as it endeavored to do in the first place. These are the propensities that define being a male praying mantis, both for the members of the species generally and the individual. The male praying mantis behaves out of the dispositions with which it is structured and which, when frustrated, represent a lack of a benefit to the particular praying mantis in question. As in the case of losing a limb, relative to the condition of having a limb, not being eaten by the female means that this male praying mantis is worse off. Thus, for living things, we cannot understand the good *for* something as being finally different from the good *of* something. The praying mantis as we have depicted him is, no doubt, an extreme example; but we dwell on it here to highlight the implications of our position.

One case remains. We might suppose some transitional evolutionary state, in which nature is transforming from one condition to another, because some surviving male praying mantises turn out to contribute more to the continued existence of members of the species than ones who get eaten. In this case, the praying mantises who survive, even though disposed differently, might be said to be contributing to the kind of thing they are; but, in light of what we just said, the resulting action is not of benefit to them individually, because it runs contrary to their structural dispositions. In this case, however, we have, in formulating the example, answered our own question, for there is, by definition, a discontinuity between the praying mantis's new end and the means for achieving it. This needs a resolution. Either there will be a transition to a new form, or the species will die out. In either case, the good for the thing and of the thing are necessarily seen as unstable and in transition and thus not a threat to the idea that the "good for" and "good of" remain together.[58] And similarly, what we noted in the second example of Socrates at the beginning of Chapter 5 might likewise be regarded as a situation of a life-form in transition or altered, requiring new standards for measuring success. In general, then, life-forms are "meant" to be an integration of "good for" and "good of."

2. An Epistemological Gap: Values Are Justified Differently from Facts

It might be replied, however, that although the foregoing examinations are all well and good, exactly how do we go from goodness being a description of X (that is, goodness being the actual, as compared with the merely potential, with respect to X) to that description being an evaluation of X? The strawberry is red, juicy, and sweet. This is what it is to be an actual, mature, and complete strawberry. We can even say that the strawberry is good in this descriptive sense; but how does being an actual, mature, and complete strawberry get one to the strawberry's being good, evaluatively speaking? Indeed, this may be the ultimate point of both Hume and Moore—namely, that what is needed to justify an evaluative judgment is fundamentally different from what is needed to justify a descriptive judgment. Accordingly, one must, somewhere in the process of justifying an evaluative judgment, either beg the question by slipping in some unsupported evaluative claim, or take recourse to some special evaluative intuition to lend support to the justification process.

Of course, there is a difference between saying regarding living things that "X is a, b, and c" and saying "X is good"; but the question is whether this difference indeed constitutes an unbridgeable epistemological gap in justifying an evaluative claim. We do not think so. In light of our discussion in the previous section, the basic

---

[58] The actual reality, as we understand it, may serve as the outcome of our hypothetical case here. The female eats the male head either to stimulate ejaculation or because she needs the nourishment to continue. So the "solution" is that the male is postured for a "willing sacrifice" but functions quite well if such a sacrifice is not needed.

answer to this question of justification is that the strawberry's being actual, as compared with being merely potential, is also a description of the strawberry *with respect to its natural function or end*—in this case, living qua strawberry. In other words, a strawberry being an actual, mature, complete strawberry is being a strawberry that has performed[59] its function or attained its end. Being red, juicy, and sweet is what it is for a strawberry to be actual, mature, complete, and thus good. This is not to deny, however, what we have noted earlier—namely, that strawberries, like many other things in nature, can be changed and developed by humans for their own purposes, and thus in turn be judged good or bad in those terms. Nor is it to deny that there have been accounts of the natural order that conflate natural teleology with anthropocentric and providential accounts of nature.[60] But there remains, nonetheless, a difference between what is a good strawberry for humans and what is good for a strawberry as such. Thus, when we note X's being actual, as compared with merely potential, with respect to its natural end or function, we are reporting how X has performed with respect to its end. We have a description that is also an evaluation. We are reporting certain facts that are, so to speak, inherently value-laden; or to put it more directly, we are reporting a case of natural goodness. We thus face no epistemological gap.

We admit that this answer puts considerable weight on the idea that living things have natural ends, but this idea is by no means indefensible.[61] Indeed, as we argued not only in the previous section but also in Chapters 1 and 5, the idea that living things have natural ends has much to recommend it. Natural teleology, as we are endorsing and using it here, is wholly "immanent," and provides

---

[59] The strawberry as a living thing has the power, if conditions are correct, to attain its actual or mature state.

[60] Indeed, Robert Boyle, one of the leading mechanical philosophers of the scientific revolution, provided in 1686 a trenchant criticism of the idea of nature as wise, benevolent, and purposeful. See Robert Boyle, *A Free Inquiry into the Vulgarly Received Notion of Nature*, ed. Edward B. Davis and Michael Hunter (Cambridge: Cambridge University Press, 1996). But as we noted in Chapter 5, natural teleology need not be tied to such a conception of nature. See also John Herman Randall, Jr., "Aristotle's Natural Teleology versus 'Design,'" in John Herman Randall, Jr., *Aristotle* (New York: Columbia University Press, 1960), pp. 225–9.

[61] See Stephen Brown's defense of natural teleology in *Moral Virtue and Nature*, chap. 2, pp. 19–44.

a non-reductive naturalistic basis for understanding good. As John Herman Randall observed regarding Aristotle's view of natural teleology:

> No kind of thing, no species, is subordinated to the purposes and interests of any other kind. In biological theory, the end served by the structure of any specific kind of living thing is the good—ultimately, the "survival"— of that kind of thing. Hence Aristotle's concern is always to examine how the structure, the way of acting, the "nature," of any species conduces toward the preservation of that species, and enables it to survive, to exist and *to continue to function in its own distinctive way.*[62]

There is, however, another way of asserting that there is an epistemological gap, and this pertains to the difference between such evaluations as "The oak tree is good" and such ethical evaluations as "Socrates is good." In other words, though one may be able to show with respect to non-human living things that some descriptions also involve evaluations, this is not the case for human beings. The difference between these two types of evaluations is too great to countenance any description of a human being also being an evaluation. Thus, we cannot in general argue as, for example, Tibor R. Machan does:

> If it is true, for example, that "good" means "life-enhancing for the agent, *qua* nature of the agent," so that say, it is good for plants to gain sunlight because sunlight enhances plant life, and if "ethically" means "chosen by the agent because it is one's good as the kind of being one is," then it can be argued objectively (not necessarily deductively) that one ought to choose to do what enhances one's life as the kind of being one is, that is, given one's nature.[63]

This manner of argument could be said to fall prey to an epistemological gap.

But is this so? It certainly does not seem obvious that this kind of argument must be wrong. To be sure, we have already provided a defense of this kind of argument in Chapter 5, and we shall soon have even more to say in defense of this way of arguing. But it should also be recognized at this point that we often describe human actions, as Bernard Williams notes,[64] with such notions as "treachery," "prom-

---

[62] Randall, *Aristotle*, p. 229 (emphasis added).

[63] Tibor R. Machan, *Objectivity: Recovering Determinate Reality in Philosophy, Science, and Everyday Life* (Burlington, VT: Ashgate, 2004), p. 78.

[64] Williams, *Ethics and the Limits of Philosophy*, p. 129. Williams argues that

ise," "brutality," and "courage" that express a "union of fact and value." There are a whole host of such expressions, so-called thick evaluative concepts, in our language. Moreover, it is not even clear that we can vindicate the evaluative concepts we use to make sense of our actions and lives, if we assume that we first note a description, full-stop, and then proceed to an evaluation.[65] Rather, some human descriptions are also evaluations. Given human language and other practices, there seems to be something terribly wrong-headed about even assuming that there is an epistemological gap involved in evaluating human beings and their activities.

Indeed, from a straightforward, common-sense perspective, not only are there many descriptions of human beings and their institutions that are also evaluations, but also the facts that constitute the human world—that is to say, the facts that make up our friendships, loves, pleasures, pains, works of artifice, art, industry, architecture, and, indeed, the world in which our daily lives unfold—are shot through with values. It is only because of what Veatch called "a sort of proofreader's mentality"[66] that one would not readily discern the various natural goods, as well as bads, of our world. They are evident! This is not to deny, of course, that there is a distinction

theorists bring the fact–value separation to language, rather than finding it there. Veatch similarly argues that theorists (especially Hume) bring a separation of fact–value to nature, rather than finding it there. See *For an Ontology of Morals*, pp. 129–30. It seems that some take the ability to consider abstractly one feature of reality apart from another to somehow entail that there is an ontological separation.

[65] Talbot Brewer, *The Retrieval of Ethics* (Oxford: Oxford University Press, 2009), p. 183, and see pp. 186–9 for a response to Simon Blackburn's argument ("Through Thick and Thin," *Proceedings of the Aristotelian Society, Supplementary Volume 66* [1992]: pp. 285–99) that thick evaluative concepts can be decomposed into descriptive and evaluative semantic components.

[66] See Veatch, *For an Ontology of Morals*, pp. 130–1; and Veatch, *Two Logics*, pp. 245–6. What this sort of proofreader's mentality is guilty of generally is not considering living things and their properties, features, and activities with respect to their natural ends or functions. More particularly, this is just what such a mentality does with regard to human beings. Now, there may be reasons for not making such a consideration. For example, suppose that one is only making a physical or chemical analysis of a living thing (or a human being). To not consider that thing and its physical or chemical properties with respect to its natural ends or functions by no means shows that that thing does not have an inherent, irreducible, and active potentiality for its mature state, and thus cannot be described as complete or incomplete, fulfilled or unfulfilled, with respect to that mature state, and thus cannot be evaluated as good or bad.

between a descriptive concept or claim and an evaluative one; but it is to say that this distinction requires no ontological separation or gap between a description of human beings and their evaluation.[67] To say that Socrates is courageous, thoughtful, and has integrity just is to note facts that involve his natural goodness.

It is only when we face a philosophical question (for example, Mackie's "Because" question), or when we have to sort out conflicts and prioritize the good and the bad, that we need to move to deeper and more comprehensive considerations. It is our contention that it is in a comprehensive view that we find the philosophical explanation—the order of being—that is implicit in how we always already operate. As said, our world is shot through with values—this is the given—and the basic ontological explanation is that beings have natures, and living ones have a telos that is the basis for what is valuable.

Regrettably, this appeal to thick evaluative concepts and common sense is not sufficient to remove the charge that there is an epistemological gap, because there may be other ways to explain the role of such concepts in human language and practices that do not depend in any manner on natural goodness. To put it bluntly, the union of fact and value in human affairs may have nothing to do with human nature or ontology.[68] So, we need to know what it is about human beings and their practices that gives rise to such basic evaluative concepts in the first place, and whether the answer is in terms of natural goodness. The fundamental issue remains, then, as to whether there is a common conceptual structure shared by the process of determining goodness and defect for a plant or an animal and the process of determining goodness and defect for a human being. The remainder of this section will concentrate on this issue.

Philippa Foot makes three important points in this regard. The first is that there is indeed a common conceptual structure to all the processes of determining goodness:

[67] As Aquinas observes: "[I]t ought to be said that it is not necessary to assume diversity in natural things from the diversity of intelligible characters or logical intentions which follow upon our manner of understanding, since the intelligible character of one and the same thing may be apprehended in diverse ways" (*ST* I, 76.3, Reply to Objection 4). This translation is taken from John P. O'Callaghan, *Thomist Realism and the Linguistic Turn: Toward a More Perfect Form of Existence* (Notre Dame, IN: University of Notre Dame Press, 2003), p. 267.

[68] Hilary Putnam has argued that a "union of fact and value" has nothing to do with ontology, but instead with our conceptual systems. See note 13.

The structure of the derivation is the same whether we derive an evaluation of the roots of a particular oak tree or the action of a particular human being. The meaning of the words "good" and "bad" is not different when used of features of plants on the one hand and humans on the other, but is rather the same as applied, in judgments of natural goodness and defect, in the case of all living things.[69]

The second is that the respective forms of goodness determined by these processes are very different, and that the goodness of a human being cannot be reduced to that of a plant or an animal:

When we think about the idea of an individual's *good* as opposed to its *goodness*, as we started to do in introducing the concept of benefit, human good must indeed be recognized as different from good in the world of plants or animals, where good consisted in success in the cycle of development, self-maintenance, and reproduction. Human good is *sui generis*.[70]

Yet, third (and as stated in the previous chapter), a common conceptual structure remains:

For there is a "natural-history story" about how human beings achieve this good as there is about how plants and animals achieve theirs. There are truths such as "Humans make clothes and build houses" that are to be compared with "Birds grow feathers and build nests"; but also propositions such as "Humans establish rules of conduct and recognize rights". To determine what is goodness and what defect of character, disposition, and choice, we must consider what human good is and how human beings live: in other words, *what kind of a living thing a human being is*.[71]

Though the matter is vastly more complicated for human beings than for plants and animals, the principle behind the reasoning used to evaluate a strawberry or an oak applies *mutatis mutandis* to human beings.[72] There are basic differences between the human world and

---

[69] Foot, *Natural Goodness*, p. 47.

[70] Ibid., p. 51.

[71] Ibid., p. 51 (emphasis added).

[72] Our account of a perfectionist normative theory developed and defended in Chapters 1 and 5 offers a perfectionist ethics that is sensitive to both the individualized and the self-directed character of human perfection. But see also Foot, *Natural Goodness*, pp. 47–51; and Rosalind Hursthouse, *On Virtue Ethics* (Oxford: Oxford University Press, 1999), pp. 217–38. Further, for a well-argued defense of Foot's and Hursthouse's views, which may or may not have an ultimate direction different from our own, see John Hacker-Wright, "Human Nature, Virtue, and Rationality," in *Aristotelian Ethics in Contemporary Perspective*, ed. Julia Peters (New York: Routledge, 2013), pp. 83–96.

the world of plants and animals; but there is, nonetheless, a common teleological dimension expressed in terms of their respective life-forms (or, more traditionally stated, their natures). In other words, what is good for an individual living being—regardless of its complexity (from amoebas to plants to animals to human beings)—is its living qua the kind[73] of thing it is. We thus can have descriptions of human beings that are also evaluations.

Yet, it will be asked: How do we determine what it is to live qua human? What is human good? To repeat, this is a far more complicated matter than what is involved for plants and animals. Further, there is more to understanding human living than merely analyzing the concepts involved. As noted, there is a natural-history story that the various sciences provide; but there are also the humanities. Further, there are the established opinions (*endoxa*), as well as the practices of one's society and culture. These opinions and practices—which are based on insights whose cognitive worth results from what they reveal about human beings—in the main provide the starting point[74] of any account of what it is to live qua human. They provide our initial understanding of generic goods and virtues. Additionally, since in the case of humans we are not concerned with determining the good of a "species," but rather with the good of an individual that belongs to the human species at a certain time, there must be an examination not only of what is known about the life-form we call human, but also of what is known about the individual.[75] Hence, as

---

[73] For a defense of such classifications, see: David S. Oderberg, *Real Essentialism* (New York: Routledge, 2007), particularly, pp. 201–40; Michael Devitt, "Resurrecting Biological Essentialism," *Philosophy of Science* 75 (July 2008): pp. 344–82; and Denis Walsh, "Evolutionary Essentialism," *British Journal of the Philosophy of Science* 57.2 (June 2006): pp. 425–48.

[74] However, these insights are not self-validating and are not short-cuts that replace the hard work of investigation and analysis of human nature. Hence, the opinions and practices based on these insights are not the ultimate justification for (and thus not necessarily the concluding point of) what it is to live qua human. We think Michael Thompson fails to make this distinction in what appears to be an attempt to show that Foot could be converted into a constructivist. See "Three Degrees of Natural Goodness," Discussion note in *Iride* (2003), available at <http://www.pitt.edu/~mthompso/>, last accessed October 2, 2015.

[75] This point is not sufficiently appreciated by Tim Lewens, "Foot note," *Analysis* 70.3 (July 2010): pp. 468–73. Nor does Lewens adequately grasp that Foot's discussion of what it is to live qua human—or, indeed, what it is for any living thing to live qua kind of thing it is—is *not* an account of what is necessary for mere survival. Further, for a response to other critics of Foot on this and related mat-

we have emphasized repeatedly in previous chapters, any account of what it is to live qua human cannot rest in a merely abstract or general perspective. There needs to be a consideration of an individual's "nexus"—the "set of circumstances, talents, endowments, interest, beliefs, and histories that descriptively characterize the individual."[76] These are vital factors in any account of human living. All of these considerations together provide the conceptual space for beginning an account of human good.

However, these responses will not suffice, because they cannot be of use if there is not first a basis for conceptually sorting what is human from what is not. Something more is required, and it is in this regard that the real definition of the nature of human beings provides assistance. To be human is to be an animal with a rational capacity. Such a capacity fundamentally involves the power to grasp the world in conceptual terms—that is to say, the power to form classifications, develop theories, formulate hypotheses, come to judgments, derive conclusions, reflect on various subjects (be they in the past, present, or future), make evaluations, develop purposes, and plan actions. This capacity is expressed in speculative reasoning (the pursuit of truth) and practical reasoning (the pursuit of human good). It is manifested in our use of language, as well as in our development of culture and conventions—and, indeed, in those practices that constitute what could be called "forms of life."[77] Rationality is the fundamental modality by which we consider and take on the issues of human life. Succinctly stated, rationality is the fundamental operating feature of the human life-form.

To be human is to be a rational animal. This definition does two things: (1) it notes that without which a human being would not exist; and (2) it notes that which distinguishes human nature from other kinds of beings. It thus provides the terms in which individual human beings can be identified as what they fundamentally are by

---

ters, see Micah Lott, "Have Elephant Seals Refuted Aristotle? Nature, Function, and Moral Goodness," *Journal of Moral Philosophy* 9 (2012): pp. 353–75.

[76] See Douglas B. Rasmussen and Douglas J. Den Uyl, *Norms of Liberty: A Perfectionist Basis for Non-Perfectionist Politics* [hereafter *NOL*] (University Park: Pennsylvania State University Press, 2005), p. 144.

[77] See Roger Teichmann, *Nature, Reason, and the Good Life: Ethics for Human Beings* (Oxford: Oxford University Press, 2011), p. xiii. Michael Thompson also calls such "forms of life" second nature (*Life and Action: Elementary Structures of Practice and Practical Thought* [Cambridge, MA: Harvard University Press, 2008], p. 208).

expressing the overall limits of the nature of such a being; but it does not provide a list of all the characteristics, features, activities, properties, and relations of a human being. (Indeed, if it did try to provide such a list, then it would defeat its very purpose and distinguish nothing.) Though there is much more to this overall account of real definitions,[78] it is in terms of this most condensed expression of human nature (or, if one prefers, "the life-form of human beings") that an account of human good is based.

Clearly, then, human good must involve the exercise of rationality in living; but, as we have discussed in earlier chapters and will do both in the next section and in Chapter 7, it is also in terms of this basic capacity that we begin to understand what it means for a human being to be a self-directing agent. Because the exercise of rationality is not automatic, it must be initiated and maintained. Being self-directed pertains to the exercise of rationality; and thus human good is different from other forms of natural goodness in its being a self-directed activity.[79] Moreover, it is the ability of humans to discern intellectually what is good for themselves that allows one to speak of what is choice-worthy and, *mutatis mutandis*, what ought to be done. It is from this starting point, together with what we have learned about human life from the sources that were noted above, that a naturalistic perfectionist ethical theory generally begins.

Our approach allows one to acknowledge that there is a common conceptual structure shared in the process of determining what is good for non-human living things and humans and, nonetheless, to emphasize that the human mode of living is neither passive nor of the one-size-fits-all variety in regard to concrete actions. It will be helpful, then, to reprise very briefly some of the central features of individualistic perfectionism, in order to add further support to Foot's claim that there is a common conceptual structure for all the processes of determining goodness.

Exercising rationality in living is what has been called "the practical life of man possessing reason."[80] This is not disembodied reason-

---

[78] See Rasmussen, "Quine and Aristotelian Essentialism," as well as Tibor R. Machan, "Epistemology and Moral Knowledge," *The Review of Metaphysics* 36 (September 1982): pp. 23–49.

[79] See Rasmussen and Den Uyl, *NOL*, p. 89.

[80] See Henry B. Veatch, *Rational Man: A Modern Interpretation of Aristotelian Ethics* (Indianapolis: Liberty Fund, 2003). This may not be Aristotle's primary conception of *eudaimonia*; that may be the activity of *theoria*.

ing, because (1) it includes exercising capacities shared with other animals, such as those for pleasure and health; and (2) it includes such activities as, for example, the pursuit of friendship and knowledge, the use and control of one's affective and conative states, and having an array of relationships with others. What our real definition's differentia, "rational," does is characterize the manner by which the development of those other faculties will be successfully actualized. As noted in Chapter 5, with our discussion of the case of Angela, human intelligence needs to be employed in discovering, achieving, maintaining, and enjoying what is good for a human being, regardless of the issue or how complex the situation might be.

It has been objected that an account of human perfection such as this, as well as the facts of human nature to which it appeals, is insufficient to provide an objective rationale for a specific ethical outlook.[81] Much depends here on what one expects from an ethical theory, because it would seem that one could say straightforwardly that human living involves certain activities—for example, the pursuit of friends, the acquisition of knowledge, and the development of dispositions (moral virtues) that require the use of one's intelligence in dealing with life's challenges—and that a human life that did not involve activities such as these would be incomplete and defective. These general standards connected to these activities provide, then, an ethical outlook. However, they are not sufficient to provide guidance in the concrete situation; and this is the central insight of individualistic perfectionism. As noted many times, human flourishing is individualized and agent-relative, not abstract, universal, or agent-neutral. The ethical life cannot be achieved by simply following rules or formal imperatives, and none of the aforementioned activities is worthwhile for the individual without the excellent use of their practical reason. It is only by exercising insight into the contingent and the particular that individuals might fashion worthwhile lives. One has to determine not only with whom one might develop a friendship,

---

[81] Christopher W. Gowans, "Virtue and Nature," *Social Philosophy & Policy* 25.1 (Winter 2008): pp. 54–5. Gowans also argues that neither Foot's nor Hursthouse's (see Hursthouse, *On Virtue Ethics*) accounts of natural goodness can provide a basis for such insights as human beings having equal moral worth and possessing equal rights. We cannot take up a defense of Foot's and Hursthouse's normative theories here; but we can refer the reader to *NOL*, where we address in detail the connection between individualistic perfectionism and the ideas that each and every human being is an end in him- or herself and the bearer of equal (basic negative) individual rights.

what forms of knowledge to pursue, and what moral virtue requires in terms of personal character, but also how all of these activities are to be coherently achieved, maintained, and enjoyed. Practical wisdom is the central virtue for the individual self-perfecting life. It is the virtue that must be present in any worthwhile life. To live in such a way is to be fundamentally a good human being.

However, this is not the place to attempt a full-blown account of the relationship between practical wisdom and human goods and virtues,[82] although we have already dealt with some of these issues in Chapters 1 and 5. Rather, the aim here has been to indicate a basis for supposing that there is a common conceptual structure used to determine what is good and defective for non-human living things, and to determine what is good and defective for human beings. This has been done. Thus, when considering possible approaches to ethics or morality, one cannot begin by claiming that a naturalistic perfectionist theory of the sort described here faces an epistemological gap, or even that important reasons have not been offered as to why there is no such gap. The existence of such a gap can by no means be assumed or considered the default position.

3. A Motivational Gap: Values Can Motivate Actions, Facts Cannot

Despite everything that has been argued, it might still be replied that a version of the naturalistic fallacy still remains. It is one thing to know that X-ing is good, but it might seem another matter to have a reason or motivation to engage in this activity. What "pull" does some activity's being good have on a human being? In other words, if we take "X-ing is good" to be a descriptive claim, how does that and that alone provide a human being with any reason or motivation to attain it?[83] What is more, this question can be asked in a more general and fundamental way—namely, "Why be ethical or moral?" Can some descriptive claim ever be sufficient to provide a basis for a human being doing what is ethical or moral? Can it provide a foun-

---

[82] See Daniel C. Russell, *Practical Intelligence and the Virtues* (Oxford: Clarendon Press, 2009) for an excellent account and defense of practical wisdom that is most genial to our own.

[83] Stephen Darwall, Allan Gibbard, and Peter Railton argue that this question constitutes a revised form of the OQA. See note 20. This section can be understood as addressing this claim, but aspects of this issue will also be treated in Chapter 7.

dation for a basic ethical imperative? More particularly, why, on a perfectionist theory, should one be ethical or moral?

The charge that a perfectionist theory faces a motivational gap comes from two different directions. On the one hand, what is generally regarded as the Humean view sees the difference between descriptive statements and statements that purport to guide conduct as revealing a gap between what human reason can discern regarding facts and what it can do by way of guiding action. As Hume famously (notoriously) remarked:

> It is not contrary to reason to prefer the destruction of the whole world to the scratching of my finger. It is not contrary to choose my total ruin, to prevent the least uneasiness of an *Indian* or person wholly unknown to me. It is as little contrary to reason to prefer even my own acknowledged lesser good to my greater, and have more affection for the former than the latter.[84]

In determining what people ultimately ought to do, judgments about what is the case may be true or false, reasonable or unreasonable; but these judgments carry no necessary connection to what people should prefer or want to do. "Reason is and ought only to be a slave to the passions, and can never pretend to any other office than to serve and obey them."[85] Thus, to revisit our classifications of basic ethical imperatives from Chapter 2, the type of imperative in which one is involved is a "Problematic Hypothetical Imperative" (PHI): *If* you want or desire to X, then you ought to engage in those activities—p, q, and r—that are necessary to X. But there is no way to show that to X is a worthwhile activity and ought to be desired. So, even if you know that p, q, and r are constitutive activities of human flourishing, and thus good for you, this would not necessarily,[86] according to the Humean, give you reason or motivation to prefer or seek them. It need not be a guide to your conduct. Your desires select your ends, and reason cannot evaluate desires.

---

[84] Hume, *A Treatise of Human Nature*, II.III.III, p. 416.

[85] Ibid., p. 415.

[86] It should not go unnoticed that the procedure by which Hume determines what is or is not contrary to reason, and thus necessary or not, as well as his entire distinction between so-called relations of ideas and matters of fact, are subject to the same sorts of objections that were used in our examination of the open-question argument. Additionally, Hume's claim that the distinction between vice and virtue is not apprehended by reason seems to rest on the dubious assumption that the ability to consider an instance of vice or virtue abstractly apart from its supervenient and relational aspects implies that they can so exist concretely. See Veatch, *For an Ontology of Morals*, pp. 125–35.

What is generally regarded as the Kantian view, on the other hand, sees no appreciable difference between the Humean and the naturalistic perfectionist approach to basic ethical imperatives. Even if it were true that every human being actually desires human flourishing, and even if it were further true that p, q, and r are activities that express such a way of living, this still does not free morality from its fundamental dependency on desires (or emotions or even attitudes). It leaves reason no role in grounding the ethical or moral life, and it opens the door to many forms of non-cognitivism.[87] Hence, the only alternative, according to the Kantian view, is the "Categorical Imperative" (CI), in which the imperatives of morality are sharply differentiated from anything that might be conditional on human nature (at least, as it pertains to beings in space and time).[88] The CI holds that one is to "*act only according to that maxim through which you can at the same time will that it become a universal law.*"[89] The CI is taken to be an expression of the formal character of reason itself and is conditional on nothing.[90] The obligatory character of p, q, and r results from the CI alone.

The naturalistic perfectionist response is, not surprisingly, to deny that the CI is the only alternative to the Humean claim that reason can never be a basic guide to human conduct. There is a middle ground between the PHI and the CI, and this is the "Assertoric Hypothetical Imperative" (AHI): *Since* human flourishing is your natural end, and since p, q, and r are constitutive activities of human flourishing, then you ought to p, q, and r. That human flourishing is one's natural end is based on a claim about what one is, and not on what one desires or chooses. Thus, desire is not fundamental in this regard. Yet, by the same token, human

---

[87] Hume woke Kant from his "dogmatic slumber" and threatened "the moral law within."

[88] Kantian ethics seems to be based on a "noumenal self"—a self free of all temporal, spatial, and empirical considerations. Indeed, it could be argued that such a noumenal self provides the basis for a categorical *end* for practical reason, and thus makes the fundamental ethical imperative for Kant assertoric and hypothetical in character. See Bloomfield, *Moral Reality*, pp. 139–40. But since we cannot take up here how best to interpret Kant, we would simply suggest that if this is so, then Kant's view of human nature is not a very plausible one.

[89] Immanuel Kant, *Groundwork of the Metaphysics of Morals*, rev. ed., trans. and ed. Mary Gregor and Jens Timmermann (Cambridge: Cambridge University Press, 2012), 4:421, p. 34.

[90] Ibid., 4:400, p. 15 and 4:415–16, pp. 28–30.

flourishing is also the object of desire, because (as was noted in previous sections) a description of the human life-form carries with it an account of what human life is *for*. Humans, like all living things, are teleological beings and have an inherent potentiality for their mature state—which is to say, they have what could be broadly called natural inclinations or desires to engage in activities that constitute their completion or fulfillment. They have a natural desire for their good.[91]

Aquinas's approach to this issue is instructive here. He held that the goodness of a thing is not only its actuality as it exists in relation to its potential, but also its actuality as it exists as the object and measure of a thing's strivings and endeavors. In other words, the goodness of a thing is indeed desired, and thus can never be considered apart from its relationship to the appetitive powers of a thing; but its goodness is not the mere result of being desired. Just as cognition establishes a relation between knower and known, and thus turns a thing into an object of knowledge, but does not thereby cause it to exist or to have the particular nature that it has, so too our desiring establishes a relation between the desirer and the desired, and thus turns something into an object of desire, but does not thereby cause it to exist or to have its particular nature. The relationship of dependence is one-way in both cases. Cognition depends on the object cognized in order for there to be truth, and desire depends on the object desired in order for there to be goodness. In both cases, the object provides the standard or measure. Of course, in our view, the object that provides the standard or measure for right desire is the life-form of individual beings, and not a divine idea they imitate.

The issue of human beings having a natural desire for their good has, of course, been recognized since Plato's *Euthyphro*. Since human beings are teleological beings, desires must involve the desire for something. Now, certainly we can have, for example, a desire to have a desire to exercise or we can have a desire to no longer have the desire for alcohol, but ultimately we cannot have a desire for a desire that has no object. If we try to conceive of a desire without an object, then the concept of desire has been made unintelligible. In so doing, one transforms the concept of a desire into something that cannot be

---

[91] Of course, this is not to say that knowing a particular activity is good for you will necessarily provide you with a reason or motivation to engage in it and, even if it did, that one would do so. We will discuss this point in greater detail shortly.

integrated or used in understanding why human beings do what they do. It loses its explanatory power.[92]

Another different, but closely related consequence of the teleological character of human beings is this: if it is claimed that, in the final analysis, all objects of desire are themselves nothing but the products of desiring in an ever-broadening circle of a desire for a desire that is for a desire, then we face a vicious infinite regress, and the very existence of desire cannot be explained. Accordingly, desiring is neither the ultimate ground nor determiner of our ends, and though natural goodness for a human being is an object of desire, that it is an object of desire is not ultimately merely the result of its being desired.

Further, if we reject the teleological character of human beings and hold that desires are primitive and without objects, how can practical reason do its work well? In such a situation, there is no way of knowing how to orient desires in relation to one another, because there is no way to compare and contrast desires. Moreover, it would not simply be that push-pin is as good (or bad) as poetry but also that there would not even be a way to determine what it is to satisfy a particular desire, let alone maximize satisfaction. If desires are ultimate and without objects, then there is fundamentally no way to differentiate one desire from another and thus no way to provide insight for their proper ordering in attaining a worthwhile life.

Non-human animals do not, of course, face any question regarding why they desire something. Indeed, the question of the nature of the relationship between desires and what is worthy desiring (that is, the desirable) is not something they confront. They are more or less hard-wired; for them, what they desire is desirable, and they follow their desires. For human beings, teleology works differently. As noted in the previous section and in Chapters 1 and 5, rationality is the basic modality in and through which the human telos is actualized, but there is nothing automatic about this process. It is from beginning to end a self-directed activity, and so it is possible for humans neither to attend to what their desires are ultimately for nor to understand what that requires in terms of the concrete character of their lives. Humans can and often do just act on their desires and indeed develop dispositions with no thought of the ultimate object of their desires or what this means for their very lives.

But what in fact must be realized is that desires are only ultimately

---

[92] See Talbot Brewer's penetrating critique of how many modern and contemporary analytic philosophers conceive of desire, *The Retrieval of Ethics*, pp. 12–67.

able to motivate us because they fall under the aspect of desirability, even if it is in most cases only the appearance of desirability. This is illustrated well by Elizabeth Anscombe's example of someone wanting a saucer of mud.[93] How could we explain or understand someone desiring a saucer of mud? Why does this desire exist? Of course, we could say that the person desires to fulfill the desire for a saucer of mud, but that only pushes our question back another step and answers nothing. Moreover, linking a desire for a saucer of mud to a network of desires that are complex, stable, and highly structured (or to some set of dispositions) might reveal what human beings typically want; but it does not establish desirability. Contrary to what James Lenman has argued, desirability does not somehow emerge from "our stable habits of desiring and liking things."[94] No, if desiring a saucer of mud is not to be pronounced senseless, then it must be explained in terms of someone seeing something good or worthwhile in obtaining it. And, of course, what is needed next, in order to understand this situation, is an insight into how such a thing could appear to be worthwhile regardless of how perverse that appearance may be. But the lesson to be drawn from this example is that desires cannot be separated from what they are ultimately for, if we are to understand their ability to motivate.

Finally, basic desires for human beings come already attached to some aspect or feature of their development or well-being; they are not simply empty vessels of motivation into which we pour desirability. Nor is the basis for the quality of desirability simply an expression, projection, or construction of a mental state.[95] The

---

[93] G. E. M. Anscombe, *Intention*, 2nd ed. (Cambridge, MA: Harvard University Press, 1963), pp. 70–8.

[94] James Lenman, "The Saucer of Mud, the Kudzu Vine and the Uxorious Cheetah: Against Neo-Aristotelian Naturalism in Metaethics," *European Journal of Analytic Philosophy* 1.2 (2005): p. 40.

[95] As well as Brewer's *The Retrieval of Ethics*, see Veatch, *For an Ontology of Morals*, pp. 114–17. Further, see Gabriele Taylor, *Deadly Vices* (Oxford: Oxford University Press, 2008), p. 62. Finally, see Edward Feser, "Being, the Good, and the Guise of the Good," in *Neo-Aristotelian Perspectives on Metaphysics*, ed. Daniel D. Novotný and Lukáš Novák (New York: Routledge, 2014), pp. 84–103; especially see pp. 95–9 for his response to the influential objections of J. David Velleman to the claim that desire exists under the aspect or guise of desirability. Feser argues that Velleman begs the question against the Aristotelian–Thomistic view of desire, in supposing that the "direction of fit" of desire cannot consist in its conformity to the world—in this case, to human good. Feser also takes up a line of argument similar to Brewer's in insisting that the reality of desire cannot be

quality of desirability "cannot consist in the occurrence of what Ryle called ghostly episodes within oneself, having an intrinsic character, presumably 'emotional' or 'attitudinal,' and being only contingently related, if at all, to their so-called objects."[96] To offer such an account of desirability is to treat desires, emotions, attitudes, and expressions as "third things" that inhabit our consciousness. As such, they would either exist in isolation from the objects they are supposed to make desirable, or they would stand in need of something else that would relate them to their objects. But this is a philosophic invention. Trying to base the quality of desirability in some mental state fails to explain what it is intended to explain[97] and is no more promising than an account of ideas as "third things" is for cognition. It fails to grasp the reality of the human situation.

A realistic *description* of a human being is seldom devoid of an *evaluative* dimension and can, as a result, most often provide a basis for guiding conduct. Of course, human beings do not pursue their good in the abstract; and the form in which they desire their flourishing is not merely biological. It is through human rationality, particularly the excellent use of practical reason, that what is worthy of pursuit in the contingent and the particular is discovered, and thus what ought to be done determined. Jonathan Jacobs makes this point nicely:

> Practical reason's prescriptivity is neither autonomous (as Kant held) nor derivative (as in a Humean account). What makes it practical is that it has a telos; it is reason that aims at what is good in the sense of both taking good as its object and having the realization of good as its aim. What makes it reason is that it can be informed by factual understanding. If it were not informed, it would be a capacity that is causally relevant to action but not prescriptively relevant. It would not be a power to acknowledge and comprehend anything counting as reason-giving or reason-making for a purposive being that acts under concepts.[98]

adequately explained in terms of some propositional attitude about some belief. Overall, Feser describes what we have called an "assertoric hypothetical imperative" as having "categorical force," because it is true that "I want what is good for me." And, in fact, this cannot be otherwise, given our nature as teleological beings.

[96] Butchvarov, *Skepticism in Ethics*, p. 57.

[97] For a powerful critique, along similar lines, of the attempt to locate desirability in pro-attitudes, but where pro-attitudes are understood as functional states, see Warren Quinn, "Putting Rationality in Its Place," in *Morality and Action* (Cambridge: Cambridge University Press, 1993), pp. 228–55.

[98] Jonathan Jacobs, *Practical Realism and Moral Psychology* (Washington, DC: Georgetown University Press, 1995), p. 55.

Rational desire is possible. What we have reason and motivation to do is ultimately grounded in facts about human life. There is, then, no motivational gap for a naturalistic perfectionist ethics of the sort that we have been describing in this chapter and developing throughout this work.

Nonetheless, it might be objected that there is still a motivational gap because, regardless of the teleological character of human nature, human beings are able to not pursue their good. We can know what is good for us in some concrete case (for example, exercising) and still have no desire to engage in it; and even if we have a desire, we can still not do it. Human beings can not only misapprehend in what their good consists, but they can also fail to consider or focus on the full context in which a particular course of conduct is being contemplated. In general, humans often fail to engage in the level of awareness required to make appropriate decisions. Further, human beings can simply "not give a damn" what they do; or they can do something *because* they know it is bad for them; or finally, they can just disengage from the activity of living altogether. However, there are three reasons for the version of naturalistic perfectionism we have been advancing *not* to take issue with these considerations. First, to have a "rational desire" is by no means guaranteed by the possession of an inherent potentiality or inclination for human maturation. *Teleology is not compulsion.* Second, the process of human self-perfection is, as we have noted before, one in which the individual human is as much the agent as the object of this activity.[99] Third, ethics proper is concerned with choice, rather than merely knowledge of human good. Indeed, this third reason was the basic point of Aristotle's rejection of the Socratic claim that virtue is knowledge. But to accept these reasons does not imply that knowledge of human good is irrelevant to human conduct or that such knowledge cannot provide reason or motivation and thus be the basis for determining what one ought to do. There is a difference, as Butchvarov has noted,[100] between asking "What ought I do?" and "What shall I do?" and these two considerations should not be confused. A naturalistic perfectionist ethics can answer the former without being required to answer the

---

[99] See Peter Simpson, *Goodness and Nature* (Dordrecht: Martinus Nijhoff, 1987), pp. 194–228.
[100] Butchvarov, *Skepticism in Ethics*, p. 50; see also Veatch, *For an Ontology of Morals*, pp. 120–2.

latter.[101] It ultimately remains up to each one of us to decide whether we shall do what we ought to do.

There is finally another issue to be considered: Has not the proposed solution to the so-called motivational gap revealed a basic difficulty? Is not the presence of a natural inclination or desire for self-perfection actually incompatible with the self-directed character of human rationality? This is a complex issue, and we will have more in response to this question in Chapter 7. However, this much can be said here: it is not necessary that human rationality be understood as setting its own context of operation, or determining what it is ultimately for. Rather, human rationality can be understood as a capacity or a power which, like all the other basic powers of a living thing, functions for the sake of that thing's actualization but, unlike many of those other powers, requires, for its exercise, effort or exertion on the part of the individual human being. If this is so, then the presence of natural inclinations or desires would not mean or imply that the operation of rationality was not something for which the individual human being was responsible. The ability of natural goodness to motivate us does not require, as Warren Quinn noted, "any 'queer' power over the will. It requires a conception of the will as the part of human reason, whose function is to choose for the best."[102] But this is, of course, to suppose that there is more than one mode of causality involved in the operations of human beings and, indeed, living things in general. To be sure, efficient causality alone is not sufficient. As we have been contending, there must be a teleological dimension; and that dimension is crucial in avoiding the so-called motivational gap.

4. Because

What, then, is our response to Mackie's metaethical challenge? What is the structure of the reasoning process that provides the "because"? To use his example, what *in the world* makes deliberate cruelty—for example, causing pain just for fun—something wrong and unworthy? From what we have argued, in both this chapter and previous ones, our answer is simply that human flourishing does not consist merely in the attainment of pleasure (or, more generally, that satisfaction

---

[101] Even if "ought" is understood entirely apart from natural goodness, being able to determine what one ought to do is still different from deciding that one shall do it.

[102] Quinn, "Putting Rationality in Its Place," p. 253.

of desire alone does not define human flourishing), and that gratui-
tous cruelty, though pleasurable to some, cannot be a constituent of
human flourishing. Indeed, such cruelty is incompatible with many of
the other constituent goods and virtues of human flourishing. There
is nothing wrong with doing something for fun, but it is wrong to do
something *just* for fun, with no thought given to anything else. Thus,
it ought *not* to be done.

Part of the reasoning behind our response is, of course, nothing
more than a version of Aquinas's first principle of practical reason:
"Good is to be done and pursued; and evil is to be avoided."[103] This
principle is based on the teleological character of human nature. It
does not tell one in what human perfection ultimately consists or
what is good in particular cases, but rather only reports the implicit
principle upon which human conduct is based. It provides the context for ethical reasoning, as we have seen in our discussion of the
alleged motivational gap and will see again in Chapter 7.

But exactly what is it about human beings and human good that
grounds this first principle, and how does it provide the "because"?
This still needs to be stated. Our basic answer in positive terms is as
follows:

a. X is a human being.
b. A human being's *ergon* (natural function) or *telos* is human flour-
    ishing.
c. Human flourishing is what is good for a human being.
d. What is good for a human being is what is choice-worthy.
e. What is choice-worthy is what ought to be done.
    Hence, X ought to pursue X's flourishing.

To emphasize again, by invoking an argument structure such as
this,[104] it is not our point that someone actually engages in such reasoning in determining what ought to be done (and, *mutatis mutandis,*

---

[103] Aquinas, *ST*, I-II, 94.2.
[104] Paul Bloomfield describes the structure of such reasoning this way: " If . . . one
       looks at human nature, one sees that there are some goals truly worth working
       for, purposes or plans toward which one ought to aim, and others one ought to
       avoid. These are facts about us, special normative facts, but facts nonetheless. If
       we were different creatures than we are, we would have different aims and pur-
       poses, but we are not and therefore do not. 'Oughts' are a subset of 'is's" (*Moral
       Reality*, p. 151). See also Bloomfield, *The Virtues of Happiness: A Theory of the
       Good Life* (Oxford: Oxford University Press, 2014) and, particularly, "Why It's
       Good to Be Good," pp. 153–231.

what ought not to be done). Indeed, there are too many details and questions of context and circumstances, let alone forms of flourishing, involved for such an argument to be useful in making a concrete decision. But if one wants to answer the sort of philosophical question that Mackie raises—that is to say, if one wants to know what it is about the world and about human beings that makes an answer possible—then one must use an overall argumentative structure of the sort that lies beneath our form of perfectionist ethics. It is our response to his *metaethical* challenge as to what in the world is signified by "because"; and it illustrates Foot's basic contention that "a moral evaluation does not stand over against the statement of a matter of fact, but rather has to do with facts about a particular subject matter."[105]

5. Conclusion

One of the goals of this chapter was to show that an individualistic perfectionist theory does not commit some so-called naturalistic fallacy. In doing this, five ways in which this alleged fallacy might be construed were considered; and in each case, the supposed fallacy was shown not to be applicable. Of course, there may be some other way of understanding this supposed fallacy that still needs to be considered. Be this as it may, it seems, at least for now, that there are no good reasons for thinking that an individualistic perfectionism that is life-centered is subject to some supposed naturalistic fallacy.

The primary goal of this chapter was to show that the so-called ontological gap that seems so pervasive in current thought is really without foundation, if we begin by understanding that the natural order consists of things that have natures. It is in terms of a thing's nature that we not only find the basis for understanding its mode and manner of existence, but also how it changes and develops.[106] In such an order, the nature of a thing can be understood as consisting of a set of inherent potentialities, and the process of change as an

---

[105] Foot, *Natural Goodness*, p. 24. Steven J. Jensen notes, "An ought-statement is in fact a certain kind of is-statement. It describes a certain kind of necessity, a necessity that applies to an agent insofar as it has an end" (*Knowing the Natural Law: From Precepts and Inclinations to Deriving Oughts* [Washington, DC: The Catholic University of America Press, 2015], p. 149).

[106] See Baruch Brody, *Identity and Essence* (Princeton: Princeton University Press, 1980).

activity that actualizes these potentialities. The relationship between potentiality and actuality is thus basic and pervasive; and in living things, we find both a basis for natural goodness and a way to begin to understand human good.

7

Toward the Primacy of Responsibility

To say that you have a reason is to say something relational, something which implies the existence of another, at least another self. It announces that you have a claim on that other, or acknowledges her claim on you. For normative claims are not the claims of a metaphysical world of values on us; they are claims we make on ourselves and each other.

Christine M. Korsgaard, "The Reason We Can Share: An Attack on the Distinction between Agent-Relative and Agent-Neutral Values," *Social Philosophy & Policy*

In order to fully grasp the exact character of individualistic perfectionism, we think it is worthwhile to contrast the theory we have developed with the thought of two very important philosophers: Stephen Darwall and Mark LeBar. We have chosen these thinkers because they are, in some fashion or other, advocates of constructivism—that is to say, the metaethical view that evaluative or normative claims are seen as true or false because they are based on principles that are constructions of moral thought, and not because they are discovered, detected, or grounded in anything real apart from such thought. We have benefited from considering these thinkers, because they have been instrumental in our clarifying the ways in which the individualist perfectionist position we hold stands apart. What follows indicates some of our reflections and conclusions in this regard.

1. Darwall

We take the works of Stephen Darwall to be one of the most prominent examples of the paradigm of respect. Anyone familiar with Darwall's work has learned from it, and we ourselves have come to understand our own views better in light of it. It would be folly to suppose that we could provide a full analysis of Darwall's views here. Instead, we seek to contrast some of his major tenets with our own, more as a way of further clarifying *our own* position, and less as a criticism of Darwall. The spirit with which we undertake the following reflections is thus one of illumination rather than depreciation.

There seem to be three major points of comparison between Darwall's work and our own. The first has to do with Darwall's understanding of Moore's "open question argument" (OQA), and his use of it to establish a wedge between our understanding of what human good is (that is, what theoretical or speculative reason may conclude) and that good's serving as a norm for human conduct (that is, its guiding the use of practical reason). The second has to do with Darwall's claim that it is neither conceptually nor metaphysically necessary that what will advance one's good is something one is thereby rationally required to seek. Third, Darwall holds that what he calls "the second-person perspective" is central to the establishment of a norm for human conduct. On this perspective, norms for human conduct are not to be found in objective states of the world, but rather through forms of social relatedness that are necessary for the appearance of such norms. More specifically, Darwall holds, similarly to Gaus, that morality arises through, and is to be understood as, a system of claims that we make upon each other (as well as ourselves). This understanding is ethically primitive. It is that in terms of which other approaches to morality are ultimately to be understood and defended. In what follows, we will expand each of these points and discuss them in relation to our approach to ethics.

MOORE's "OPEN-QUESTION ARGUMENT" VERSUS HUMAN GOOD AS NORM FOR CONDUCT

Darwall thinks that what is legitimate about and crucial to Moore's OQA is that the good is a norm for human conduct. It makes a claim upon our conduct. If the good were ultimately understood in terms of something other than its being choice-worthy, and thus something other than what ought to be done, then there would be a gap between understanding the good this way and there being a reason or basis for attaining the good. Darwall holds that if the good were thought of as simply a description of reality, then it would have no normativity. In effect, he says, there would be no normative tie between the good and the agent, because the good would involve no ought and would make no claim upon the agent's conduct: "For anything characterized in non-normative terms, we can sensibly ask whether there is any reason to choose or pursue it, or deny without contradiction

247

or conceptual confusion that there is any reason to do so."[1] Since there is nothing in the natural or metaphysical order that constitutes a *"brute* ought to *be,"*[2] any account of the good in terms of such an order will leave open the question of why the good should be done. This is the crux of Moore's claim that the good and, hence, the normative must be *sui generis* in character; and it is this part of Moore's legacy that Darwall applauds.

The part of Moore's approach to ethics that Darwall deplores is Moore's modeling of human agency on a so-called naïve, first-person perspective that sees practical reason as being regulated by an agent-independent truth[3] regarding what the world should be. According to this perspective, we act to bring about what we desire; and our desires are for what is desirable, or at least apparently so. This model further conceives of practical reason as purely instrumental. That is, it determines what conduct ought to be done by whether or not it achieves the good. Darwall calls this "definitional consequentialism"[4] and claims that this approach determines the worth of actions qua actions "entirely in terms of their power to bring about intrinsically valuable *existents* or states including, perhaps, the intrinsically valuable state of that act's being performed."[5] In short, it "reduces ought to do's to ought to *be's.*"[6] It is here, however, that Darwall turns the OQA against Moore's own account of practical reason. The normative character of the good and its ability to be a guide for practical reason cannot be found merely in some existential state, even if that state is intrinsically good. Rather, the good's choice-worthy character must result from a norm that can appeal to our practical reason. Yet, for humans, practical reason is "free." Indeed, a norm could not be a norm if it were not possible to flout; and thus it must be recognized that practical reason has no "substantive aim" in the way that theoretical or speculative reason might be said to have truth as

---

[1] Stephen Darwall, "Moore, Normativity, and Intrinsic Value," *Ethics* 113 (April 2003): p. 485.

[2] Ibid., p. 478.

[3] On this view, an agent-independent truth is one that is not determined by what one thinks, feels, or chooses; but it does not follow from this (as Darwall appears to assume) that the normative reality that provides the basis for this truth is not essentially related to what *and* who an individual human agent is. We will discuss this point later.

[4] Darwall, "Moore, Normativity, and Intrinsic Value," p. 471.

[5] Ibid., p. 477.

[6] Ibid., p. 477 (emphasis added).

its substantive aim. We cannot find the needed normativity from the first-person perspective, because there is nothing in an existential state that can provide the needed normativity. Such a state cannot provide an answer as to what the agent or practical reasoner should do. Darwall describes this needed normativity as "agent-relative" in character.[7] The source of this needed normativity must lie somewhere else.

Darwall's claim that the needed normativity results from our reflection on ourselves as "free" practical reasoners will be considered in the following subsections; but here we must note how we differ from Darwall on these foregoing claims, and how we might respond to some of his concerns. What follows is based on what has been argued throughout this book, and particularly in the preceding two chapters, as well as on the overview of individualistic perfectionism that was presented in Chapter 1.

We have argued that human good is not merely an existential state, but an actuality, an activity, and a *telos*. Moreover, human good is essentially related to some person or other and always exists in an individualized manner. In other words, human good arises, obtains, and exists in relation to a person's immanent activities that constitute the actualizing of potentialities crucial to both who and what that individual human being is. Thus, our approach is very different from the Moorean view of goodness that Darwall provides.

We certainly agree that the good must be something choice-worthy if it is to be a norm for human action; but we do not think that this in any way requires that human good's status as a norm cannot be due to certain facts about reality, particularly human nature. We see the first-person perspective not as naïve, but as fundamental and, indeed, do think of human good as standing as the regulating standard for practical reason, just as truth stands as the standard for theoretical or speculative reason. In other words, the "substantive aim" of theoretical or speculative reason is truth; and for practical reason, it is human good (what we call human flourishing).[8] Our justification for

---

[7] Ibid., p. 471. But Darwall thinks of agent-relative obligation only in deontological terms that he wants to ground in the making and entertaining of claims second-personally. We have, throughout this work, presented an alternative to conceiving agent-relativity in deontological terms, and we will discuss the alternative again below.

[8] A clarification and a qualification are required here: speculative and practical reason are not two separate powers (Aquinas, *Summa Theologiae* [hereafter *ST*], I, 79.11, trans. Fathers of English Dominican Province [Benziger Bros. ed.,

making these claims, and the crucial point at issue here between us and Darwall, is found in how practical reason can be a self-directed activity[9] that is essential to the very nature of human flourishing and, nonetheless, can have an end or function set by human nature. Simply put, the point at issue is how can practical reason be self-directed or "free" and, yet, teleological? We hold that the first step in the answer to this question is that the self-directed exercise of practical reason is the exercise of one of a set of powers that makes a human being a living organism, and as such is to be understood in terms of a human being's inherent, overall, and irreducible potentiality for his or her mature state—namely, human flourishing. Thus, there is something practical reason is naturally *for*, and this orientation can be construed as giving direction to practical reason, but not determining it in a manner that could be likened to the effects of efficient causality.

Rather (and this is the second step in our answer to this question), this orientation is to be understood in terms of what a human being is as a living thing. Humans have powers that have an inherent potentiality for their mature state, as we argued in the previous chapters; and the potentiality of these powers is not reducible without remainder to the potentialities that are found in the material elements that compose living things. Since the self-directed exercise of practical reason is one of these non-reducible powers, it, too, functions for the sake of maturity. The biocentric context provides roles for formal *and* final causality to play in understanding the character of practical reason. They explain the directive (but not directing) character that human flourishing as our telos has for our exercise of practical reason. It is something to which we are naturally drawn—as something our choices are potentially for—and thus is why practical reason is not itself the source of what it is ultimately *for*. Our flourishing is not

---

1947, available at <http://dhspriory.org/thomas/summa/FP.html>, last accessed October 2, 2015]). The former is simply human reason concerned with truth, and the latter is human reason concerned with means and ends—that is, with either artistic or technical production or attaining human good. For Aristotle, *phronēsis* is "a state [of the soul] involving truth and reason concerned with action regarding things that are good and bad for a human being" (*Nicomachean Ethics*, VI 5 1140b 4–6) and is what we call practical wisdom. This is Fred D. Miller, Jr.'s translation. See *Nature, Justice, and Rights in Aristotle's* Politics (Oxford: Clarendon Press, 1995), p. 10.

[9] As we have noted in previous chapters, speculative or theoretical reason is also self-directed, which will figure into our second point of comparison with Darwall below.

something to which we are driven; and thus there is, in this account, conceptual space for saying we are "free." Our flourishing is inherently a function of the exercise of our agency (that is, of the exercise of both theoretical [or speculative] and practical reason) and, yet, is not defined by the mere act of choice itself.

We are thus "free" agents in the sense that there remains something that an individual human being must do for him- or herself. An individual human being must initiate and maintain his or her practical reason. Exercising practical reason is not something that happens to human beings; it is something we do. Here is where efficient causality plays its role in self-direction. We are the efficient cause of the exercise of practical reason. That we are the efficient cause affords a foundation for the idea that self-direction is the central activity through which practical reason can make human flourishing an actuality. That we are the efficient cause also affords a basis for holding ourselves responsible, because it is by failing to exercise our practical reason (or, indeed, our theoretical or speculative reason) that we are ultimately turned away from our telos.

The third step in explaining how practical reason can be self-directed and, yet, teleological in character is the realization that there are many modes of causality involved in understanding practical reason. If we think only in terms of efficient causality, then every deviation from anything posited as an end would ipso facto indicate that it is not an end. But there is no obvious reason to so confine our understanding of causality. The self-directed exercise of practical reason is not reducible to some string of efficient causes; but neither is it some primitive, inexplicable act that creates its own context or, as we shall see, norms. We are flesh-and-blood agents that are the efficient causes by which we attain our telos; but we do not, through our agency, create the potentiality for either our telos or our ontological context. Self-directedness involves efficient, formal, and final causality. Hence, formal and final causality must be considered, as well.[10]

Darwall thinks that a consequentialistic theory of obligation is inadequate to the task of grasping the worthiness of actions. This is so because, for consequentialism, the obligatory character of actions results from their entirely instrumental character—that is, they are simply means to some inherent good. We agree that such a consequentialistic view does not suffice. However, it is not that

---

[10] See Edward Pols, *Mind Regained* (Ithaca, NY: Cornell University Press, 1998).

consequences have no role in determining obligations; it is just that they are not foundational.[11] But to grant this point does not rule out practical reason's needing to serve an ultimate end or our obligations' being determined by how they relate to that end. As we have maintained throughout this work, human flourishing is our ultimate end; but it is neither dominant nor monistic. Instead, it is a complex activity that comprises many other activities; and these activities— for example, cultivating moral virtues—are worthwhile not because they are simply means to human flourishing, but rather because they are each expressions of what it is to so flourish. Thus, there is no need to invoke a consequentialistic view of the sort Darwall describes to explain why the constituent activities of human flourishing as an inclusive good are worthwhile and ought to be taken. Human flourishing is the ultimate inherent good *and* a complex set of worthwhile activities. So, one can conceive of practical reasoning serving an ultimate end, without having to subscribe to the sort of consequentialism Darwall deplores.

Ultimately speaking, "ought to be's" are "ought to do's." This is possible because the ultimate end is, on our account, a way of living. Such an ultimate end is essentially the life of some person or other and, as such, is not only an actuality but an activity. It is found particularly in the self-directed exercise of practical reason, and not in some state or condition of existence considered apart from human agency. Indeed, the life of practical wisdom is just that perfected state in which acting in an appropriate or right manner has been initiated and maintained by the individual agent. Thus, human good is an activity that is an actuality whose existence is dependent upon our self-direction. So, on our view, an ultimate end does not need to invoke a consequentialistic view to explain why its constituent activities are worthwhile and ought to be taken; nor is it simply an activity in which the agent is merely the means to its performance; nor is it a mere existential state. Rather, our human good, our very flourishing, just is each of us, as an agent, engaging in the activity of actualizing or perfecting him- or herself: the actuality, the activity, the telos, and the individual human agent are one. As we argued in Chapter 1 and elsewhere in this work, the individual human being is both the agent and the object of self-perfection. Thus, the view of moral guidance and agent-relativity that Darwall offers is not the only alternative to

[11] Philippa Foot, *Natural Goodness* (Oxford: Clarendon Press, 2001), pp. 48–51. See also our discussion of this point in our account of inclusivity in Chapter 1.

consequentialism (and its failure to appreciate the human agent) that he so roundly, and soundly, rejects.

Finally, the observations from the previous two paragraphs bring us to an assumption about what it is for an activity to be objectively and inherently worthwhile or good that needs to be made explicit. Simply put, Darwall thinks that what is to be so worthwhile or good cannot be something that is the welfare of, or good for, someone. It must be agent-neutral. Indeed, he states that "worth or worthiness is not a form of welfare or goodness *for* anyone."[12] Thus, Darwall thinks that if there is an objective, inherently good or worthwhile activity that constitutes the substantive aim of practical reason, then it bears no essential relation to the agent. It cannot be agent-relative and make any claim on this agent's conduct.[13] This is, however, not the case for our account of human flourishing, as we made clear in our discussion of agent-relativity in Chapters 1, 2, and 5. But we will have more to say about this matter when we take up our discussion of the second-person perspective in the last subsection of our comparison.

No Rational Obligation to Seek Human Good

As a result of his understanding of Moore's OQA, Darwall believes it is neither conceptually nor metaphysically necessary that one is rationally required to seek whatever will advance one's good. "The proposition that an act would bring about the most valuable outcomes is neither identical with nor entails the proposition that the agent should perform the act (all things considered)."[14] The required normativity for conduct cannot be found in the first-person perspective, but must be found in norms consonant with the freedom of practical reason.

---

12 Stephen Darwall, "Self-Interest and Self-Concern," *Social Philosophy and Policy* 14.1 (Winter 1997): p. 177. He also states here that perfectionist theories are most naturally viewed as theories of worth.

13 This assumption is a crucial feature of his criticism of the first-person perspective: If Darwall can separate what is good or worthy or obligatory from the agent, then something else will be needed to link them back to the agent's own concerns and desires. Indeed, this separation, if successful, is the basis for Darwall's later claim that in order for the agent to be subject to moral obligation, the second-person perspective must be foundational.

14 Stephen Darwall, *The Second-Person Standpoint: Morality, Respect, and Accountability* [hereafter *SPS*] (Cambridge, MA: Harvard University Press, 2006), p. 286.

The only norms that will be consonant with such freedom, however, are norms grounded in free practical reflection itself.

Darwall attempts to show how such a grounding is possible by asking us to consider the kinds of claims that we can make reciprocally on one another—for example, when I make a claim, from a request to a demand, that you remove your foot from my toe. This claim is not based on trying to attain some good or avoid some evil. Rather, I would be making a personal claim on *you*; and my ability and standing to make this second-personal address would give you a reason to remove your foot. You would regard my claim as a reasonable one that a free and rational agent would make to another, and part of a framework of reasons that would provide mutual accountability.

The viability of this claim on another person would not, for Darwall, be based on what we do when we provide the evidence for a theoretical or speculative claim. I am not providing "epistemic access" to some truth about intrinsic value that would determine the aim of your practical reason. Rather, in asking you to remove your foot from my toe, I am engaging in an *"authoritative expression of will."*[15] To take up—or consider—this sort of claim is to presuppose that the other can act on reasons that have nothing to do with trying to attain some good outcome, and it is to presuppose the autonomy of both the addresser's and addressee's wills.

Darwall claims that once we grasp our agency, our freedom, our autonomy, we note that what

> seemed to be true from a naïve practical standpoint, that action has the substantive aim of bringing about valuable outcomes, is an illusion. If action had bringing about valuable outcomes as its substantive aim, then it would be simply impossible freely and self-consciously to act against this aim, just as to believe in the face of facts of what one regards as conclusive evidence to the contrary.[16]

Ethical claims can have the normativity that the OQA demands only if they are grounded in norms that guide free rational agents—that is, only if they are grounded upon agents who can act independently of a consideration of outcomes. The second-person standpoint, and the ethics of respect, is foundational for Darwall because it is the only way to express free agency.

We would like to concentrate a little more on what seems to

---

[15] Darwall, "Moore, Normativity, and Intrinsic Value," p. 487.
[16] Darwall, *SPS*, p. 290.

be the lynchpin in Darwall's argument—namely, his claim that if practical reason had a substantive aim of attaining an outcome or end, then it would be impossible to freely and self-consciously act against this aim. Darwall amplifies what he means by "freely and self-consciously" in a footnote:

> Although we seem to be able to believe contrary to what we *believe* is better evidence, it is by no means clear that we can believe contrary to what we are then *seeing* as better evidence. And something comparable would be true of action if it had the substantive aim of bringing about intrinsically valuable outcomes.[17]

Yet, there are three problems here. The first two are internal to Darwall's own account. First, "seeing as *better* evidence" is itself an evaluation and is, at least implicitly, a judgment or belief, because the notion of "better" requires some sort of judgment or belief. Thus, the contrast Darwall seeks to establish between believing and seeing does not stand up on its own terms. Second, it is true that *whatever* we see as so, we must see as so—at least, at the time we see it. But Darwall has not shown that this cannot be true, as well, for what we see as good, worthy, or obligatory. Of course, he wants to claim that if this were true for what we see as good, worthy, or obligatory, then we could not later freely and self-consciously disregard what we see as good, worthy, or obligatory. However, such disregard is just as possible with respect to anything else we see as so. To say that we see something as so does not show that we cannot freely and self-consciously disregard what we see as so. Seeing as so is still a conceptual activity that we initiate, and there is nothing that compels us to initiate it or to continue to engage in it. To disregard what we see as true is just as possible as to disregard what we see as good, worthy, or obligatory. It is perfectly possible for one to let the focus on what one sees as so to change, allowing things to be more generally (or more particularly) viewed, or letting different factors become objects for attention rather than the current ones. Even if our focus does not change, it is also possible not to consider what we see as so. Letting one's awareness blur, failing to think about it until tomorrow, or disregarding continually all consideration of evidence are quite common ways to fail to engage conceptually. Effectively, we can, by these and other ways, fail to see something as so. That is to say, we can fail to grasp, discern, judge, infer, entertain, accept, or understand anything

[17] Ibid., p. 290 n23.

that is an object of our awareness, *including not only our seeing something as so, but also the very failure to see our seeing something as so*! Indeed, people exhibit these sorts of failings all the time; and there is nothing privileged about self-consciousness. The colloquial expression for this is: "Not letting the left-hand know what the right-hand is doing." Thus, the type of freedom Darwall wants to attribute to practical reason seems just as prevalent in theoretical or speculative reason; and yet he does not want to deny that truth (or objective probability) is the standard or goal for these forms of reason. But if this is so, then, by the same considerations, human good could be the standard or goal for practical reason.

We certainly view human freedom as pertaining not only to our conduct but, more fundamentally, to human reason itself. The act of using one's reason (whether it is practical or not) is an exercise of self-direction and, conversely, the act of self-direction is an exercise of reason. To note once more what Aquinas has said on this matter: "Man is master of his actions through his reason and will; whence too, the free will is defined as 'the faculty and will of reason.'"[18] Self-direction and the exercise of reason are not separate acts of two isolated capacities, but distinct aspects of the same conscious act. Human reason[19] is, in its very essence, a self-directed activity. Freedom, agency, or choice just is self-direction and, as noted in the previous paragraph, there are many ways by which we can fail to exercise our reason. Indeed, our fundamental responsibility consists in keeping ourselves in appropriate focus (or at the needed level of awareness); and this, of course, is a never-ending task that varies continually with subject matter and context. Yet, neither is self-direction autonomy, as Kant or Darwall would define it. Self-direction is, as we have noted in previous chapters, simply the act of bringing to bear one's reason and judgment on one's surroundings, making plans to act within and upon them, and conducting oneself accordingly.[20] It

---

[18] Aquinas, *ST*, I-II, 1.1, trans. Fathers of English Dominican Province (Benziger Bros. ed., 1947, available at <http://dhspriory.org/thomas/summa/FP.html>, last accessed October 2, 2015). See also Ayn Rand's discussion of the relationship between agency and human reason in *Atlas Shrugged* (New York: Random House, 1957), pp. 1012–13.

[19] As should be clear, we are speaking of both theoretical (speculative) reason and practical reason.

[20] Douglas B. Rasmussen and Douglas J. Den Uyl, *Norms of Liberty: A Perfectionist Basis for Non-Perfectionist Politics* (University Park: Pennsylvania State University Press, 2005), pp. 88–9.

may or may not issue in the development of proper dispositions or conduct.

Darwall assumes, however, that human freedom is truly possible only if that freedom is the source of its very norms. Indeed, this seems to be the basic sense of "free" that underlies his entire argument. It is Kantian in character. That is to say, we give norms to ourselves. We are our own lawgivers. But this brings us to the third problem. Why must one accept this Kantian sense of "free"? Darwall claims that unless we are free in this sense, we will lose our agency and any basis for what we ought to do. Yet, why must this be so? We have already discussed this claim at some length and have offered an alternative, neo-Aristotelian view of freedom. On that view, we are agents from beginning to end, and there is nothing that compels us to know what is true or to achieve what is good. It is possible to understand human freedom as pertaining to our initiating the effort to achieve some specific object of awareness or concrete object of conduct, without denying that these activities must have an object that they do not themselves ultimately create. In sum, it is possible that we are free to initiate the effort to discover and achieve the concrete form of our human good but, nonetheless, *not* free from the normative applicability of human good for the activities we undertake.[21] Indeed, we are capable, in the concrete, of rejecting all norms for human reason— even human flourishing itself—but that does not make us any less human or any less subject to what our telos requires. It also, incidentally, does not make us any *less* free than the Kantian version of freedom, where worthiness or some other deontic, agent-independent standard is relied upon to measure our conduct.

One other matter remains to be considered, and this is whether the OQA itself might not entrap Darwall's own second-person standpoint. Even if we assume this view of morality is right, we still have the question: "Why should we care? Even if dignity, worth, and

---

[21] We interpret F. C. Copleston to be making more or less this very point when he says in his discussion of Aquinas's basic moral imperative: "The moral imperative says, 'You necessarily seek this end because you are what you are, a human being; therefore you ought to do this and not to do that.' In this sense, the imperative is unconditional and absolute. Kant would call it an *assertoric hypothetical imperative*. . . . According to . . . [Aquinas], all seek 'happiness' in an *indeterminate* sense. And the moral imperative directs the taking of means to that end. But among the means are the *discovery* of what 'happiness' signifies in the concrete and the conscious willing of it as thus *concretely conceived*" (*Aquinas* [London: Penguin, 1991], p. 225 [emphasis added]).

mutual accountability are presupposed by our giving and receiving moral claims, this only shows, at most, what is logically involved, and does not show why one ought to care. How does one derive an "ought" from a "must"? Or, put slightly differently, how does one get a motivational "must" from a logical "must"? Of course, it might be replied that all one needs is a reason, because an ethical obligation per se is a matter of what follows from our reasoning; and this is not the same as motivation, which is an empirical and contingent matter. But unless one assumes that human beings are noumenal selves, this response reveals just what is wrong with the constructivist approach. It confuses or conflates reasoning with reality. In this case, it confuses or conflates what is a logical necessity (be it theoretical or practical) with a psychological necessity.[22] This brings us to our third point of comparison. Let us now consider Darwall's approach to this issue and his account of rational caring.

Second-Person Perspective as Basis for a Norm of Conduct

Our second point of comparison noted that, for Darwall, the "second-person perspective" is central to the establishment of a norm for human conduct. Norms are to be found not in objective states of the world, but rather in forms of social relatedness that are necessary for their appearance. In our discussions of the first two points of comparison, we have seen the basis for this claim about the need to look elsewhere than in objective states of the world for the foundation of ethical norms. As we have already seen, this is a complicated business; and Darwall has an elaborate account of the second-person perspective that cannot be fully appreciated or analyzed here. However, we believe we can get a good handle on what is of relevance to our discussion by considering Darwall's discussion of caring.

As we noted earlier in our discussion of the first two points, an intrinsic good that delineated an appropriate form of social relatedness (including one's relationship with oneself) would not by itself imply that one ought to pursue it. Consequently, one must find some other factor to provide a motivating reason for pursuit of such a good. As it turns out, it is not motivation per se that will ultimately be acceptable here, but a certain type of motivation—namely, what

---

[22] See G. E. M. Anscombe, "Practical Inference," in *Virtues and Reasons: Philippa Foot and Moral Theory*, ed. Rosalind Hursthouse, Gavin Lawrence, and Warren Quinn (Oxford: Clarendon Press, 1995), pp. 1–34.

Darwall calls "caring." While there must be some affective component for motivation to occur, not every affective state will qualify. Self-interest, for example, might be motivating; but it is not the right type of motivation for an *ethical* norm. In a passage we regard as central to Darwall's perspective, and one in which we may begin to see the distance between his own theory and ours, he notes the following:

> On a rational-care theory, self-interest is simply a person's interest, viewed as his own, and its normative claim is independent of its being his own. In caring about oneself in the way that gives rise to the desire to promote one's good *for one's own sake*, one sees one's good as worth promoting in seeing oneself as care-worthy. This is not an attitude *de se*. One values oneself, and one's interest, from a perspective one can share with anyone who can care.[23]

We might ask why promoting the "good for one's own sake" is not sufficient in itself to count as ethical motivation, but presumably that is because there is no basis upon which to differentiate care from care-worthiness. If, *pace* Darwall, promoting one's own good for one's own sake *were* sufficient to count as ethically normative, then the interpersonal would seem to be either a derivative notion or some other dimension of ethics not captured by notions of promoting one's own good. Darwall, like us, is not fundamentally a dualist or an analogist who advocates multiple valid and mutually exclusive understandings of what qualifies as ethical. For Darwall, therefore, an ethical norm is one that is *foundationally* interpersonal; and his task is to find a standard that retains that feature. Obviously, it appears that a teleological perspective similar to the kind we have advanced here will not do, however other-oriented it may be.[24] Thus, motivating the agent and, at the same time, finding some interpersonal dimension from which ethical norms can be derived is the requisite combination. Simply knowing the good in itself is not sufficient, even if that good were to apply to all; but having some desire for an end is not sufficient by itself either. We must find a way to merge these two dimensions, and that merger comes through care-worthiness or rational caring.

---

[23] Darwall, "Self-Interest and Self-Concern," p. 174.

[24] It is clear from what has gone earlier that our view of being a social animal as part of our nature builds interpersonality into our perspective. However, is it also clear that we *would* allow it to be possible to say that pursuing one's own good because it is one's own good *is* ethical, since that is the foundation of value for the teleologist.

In this regard, Darwall wishes to employ the concept of estima-bility, which will give us an affective turn toward worthiness, while at the same time including motivation, without thereby reducing itself to some form of first-person interest. To regard something as estimable is to be motivated toward it, but for reasons that are not reducible merely to one's interest, since what is estimable seems to stand outside oneself and to be something any agent can appreciate. Similarly *merely* caring for another, in the usual parlance of caring, could certainly be considered just another form of first-person inter-est, since it is directed toward one's own end, even though the object of interest is not oneself. Hence, it is not that the object be different from oneself that matters here, but rather that the aspirational object be something inherently interpersonal. Things worthy in themselves are inherently interpersonal in this way because of their universal estimability. Rational-caring, as it turns out, is a universalized form of caring which can be entered into by any agent capable of caring in the first place, and which serves to ground the normative appropri-ateness of any agent's caring.

Perhaps we can explore the point better by noting the connection and difference for Darwall between welfare and worth. An interest-ing feature of the difference between these two is that welfare is something that can be promoted or produced, whereas worth (or merit) can only be appreciated or expressed.[25] And this very differ-ence is a function of the fact that whereas welfare can be, and nor-mally is, agent-relative, worth and merit are agent-neutral.

> Unlike welfare, merit and worth are not value *for* anyone. Something enhances welfare by being good *for someone*, but there is no such thing as merit or worth for someone, except in the sense of someone think-ing something has merit or worth. There is only merit or worth period. Consequently, if worth or merit is normative for distinctive evaluative attitudes, they must be normative for such attitudes in *anyone*, norma-tive for such attitudes *as from anyone's perspective* . . . Because they are not appreciated or regarded from any *particular* standpoint, merit and worth can be *common* values—they and their appreciation can be shared. Moreover, appreciating these values through shared valuable activity makes possible distinctive forms of valuable relationship, through which the agent-neutral value of these activities is both confirmed and ramified.[26]

---

[25] Stephen Darwall, *Welfare and Rational Caring* (Princeton: Princeton University Press, 2010), p. 89 *passim*.
[26] Ibid., pp. 98–9.

The upshot of this distinction is that ethical caring is not the desire to promote what the agent holds to be her welfare, but rather the desire to promote what is regarded to be her welfare from an agent-neutral perspective.[27] "According to a rational care account, we make assessments of welfare, not from the (agent-relative) perspective of the person whose welfare is in question, but from the (agent-neutral) perspective of someone who cares for her."[28] We come to care for others in an ethical way when we promote for that person (or ourselves) what is estimable and thus worthy. A person's welfare is enhanced *for that person* "through active engagement with and appreciation of values whose worth transcends their capacity to benefit (either extrinsically or intrinsically). The contribution to welfare comes through the *appreciative rapport* with the values and the things that

---

[27] Elsewhere ("Self-Interest and Self-Concern," pp. 173ff.), in the example of Sheila, Darwall drives a wedge between Sheila's own desires and what it means to care about her well-being. One of the keys here is that a person's own interests make no necessary normative claim on anyone who cares about the person in question, including the person herself. This is mainly because we can all recognize cases where the person's expressed interests about what would be good for her diverge from what someone who cares for that person would regard as being good for that person, that is, from what would actually serve that person's well-being. In Sheila's case, she is unwilling to divert even a few dollars away from a cause in which she believes, in order to rescue her failing health (or even to accept such from others for that purpose). One who cares about Sheila, including Sheila herself, if she could reflect dispassionately about her own situation, would find such fanaticism to be contrary to true caring. The key move here seems to be that simply from the fact that one desires X, nothing normative can be inferred about whether X is really "in one's interest." In what follows, we explore further the reasons for this position. For now, we can note that Darwall's position bumps up against the fundamentals of a paradigmatic understanding of the nature of ethics. The responsibility paradigm that we adhere to does put normativity into one's desires, after all, precisely because that is the locus and material of responsibility. One's desires can be mistaken; but that they are one's own makes one responsible for them, implying both that others can never assume an equality of responsibility for those desires with the possessor of them, and that it is a mistake to hold that *any* caring agent's concern for someone's well-being is equivalent to that of any other agent. Hence, to put the matter in Darwall's language of the Sheila example, o1 (where she doesn't pay for her health) rather than o2 (where someone does) may finally be the correct conclusion to what is in Sheila's interest, because she is the only one to whom the choice between o1 versus o2 (or vice versa) applies. This is the difference between something being *for* her sake, as Darwall would have it, and something *being* her sake as we would have it.

[28] Darwall, *Welfare and Rational Caring*, p. 103.

have them."[29] Consequently, a person's desires, choices, aspirations, and goals may have nothing whatsoever to do with that person's welfare, even should that person benefit by satisfying those desires, making those choices, realizing those aspirations, or achieving those goals. The person's welfare would have to do with whether she gained some rapport with, and thereby endeavored to instantiate, the appropriate goods, those goods being largely the list of generic goods we ourselves might identify, goods such as knowledge, friendship, health, aesthetic experience, and the like. As we shall see momentarily, for us, welfare and benefit are going to be more closely aligned than we find here in Darwall, since the agent-relative conception of benefit is inherently a factor in what one must mean by "welfare."

Another way of noting the difference between the way Darwall looks at those ethical goods and the way we do is simply stated by him when he notes that one "has reason to care for *himself*. And he has reason to care for himself because he, like any person, has *worth*—he matters."[30] Darwall certainly expresses an ethics of respect in giving a central role to worth; but from the point of view of an ethics of responsibility, a person's worth is a function of his exercising the reasons he has to care for himself, and not of his having reasons to care for himself because he has worth. Darwall sees himself as being consistent with a certain interpretation of the Aristotelian tradition; nonetheless, he rejects its underlying nature. "What we are prepared to count as perfecting or cultivating ourselves itself depends on what we can see as developing our powers to appreciate values, which cannot in turn reduce to the value of developing those very powers."[31] Perfection could not "reduce" to the value of developing our powers in a Darwallian universe, because teleology—the central feature of an Aristotelian ethics—has been rejected, thus removing the possibility of moral values being, in any form, objects of desire. Instead, Darwall needs something to "pull" one toward the good which would, at the same time, keep values from becoming simply objects of desires. *Sans* teleology, the needed goods must take on an independence of their own, as if they were detachable from the persons whose goods they are.[32] They pull

---

[29] Ibid., p. 76.
[30] Ibid., p. 83.
[31] Ibid., p. 118 n14.
[32] Darwall allows that a "defensible teleological metaphysics" might offer an alternative to the view he takes here, in ibid., p. 118 n15.

because of their agent-neutral estimability, and not because they are realizing an inherent potentiality of the agent. In this regard, Darwall might be said to have a passive conception of worth and merit, where appreciation is the modality of their expression, rather than of their being manifest through a process of activity. This must be so to achieve the universality of value that agent-neutrality requires. For if worth and merit were a function of the active realization of inherent ends, then the possibility exists that a given realization may not be the same as, or transferrable to, that of another. But with appreciation as our modality, the same value is open to appreciation in the same way by all.

Now, we also would not suggest that the object of any desire, simply in virtue of the fact that it is an object of desire, is thereby morally good. We would hold, however, that cultivating ourselves does finally "reduce" to the developing of our powers; and that has sometimes been expressed historically in terms of appetites and desires. In any case, those powers are measured in terms of what promotes our natural end. The additional act of estimability—that is, appreciating a good in such a way as any other agent might do so— necessarily offers us some other standard besides end-realization as a determinant of moral good terms such as "welfare" or "perfection." Indeed, it often seems in Darwall that the appreciation of the good in moral conduct supersedes its realization, whereas we believe the Aristotelian position is exactly the reverse. In the Aristotelian position, including our own, appreciation is not the pull that motivates moral action, but a benefit of having undertaken it. This last point is not to say we cannot be drawn to what is estimable, but rather that estimability is a function of our ends, meaning that its appropriateness is defined by those ends, and that the final status of estimability as a value is a function of those ends having been achieved. Put this way, it may thus be the case that estimability as a moral term can only be fully appropriate with respect to what may *not* be shared with others. A bit of unpacking of this notion seems to be called for here, and we can do this best by looking at "Golub's smile."

In discussing what Darwall rightly terms the "Aristotelian thesis"— namely, "that the good life consists of excellent . . . activity,"[33]—he notes the following:

---

[33] This quote comes from ibid., p. 75. The ellipses leave out the following: "(meritorious or worthy)." We leave out this parenthetical phrase because the meaning of these terms is precisely what is at issue here. Most simply put, the difference lies

I think of a photograph I clipped from the *New York Times* as vividly depicting this claim [the Aristotelian thesis]. It shows a pianist, David Golub, accompanying two vocalists . . . at a tribute to Marilyn Horne. All three artists are in fine form, exercising themselves at the height of their powers. The reason I saved the photo, however, is Mr. Golub's face. He is positively grinning. . . . Mr. Golub's delight is a sign of his activity's value, not what makes it good. His pleasure, in Aristotle's words, "completes the activity . . . as an end which supervenes as the bloom of youth does on those in the flower of their age."[34]

Darwall notes that, with the Aristotelian thesis, the human good derives from certain activities, but that beyond the valuing of the activity itself is the *appreciation* of the value of the activity which, as it turns out, is really the basis for speaking about a person's welfare:

My claim will be that a person's welfare is enhanced, her life is made better *for her*, through active engagement with and appreciation of values whose worth transcends their capacity to benefit (extrinsically or intrinsically). The benefit or contribution to welfare comes through the *appreciative rapport* with the values and the things that have them.[35]

In essence, then, as we noted above, certain things have value apart from any particular act of expression of that value; and it is our connection with this form of the value—and not its instantiation—that finally justifies us in referring to that person's welfare. The "appreciative rapport" with this further dimension entitles us to say that value V makes a person's life better. We presumably would not be justified in saying so without that rapport, or on the basis of the realization of ends alone. It would seem, therefore, that we are so entitled to speak of a person's life being better because, without this further dimension—that is, with only the activity itself—we could never get out of the first-person perspective to that of others, thus making it impossible to offer any generalizable normative prescriptions or to draw any generalizable normative conclusions.

The above-cited passage from Darwall has, however, a certain ambiguity attached to it—namely, whether we are speaking of the very meaning of discussing a person's welfare, or of just an addition to it. To this point in our discussion, we have been searching for the

---

in Darwall's agent-neutral rendering of them and our agent-relative use of them. But it is, nonetheless, correct to define the Aristotelian thesis in terms of excellent activity.

[34] Ibid., pp. 75–6.
[35] Ibid., p. 76.

basis of ascribing welfare to a person per se. The foregoing passage, however, speaks of "enhancing" a person's life. This would suggest that the standard for determining a person's welfare lies elsewhere, and that having an appreciative rapport is but a further enrichment of what is otherwise fundamentally contributory to a person's welfare. If having this appreciative rapport was, after all, simply an addition to something else, then it would be hard to say anything against it. But such a claim would neither be very novel, nor of much use in helping us decide just what exactly does define a person's welfare. It seems to us, from all we have considered above, that the claim Darwall is making is much stronger, and that the benefit one receives from performing an action (any action) is not sufficient for saying those actions contribute to one's welfare.[36] That can only be done once we have established the appreciative rapport with something inherently valuable; and that appreciative rapport is our basis for ascribing welfare at all.

To get at how Darwall's approach fails to capture the nature of welfare, we might turn to what we would call "Deborah's Frown." Deborah (the daughter of one of us) was, shall we say, "parentally encouraged" to take piano lessons. She dutifully attended her lessons and was able to play a number of pieces well. At some point, she, along with the other students, was asked to play in a recital. The image one of us has of that event is listening to the piece being played almost flawlessly, with not only no sign of pleasure upon her face, but a rather unhappy frown. Whereas Golub relished the music and his accomplishment in playing it, Deborah's experience was a joyless and rather tedious mechanical exhibition of some competence. It would be wrong to say that Deborah took no pride in being able to play the piece, or even that she was unappreciative of the value of the music. But it would certainly seem far-fetched to say her life was enhanced much by the experience. It is possible her life may have even been diminished in some ways by the experience. Deborah never took another piano lesson and, so far as we know, has never since played the piano.

Part of the problem here can be traced to Darwall's central claim with which we opened our discussion of the third point of

---

[36] Darwall notes that, "I don't question that he [Golub] appreciates the merit of his playing, but I doubt that this is the main object of his delight. Rather, I imagine that what his smile primarily reveals is an appreciation of values that *make* music-making a noble pursuit" (ibid., p. 77).

comparison—namely: "self-interest is simply a person's interest, viewed as his own, and its normative claim is independent of its being his own." It is the last part of this clause that we object to. The normative claim is exactly *not* independent of "its being his own." Indeed, in the most important sense, the normative claim does not arise at all in independence from "his own." Saying this may also implicate us in holding—*pace* a claim made in another passage from Darwall cited above—that merit and worth can indeed be "for someone." The push toward, and requirement of, agent-neutrality is, we believe, responsible for both of Darwall's claims and is consistent with them; but that foundation is quite contrary to our own.

As we have seen throughout this chapter and elsewhere, one need not and should not adopt the agent-neutral perspective. There is, however, a certain intuitive plausibility to Darwall's claims about merit and worth that we need to examine through the perspective of our own theory. We might begin by noting that worth may not, after all, be so distinct from individuals because, although we can consider certain values, say knowledge, in the abstract and in a way others can enter into as well, we can still also meaningfully ask "for whom" about that very same value. David Norton puts this best when discussing a claim of Mill's:

> When Mill says "It is better to be Socrates dissatisfied than a fool satisfied," we must once again ask, "For whom?" And we reject the answer implied by Mill, "For everyone" (Mill would restrict this to everyone who has the intellectual capacity; but in Mill's terms it would clearly be better if everyone had the intellectual capacity). Certainly it is better for Socrates to be Socrates. But for Mill to be Socrates (or try to be, since the proposal constitutes an impossibility) is distinctly worse than for Mill to be Mill, and correspondingly for you and for me.[37]

So, although we are quite capable of appreciating the insights and intelligence of Socrates, that is some distance from saying that the values of Socrates should be our own. Better for Deborah to be Deborah dissatisfied than to be Golub satisfied. If we grant this, then what accounts for the intuitive appeal of Darwall's claim that merit and worth are somehow of value independently from the agent?

The answer to this last question, of course, lies in treating merit and worth as if they attach only to generic goods. Certainly it is true

---

[37] David L. Norton, *Personal Destinies: A Philosophy of Ethical Individualism* (Princeton: Princeton University Press, 1976), p. 219.

to say that merit and worth do attach to generic goods. Given what we know about human nature, human living, human maturation, and the like, it is perfectly sensible to speak of generic goods such as knowledge, aesthetic experiences, health, and the like as having application to persons. Indeed, insofar as one is human, there is even some normativity upon the individual in such claims. Moreover, some of the value of these goods would certainly express themselves in an appreciative rapport that would have some independence from the individual. Deborah, no doubt, could appreciate Golub's smile, even if she could not put one on her own face while playing the same piece of music. One might object that if Deborah had the same skills and talents as Golub, she would have more of a smile. Again, there is truth in this; but what would not follow would be that any such "smile" would be the same as Golub's, or that it would be appropriate for Deborah to pursue his smile. Doing so might just be an extreme distraction for Deborah, however much bigger her smile became.

Generic goods do have normative force upon us—not because of our rapport with something inherently good, however, but because of their connection with, and possible contribution to, human nature and maturation. Their value, in other words, is due to the role they *actually* play in our achieving our telos which, as we have noted here and elsewhere, is an individual affair. The *actual* worth of the piece of music Golub is playing is very much tied to Golub, and severally to any other persons under consideration who might be playing the piece, as having more or less worth relative to them. Except in the way just described, the worth of the music does not stand apart from individuals—unless, perhaps, one is offering some sort of social generalization about what might normally be of value to persons,[38] or one is focused solely upon the level of generic goods.[39] Ordinary language does not really contradict this point either. When we say "it isn't worth it to me," we are often saying both that we do not

---

[38] Of course, if the primary function of ethics is to be a tool of social management, then such a conclusion about the individuality of ultimate worth would be rather disappointing, for that would mean we would have to elide individual differences for the sake of gaining social control.

[39] David Norton speaks of the "complementarity of excellences" and of how it is possible for an individual to "recognize and affirm values different from his own" (*Personal Destinies*, p. 13). At the level of generic goods alone, merit and worth are, as Darwall suggests, "independent" of the agents. But generic goods alone are a long way from a complete account of moral value.

want to pursue it, and yet that we understand fully well why others might. In short, one's welfare is, after all, "reducible" "to the value of developing those very powers" of self-development. The appreciative rapport one has with what is of worth and merit is itself a part of those powers.

2. LeBar

We now turn to a form of constructivism, with whose conclusions, in contrast to those of Darwall, we are highly sympathetic, because it issues in a vision of practical moral action similar to our own. This is the work of Mark LeBar. In his deep and powerful book, *The Value of Living Well*,[40] LeBar provides an account of virtue *eudaimonism* as our ultimate end that explains many of the features that our own account of individualistic perfectionism has from the beginning sought to defend and make clear. When we discuss the entrepreneurial character of human flourishing in the next chapter, we will consider some of these features in detail. But our concern in this chapter is primarily metaethical, and so it is with LeBar's constructivism that we will be occupied.

A good place to begin is with LeBar's analysis of Julia Annas's view of what is involved in appealing to the nature of living things as the ground for normativity. Annas states:

> The normativity of our ethical discourse is not something which emerges mysteriously with humans and can only be projected back, in an anthropomorphic way onto trees, their roots. Rather, we *find normativity* in the realm of living things, plants and animals already.[41]

According to LeBar, "we are able 'to find normativity' in other living things only by putting it there ourselves, in our active deployment of action-guiding norms in interpreting nature."[42] Though he suggests his reading of Annas is compatible with what she states, we find LeBar's view to be the very position that she is rejecting. Indeed, he claims that his target is the idea that "nature can itself some-

---

[40] Mark LeBar, *The Value of Living Well* [hereafter, *VLW*] (Oxford: Oxford University Press, 2013).

[41] Julia Annas, "Virtue Ethics: What Kind of Naturalism?" in *Virtue Ethics Old and New*, ed. Stephen M. Gardiner (Ithaca, NY: Cornell University Press, 2005), p. 13, quoted in LeBar, *VLW*, p. 142 (emphasis added by LeBar).

[42] LeBar, *VLW*, p. 142.

how characterize the norms for success in practical rationality."[43] Perhaps, however, the real issue behind LeBar's analysis of Annas's view is revealed when he states: "If nature gives us a kind of a map, or supplies premises, about how we should reason practically, that still leaves us short of normative guidance in how to read the map or draw inferences from the premises."[44] Moreover, he claims that it is very difficult to understand Aristotle's claim that virtue aims at some mean "relative to us," if one understands that mean to be determined by something we recognize or discover.[45] LeBar's points seem, then, to be that: (1) even if the nature of a living thing were to give us an account of what is good for a particular living thing—including ourselves—that would not give us any reason to attain this good; (2) even if what is good for us were our natural end, we could not really know it, because nature does not tell us how to understand and use that end to determine what is good for us as individuals; and (3) overall, we need a direction in which we are going in order to read the map or to make the inferences that will guide our conduct. Thus, it seems fair to say (and we will add to this conclusion as we proceed) that LeBar does not find normativity in the nature of living things, because he does not see that nature as capable of providing any end or goal for human conduct; and even if it were, he does not see such an end or goal as being compatible with either human rationality or, indeed, with the individualized character of human good.

LeBar instead seeks to provide a constructivist account of ethical norms: true normative practical judgments represent a normative reality, but not any kind of reality that exists independently of our exercise of practical judgment.[46] It is not merely that LeBar regards the exercise of practical judgments as necessary for achievement or actualization of the normative reality that makes a normative judgment true, but rather that there is no normative reality that exists in any sense without the exercise of practical judgment. The normative reality that makes a normative practical judgment true is not "ontologically prior to and independent of our exercise of practical judgment."[47] LeBar insists, nonetheless, that while values are objective properties, they are response-dependent "in that the

---

[43] Ibid., p. 142.
[44] Ibid., p. 142.
[45] Ibid., pp. 127–8.
[46] Ibid., p. 114.
[47] Ibid., p. 118.

characterization we must give of them metaphysically makes essential reference to our responses to them."[48] These responses include everything from our practical judgment of what is fitting for us, to our attitudes and actions that follow both from such judgments as well as from our process of critical reflection about our attitudes and reactions. In general, LeBar defends his version of constructivism by appealing to the idea of best explanation. He believes that his account of constructivism is a coherent and satisfying explanation of both "our natures as normatively sensitive animals, and how the world must be for us to make sense of those natures."[49]

LeBar's reasons for thinking that normative realities cannot exist independently of the exercise of such judgment owe much to J. L. Mackie's skepticism about how there could be anything in reality that could support a normative truth.[50] We have already considered Mackie's skepticism, as well as many of the issues related to his doubts, in our chapter entitled "Because," and so we do not need to reprise what we have said in showing how Mackie's doubts are not applicable to the type of ethical view we espouse. We need, nonetheless, to consider LeBar's reasons for thinking that norms cannot be found in reality apart from the exercise of practical judgments.

Though human beings are certainly capable of observing their own or others' conduct in order to see how well it meets normative standards, this perspective is not fundamental for LeBar. What is fundamental is that human beings are agents who live by making choices. He holds that the "practical point of view" (also called "the deliberative perspective") is prior to the mere observational and descriptive (also called "the critical perspective"), because what is crucial to an ethical reality or norm is that it is for action-guidance.[51] It is our being successful as authors of the conduct that makes our lives worthwhile—or, as we have termed it, the self-directed character of the flourishing life—that makes the practical perspective fundamental. We need norms for acting in this sense, and it is here that LeBar finds wanting the idea that ethical norms exist apart from the exercise of practical judgment. He holds that a judgment that a certain action satisfies normative criteria provides in itself no action-

[48] Ibid., p. 121.
[49] Ibid., p. 112.
[50] Ibid., p. 168.
[51] Ibid., pp. 136–7 and 171–5.

guidance.[52] This judgment may be true; but one could still ask: "But why should I do that?" In effect, it is (and always will be) open to question. LeBar quotes Christine Korsgaard, who claims that "the ability to act is something like the ability to read a map and that ability cannot be given by another map."[53] If there are to be normative standards that are action-guiding, they cannot be thought of as independent of our engaging in practical rationality, because such action-guiding norms cannot be something we merely recognize as realities. They must have some claim on our conduct—some way to provide guidance. Thus, for LeBar, it is impossible for there to be a norm that exists apart from the exercise of practical judgment and, at the same time, provides direction for what we do.

This is not, however, much of an argument for making a constructivist turn, because it simply assumes what it seeks to establish—namely, that there are no action-guiding norms existing independent of practical judgment. This is the basic point at issue; and we have, in previous chapters, provided reasons to reject this assumption. Later, we will briefly return to our central reason for thinking there are action-guiding norms independent of practical judgment. But before doing so, it should be inquired: What reasons does LeBar have for rejecting the possibility that there are action-guiding norms existing apart from the exercise of practical judgment?

In his examination of Richard Kraut's idea that what is good for living things is a cognition-independent relationship of suitability (or "match") between a living thing and what is good for it, LeBar comes up with three reasons to reject such a normative reality. His first reason is that such a view as Kraut's commits one to populating reality with a "fabulously rich ontology of normative facts,"[54] which is a fantastic and highly dubious ontological commitment. His second reason is that such a view cannot do justice to the particular and concrete character of normative guidance without abandoning the role of abstract and universal norms; and thus that it fails to provide an adequate account of what we do as practical reasoners. Finally, if a view such as Kraut's holds that normative facts supervene on non-normative ones, this would also seem to require that

---

[52] Ibid., p. 141.

[53] Ibid., p. 140; Christine Korsgaard, "Realism and Constructivism in Twentieth Century Moral Philosophy," in *Philosophy in America at the Turn of the Century* (Charlottesville, VA: Philosophy Documentation Center, 2003), p. 110.

[54] LeBar, *VLW*, p. 167.

if the non-normative subvening facts are identical, then so must be these normative facts. But why must this be so? What guarantees such a neat fit between the normative and the non-normative? Or must there be an acknowledgment of the role of practical judgments in providing normative realities or facts?

Now, our interest here is not with Kraut's views in particular, but only with the general claim by LeBar that if there are norms that exist apart from the exercise of practical judgment—what LeBar calls "recognitionalism"—then these three seemingly untoward consequences follow. We will consider whether they do.

COGNITION-INDEPENDENT HUMAN GOOD REQUIRES BLOATED ONTOLOGY

It may be one thing to say that exercise is good for a dog, or that being a physician is a vocation to which one may be suited, given one's natural abilities and interests; but for more complex matters such as mulling over whether it would be better to accept a new job offer, practical reasoning quite often involves the consideration of counterfactuals. For example, what if the new job, which is riskier than the old one, pays more? Or, what if the new job gives you more authority and control than you currently experience? Would that make it more suitable for you? LeBar rightly holds that considerations such as these are the stuff of which much practical reasoning is made, and that one needs canons by which to determine the better choice. Yet, LeBar claims that a view such as Kraut's requires that for every counterfactual, there must be a match in reality which grounds a canon.

> And that means the world must be populated by at least as many facts about matches as . . . [one] is capable of imagining, *without the fact that . . . [one] is imagining them playing any role in their existence.*[55]

But this claim does not follow. One's ability to conceive, consider, suppose, or imagine a state of affairs does not require that what is so mentally entertained actually exists. It is perfectly possible to hold that norms are explained by relationships of suitability that exist apart from the exercise of practical judgment, without holding that whenever one considers or conceives of a situation—such as one regarding the conditions that constitute such relationships of suit-

[55] Ibid., p. 167.

ability that is different from what currently exists (for example, what *if* the job offer paid more than it does?)—there is a corresponding reality answering to that consideration or conception. To assume this not only smacks of a crude form of Platonism, but also seems to confuse conceiving of something with asserting that something exists. To conceive of what would be suitable under certain conditions is not the same as to assert that that situation exists.

It may be, however, that Kraut's view does involve a form of Platonism, but no compelling reason has been given for adopting a Platonic view of normative realities. It is perfectly possible to hold that relationships of suitability are discovered and not constructed, without assuming an isomorphism between these normative realities and what is considered or contemplated as suitable in various circumstances. Simply put, there need not be a normative reality corresponding to every normative concept, in order for such concepts to be ultimately of or about a normative reality. The process of abstraction is almost always much more involved. Further, what exists need not be confined to what is actual, but can also involve what is potential; and thus reality can involve change and development. Finally, it may also be that LeBar is held captive by the belief that our cognition of a normative reality is like having a fixed picture of that reality, one that does not reveal its dynamic character—for example, as a relationship of potentiality to actuality. But again, no reason has been provided for adopting this view of cognition. Consequently, LeBar's objection misfires.

COGNITION-INDEPENDENT HUMAN GOOD CANNOT EXPLAIN PRACTICAL REASON

Though Kraut and LeBar (as do we) see what is fitting or suitable as grounded in the particular situation—that is, in the relationship between an individual human being (or some living thing) and some aspect of reality—LeBar holds that such relationships of suitability (or "matches") are not discovered, but instead are constructed by the exercise of practical wisdom. He argues that if they were discovered, then what is discovered would end any justificatory story and make it unnecessary for us to reflect on or cite the particular features of the circumstances of our actions that warrant them.[56] In effect, we would not need to show why our actions are justified. But this is not,

---

[56] Ibid., p. 168.

of course, what we do when we reason about our actions. Rather, when we show how the particular features of the circumstances of our actions warrant them, we move from the particular to the general. We reason abstractly and universally. Indeed, LeBar is correct in this respect: we must employ a "middle term." We must connect a particular action to some feature of our normative lives that justifies what we do. But these considerations are not sufficient to show an incompatibility between the relationship of suitability being something that we discover and its being able to provide a justification. The fact that, in the process of justifying one's actions in terms of a relationship of suitability, one must reason abstractly or universally does not show that what one is reasoning about—in this case, the relationship of suitability—has been constructed. Our practical judgments can be *of* a reality without having to *be* that reality. Nor do these considerations imply that such a relationship cannot be the object of reflection, discussion, or debate. That is to say, that we discover a relationship of suitability does not mean or imply that it is simply "read off" reality in some isomorphic manner, as if there were some map[57] or rule book provided by reality. Discovering the character of a normative reality is no less complicated or involved than is the discovery process for any other reality, and it requires as much ingenuity and skill. But again, generally speaking, there is nothing about the complexity and difficulty of the discovery process or the insight employed in that process that requires a specifically normative reality to be something constructed by practical judgment. LeBar confuses one's *constructing* a judgment about what is good or ought to be done with that judgment's *constituting* what is good or what ought to be done.[58]

In addition, it is by no means clear how the relationship of suitability being something that is grounded in the *particular* situation that we discover is incompatible with its being able to provide a justification. Surely, the argument cannot be that because we reason abstractly and universally, then what is discovered must be abstract and universal. If that were the argument, then it would be a case of confusing the mode of cognition of something with the manner of existence of what is cognized. So, what is really the argument here? It might be the case that, on the one hand, LeBar assumes that the particulars in which a relationship of suitability is nested are ultimately

---

[57] We will have more to say about the map analogy at the end of this section.
[58] We shall see more evidence of this shortly.

"bare," with no form or character, and thus can provide no basis for justification. But if this is so, then an argument needs to be mounted for this assumption. Further, if the particulars are bare, then that also raises the question of just how the relationship of suitability derives its character. Of course, LeBar could claim that the character of this relationship owes nothing to the particulars in which it is nested; but if that is so, then one wonders what would be the point of his own claim to offer a *particularist* account of virtue eudaimonism.[59] On the other hand, if the particulars are not bare, if they do have form or character, then the impetus to make the Kantian ploy and suppose that practical judgments provide a relationship of suitability with its normative character is reduced, because now there is the possibility that the form or character of the particulars provides the basis for justification. Be this as it may, LeBar has not shown that grounding relationships of suitability in particulars that exist independently of the exercise of practical judgment fails to provide an adequate account of what we do as practical reasoners.

COGNITION-INDEPENDENT HUMAN GOOD CANNOT EXPLAIN SUPERVENIENCE

Kraut and LeBar hold that what is good or suitable or fitting supervenes on non-normative properties, and what is good or suitable or fitting cannot differ without some difference in the subvening non-normative properties. But LeBar holds that the explanation of what makes it true that certain non-normative properties underlie certain normative properties cannot be provided by the idea that normative realities exist independently of the exercise of practical judgment. Apart from the awareness of responsive beings like us, there can be no explanation of the necessary connection between supervening normative properties and subvening non-normative properties. It must be accepted as a simple, brute fact. In a world governed by causality, he claims that it can, at best, be only a happy accident that there are normative realities suited to our needs or good *for* us. In effect, there is no explanation of how a normative reality could be an agent-relative norm. But these claims by LeBar are not so much arguments as they are simply assertions of a metaphysical thesis from which he builds his brand of constructivism. In making these claims, he ignores possibilities for which we have argued in previous chapters—namely,

---

[59] LeBar, *VLW*, pp. 179–80.

the role of the centrality of life in understanding the necessary connection between normative and certain non-normative or descriptive properties, the role of the dynamic character of living things (as expressed in terms of the relationship of potentiality to actuality) in grasping the good of a living thing, and the crucial role of teleology in explaining the causality of living things and the normative character of life itself. By ignoring these possibilities, LeBar assumes that a relationship of supervenience between normative realities (for example, the good of a strawberry plant or the good of a human being) and non-normative or descriptive realities (for example, a strawberry plant developing red, juicy, and sweet berries or a human being choosing courageously) is static, and thus affords no way for a normative reality to be agent-relative in character, except through human responses. But as we have indicated, there are more possible sources of explanation of the relationship of supervenience than LeBar is willing to grant.

Even if we leave these considerations aside, however, it is by no means clear that LeBar's constructivism provides the best explanation of the necessary connection between normative and non-normative or descriptive properties. LeBar thinks that his version of constructivism can provide an explanation of the necessary connection between normative and non-normative or descriptive properties, because "facts about *us* as judgers are part of the subvenience base."[60] Further, he states:

> Our practical judgments take the form of a response to sets of conditions we see as relevant to our choice and action—as calling for a practical response. The wise judgments we make *determine* (as a matter of metaphysical fact) what normative responses supervene on those conditions, in the sense that the fittingness of a response to a set of conditions with features $F_1, F_2, F_3, \ldots F_n$ necessitates the fittingness of the same response in any other case in which those features are all and only the relevant conditions. . . . Our judgments *establish* a supervenience relation. That relation is constituted (or constructed) by the exercise of our capacity for normative judgment. That removes much of the mystery as to why the supervenience of the normative approach upon the natural would be a necessary element in conceptual mastery of the idea of the normative.[61]

But does this really remove the mystery? Is the role of human judgment in establishing the supervenience relation any less a brute fact

---

[60] Ibid., p. 213.
[61] Ibid., p. 215.

than normative realities existing apart from such judgments? LeBar claims that we need to judge. But why is this so? Is the judgment that we need to judge itself something that has been constructed by the exercise of our capacity for normative judgment? Is the exercise of our capacity for normative judgment self-justifying? Must we judge, and how are we to understand this "must"? Is it only a logical "must," or is it also moral, and why does it motivate us? What is it that determines what is relevant to our choice and action? What makes our judgments wise? What makes our responses fitting? What is it about human beings that makes us capable of normative thought and action, and how can we possibly be part of a larger reality that is viewed as having no normative features whatsoever? Could we be mistaken in thinking of normativity as an ineliminable feature of the human world? Could not (à la Mackie) all our normative claims just be in error? There are many unanswered questions here that need to be answered—indeed, too many to allow us to conclude at this point that LeBar's constructivism is the better explanation of the supervenience relation than alternative explanations, especially the one we advanced in the previous chapters.

Yet, maybe the most important question for our purposes is this: Do we simply invent our standards? LeBar is sensitive to this concern. When discussing the wise agent who considers fittingness of particular responses to particular concrete sets of conditions, he admits that "it is the judgment of that agent himself that constructs, or constitutes, the normative truth in question . . . "; but he quickly adds that this judgment can secure a "public" character as a result of the constraints "imposed by the supervenience requirement . . . and the capacity for interpersonal criticism and justification made possible by that requirement . . . ." He claims this vindicates calling the wise agent's judgment a "'discovery.'"[62] Further, he adds to the constraints on the wise agent's judgment that his reasons must be intelligible; and he defines publicity as intelligibility, where intelligibility is understood as being able to fit a reason into a hierarchy of ends sought for the sake of living well.[63] Overall, LeBar sees supervenience and publicity as formal demands that a practical judgment must meet, and fittingness as a substantive one.[64]

---

[62] Ibid., p. 220. Note here LeBar's identification of constituting with constructing as well as his scare quotes on the word *discovery*.

[63] Ibid., p. 224.

[64] Ibid., p. 228.

We cannot engage here in a full examination of everything that is involved in LeBar's most sophisticated response, but we can note simply that, despite making every effort to explain how his constructivist account can provide constraints on a wise agent's practical judgments of fittingness, these constraints remain unexplained. They are so because they are understood in terms of what is involved in the exercise of reflective practical rationality itself, without any appeal to a normative basis that exists apart from practical rationality. LeBar states that "the wise agent just does get it right (that's what it is to be so wise) . . . . The objective constraints on the wise agent's scope of vision are just those constraints available to him from the critical perspective he has . . . . "[65] But what is the source of these constraints? Are there constraints because the wise agent judges something as fitting, or does he so judge because of the constraints? LeBar's response to such a Euthyphro-like question is to hold that these constraints result from two sources: first, the *notion* we have of the virtues that constitute the good life; and second, the critical perspective a wise agent's judgment takes on settled intuitions.[66] And if it is asked, "Why do we have the intuitions that we do?" LeBar answers that "these intuitions just are the internalized outputs of deliberative judgments that pass critical scrutiny."[67] This answer will not do, however. Since critical scrutiny provides only formal criteria, what one wants to know is: Why should these "internalized outputs" be regarded as substantively ultimate? Not only: Why does the practically wise agent think that certain virtues are involved in the good life? but also: Why, in the particular case, is this virtue called for, or that practice rejected? This is the basic lacuna in LeBar's approach.

It might be replied, however, that such questions assume that ontology is relevant for ethics, and that this is the very thing that LeBar is rejecting; but we do not think that that is what he is doing.[68] Rather, it seems that LeBar is arguing that his metaphysi-

---

[65] Ibid., p. 230.

[66] Ibid., p. 293. It is important to note here that LeBar defines what is public in terms of what is intelligible, and he holds that it is possible for one to have an intelligible end that is not shared by others. Critical scrutiny requires that an end be shar*able*, but not necessarily shared. This is part of what LeBar means by calling publicity a formal requirement of practical judgment. See ibid., pp. 224–8.

[67] Ibid., p. 294.

[68] If his response, contrary to what we think, does involves an appeal to the primacy of practice over ontology, then we would, of course, respond, as we have earlier in "Tethering I," as well as in Douglas B. Rasmussen, "The Importance

cal account of the nature of normative realities is better than other accounts. If this is so, then he needs to show why the reflections of practical rationality are basic for explaining the nature of normative realities—that they are, in effect, the point where explanation ends—and thus why the desire to have answers to questions of the kind just asked are not appropriate. Of course, LeBar's reason for thinking that these questions are not appropriate, and that the reflections of practical rationality are basic, has to do with his conception of the relationship between human choice and natural teleology. So, it is to that issue that we shall now return.

Because LeBar's account leaves out natural teleology, it seems to him that the only possible way we can justify our normative judgments and provide a response to someone like Mackie is by positing normative realities that we "construct." Indeed, there is very little or no discussion of teleology by LeBar;[69] and when he does introduce the notion of ends, he starts with Kant: "An end is an object of choice (of a rational being), through the representation of which choice is determined to an action to bring it about."[70] Ends come about because of practical rationality. But if this is so, then the actions of anything that does not engage in choice or practical reasoning would not involve ends. There would be nothing about the nature of non-human living things—from amoebas to plants to animals—that would be end-oriented. They would have no natural ends.[71] But as we have seen from our previous chapters, there are good ontological reasons to think that living beings do have natural ends. More importantly, however, to LeBar, it does not seem necessary to situate human agency and practical rationality in this larger context. The greater reality of which human beings are a part is ignored. Rather, he contends that we cannot fully appreciate human agency unless

---

of Metaphysical Realism for Ethical Knowledge," *Social Philosophy and Policy* 25.1 (2008): pp. 56–99, that public reason and practice are not an adequate account of ethical knowledge.

[69] There is no discussion of natural teleology, and "teleology" is indexed only once. Nowhere is there a discussion of how a life-based natural teleology might meet Mackie's concerns.

[70] LeBar, *VLW*, p. 10.

[71] On this view, one might speak "as if" they had natural ends, but there would be nothing in reality and the causal order that would be teleological in character. The most incredible use of the "as if" methodology by LeBar is possibly his claim that exercise is good for a dog not because of what a dog is, but because of the exercise of our rational capacities in judging a dog. See LeBar, *VLW*, p. 264.

we see it as operating in a manner that is radically different from the way other living things act. He thus thinks that if human beings have natural ends in the way other living things do, then it would be incompatible with the robust sense of agency that characterizes human conduct. He thinks we would be "essentially passive," and our actions would take place just as "the phototropic behavior of various plants follows naturally from their sensitivity to light."[72] But clearly this is a false alternative. Human beings can have ends due to their nature as living beings without having to assume, as Tibor R. Machan once put it, that human flourishing is the same as the flourishing of a rosebush.

If our ultimate end is a normative reality that does not owe either its nature or existence to our practical judgments, then there is, of course, a sense in which we are cognitively passive. Our cognition is *of* this reality; and thus, in a fundamental ontological sense, existence is primary and cognition secondary. We most certainly accept this claim. Indeed, we insist upon it. But to say this does not mean or imply that the activity of discovering or recognizing in what our ultimate end consists, or how this end will be achieved, maintained, and enjoyed, is essentially passive. In its essence, human cognition—be it speculative or practical reason—is both about something other than itself *and* self-directed.

To repeat what we noted in Chapter 6, human rationality is fundamentally the power to grasp the world in conceptual terms. Discovering in what one's human good consists and determining how to achieve it is a complex cognitive achievement that would never exist if we were epistemologically passive. But to admit that we are epistemologically active does not show that the activity of knowing one's human good is the source of its very character or existence. That is to say, it does not show that practical rationality is the fundamental ontological ground for the nature and existence of the canons by which the wise practical agent judges. LeBar has failed to show that there is a fundamental incompatibility in holding that normative realities do not owe their nature and existence to the exercise of practical judgments and in holding that practical judgments are essentially active or self-directed.

It seems that the fundamental issue between us and LeBar is whether it is possible for our ultimate end to be discovered or recognized by human rationality and also be a guide for human action—in

---

[72] Ibid., p. 55.

effect, whether it is possible for practical reason to have an ultimate end that it itself did not create but, nonetheless, serves. We have indicated above that there is nothing about having an ultimate end we discover or recognize that requires our practical judgments to be epistemologically passive. To recall what we noted in Chapter 1, the process of human flourishing is, from beginning to end, a "do-it-yourself job."[73] Further, we have also argued in previous chapters that the activities of living things are inherently end-oriented, and that since human beings are living things, our activities—including our rationality—need to be understood in a teleological manner. Our ultimate end, which practical reason serves, is not ultimately grounded, then, in the reflections of practical rationality, but in *what* and *who* we are. Our ultimate end is a natural end; and unless one wants to treat human beings as noumenal selves that stand outside the rest of nature (and LeBar has not presented compelling reasons for so assuming), then there are no good grounds for thinking that our practical judgments are to be understood apart from natural teleology. Finally, to consider that the nature and existence of our ultimate end is ontologically prior to and independent of the reflections of practical judgment is not to indicate that we are—as we have argued throughout this entire work and especially in this chapter—anything less than beings that need to develop the dispositions that will allow us to attain our human goods. We need to make virtue second nature. Nor would any of these considerations demand that this process occur apart from language, convention, and culture, or result in anything incompatible with the highly individualized character of our human good.

It is important to note here a difference between how we and LeBar understand what it means to make virtue "second nature." We both understand second nature to be the habits we develop through our choices to conduct ourselves in various ways; but LeBar sees the establishment of virtuous habits as *transforming* first nature, whereas we see it as *actualizing* it. We do so not because we think every human desire necessarily tracks what is good for us, but because we see desires, like all the basic capacities of our first nature, as being for the sake of our maturation or perfection. In other words, a life in which virtue has been made second nature is a life in which first nature has been actualized, and not simply changed or transformed;

---

[73] Henry B. Veatch, *Human Rights: Fact or Fancy?* (Baton Rouge: Louisiana State University Press, 1985), p. 84.

and it is the end of our first nature that determines what it is for us to be actualized.

To return to the analogy LeBar introduced: we need to create maps to guide our conduct; and these maps can be of various kinds that issue in different types of normative guidance, depending on what aspect of our nature is the object of our focus. We do not start with maps, however, but with the fact that we are already on the road, headed in some direction. So, the reason we create maps in the first place is to attain our human good, which is our ultimate end (and which is constituted by many final ends of which knowledge is but one); and the adequacy of our maps is based finally on our nature and the ontological context in which we operate. What is second nature is neither independent nor constitutive of first nature, any more than maps are independent or constitutive of the reality they seek to express. Just as it is an error to hold that maps are ontologically prior to and independent of the realities they intend to convey, so it is an error to hold that practical rationality is ontologically prior to and independent of normative realities which its function is to judge.

3. Conclusion

We hold that there is an alternative view of practical rationality and human good to the one LeBar presents. We can be both the agent and the object of the activity of self-perfection, without having to assume that the standard by which this process is judged—namely, our ultimate end—owes its existence and nature to this very process. In other words, we do not have to adopt constructivism. The appeal of constructivism, as we have seen, is that it appears to make us the authors of our own moral universe and, thus, preserves our freedom. In contrast to our arguments above showing that the teleological eudaimonist position is compatible with at least a certain type of human freedom, however, we have also witnessed the juridical drift constructivism induces—a drift that moves value away from the individual and, thus, the freedom of the individual. Darwall embraces this drift, while LeBar struggles against it. Either way, constructivism rationalizes value such that what looks like freedom initially is, at best, a freedom not for the agent herself, but for something else, such as "the public." By contrast, since the essential purpose of ethics must be personal flourishing, rather than adherence to certain types of generalized norms, centralizing the good within the agent, rather than in some notion of inherent worthiness or publicity, is to emphasize the primacy of personal responsibility. We now turn to some further reflections on what it means to be a responsible flourisher in practice.

8

The Entrepreneur as Moral Hero

The mature lifetime of the integral individual is a single act, spread over time by the condition of existence that a thing cannot present itself all at once. But in a profound sense, integrity hereby abolishes time by containing its past and its future in its present.

David L. Norton, *Personal Destinies*

The deliberately provocative title of this chapter is not meant to suggest that business is somehow a superior form of activity relative to other occupations. The value of any pursuit, as should be clear by now, is a function of individuals and their various talents and circumstances. Rather, our point will be that although we have been operating at a theoretical plane throughout this work, moral theory is meant, finally, to issue in action—and, therefore, that some of the essential features of market entrepreneurship are also essential components of ethical conduct as we have been advancing it here. So, the question now becomes: What general models of action are best suited to the type of moral theory we are advocating? We noted in the last chapter that Darwall claims that modern ethical theory and practice is essentially juridical. This claim is no doubt accurate; but it does not follow that it represents the only, or even the best, way to understand morality. We have tried to offer in the preceding chapters an alternative perspective—one that might be called an "evaluational" approach to moral action, in opposition to the "juridical." The contrast between the evaluational and the juridical forms may generally map onto our two basic paradigms of an ethics of responsibility and an ethics of respect, with the juridical being more likely to be found in the latter and the evaluational in the former.

In general, the juridical form seeks to render ethical prescriptions in terms of universal claims or rules grounded in a theory of value that is at least partially agent-independent,[1] if not directly agent-

---

[1] By "agent," we mean existing acting agents or what Kant might call phenomenal selves. Noumenal selves are thus at least partially agent-independent or agent-neutral.

neutral. The object of moral action, then, is to find the rule or norm that covers the kind of case at issue and to direct one's conduct according to that rule or norm. The evaluational form, by contrast, is grounded in an agent-relative understanding of value that issues in evaluative judgments which may or may not be applicable to other agents—the applicability to other agents being of derivative concern, at best. Consequently, the object of action here is to assess which course(s) of action is either conducive to or expressive of values appropriate to and perfective of the individual human agent within a given environment.

As we noted, in our Introduction and elsewhere, the juridical form tends to manifest itself in terms of universalized obligations, resulting in a structural identity between politics and ethics. Both of the main forms of ethical theory today—namely, Kantian deontologism and utilitarianism—are juridical: the Kantian, because it explicitly seeks categorical imperatives; the utilitarian, because the requirement to maximize overall social utility itself functions as a categorical imperative—the calculations being a mere means to a generalized prescription.[2] The evaluational approach, as we see it, manifests itself in normative judgments applicable to specific persons and their situations through insights into those situations informed by example, past experience, and principles of conduct. Functionally, the juridical form manifests itself as a form of social management, with individuals being commonly directed to similar actions in like circumstances by the universalized normative rule(s) they are bound to follow. It is prescriptive in nature. By contrast, the evaluational form is not, in the first instance, concerned with regulating social behavior. Instead, it functions as a tool for individual well-being, as guided by principles and exemplars of conduct. It is judgmental in form, in the non-pejorative sense of "judgmental"—that is, "as a judgment." Whether a given normative insight that is appropriate for A is also appropriate for B, even in like situations, is of little theoretical concern to the evaluational ethicist, unless a particular problem calls for it, such as in establishing rules for the social/political order.[3]

---

[2] This was noted long ago by Henry B. Veatch, *Human Rights: Fact or Fancy?* (Baton Rouge: Louisiana State University Press, 1985), p. 33.

[3] It is important to note that a significant part of one's life as a human being involves interaction with others through the construction of social institutions. In these circumstances, institutions will often operate in terms of rules that must apply, in juridical fashion, to all in the same way under similar circumstances.

The meaning, and sometimes even the phenomenological characteristics, of ordinary moral experiences is understood in light of the larger theoretical frameworks that might be applied to them. Darwall, for example, shows that the moral characteristics of the ordinary experience of acting in one's interest are not reducible to the good that results for the agent, despite appearances to the contrary. We, by contrast, would see the respect one may owe to another as a function of what it means to live well as a person, and not as something outside of the good present in the relationship. In both cases, our ordinary experience needs to be accounted for in some way by the theory; but also it would be mistaken to suppose that the theory in no way influences one's experiences, however ordinary. If one, for example, has a religious conviction, an ordinary experience—say, eating a certain food—can take on a meaning which that same action would not have without that conviction. There is no reason to believe moral frameworks are any different in this regard. The point is important, because moral theories, at least by implication, have their heroes. For the juridical form, the hero would be the person who is righteous. For the evaluational form, the hero is the person who is insightful or, as we shall try to detail below, entrepreneurial. In the entrepreneurial mode, the object of investigation is less to come up with prescriptions for conduct than to arrive at meaningful reflection upon it.

1. On the Analogy between Entrepreneurship and Ethical Conduct

The analogy developed here was anticipated by us some time ago,[4] but we are by no means the only ones to suggest that some charac-

---

Needless to say, and as noted just below, the explanation of how to understand such relationships morally will depend on whether one has adopted an ethics of responsibility or an ethics of respect.

[4] "There is a parallel between an argument that [Ludwig von] Mises and [F. A.] Hayek used to show that socialist economies could not efficiently coordinate the production and exchange of goods and services and an Aristotelian argument against rationalistic accounts of the good life. Just as central planners do not have access to the contingent and particular facts that individuals do in exercising the 'entrepreneurial insight' that moves free markets toward equilibrium so too speculative insight into the nature of the human good is not sufficient for a person's well-being to be achieved. . . . Thus, there is a creative role for the individual to play in *discovering* the individuative content that gives reality to the good life

teristics of entrepreneurship might have strong analogs in ethical conduct.[5] Perhaps, however, our way of connecting these characteristics to a general ethical theory gives them some additional emphasis and importance. In any case, chief among the characteristics worth noting initially is one involved in a pair of important distinctions: just as it is fundamental not to confuse entrepreneurial insight with an optimization process in a market setting, neither is ethical insight primarily an optimization process. Regarding the former, as Scott Shane and S. Venkataraman note, following Israel Kirzner, optimization in the marketplace involves a more efficient use of already-employed means to ends. Entrepreneurial insight, by contrast, identifies new means to ends.[6] In this connection, we have seen a number of different thinkers, when characterizing a teleological perfectionist ethic, endeavoring to render the pursuit of our final end as essentially an optimization process. Knowing what our end is, so it is said, will leave us only the task of utilizing the means at our disposal to effectively achieve that end. Yet, as we have tried to show in our various discussions of freedom and self-direction, our end of a perfecting or flourishing life is not like one of using known resources in their most effective manner. Rather, the perfecting is more like discovering means available to such an end that are as yet unknown, or only partially known, to us. Moreover, once those means are discovered, it is equally mistaken to suppose that efficient usage is the only remaining challenge. Because perfecting or flourishing is not a passive state but

philosophers abstractly describe. It is the creativity of human beings, not only in the creation of wealth *but in making moral character*, that a system based on political and economic liberty helps to make possible" (Douglas B. Rasmussen, "Review of Michael Novak's *The Catholic Ethics and Spirit of Democratic Capitalism*," *The American Catholic Philosophical Quarterly* 68.4 [Autumn 1994]: pp. 559–60 [emphasis added]).

[5] See, for example, *Virtues in Entrepreneurship*, ed. Nils Karlson, Mikolaj Norek, and Karl Wennberg (Stockholm: Ratio, 2015). This collection of essays largely explores how virtues apply to entrepreneurship, whereas what follows here is concerned with the application of entrepreneurship to understanding ethical conduct. In this latter vein, see Jared Meyer, "The Moral Perfectionist," in *Steve Jobs and Philosophy*, ed. Shawn Klein (Chicago: Open Court, 2015).

[6] Scott Shane and S. Venkataraman, "The Promise of Entrepreneurship as a Field of Research," *Academy of Management Review* 25.1 (2000): p. 220. We will rely heavily on this article in what follows. The two classic works on entrepreneurship are Israel Kirzner's *Competition and Entrepreneurship* (Chicago: University of Chicago Press, 1973) and Joseph Schumpeter's *Capitalism, Socialism, and Democracy* (New York: Harper and Row, 1934).

an activity, there is virtually a constant reassessment of the adequacy and appropriateness of the means; this, as a consequence, suggests openness and alertness to new opportunities amidst changing circumstances. Finally, optimization suggests efficiency along only one dimension, but flourishing (at least in our view) is inclusive of multiple dimensions. If we are optimizing in any sense when flourishing, it is across dimensions and not within one.

In the ethical context, then, perhaps even more so than in the market context, the connection between resources and ends is not linear. It may be, for example, that by wasting less of a certain input, one will be able to produce more of a certain product, just as by eating less of a certain kind of food in one's pantry, one may become healthier. But such linear examples fail to capture entrepreneurial insight in either markets or ethics for, as we noted, it is discovering as yet *unrealized* resources for the product in question, or similarly gaining new insights into better nutrition, that more closely corresponds to entrepreneurial insight in these cases.[7] In the ethical situation, however, a good like health is never understood in isolation from other goods and thus is not simply optimized in isolation. No doubt, each of us could spend more time at the gym; but the time spent there is time lost somewhere else.[8] The object in ethics, then, is actually *not* to optimize—at least not with respect to any given good—but, rather, to integrate or synthesize properly.

The identification of resources is thus one thing; the follow-up process of optimizing them is another. In market situations, the resources involved in any optimization process are generally material ones. In ethics, by contrast, the "resources" are either largely not, or not at all, material resources. Rather, they are typically forms of activities such as the deployment of certain dispositions of character or the exercise of suitable mental habits or the application of insight and judgment— all of which may, of course, thereby be applied to, or involve, material goods. With these types of "resources," the process can be even less one of optimization than with the coordination of material resources,

---

[7] It should be noted that while we find the basic distinction between optimization and entrepreneurship helpful, there is some ambiguity attached to the distinction that needs clarification, and such clarification is not always manifest in the business literature. The *recognition* of a more efficient means seems to us an entrepreneurial insight, even if the process of optimizing is not. This is because the opportunity to recognize an efficiency seems no different than the recognition of any opportunity.

[8] We will take up the discussion of "opportunity costs" later in this chapter.

because these ethical resources are both more complex in nature and more subject to variation and degree. As a consequence, their integration, even when identified, is more of a matter of fittingness than optimization. No doubt, this need for "fittingness" is a function of the wider context that surrounds ethical insight, rather than the context that surrounds market insight. We shall speak of this matter again momentarily. The general point is to note that, while there is certainly some optimization in the taking of any action, ethical action is not primarily about optimization in the form of "being all you can be," but rather in the form of "being all you would be."

If the foregoing is accurate, individuals in an ethical setting would constantly monitor, evaluate, and adjust any mix of resources as they go along, in order for their actions to be a function of a coherent set of plans and endeavors. Among the resources at one's disposal, upon which one may call to ensure that coherence, are certain dispositions of character (virtues). In ethical theory, it is not uncommon to think of the exercise of virtues along a generally juridical model as being defined dispositions that exert themselves (or ought to) in certain prescribed ways under similar circumstances. Yet, while the development of steady dispositions is indeed central to virtue, once the dimension of practical wisdom is added—and the analogy we are drawing here to entrepreneurship is, after all, about helping to clarify the nature of practical wisdom—then the juridical perspective largely recedes. One's disposition toward generosity, for instance, must be weighed along with one's disposition for, say, justice. It is not, for example, the case that a situation S simply calls for an exercise of the virtue of generosity G; nor is it the case that S at time t_2 must call for the same G as does S at t_1. If one gives money to a beggar on one corner of the block, it does not follow that one must do so at the next corner, even though the only difference between them is t_n. The exercise of any given disposition must be weighed not only against differing circumstances, but also against other available dispositions and plans, such as simply the need to have enough remaining cash to pay for one's fare home. It is thus not the case that in being just or generous, one is simply waiting for an appropriate circumstance in which to manifest such virtues. Rather, the activation and integration of our dispositions are filtered through practical wisdom, which judges applicability, degrees of appropriateness, and general fittingness. A juridical model would tend to employ practical wisdom mainly to determine applicability, most likely of a rule, rather than a disposition, that applies across like cases. The evaluational model we are using here, however, would judge applicability, degree, and coherency of available and appropriate resources, without the burden or pretext of universalizability. The object here is integrity of action, not consistency.[9]

In discussing the field of entrepreneurship studies and entrepreneurship itself, Shane and Venkataraman note that "entrepreneurship involves the nexus of two phenomena: the presence of lucrative opportunities and the presence of enterprising individuals."[10] In presenting the dimensions of this nexus, these authors consider individuals as they face opportunities in the market under three different aspects: (1) the sources of the opportunities; (2) the process of discovery and evaluation of those opportunities; and (3) the exploitation of those opportunities. While there are certainly *dis*analogies between the market entrepreneur and the ethical actor,[11] these basic categories from a market model can, nonetheless, serve our analysis of ethical conduct. We shall, therefore, employ these three concepts in what follows below.

Sources of Opportunities

Shane and Venkataraman note that opportunities are "objective phenomena."[12] In the ethical arena, as we have discussed it here,

---

[9] This is not to say, however, that general principles are to be ignored for the sake of some sort of particularism. As Elaine Sternberg has reminded us, integrity of action and character do presuppose, exhibit, and require consistency within the individual's life: virtuous action stems from a "firm and settled character," which would seem to preclude random, arbitrary, or whimsical variations. Principles help the process of preclusion. Rather, what needs to be excluded is a rigid or mechanical application of rules, and a failure properly to take into account the full complexity of actual situations.

[10] Shane and Venkataraman, "The Promise of Entrepreneurship as a Field of Research," p. 218.

[11] Shane and Venkataraman note, for example, that market entrepreneurship tends to be transitory and not a stable characteristic of market actors (ibid., pp. 218–19). Needless to say, when speaking of something like an ethical virtue, we are talking about a stable disposition, as Aristotle noted long ago. There may, nonetheless, be some similarities, even in this case. The transitory characteristic of entrepreneurship in the market may have to do with the need to exploit an opportunity once recognized. Such exploitation leads one out of the entrepreneurial mode and into the development mode, which may take time. Similarly, moral lives go more smoothly with habituation and the linking properties of principles, as we noted in an earlier chapter. What we may become rests on a foundation of what we are.

[12] Ibid., p. 220.

the situation is quite analogous. While some ethical theories would subjectivize the ultimate source of moral "opportunity" within the agent's reason or will,[13] the sort of perfectionism we have advanced— namely, teleological *eudaimonism*—roots moral opportunity within an objective human nature embedded in an external environment. In the "The Perfectionist Turn" and "Because" chapters, we endeavored to lay this out in some detail. Of course, because human beings do not exist in isolation from their environment, characteristics of that environment in their relation to our nature are part of the very meaning of the objective dimension of our ethical theory, and thus a source of ethical "opportunity." In our framework, then, ethical conduct is not fundamentally a matter of going from "inner" states (for example, intention, will, or disposition) to "outward" action, but rather more the reverse. "Outward" factors or conditions lead to "inner" resolutions and plans of action.[14] In this respect, the objective features—namely, one's own nature and circumstances, jointly considered—constitute the sources of ethical opportunity. Of course, the actions we take in light of those opportunities will have implications, effects, and outcomes that become part of a landscape of opportunities. The landscape may become complicated, but it is no less objective for that. The question still remains, however, as to what is the context for what we are calling "ethical opportunity."

To speak of our nature and the circumstances in which that nature may manifest itself is to point to (objective) factors that define a context which gives activities meaning. In a market setting, entrepreneurial insight and activity are made meaningful in the context of pursuing a profit or, if profitability is too narrowly an economic term, a context of pursuing that which directly contributes to advancing one's interest in some way. Thus, the success of entrepreneurial activity in the market is measured by profitability; but if self-interest, more generally, were our measure, then entrepreneurship could apply to virtually any sort of activity beyond the market, such as politics or sports, provided one is discovering a means to advancing one's interest. In an ethical setting, however, it seems too narrow to define the ethical context as self-interest. Rather, in ethics, the analog to a profit (business) context could be said to be one's "life as a whole." In ethics, then, life as a whole is the context, and flourishing

---

[13] We distinguish this from subjectivism, which relativizes the good completely to the individual's desires or aspirations.

[14] Included in "outward," in this context, is one's own nature.

is the measure of success within that context. "Life as a whole" might be misunderstood as being purely a chronological reference—that is, a reference to one's whole life over time. Yet, it is difficult or impossible to know where one will be at some future point; and one's life is not simply its ending. So, for ethics, the more appropriate understanding would be the "whole of one's life." At any given time, one always carries all the various aspects of one's life—that is, one carries a whole life. Hence, the whole of one's life can be a context for action, no matter how immediate or particular the object of action may be. Indeed, in developing this analogy between entrepreneurship and the ethical agent, we are rejecting the idea that individual human perfection or flourishing is confined to some future state. As David Norton put it, "*Eudaimonism* consists not in living for the future, but in subsuming one's future within one's present."[15] Just as the entrepreneur measures success against a standard of profitability, so an agent would measure ethical success in terms of achieving an integral unity that is the defining quality of one's life as a whole, or one's whole life.

With the context of ethics being the whole of one's life, there cannot be truly ethical entrepreneurship in one area of one's life to the exclusion of the others, because successful practical reasoning considers the whole of one's life, not just a part of it. One could, of course, be entrepreneurial and advance one's interests in one aspect of one's life—say one's social life—to the exclusion of other aspects. But ethical entrepreneurship in its appropriate context would consider one's social life in terms of one's life as a whole; thus, one's interests in one area need to be considered in terms of one's interests, aspirations, and dispositions elsewhere. These would include such matters as one's health, learning, private life, family life, civic life, and the like. Unless one is going to define "self-interest" as meaning the same thing as general flourishing, ethical opportunities take into account the sum of one's opportunities as they contribute to an understanding of one's life as a whole, not just part of it. Why must that be the case? The reason is that our *telos* is not about one feature of our existence, but arises from our nature generally, as we hope to have indicated in earlier chapters.[16] Our telos is not, in other words,

---

[15] David L. Norton, *Personal Destinies: A Philosophy of Ethical Individualism* (Princeton: Princeton University Press, 1976), p. 237.

[16] We take this view of the holistic context of ethical opportunity to be a kind of neo-Aristotelian updating of the doctrine of the "unity of the virtues," especially

simply to maximize our health, our social standing, our intellect, or any other dispositional feature of our nature. Rather, our telos consists in maturity or fulfillment, which are themselves concepts implying integrated development and action regarding an array of dispositions, talents, and judgments. Our point here addresses why we spoke earlier of "fittingness" as being so important to realizing that ethical opportunity should not be understood as an optimization process. The problem is less one of getting more out of something than it is of realizing how to fashion that "something" in the first place, in light of a multiplicity of factors.

With the appropriate contexts now in mind, one notices that typically, in market settings, entrepreneurial opportunities are often a function of an existing disequilibrium. One might notice, for example, that by employing alternative resources, one can produce a good at a cost below a current price and realize a profit from so doing. Entrepreneurship in the market provides course-correction to the market. The analog here in ethics may equally be a recognition of a need for course-correction of one's actions. One might notice, for example, some version of "working too hard," to the neglect of other important factors of one's life, such as family, friends, civic responsibilities, or even such things as one's own talents or the care with which one undertakes any of these. With the context being one's life as a whole, a constant monitoring of the various dimensions of that life is needed to equilibrate its various dimensions, much as a market needs equilibration, and for similar reasons. Markets in disequilibrium waste or neglect resources that might otherwise have been more fully exploited. There is no reason to suppose that the resources of one's life are any less subject to waste or neglect, and thus any less a possible source of opportunities.

The idea of monitoring the resources that go into fashioning a life for ourselves naturally leads us to the second main category of analysis, namely, the process of discovery and the evaluation of opportunities. Before taking that step, however, we need to emphasize a point about the objectivity of ethical opportunity in another way—namely, the social. Since Plato's discussion of the Ring of

---

if virtues are seen as certain types of actions and not simply dispositions of character. This is because for actions to be meaningful, a context for understanding them is needed whereas, for dispositions, such is not the case. For an interesting related discussion see Howard J. Curzer, *Aristotle & the Virtues* (Oxford: Oxford University Press, 2012), pp. 293ff. on the reciprocity of virtue.

Gyges in *The Republic*, philosophers have recognized that there can be "opportunities" that have to do with advancing oneself at the expense of others. Recently, the term "golden opportunities" has been appropriated to label such "opportunities" where one is in a position to take advantage of another without detection, by violating or diminishing a trust relationship between them.[17] This "opportunity" is especially available in what David C. Rose labels "third degree opportunism."[18] In these cases, we are speaking of a contractual relationship which inherently and intentionally lacks specificity in a number of areas of the relationship, in order to allow an agent the flexibility to adapt to needed changes and circumstances. A boss might have such an arrangement with his employee, where neither every action of the employee was defined in advance, nor was it desirable to do so. As Rose points out, these relationships "are by definition beyond the reach of institutional mechanisms that work through external incentives."[19] Another way of putting this point is to say that one individual is counting on another not to take advantage of a trust between them.

However poorly a society might progress if third-degree opportunism were prevalent, it might seem, on our account, that such forms of opportunism could be objective opportunities for one to exploit. Of course, one is immediately tempted to respond that such opportunities would not be ethical ones. That answer is, no doubt, correct; but from what we have said to this point, it may not be clear why exploiting a "golden opportunity," where one's advantage comes at the expense of another, has to be a detriment to "the whole of one's life." A detailed response cannot be offered here; but the seeds of one are contained in the explanation of the problem—namely, "the whole of one's life." The whole of one's life includes one's relations with others and, perhaps more importantly, what kind of person one is to be and become. It is usually when one narrows down one's attention from the whole of one's life to part of it that an opportunity is seen as a "golden" one. Hence, the unethical nature of taking advantage of such an "opportunity" is neither simply a function of its violating a social norm, nor even due to its possible effect upon the

---

[17] David C. Rose, in *The Moral Foundations of Economic Behavior* (Oxford: Oxford University Press, 2011), p. 6, credits Robert Frank with the term, but uses it himself in connection with "third degree opportunism."

[18] Compare ibid., pp. 35ff.

[19] Ibid., p. 6.

rest of society or upon one's character per se. The unethical aspect of the "opportunity" comes from its inducement toward narrowness of focus and, hence, of the truncating of practical wisdom, such that one's efforts are diverted from the building of an appropriate character for one's life as a whole. We are repelled by third-degree forms of opportunism, not simply because the mutual understanding of trust is violated, but also because it puts the relationship we have with ourselves as a whole in disequilibrium by eroding what we ought to be in our relations with others generally. In other words, what we owe to others should line up with what we owe to ourselves (trust-worthiness); and the exercise of third-degree opportunism removes that balance.[20]

Objectivity, then, is always circumscribed by a normative framework. In the market, that normative framework is a narrow but well-defined one—namely, the pursuit of profit. Success or failure in the use of resources is measured by profitability, and thus profitability is a norm for market conduct. Profitability is itself thought to be constrained by ethical norms.[21] One might be profitable, for example, in the sale and purchase of babies; but the immorality of the practice would forbid it. Similarly, one might make profits through acts which compromise some deeply held value; but presumably, the "gain" at the expense of one's integrity would be morally condemned. Although such points are well-taken, and human flourishing is a broader and more fundamental normative context than mere profitability, such contrasting cases are more misleading than instructive. We see profitability in a market context, where the metanorms relevant to trade and exchange are present and functional,[22] as being an extension of the requirements for human flourishing, and not as something in inherent conflict with it. This is because market profitability typically represents enhanced value-realization, even if measured in monetary terms. That there are possible pathologies connected to the process, such as greed and "golden opportunities," does not thereby diminish the inherent value-enhancement of ordinary market entrepreneurial

---

[20] For a related approach to this issue, see Paul Bloomfield, *The Virtues of Happiness: A Theory of the Good Life* (Oxford: Oxford University Press, 2014).

[21] For a neo-Aristotelian analysis of what they are, see Elaine Sternberg, *Just Business: Business Ethics in Action*, 2nd ed. (Oxford: Oxford University Press, 2000).

[22] See Douglas B. Rasmussen and Douglas J. Den Uyl, "Making Room for Business Ethics: Rights as Metanorms for Market and Moral Values," *The Journal of Private Enterprise* 24.2 (Spring 2009): pp. 1–19.

actions. As a consequence, profit-making in the market should be regarded as an inherently legitimate form of ethical expression lying on a continuum of value-enhancement that marks the actual living of a flourishing life.

DISCOVERY AND EVALUATION OF OPPORTUNITIES

This process is, no doubt, the central category in our evaluational ethics of responsibility. With practical *wisdom* at the center of ethical theory and conduct, we have placed the bulk of the weight of the moral enterprise upon our rational natures: it is they that are calling for fulfillment and exercise in cases of moral action. Shane and Venkataraman note that the discovery and evaluation of opportunities in market entrepreneurship depend upon two factors, both of which are cognitive: the possession of prior information necessary to identify an opportunity, and the cognitive properties necessary to evaluate it.[23] With respect to the first, knowledge as a generic good is one of the central human goods. The disposition to know is itself a generic human trait. But, of course, the object of ethics is action; and action is undertaken by individuals. Hence, knowledge regarding action must ultimately be more individuative than generic. Indeed, the latter form of knowledge can be approached by experience with the former sort (similar to induction); but the reverse is seldom the case, since generic knowledge alone does not speak to any specific individual. The so-called Aristotelian "practical syllogism," where a universal is applied to the particular, still requires the minor premise in order for a conclusion about action to be realized and thus for action to occur.

All this is to say that knowledge needs to be tailored to the individual and to that individual's circumstances for effective action to take place, where "effective action" is understood as action that contributes to or is expressive of the individual's flourishing. If moral opportunities are situations where certain actions will contribute to human flourishing of self or others, then identifying situations where such contributions can be made may depend upon something like "prior information." Yet, this last point seems somewhat inapplicable to moral matters, because we tend to think of morality in binary terms: either X is moral, or it is not moral. In other words, if

---

[23] Shane and Venkataraman, "The Promise of Entrepreneurship as a Field of Research," p. 222.

something violates a moral norm, little prior information is needed to identify the violation and pronounce it wrong (or vice versa, in the case of moral propriety). We do not, for example, need much prior information to discern whether a lie is wrong or right, only whether what was said was true, and what was the intention behind it. While it is the case that people can pass moral judgments with little or no "prior knowledge" (besides the norm in question), the critical moral issues that contribute significantly to flourishing and well-being are seldom so simple as to whether a lie was told or not. Communism and socialism are lies with respect both to what contributes to prosperity and to what respects human dignity; but experience and knowledge of the workings of social orders would be significantly helpful in rebutting the pretenses of such positions.[24] Even in less dramatic or complex contexts, a "lie" might be excusable in certain situations; but determining that situation correctly may, again, require experience and prior knowledge about human conduct, feelings, and appropriate contexts. We have all experienced the child who blurts out the truth, when perhaps a "lie" would have contributed more to the well-being of all. Hence, we consider so-called moral norms to be just as much resources for action as reasons for action. A rejection of a juridical model of ethics in favor of a responsibility model does not reject moral norms, but it does require that they be measured against the standard of contributions to human flourishing.

The market entrepreneur, of course, uses knowledge to spot potential opportunities that can produce profitable outcomes in a competitive environment. To successfully see in a market what others may not be seeing is obviously likely only if one is not a new player in that market, or if one is lucky. But as F. A. Hayek notes, the process of being in a competitive environment is itself a discovery process.[25] In a competitive market, competition produces signals through the price mechanism about the relative values people in that market have for what is being offered. Hayek stresses that a competitive market is not one that conforms to an ordered hierarchy of values but, instead, is one in which no overarching set of values is either produced or conformed to. Individuals may retain a hierarchy of values; but in

---

[24] If one does not share our political perspective, an equivalent observation might be tried by replacing communism or socialism with whatever ideology would benefit from experience.

[25] F. A. Hayek, "The Use of Knowledge in Society," *The American Economic Review* 35.4 (September 1945): pp. 519–30.

their interaction with numerous others, no designed or contemplated resulting value hierarchy obtains over the whole social order.[26] Ethics would seem, by contrast, not to have the benefit of a market through which ethical judgments could be evaluated, precisely because ethical judgments define value and seem relatively invariable as to their worth (the value of an ethical norm upon which judgments are based does not seem to fluctuate). Moreover, ethics would seem to be defined by an overarching hierarchy of pre-existing values that define the domain of ethical judgments, and such a hierarchy is not present in the Hayekian market order. Yet, is it necessarily the case that hierarchical value structures are central to ethics in a way that is dissimilar to markets? Or, could there, instead, be an analog in ethics to the motivating force of entrepreneurial profits in a market situation, for discovering ways toward the improved use of resources?

In answering these questions, let us begin by correcting a possible mistaken inference about the market and values. Markets do prioritize values to some degree by rejecting fraud and force in exchange relationships, and possibly, also, by giving importance to trust and cooperation. Hence, there is some kind of ordered value hierarchy even when speaking of markets, though there may be no anticipated or foreseen pattern to the outcomes that result from the respect of these values. No doubt, this is not the kind of value hierarchy Hayek was referring to; and no doubt, some ethicists would say that the particular values just mentioned are hardly a complete list, or even a list of the deepest and most important values. In both of these cases, we would agree. But saying that calls upon us to reflect further on our context. In the case of the market, we are talking about an unknown number of individuals who are engaged in trade, and most of whom are strangers to each other. To engage in trade, certain "rules of the game" need to be followed, or peaceful exchange will not occur. Ethical norms are, no doubt, wider and, in some sense, prior to market values; but the exercise of those norms still typically takes place in a social context. So, although refraining from force and fraud may not be the highest of values or the only ones, those norms may still be the most important for establishing a *political* context, where the possibility of pursuing any values is secured. As a result, the value structures for markets and politics, as we have argued in *Norms of Liberty*,[27] are roughly the same. The point here, though, is

---

[26] Ibid., pp. 519–30.

[27] Douglas B. Rasmussen and Douglas J. Den Uyl, *Norms of Liberty: A Perfectionist*

to note that entrepreneurs are dependent upon, if not accepting of, a certain value hierarchy in the world in which they act. Ethical actors are no different in this regard, and for the same reasons: ethical actors also need an appropriate social context so that ethical action can take place. Similarly, entrepreneurs might pursue profit to the exclusion of all other values; but then, ethical actors might pursue one value to the exclusion of others, as well. Perhaps now, then, we must grapple with the difference between the limited pursuit of a value (profit) undertaken by the entrepreneur and the much more expansive pursuit of values undertaken by the ethical actor. The difference seems to be that ethical actors must have the full range of their life values before them, while entrepreneurs need only concentrate on profits.

Before becoming too carried away with this difference, however, we might note, first of all, that entrepreneurs are acting agents; and unless their pursuit of profits has become pathological, they are pursuing them to fashion a life for themselves. Likewise, ethical agents do not act in abstraction from society or the material world. So, in this regard, entrepreneurs are in pursuit of an answer to the basic ethical question of what kind of life one should fashion for oneself, and ethical agents are asking themselves how they can transform the world around them to accomplish that same end. The former quest could compel one to consider one's pursuits in light of all others, and the latter to discover opportunities that produce benefits not yet exploited. Yet, this level of similarity perhaps strikes one as a bit abstract and facile. It would seem best to concentrate for a moment on just what we are talking about when speaking of "profit," and whether that has any ethical analog.

As we shall use "profit" here, we are not referring to the monetary result of some entrepreneurial activity. Rather, generally following F. A. Hayek, James Buchanan, and Israel Kirzner, profit refers to the added value that results from a redeployment of resources, as a consequence of an insight into their possible use. In the marketplace, the monetary outcome is a signal of the degree of success of one's insight—that is, the degree of profit.[28] But value must first

---

Basis for Non-Perfectionist Politics [hereafter *NOL*] (University Park: Pennsylvania State University Press, 2005), p. 288; and Rasmussen and Den Uyl, "Visible and Invisible Hands," *The Freeman: Ideas on Liberty* (April 2007): pp. 37–40.

[28] Perhaps something like "happiness" or "efficacy" would mark the degree of benefit in ethical action.

be discovered, so discovery itself becomes a key concept in market entrepreneurship. It is a concept seemingly absent in ethics, because the normative rules or principles are thought "to be there." In the market situation, by contrast, what is discovered is an insight into how to integrate resources in a manner different from the way they are currently being integrated, in a form not yet seen by others. One might, for example, realize that a given output can be more efficiently produced at less cost than is presently the case, thus allowing for the sale of the good at a lower price. Or one might notice that if something is simply offered in a different way, more people are attracted to it, thus increasing sales. Competition, as Hayek notes, increases the *incentive* to look for better alternative resource uses, while also offering more alternatives to evaluate and consider. Without competition, one might be satisfied with current dispositions, making the variety of ideas to evaluate much more limited. In ethics, again by way of contrast, there seems to be little room for innovation; and discovery—in the sense of finding what others have not seen before—even appears anathema to ethics. After all, it would seem that it is precisely those rules we all understand that are applicable to ethics, not some principle or norm no one has yet discovered. Yet, we should pause to note that even if ethics was simply a matter of applying rules to situations, doing so may sometimes demand a degree of subtlety and, thus, innovation, analogous to the insight required by entrepreneurial activity.

In regard to market entrepreneurship, Buchanan notes that a significant feature of entrepreneurship in the market is disappointment;[29] and that, too, would seem to be inapplicable to ethical processes. The market actor approaches the world with certain expectations and takes actions believing in certain outcomes, based upon how she judges the world to work. Yet, those expectations are often frustrated and unrealized. In such a process, there is "disappointment" with the results, and then a search for alternatives. If "disappointment" could be described simply as a response to an unrealized expectation, however, it need not connote something negative. An

---

[29] James Buchanan, "Resource Allocation and Entrepreneurship," in *The Collected Works of James M. Buchanan*, Vol. 12 (Indianapolis: Liberty Fund, 2000), pp. 160ff. F. A. Hayek mentions this also: "its [competition's] salutary effects must manifest themselves by frustrating certain intentions and disappointing certain expectations" ("Competition as a Discovery Procedure," trans., Marcellus S. Snow, *The Quarterly Journal of Austrian Economics* 5.3 [Summer 2002]: p. 10).

expectation that a certain combination of resources will produce a certain result (whether one is employing those resources oneself or another is doing so) could be "disappointed" merely to the extent that one sees another (better) way to deploy those same resources. There is, in other words, a discontinuity between expectation and result, the response to which we are labeling "disappointment." In this respect, insight would be a function of "disappointment," without carrying with it all the negative connotations normally associated with the term "disappointment." It is important to bring out this point, because entrepreneurship is not an academic exercise, but takes place among agents already engaged in the use of resources. They gain their insights in the course of practice, and not from a philosopher's armchair. In other words, they are continually monitoring actual actions, rather than simply contemplating various scenarios in a setting removed from practical activity. Consequently, "disappointment" in practice does not necessarily imply dissatisfaction, as it might if one's vision of something were frustrated. Indeed, "disappointment" might produce the opposite, if one sees a superior alternative.

Now, if ethical actors are, indeed, actors and not ethical theorists—meaning, they are actually engaged in practical activity, and not simply contemplating possible scenarios of action—then discovery and disappointment would seem to be every bit a part of the ethical enterprise as of the entrepreneurial. In either case, knowing what one should do does not come packaged neatly with ready-made solutions to the problems actors face; nor is one likely to develop appropriate insights abstracted from the concrete situations. Indeed, even if some norms and principles are familiar and available for consideration, multiple principles can conflict or be in tension; and the successful moral actor is one who negotiates them well. It does not take much imagination to appreciate this last point. One might, for example, have promised one's mother to visit her on Sunday. When Sunday arrives, however, one receives a call offering a business opportunity that must be taken advantage of on that day, or the opportunity will be lost. One obviously has obligations to one's mother; yet one has obligations to oneself, as well. There are many possible scenarios for trying to resolve this tension: for instance, one might imagine asking one's mother to relieve one of the promise or seeing one's mother in the evening instead of during the day. Indeed, the relative costs of doing one of the actions to the complete exclusion of the other could be weighed as well; and no a priori solution seems plausible, however many moralists there might be who claim promises trump every-thing. By the same token, there are alternatives under these same moral principles that are obviously bad ones—such as taking the business opportunity while making no effort to contact one's mother, or simply ignoring the business opportunity altogether, because one "made a promise." Our point here is not to rehearse scenarios, but to suggest that actions in the real world are complex, and that the successful actors in ethics and markets are those who consider all the available alternatives and find ways to either eliminate or lessen conflict among existing forces or principles.

If the foregoing is correct, then ethics is ultimately better modeled on exemplars than upon rules, as Aristotle seems to have under-stood.[30] We will mention this again below; but here we are saying that if we displace the juridical model of trying to establish conform-ity of rules, and thus behavior, as the goal of ethics, and substitute instead a perfectionist standard of personal fulfillment, then exem-plars become significantly more central. Just as successful market players serve better than manuals for action as models for other entrepreneurs, ethical "entrepreneurs" serve better than do norms of conduct alone, and for the same reason: they have managed, through disappointment, to discover ways worth emulating by others. In this respect, a morally profitable action would be one where the expecta-tion (or presence) of a tension among principles is removed or dimin-ished, such that the costs to one's integrity are thereby minimized or eliminated.

If our analysis of the role of discovery in ethics is plausible, we would be pushing the paradigm of ethics away from a view which sees ethics as primarily defining *constraints* upon living, and toward a view which sees ethics as both an aid to and an expression of actu-ally living well. One reason it might be difficult to see discovery and innovation in ethics is because ethics, on the former view, is essen-tially self-contained and primarily concerned with the permissible or obligatory, as opposed to the impermissible or arbitrary. If there is a "living well" in this approach, it comes through the act of taking those obligatory actions for their own sake—that is, internalizing them because they are ethical. And because the norms are seen ulti-mately as constraints upon action—or at least as regulatory—they trump all other considerations for conduct. In this respect, life tends to go on around, or in compliance with, the constraints set by ethical

---

[30] For example, Aristotle, *Nicomachean Ethics*, 1105b 5–14.

norms, rather than through them; and any compliance with those norms has value quite independently of its contribution to living well. Hence, compliance has its value in terms of ethics alone, unlike a teleological framework such as ours, where ethical conduct is given value in light of its contribution to our telos.[31] Our point here is to suggest that any initial reservations about the analogy between ethical conduct and the dimensions of entrepreneurship we have been discussing may be a function of one's having a certain perspective on ethics that differs from the one we have been advancing. As we argued in Part I of this book, once the necessity of the juridical form is abandoned, a certain sense of liberation accrues, for ethics becomes an aid to living, not a restriction upon it.

A second reservation may have to do with the difference between action in a market setting, where one's "success" would seem to be a function of others, and ethics, where "success" seems ultimately a function of oneself. After all, in a market setting, one's "discovery" and resulting profit is, in the end, a function of whether others appreciate the outcome made possible by that discovery, to such an extent that they divert some of their own resources toward the entrepreneur's product. It is even conceivable that the entrepreneur could personally find little value in the very product she produced, and succeeds simply because others happen to find value there. It is hard to imagine similar "success" in an ethical context. Our purpose here, however, is not to suggest that every component of entrepreneurship has an analog in ethics, but only that some key elements do and, thus, how noticing these can be instructive.

We have commented above on profit. Let us grant here that even if it were possible in a market setting to make a profit with a product one does not use oneself, ethical success cannot be found with an indifference toward the values one pursues and expresses. In ethics, one's "product" and one's values are the same, the former not being instrumental to the latter. Given our individualism, we are not likely to find much merit in an approach that sees final confirmation of ethical success in the opinions of others. Ethics *could* be conceived like

---

[31] We are not suggesting that no ethical norms are constraining, or that constraining norms do not qualify as "ethical." Instead, our point is to attack again what we called "equinormativity" (see Rasmussen and Den Uyl, *NOL*, pp. 33–41), and to suggest that norms and principles are not all reducible to one type, but instead have different characteristics, depending on their function, which is ultimately determined with reference to our telos of flourishing.

a market where values are "traded," and norms are the "prices" that result from the intersubjectivity of normative trading. Perhaps this is a way of reading Adam Smith; and perhaps there are interesting analogies to be drawn, in this connection, with market entrepreneurship. Yet, our individualistic teleological eudaimonism must here, at least for the moment, move us in a different direction. Consequently, what seems to us worth exploring a bit further is the nature of discovery in the market, as it might relate to the type of ethics we are advocating.

In pursuit of the aforementioned end, the key concepts we have yet to explore in an ethical context, yet frequently mentioned in connection with entrepreneurship in a market context, are risk, uncertainty, and discontinuity. When these concepts are properly considered, it becomes significantly less clear that the defining characteristics of entrepreneurs, even in a market setting, are a function of others, though their profit might be. Instead, it is almost *in spite* of others that entrepreneurs exhibit their entrepreneurship. We can begin to see this point if we start with discontinuity. The market entrepreneur notices a discontinuity between, let us say, prices in one place and those in another for the same good. Buchanan argues[32] that this situation presents an opportunity for "economic arbitrage" to the advantage of all parties. What the entrepreneur has discovered is a way of eliminating the discrepancy between the prices, by purchasing at one price and selling at another, such that the overall market effect is to close the difference between them. In other cases, a discontinuity might be closed by a product innovation that reconciles the distance between two related, though conflicting, desires. For example, one might have not only the desire to travel from point A to point B, but also the desire not to take too much time or trouble to do so. Under current conditions, time and trouble either restrict travel or make it unpleasant to do so. In this case, an entrepreneur might discover a quicker, more pleasant means of traveling, such that the incompatibility between the two desires is significantly diminished. In all such cases of entrepreneurship, a (to some degree) reconcilable discrepancy between discontinuous, but potentially related, factors is achieved.[33]

---

[32] James M. Buchanan and Alberto di Pierro, "Cognition, Choice, and Entrepreneurship," in *The Collected Works of James M. Buchanan*, Vol. 12 (Indianapolis: Liberty Fund, 2000), p. 150.

[33] A discrepancy can also exist between two as yet unrelated factors, which have the potential for a relationship—unrecognized, until an entrepreneur joins them—to consumer satisfaction. A recent example might be bacon and ice cream!

Yet, the reconciliation of a discrepancy, or the recognition of a discontinuity, carries with it two other factors that help individualize the entrepreneur's act and set it apart from the perceptions of others—namely, risk and uncertainty. It seems evident that if something new is being offered by entrepreneurs, there must be an accompanying degree of uncertainty about its outcome or reception. It is here that entrepreneurs invest—that is, risk—themselves in their plans of action. For others may see exactly the same facts and, indeed, the entrepreneur may even describe those same facts to others; yet, despite this observation or description, those others choose not to invest themselves in the described opportunity, because they fail to see the discrepancy in quite the same way. In this regard, the entrepreneur "stands alone" in distinction from others, and perhaps even stands contrary to their support and understanding. Because of this, it is possible to suggest that the discovery of which we are speaking is generally closer to a creation than an insight and, thus, is a basis for Schumpeter's famously describing entrepreneurship as "*creative destruction.*" Buchanan, however, puts our point better:

> There exists basic uncertainty, at the cognitive level, about the set of possibles that might be realized upon choice or consequent to choice. In a very real sense, the entrepreneur creates his own opportunity set and the act of choice enters a new world that unfolds with choice itself. When this point is recognized, formal theories of probability have little or no contribution to make to our understanding of entrepreneurial choice.[34]

There is thus not some "fact" out there that is visible to the entrepreneur and either invisible to or simply unrecognized by others. Rather, what one has is an imaginative reordering or reconnecting of facts or processes that may be potentially visible to all, but which, for whatever reason, others do not imagine or are unwilling to imagine. That is why entrepreneurs not only stand alone but also attach themselves to the outcome in a way that goes well beyond mere recognition of an opportunity. As Buchanan says above, the choice is itself opportunity-creating, and not merely the terminus of a set of perspectives.

Yet, however true the foregoing may be for market processes, ethics would seem to involve little risk or uncertainty, except perhaps with respect to the consequences that may be produced by any given ethical action. Certainly, it seems odd to say that in doing what is right, one puts at risk the right thing to do, or that a sense

---

[34] Buchanan and di Pierro, "Cognition, Choice, and Entrepreneurship," p. 150.

of uncertainty describes our insight when we see something as right (or wrong), or even that ethical action is a creative act. Moreover, continuity—at least, of appropriate principles—seems the better description of the flow of ethical conduct than does discontinuity. While all these points are certainly true in some fashion—and, again, without endeavoring to overstretch the analogy—perhaps there are important dimensions of ethical conduct that are, nevertheless, characterized by risk, uncertainty, and discontinuity. We can perhaps take our bearings on this from our preceding discussion of profit. There we saw that the essence of "profitability" was integrity; and with integrity as our standard, the concepts with which we have been dealing do, indeed, become more relevant.

Integrity, as the term suggests, involves integrating one's values and principles in such a way that they both cohere and functionally contribute to one's flourishing, either in developing it or maintaining it. As we have suggested above, what is directly relevant here is that our circumstances continuously challenge the continuity of our values and principles in two ways: by providing impediments to the successful realization of those values and principles, and by offering attractive alternatives that demand consideration as to their fit within our own lives. Because a given value or principle is not monadic, each one we might adopt will have some effect upon others. And if we are engaged in a project of considering our life as a whole, the degree to which values are so affected is the degree of risk we confront. The successful market entrepreneur not only takes risks, but also manages them—as does the successful ethical actor. The point here is not to entrench values in the face of alternatives, or to challenge their realization, but to consider their value in light of their impact upon other values and principles. Successfully integrating values in one's life is no less a reconciliation of discontinuities than is market entrepreneurship. For the ethical actor, then, risk in regard to values lies somewhere between dogmatism and incontinence, which is why we admire the agent who is both adaptable and principled: that agent both takes and manages risk.

Uncertainty is no different in this regard. Unless one is a dogmatist, uncertainty accompanies risk because, in a complex, changeable environment, one faces uncertainty, not only in the assessment of alternatives, but also in their adoption. This uncertainty is what necessitates practical wisdom. In other words, uncertainty demands that we monitor our conduct and reflect upon the various synergies and discontinuities that may result from any course of action we take. The market entrepreneur confronts a world of diverse activities and investment possibilities which carry with them a social value in terms of relative prices which must be evaluated. Similarly, the ethical actor is confronted with a myriad of choices whose "prices" are the cost to be paid in maintaining his or her "value universe," when investing in any possible alternative. In ethics, perhaps, we have more aids, in the form of ethical principles, to making such choices than we do in the market. But as we noted above, principles are themselves subject to the problem of successful integration, and thereby continue to demand practical wisdom of the agent.

At this point, in order to correct a possible misimpression, we should return to our earlier dismissal of analogizing ethical conduct to trade. The individualized character of one's human flourishing is not to be understood in isolation from other actors. As social animals, a significant part of our flourishing is concerned with sociability, ranging from cooperation to friendship. The core question in ethics is still: "What is one to do with *one's own* life?" but one's own life is very much tied up with the lives of others. In this regard, as numerous authors from Adam Smith to Jonathan Haidt have pointed out, our conduct is filled with acts of reciprocity and, as such, we are continually traders in value. In this regard, also, one faces a "marketplace" of values which, depending on one's choices, implicate one in various forms of reciprocity that are a function of the deeds individuals do for one another. Norms for particular forms of reciprocal engagement may develop concerning the appropriate "payment" due; but our being exchangers of value as we relate to others also means that opportunities are there for entrepreneurial engagements. Certainly, the terms with which we have been working, such as risk, uncertainty, discontinuity, profit, and the like, are applicable to interpersonal relations, for managing our relations with others has many of the same value dimensions as managing our relationship with ourselves.

One might continue to object that, unlike the market where everything is instrumentalized, including one's relations with others (since the end is profit, not the relationship itself), ethical conduct never instrumentalizes the other in any reciprocal arrangement. We would object to this characterization of the market.[35] Laying that issue

---

[35] We would hold that honest trading actually shows respect for, rather than instrumentalizes, the other. It assumes that another is a responsible agent capable of managing his or her value universe.

aside, however, it is important to recognize that reciprocal relations among persons are essentially explorations of potential combinations of values, and that those combinations carry with them not only risks and uncertainties, but opportunities for unique connections, as well. The achievement of a friendship, for example, is a process in which one faces possible failure, unimagined benefits, disruptions, and both challenges to and enhancements of one's integrity vis-à-vis one's responsibilities to others. The notion that something like a friendship is just "good" ignores the fact that friendships are activities and, like all activities, prone to dissolution, failure, stresses, and the like, as well as potentially productive of immense benefits. The maintenance of a friendship may, for example, call upon one to lessen investments in other parts of one's life that pose the same issues for practical wisdom as any other pursuit of value.

In short, the entrepreneurial discovery of means to reconcile discontinuities with innovative restructurings of value relationships seems to us to be as central to living the ethical life as it is to living the commercial one. This conclusion leads us to the third and final dimension of entrepreneurship, which Shane and Venkataraman refer to as the "exploitation of entrepreneurial opportunities."[36]

EXPLOITATION OF OPPORTUNITIES

For Shane and Venkataraman, this issue primarily concerns the propensity of an individual to act upon entrepreneurial insights. As they note:

> The exploitation of an entrepreneurial opportunity requires the entrepreneur to believe that the expected value of the entrepreneurial profit will be large enough to compensate for the opportunity cost of other alternatives (including the loss of leisure), the lack of liquidity of the investment of time and money, and a premium for bearing uncertainty.[37]

In ethical life, also, the tendency is to conform to predominating values and norms, unless the perceived value of deviating is high enough to encourage alternative actions. We might be inclined to believe that "alternative actions" in an ethical context means *unethical* action but, as we have seen above, such is not the case. Ethical

---

[36] Shane and Venkataraman, "The Promise of Entrepreneurship as a Field of Research," pp. 222ff.

[37] Ibid., pp. 222–3. In this connection, they reference Kirzner and Schumpeter.

actions, despite our inclinations to think otherwise, are often not binary—that is, not either right or wrong. Aristotle was closer to the truth when he suggested, during his discussion of the doctrine of the mean, that most ethical actions involve "the more" or "the less." Yet, even if, in the end, there is only one right answer in a given situation, our advocacy of ethical individualism indicates that most generalized descriptions of ethical conduct will need to recognize pluralism, making binary pronouncements generally inaccurate or misleading. There are "opportunity costs"[38] involved in adhering to principles or norms, such that both adherence to and deviations from them have to be evaluated. Typically, we are most likely to "go along" with certain commonly accepted norms, if the value of not doing so is not high enough and, typically, the most generally accepted and prevalent norms harden into obligations that weigh significantly in our assessment of the "costs" of an action. And in interpersonal relations, we have the additional motivational factor of *wanting* to go along, which also increases the cost of any deviation. Consequently, most of our time is spent conforming to social rules and, given the need for order in society, it is a good thing that we do. Analogously, most of our commercial relations as consumers are routine patterns of trade involving the receipt and spending of income. We have varying degrees of alertness to entrepreneurial opportunities, but the bulk of our activities are within established routines. Shane and Venkataraman note that the decision to exploit an entrepreneurial opportunity has a lot to do with degrees of confidence and optimism possessed by individuals. Similarly, we should have little trouble imagining that, on one end, there are those who conform to rules without question and, on the other, those who seek out new opportunities for ethical growth and expression. We have all witnessed those who always seem to want to do good for both others and themselves, and those who would rather not think beyond what is required of them. Indeed, we might regard the former as "moral optimists," in their desire to make their world a "better place." But Shane and Venkataraman offer a caveat in this connection that is worth our attention, as well: "The attributes that increase the probability of opportunity exploitation do not necessarily increase the

---

[38] See Mark LeBar, *The Value of Living Well* (Oxford: Oxford University Press, 2013), pp. 12–13 and Daniel C. Russell, *Happiness for Humans* (Oxford: Oxford University Press, 2012), p. 27.

probability of success."[39] The same is true, of course, in ethics. The desire to do good is not a guarantee that good will actually be done. And as Adam Smith has noted,[40] the goodness of an intention can be completely overshadowed by bad consequences, just as questionable motives can be overridden by good consequences. The point is that since we are in the world of action, success counts for a great deal, whether in ethics or commerce. But even more important than outcomes, from our point of view, is the need for practical wisdom, which the aforementioned comment from Shane and Venkataraman implies is necessary for both entrepreneurship and, we would argue, ethics.

Apart from just noting the similarities between what might be said about the exploitation of opportunities in entrepreneurship and in ethics, we have spent a moment on this third dimension of comparison, because it helps highlight the idea that the notion of "opportunity" might have a place in ethics, thus driving a wedge between ethics and the idea of a static world of adherence (or lack thereof) to rules of conduct. If Buchanan's comment about entrepreneurs in some real sense creating opportunities is true, we want to see how central that might be in a conception of ethics such as the one we have been articulating all along. In a way, that must be our concluding thought, to which we now turn.

2. The Importance of the Analogy between Entrepreneur and Ethical Agent

Even if we suppose that our foregoing analogy between the entrepreneurial and the ethical agent has been successful, the question remains as to what has been gained by this exercise. It may seem that we have done little to enhance our understanding of either the entrepreneur or the ethical agent. No doubt, there is truth in that objection; but our purpose in using the analogy has been less to understand these respective agents than to gain some insight into the nature of ethics itself. Indeed, our overall thesis has been that the paradigm for ethics most often adhered to and theorized about by its exponents today is by no means the only one, much less the decisive one. There is an

---

[39] Shane and Venkataraman, "The Promise of Entrepreneurship as a Field of Research," p. 224.

[40] Adam Smith, *The Theory of Moral Sentiments*, ed. D. D. Raphael and A. L. Macfie (Indianapolis: Liberty Fund, 1984), II.iii.2 and II.iii.3.

alternative approach and grounding, and getting some further sense of what that alternative might imply has been our mission here. We have described that mission earlier as advancing the idea of an individualistic perfectionism grounded in the nature of human beings, but issuing in an agent-relative understanding of the good and, thus, the possibility for moral pluralism in its prescriptive conclusions. As such, there is no a priori reason to assume that because A is good for person P, A is thereby good for Q—or that if action T is right for P, T is also right for Q. That would have to be shown, and we have given reasons earlier for being suspicious of universalizing claims that would require either A or T to be applicable equally to P and Q. This way of understanding ethics has opened a door to an ethical world that our entrepreneurship analogy begs us to enter.

Consider a situation where a "lawyer" and an "economist" are given the same problem to solve. The terms "lawyer" and "economist" (henceforth, simply L and E) are in quotes, because we are referring to a pattern of action most characteristic of a general type, and not necessarily to how an actual individual in one or the other category might behave in a concrete situation. First of all, both would identify the problem, which, let us say, involves the over-use of a piece of land. L would begin by looking for existing rules that might be applied to solve the problem, or perhaps by imagining some rules that might define how individuals connected to the land should behave toward it. These rules might include directives for usage or definitions of the ways in which the land can be further developed and used (or both), all with a goal in mind of reducing the over-usage. In essence, the goal of L would be to articulate, in prescriptive terms, acceptable and unacceptable forms of behavior and the obligations that arise therefrom. Individuals would look to these rules to know what they should be doing.

E, by contrast, would not be particularly interested in defining specific forms of conduct with which individuals should be abiding. Instead, E's approach would be to alter incentives and allow individuals to decide for themselves what forms of behavior to adopt, according to their own assessment of the relevant costs. Often, this would take the form of simply internalizing externalities, so that those who reap benefits also bear associated costs. Under such a regime, some will continue to behave in the "bad" ways that seem to run contrary to the newly created incentives, while others will begin to respond to those incentives and alter their behavior accordingly. At the margins, changes will reflect the existing incentives. Overall, we would expect better management of the land when there is no form of conduct dictated for each individual, and some individuals are allowed to be "bad." There is room for entrepreneurship in this world, because not knowing how any given individual will or must behave leaves open the possibility for innovation with respect to how things are done. Yet, notice that, in this world, there seems to be no singular "right" or "wrong"—only more or less of some kind of behavior or other.

In the language of regulation theory, L's world could be said to be design-based, whereas E's world is performance-based. In L's world, people do things either the right way or the wrong way, with ambiguity and discretion being the only forms of open-endedness. Though the tendency of reasoning here may not call for the removal of all discretion, ambiguity is, on the other hand, regarded as a fault in the design of the rules. In E's world, by contrast, virtually all is discretion, and "ambiguity" provides opportunity. The chief evil in E's world is having costs and benefits "leak," that is, to not actually be borne by the particular agents who take the actions. That is the central evil in E's world, because individuals can only efficiently adjust their conduct if the costs and benefits are clearly defined *for that particular individual*, thus also determining the actual effect of any incentives that may be present.

Of the two worlds we have just outlined, the "feel" of the individualist perfectionist (IP) ethical world we have been advocating would be much more like the "amoral" world of E, than it would be like L's juridical order. In the IP world we have advanced, what ethics offers is not a litany of prescriptions but, rather, open-ended principles coupled with dispositional goals which are designed to facilitate action in a variety of unknown circumstances as coordinated by practical wisdom. In E's world, we do not know exactly what any given individual will do, or even should do; and thus, we do not know how that world will look overall. We do not know because, in our example, it is trade rather than obligation that typically marks the exchanges between the agents in E's world. In L's world, by contrast, we know how people will behave if they abide by the rules that define appropriate conduct. We also know the terms under which individuals will relate to each other, because those will also be defined as part of the endeavor to remove "ambiguity." Of course, as we noted at the very beginning of this chapter, the juridical approach of L generally stands opposed to the evaluative orientation of E. As we also noted, L's world seems closer to the typical model of ethical reasoning than is E's. However, we need to explore the matter further, because the entrepreneurial analogy we have been working with is clearly more at home in E's world. Is that world sufficiently normative in nature to qualify as "ethical"?

One objection to our foregoing presentation of the two worlds could be that both are ultimately captured by the juridical. After all, any rules passed or adopted in L's world to solve the problem would have to conform to what was ethical—meaning that those overarching ethical rules which would govern the newly adopted ones could themselves be viewed according to the juridical model and thus fit comfortably within L's world. But it looks like the same could also be said about E's world! Whatever incentives are put in place, as well as the actions they produce, would presumably have to conform to the requirements of ethics which, in turn, would have an L-world list of rules to which the incentives would have to conform. In essence, E's world is a world of "nudging," where the goals and behaviors encouraged will be designed according to preconceived moral rules and notions of what is good. It may be no accident that the notion of "nudging," as applied to social issues, was developed by two law school professors![41] In essence, then, E's world is really just what might happen within the discretionary interstices of L's world.

The foregoing objection is a very useful one, because it is both telling and helpful. It is telling because, presumably, E *would be* subject to ethical constraints to which his design and his agents would have to conform. The objection is useful, because it points us to a dimension of the original problem that, in turn, helps us identify something fundamental about our approach versus the alternatives. What L and E have in common is that they both have been effectively given, by the example, the authority to organize society according to some specified goal. What they seem to differ on is merely the means to that end. But suppose we eliminate the common denominator and imagine that there is no specific problem to be solved—not even a mandate to organize society in some way for any particular end—and, instead, only an approach to problems generally. What might each of our two worlds offer under *these* conditions? Is it even possible to conceive of ethics, without making the central problem one of managing our relations with others? In the case of L's way of thinking about the world, the answer to this latter question would

---

41 Richard H. Thaler and Cass R. Sunstein, authors of *Nudge: Improving Decisions about Health, Wealth, and Happiness* (New York: Penguin, 2008).

seem to be "no," because the juridical world of rules is inherently other-oriented—that is, fundamentally concerned about defining relations among persons. As such, L's world would tend to cash itself out either through defining the terms of appropriate social cooperation, or discovering the characteristics that are expressive of giving persons the respect their dignity requires, or both. In the case of social cooperation, the rules would be designed or promoted based upon their contribution toward encouraging social cooperation. There might be some procedural values to help the process along, such as respecting autonomy or being democratic; but ultimately, the value of these procedural values would rest in their ability to produce successful rules of cooperation. Here, appropriate actions do matter.

In the second case, that of respecting dignity, the rules are adopted "for their own sake" —namely, because they are inherently expressive of human dignity. Modern-day ethical theorists tend to suppose that both forms (cooperation and respect) are at least compatible, if not identical; but the two are not the same. It is conceivable that the two might even conflict—a cooperative solution not exhibiting the proper or sufficient respect for dignity—and in such cases, we suspect that a juridical model would tend to favor dignity over cooperation.[42] In any case, the central value in this world is attitude, rather than action. Although respect can be demonstrated through action, the presumption is that for behaviors to qualify as moral, they must reflect the appropriate attitudes toward others. Since the fundamental ethical problem, in both cases, is how we should conduct ourselves with respect to others, both of these forms fall under what we called much earlier the paradigm of respect.

The removal of a specific purpose, such as we started with in discussing L's and E's worlds, does not, *pace* the presumptions of L, require some more generalized social goal or form of social management. We can imagine agents acting, even with the intention of doing some social good, without their actions having to fulfill, or be justified in terms of, some overall social purpose. And although L might concede that point, he would likely also suggest that doing so

---

[42] Pornography might be such an example. The cooperative solution might be to let persons participate in pornography as they wish; but doing so might, nonetheless, fail to respect the dignity of women. Even if the subjects are "willing" participants, that could simply be a sign of their own failure to respect their dignity. Hence, the "cooperative" solution always seems answerable to the dignity solution.

is either a form of amorality or a myopic perspective that is subtly ignoring the ethical. However, our endeavor to analogize the entrepreneur with the ethical hero is just to make E's world an ethical world. The key to doing so is not only to abandon the notion that ethical actions are necessarily, or even primarily, rule governed,[43] but also to abandon the notion that ethics, in the first instance, is about managing social relations. If both of these are abandoned, then we can start building upon a foundation that gives ethical substance to actions that are self perfective, rather than because they show respect for oneself or others, or contribute to social harmony. Both worlds, it might be said, adequately give an intelligible answer to what one ought to do. Entrepreneurs, however, have been our heroes in this chapter—not because we wish their actions to be outside of society, but because their actions can be conceived independently of existing social patterns. The entrepreneurial dimensions of their choices are, almost by definition, in contrast to social propensities which exhibit themselves elsewhere. As Buchanan noted, the opportunity set is virtually *created* by the entrepreneur,[44] and seeing that relevance for the ethical actor is the essence of IP. E's world, then, is a world of open-endedness.

In L's world, by contrast, the direction of ethical success lies in a movement to the center, that is, in an effort toward the acceptance of norms that can be made common to all. Ideally, in that world, norms would finally become internalized, with all individuals helping to enforce the accepted norms through "punishment" of deviant forms of conduct.[45] So, although individualism might be valued under non-ethical or supererogatory conditions (for example, fashion, personality, career choice, etc.), to think ethically in L's world just is to think in terms that must apply to us all—that is, in terms of our common core of norms and values. Whether the end is cooperation or respect or both, the perspective here is a global one, always seeking to cover all relevant moral agents. One great advantage of this perspective is how well it adheres to the intuitive idea that morality is something to which we must conform, rather than something we create or do

---

[43] One must keep in mind that not being rule governed is not equivalent to not being governed by principle.

[44] See note 34 above.

[45] See Gerald Gaus, *The Order of Public Reason: A Theory of Freedom and Morality in a Diverse and Bounded World* (Cambridge: Cambridge University Press, 2011), chap. 11.

on our own. We cannot innovate with respect to morality, because its source lies outside of any one of us and is thus bigger than us as individuals. This feature helps keep it from lapsing into subjectivism and maintains its usefulness as a device for social management and control.

In the ethical world pictured by E, however, ethical success is what occurs at the margins, not the center. To say this is not, of course, to discount the importance of the center. Indeed, the whole notion of there being a margin depends first upon understanding what is at the center. But in an IP ethics such as the one we are advancing, the norms at the center are a *resource* for action, rather than a necessary determinant of it. The common core becomes the basis upon which individuation builds, and the place where deviations can present themselves as new candidates for the center. In this regard, the economist's saying that "all change occurs at the margins" is no less true of ethics than of economics. That phrase, usually connected to the notion that "rational people think at the margin," suggests first that changes tend to be incremental, and second that being rational means recognizing that "sunk costs" are sunk and that one needs to look at what will actually impact the next action. If our common core of normative values is our ethical "sunk costs," then the role of practical wisdom is to assess what may impact the next action, in light of those costs, in ways that best contribute to flourishing. Unlike in L's world, where every decision has global import, the process here at the ethical margin is incremental, in the sense that some conclusion of practical reason is not necessarily a conclusion for all practical reasoners. Certainly, in cases where one's own particular well-being is at issue, such a statement about practical reason seems obvious. But as we have seen, even in cases where others are involved, there may be multiple possible solutions; and the openness to such a possibility is the virtue of E's world. In general, then, what gives motion to this world is an individual's practical innovation about how to act in a given situation, rather than that individual's endeavoring to help reinforce the core.

It is important to emphasize again a point we have made before—namely, that individualism here is not the same as subjectivism. The process of ethical "innovation" we are discussing is thus neither simply a discovery of one's strongest and most recent desire, nor the articulation of one's preference function, nor any act of choice one happens to prefer because it is the one preferred. The context of our discussion is, rather, that of the use of practical wisdom which, as we understand it, requires a serious reflection upon what will contribute to well-being. Precisely because morality, as ordinarily practiced, most often exhibits the characteristics of L's world, where people "knowing" what is right or wrong either do the right thing or not, we tend to think of innovation as absent from morality. Yet, if the common core is regarded as a resource for action, rather than the end of action itself, then there is, in principle, an openness to innovation regarding diverse courses of action not otherwise desirable under the juridical format of L's world. That openness is not equivalent to subjectivism.

And at this stage, it is important also to remember what we showed in Part I—namely, that we are here talking about ethics, not politics. Political norms must be juridical because their very purpose is to set a context for all of us, thus making deviations a threat to that very context. But politics, as we have extensively argued, has only the limited function of setting the context for moral action to occur, and not the further purpose of commanding or encouraging moral conduct itself. The juridical model unfortunately encourages the easy slide from politics to ethics, because its law-like properties replicate the characteristics of the tools politics needs to accomplish its ends (for example, universality, obligatoriness, intolerance of deviation, social control and constraint, etc.). If, however, we simply opt out of the framework of respect and into the framework of responsibility, the same phenomena of ordinary moral experience take on a differ-ent coloring, one which we are trying to evoke in these very com-ments. For example, while in the world of E, framed by an ethics of responsibility, there are also groups with rules and obligatory norms, within which one finds oneself or chooses to participate, their value must always be understood in light of the primary purpose of decid-ing what to make of oneself.

We have lionized entrepreneurs in this chapter precisely in order to fix a different paradigm of thinking about ethics. Entrepreneurs are, in a way, the quintessential individualists; but such persons neither exist in isolation, nor remake themselves completely at every moment. Entrepreneurs, ironically enough, are tested by reality in a way juridical thinkers are not. The latter believe their rules can shape the world, whereas the former believe any rules worth follow-ing are shaped by the world. Juridical thinkers hold that rules, once formulated properly, can be imposed on a society that is more or less receptive but which, in the end, is inherently suited to their imposi-tion, because their proper formulation is itself sufficient for their acceptance. Karl Brunner puts this point well when he notes about today's moralist:

> The conception implicit in the posture of moral indignation views the world as a structure-less, amorphous mass to be shaped in the light of our values. The environment appears like clay in the hands of a potter. And our "knowledge of values" is deemed sufficient to impose the true form on our matter.[46]

In this regard, the world of E has helped us see that virtually the reverse is true—namely, that the rules that become rooted evolve and grow in incremental ways, due to the experience and choices of acting agents. Generalized norms are the consequence, not the cause or source, of moral action. By contrast, as Kant so correctly put it with respect to the juridical model, moral principles in L's world are inherently legislative.[47] In E's world, however, they are legitimated.

Because of our endeavor to turn the way in which one looks at the moral universe more toward what we have been calling E's world, the philosophers of ethics after whom we have most patterned ourselves are Aristotle and Spinoza and, to a lesser degree, some of the Scottish Enlightenment figures such as Hume and Smith. In these thinkers, we find advice, exemplars, principles, and recommendations, but little in the way of commands or rules or duties. Although some of these thinkers might not accept our premises, their propensities are less juridical than those of contemporary ethicists. This is either because the former did not completely socialize ethics, or because they allowed for the a posteriority of rules and norms, or both. We have highlighted the entrepreneur because, for endeavoring to push moral thinking in the direction of individualism, no better modern exemplar exists. Entrepreneurs are in society, and even dependent upon society, but not completely *of* society. As entrepreneurs stand apart, they remind us that ethics has, as its subject, living a good life; but good lives are lived by individuals. Individuals who "do the right thing" might qualify as ethical individuals in the juridical model; but they have yet to do so in the evaluative one, however useful and necessary such behavior might be. It is one's own act of exercising practical reason that moves one into the ethical realm, for even in

---

[46] Karl Brunner, "Knowledge, Values and the Choice of Economic Organization," *Kyklos* 23 (1970): p. 576.

[47] See, for example, Immanuel Kant, "Introduction to the Metaphysics of Morals," in *The Metaphysics of Morals*, trans. and ed. Mary Gregor (Cambridge: Cambridge University Press, 1996), Sec. IV, pp. 20ff.

conformity to some set of established rules, ethical conduct only occurs when one conforms because one understands it is appropriate to conform. Anything short of that understanding might not remove the action's value, abstractly considered; but it would remove any claim to ethical conduct. This is because, as we have tried to show, our telos is the excellent exercise of practical reason, and the defining foundation of the good and the right is an individualized affair.

3. Conclusion

It has been our contention from the very beginning of this work that only the framework of responsibility sufficiently recognizes both the individualized character of the good and the burden it places upon the ethical actor. And such an outlook does place a burden on the ethical actor—the burden of having no one else to answer to about how one's life has been conducted—just as risk is imposed on the solitary entrepreneur in undertaking a new venture. One can attempt to collectivize oneself and see one's ethical responsibilities solely in terms of living according to the norms detailing appropriate respect for others and thus, as J. S. Mill put it,[48] come to see oneself and one's own good completely in those terms. Or one can come to recognize that, however much one endeavors to socialize oneself, one can never escape oneself and, thus, the responsibility for deciding how one ought to conduct oneself and oneself alone. *Socialism is no more successful in ethics than in economics, and for similar reasons: it sacrifices the future to the present by discouraging innovation and inverts the source of positive marginal change by moving it from the individual to society. Ethical wealth, like economic wealth, will be a function of the degree to which individuals take it upon themselves to produce good lives.*

---

[48] See John Stuart Mill, "What Utilitarianism Is," in *Utilitarianism*, 2nd edn, ed. Oskar Piest (New York: Liberal Arts Press, 1957), chap. 2.

Afterword: Big Morality

When all is said and done, perhaps the problem nagging all forms of eudaimonistic virtue or perfectionist ethics within the Aristotelian tradition might be the problem of "big morality." Given the focus in such theories upon the agent's own flourishing, one wonders whether this type of ethics can ever capture moral experience that seems to be "global" in proportions. Here we might be thinking of something like an evil so great, it does not seem possible to appreciate its depth by saying that it results from a "failing to flourish," or that it exemplifies actions which "impede flourishing." The examples of Hitler, Stalin, or Mao come to mind. The horrific nature of their actions is so profoundly devastating that it seems almost insulting to our moral sensibilities to think that the depth of their evil can be measured by reference to a lack of flourishing. The reverse may hold as well. There could be some moral goods that go beyond what seems necessary to support or even encourage flourishing of particular individuals or groups of them. Perhaps Jesus, Socrates, or some other saint-like person in one's pantheon of moral exemplars would come to mind in this connection. Either way, flourishing, especially when it is as individualized as we would have it in our foregoing arguments, seems somehow small when paired with the kind of evil or goodness that transcends particular circumstances and times and places.

The problem of big morality thus resurrects the old charge leveled against eudaimonistic ethical theories that, by not appreciating the other and by being too focused upon the self, they are too narrow. Various ethical theorists in the eudaimonistic tradition, including ourselves, have given responses to this charge; and these responses are, in their own way, no doubt adequate and successful. But with big morality, there seems to be a remainder. Yes, sociality is both necessary and important for flourishing, but we are talking here about deeds that go beyond the encouragement or destruction of sociality. Eudaimonistic theories may be adequate for ordinary moral discourse, but that's precisely the problem: How well do they really do with the extraordinary? And are not any problems with a "remainder" an indication of something wrong at the core? Aristotle himself may have been suggesting the problem when he banished beasts and gods from the polis.[1] And Adam Smith may have been the first one to explicitly notice the distinction between ordinary and extraordinary morality when he distinguished "superior prudence" from the ordinary sort.[2] In his account, there are just some extraordinary individuals and/or circumstances that lie outside the realm of ordinary moral discourse. These extraordinary individuals and circumstances are analogous to those addressed by ordinary morality, but do not themselves quite fit there. How do we account for these extraordinary situations or individuals within a eudaimonistic or perfectionist framework?

One possibility, as Elie Wiesel has noted, is to say we cannot.[3] Some evils are so horrendous that we really cannot explain or grasp them. Yet, such a position is likely to apply to more than one type of moral theory, not just the eudaimonistic class of theories to which we subscribe. Another possibility is to appeal to transcendence. The phenomena of which we speak cannot be accounted for, unless we posit that the moral realm extends beyond the human to dimensions of being that transcend our limited existence and thereby covers ordinary moral experience as well as the extraordinary. Thus, the transcendent good might be accompanied by a transcendent evil bigger than ordinary morality can encompass. This, too, is an answer that would supervene upon more than just eudaimonistic theories. As an alternative to these two "solutions" (insolvability and transcendence), one might instead try to address the problem by positing the existence of two moral orders that are only analogous to each other. Perhaps one of these three approaches is, in the end, the only way to view the phenomena in question. And although we cannot address the problem fully in our brief closing comments here, it might, nonetheless, be instructive to say something about it. For if we cannot say anything to relieve the intuition that something is narrowly self-centered about a eudaimonistic ethics—and big morality keeps

---

[1] Aristotle, *Politics*, 1253a 27–9.

[2] Adam Smith, *The Theory of Moral Sentiments*, ed. D. D. Raphael and A. L. Macfie (Indianapolis: Liberty Fund, 1984), VI.i.14, 15.

[3] See, for example, Elie Wiesel's speech "The Perils of Indifference: Lessons From A Violent Century," lecture 7 of the White House Millennium Lecture series, given on April 12, 1999, available at <https://www.youtube.com/watch?v=ldylvNscW54>, last accessed October 6, 2015.

highlighting that intuition, no matter what the responses proffered by eudaimonists—then perhaps we can be instructed by attempting to tackle the problem head-on with our theory. We believe that Mark LeBar has sensed the same issue as he closes his own account of eudaimonistic ethics. In the end, however, it is exactly what LeBar wants to run away from that we wish to embrace and, in addition to showing that we can further highlight the differences between constructivist and non-constructivist eudaimonistic theories, to say something further about our own theory and about big morality, as well.

LeBar frames the problem in terms of respect for persons and, given that we opened this work with some reflections on that issue, it seems equally fitting to close it there. LeBar notes that Plato claims[4] that the reason for not doing immoral things, particularly things that harm others, such as killing, rape, theft, and the like, is that doing so will disrupt the balance, unity, or harmony of the soul. Such a reason clearly cannot explain why we should not do such things, so LeBar argues, at least in part because it is too self-centered. As he notes, it is the effects upon the *victim* that matter here, not the agent herself. Even if the unity or harmony of one's soul were not affected, the immorality of such actions would remain, and one would need to be advised to avoid such actions. We must look elsewhere, then, to solve the problem; and doing so requires reasons that refer exclusively to respect for the victims, and not to (or simply to) the effects upon the agent.

One can see at a glance, no doubt, why the issue here is more of a problem for us than it is for eudaimonists like LeBar. LeBar's constructivism turns out to be his salvation whereas, for our theory, that path is closed. In simplest terms, flourishing for LeBar involves giving ourselves reasons to act in certain ways. The norms of morality come through reason-giving. Yet, giving ourselves reasons to act in certain ways in order to achieve or enhance our own self-flourishing seems too self-focused to account for all of morality. Hence, the problem of ever getting to the victim and away from ourselves in the cases we are now considering. But this problem could be solved if others can also give us reasons for acting in certain ways, because then it is not just us that we are answering to, but those others as well. Once others can give us reasons for acting, chances are good that we can then consider the victim for the victim's sake and derive norms accord-

---

[4] Plato, *The Republic*, 442e–443a.

ingly. Contrast this with what appears to be our approach and thus our problem. If the deployment of practical wisdom is our *telos* and thus the measure of right and wrong, we never seem to be getting to the victim, but only once again to our own use of practical reason— that is, to whether we ourselves are using our own practical wisdom correctly or not. That does not seem very distant, if it is distant at all, from Plato's claim that the reason to avoid immorality is its effects upon the unity or harmony of our own souls.

As we just noted, LeBar wants to run away from the "Platonic" "self-referring argument" (SRA),[5] whereas we desire to (and perhaps must) embrace it. In this regard, it is important to realize that LeBar, as well as ourselves and Plato, is speaking of a second-person relationship, not a third-person one. In other words, we are not speaking of a situation where one observes another doing harm to a third party, but rather a situation where one is the potential agent of the harm and must consider the right reasons to refrain from it. LeBar's solution, reminiscent of Darwall's, is that we are accountable to others because others give us reasons for our actions that manifest themselves as certain expressions of respect for those others. When we treat others, for example, in harmful ways, we disrespect them, which violates the reasons others have given us to accord them that respect. Notice that this giving of reasons maintains the constructivist approach, since now it is simply the case that we have two modalities (ourselves and others) for constructing reasons for ourselves. Yet, even if we grant to LeBar that others can give us reasons for actions, we do not yet know why those reasons trump the reasons we give ourselves. To him, and perhaps to us all, it seems intuitively clear that however much better off I might be with you out of the way, not murdering you trumps any benefits I might otherwise obtain. Yet, however intuitively clear all this may seem to be, the question still remains as to how to determine when the reasons given by others take precedence over reasons given to oneself. We shall come back to this question again momentarily when we mention rights. For now, the problem we are addressing is this: How do we justify one's having concern for the effects of one's actions on others, if not simply in terms of the instrumental effects of one's actions upon oneself? LeBar avoids this problem by allowing others to be givers of reasons to oneself—that is, reasons for respect. Our argument, by contrast,

---

[5] Mark LeBar, *The Value of Living Well* [hereafter, *VLW*] (Oxford: Oxford University Press, 2013), chap. 12.

will be that it is the reasons we have, and not those given to us by ourselves or others, that matter here; and that in the end, these reasons can only be SRAs, because we, as individuals, are the agents of our actions and responsible to ourselves.

What exactly does LeBar mean by others giving us reasons? He notes that "we understand reasons of respect to arise when and because we *give to others* the authority to *give to ourselves* reasons, and to hold us accountable for acting on those reasons."[6] But, of course, if it is we who are giving others authority to give us reasons, then the nature and degree of that authority must come under the purview of our own practical wisdom and thus remain, in some sense, "self-referring." If, for example, in trying to quit smoking, one gives another the authority to throw away his cigarettes or to chastise him when he backslides, this authority must still be understood in light of the giver's own practical wisdom. The other person, afterwards, does give one reasons to act in certain ways (and one should respect the authority one has delegated); and the effects upon the other should, indeed, be at least some, if not a large part, of our concerns about any violation of the delegation of that authority. And yet, none of this, finally, exists outside of the framework of one's own practical wisdom and flourishing. Clearly, then, this seems not the kind of thing LeBar is seeking when he talks about giving others the authority to give us reasons. Yet, if others are ends in themselves *irrespective* of ourselves, then the centrality of the flourishing project itself seems lost. Rather, our moral world, according to LeBar, would seem to consist in self-giving reasons and other-giving reasons for *our* actions. But as we asked earlier, how do we sort out the priorities between them?

Here, LeBar would no doubt rely on the reflections of so-called wise practical reasoners or agents on "settled" intuitions, in the attempt to find a Rawlsian-like equilibrium between those intuitions and novel or difficult cases.[7] This would keep the object of our judgment from being too self-referring and allow for us to have reasons that come from others, yet not be *special* grants of authority, as in the smoking case. Instead, they would be general grants against certain kinds of harm. We spoke of this appeal to intuitions that are "internalized outputs of deliberative judgments that pass critical scrutiny"[8]

[6] Ibid., p. 310.
[7] Ibid., p. 293.
[8] Ibid., p. 294.

in Chapter 7. We noted that critical scrutiny provides only formal criteria, and that the basic lacuna in LeBar's constructivist approach was the failure to provide an answer as to why one should regard these "internalized outputs" as substantively ultimate. Yet, what is needed here is a standard for deciding between self- and other-giving reasons. If we are to avoid lapsing into subjectivist intuitions or an ever-widening circle of appealing to reasons for reasons, some such sort of standard must be employed. Of course, having the need for such a standard does not preclude the application of a non-constructivist standard such as our own.

Still, the key concept here seems to be connected to what it means to "give." What is involved in the "giving" of authority and reasons? Why not just say others *have* this authority or one *has* reasons for doing such and such? One of LeBar's main answers to this concern is that "in essence we have reasons of respect because it is *good for us* to think that we do." And, "we have reasons to act in virtue of our exercise of judgment that certain ways of living our lives and choosing what to do make for better lives than others."[9] Now, the interesting thing about these answers is that they are the same ones we would provide! For us, once one understands human nature and the nature of human sociality, certain general norms may follow from that understanding that the person of practical wisdom would recognize and follow. But there is no "giving" here; one *has* these reasons because they represent insights into the nature and meaning of our telos and the norms implied by it for our interactions with others. Our reasons for acting are not constructed, but recognized; they are not given, but deployed. Yet, LeBar too seems to want to capture this same sense of things when he says this respect is basically "two hatted," meaning that once we add another person to the picture, respect "is constitutive of *the way we arrive at* these reasons" and "arises from the way we see others as sources of reasons for us."[10] Nothing in these statements seems to require a rejection of our own approach. However, like Darwall, who is cited in this connection, LeBar sees adding another person as changing the very character of the reasons. We no longer recognize reasons for actions, but must authorize them.

LeBar's Kantian move to have a standard beyond ourselves which, nevertheless, we ultimately originate, is a way of trying to move us

---

[9] Ibid., p. 312.
[10] Ibid., pp. 314–15.

off the center of self and on to respect for others. Yet, we are not, for LeBar, giving *ourselves* the rule of respecting others, as some Kantians might have it, but instead are giving others the authority to thereby give us reasons. Presumably, they cannot just have this authority, or we will lose the connection to ourselves altogether; and that, as noted above, would sever the connection to the framework of flourishing. Yet, we must actually give them the authority to give us reasons, in order to move the object of concern toward them, away from us, and to keep the constructivism intact. Our response so far, by contrast, has been to note that nothing need be given to anyone here; and that we do not easily escape the SRA as long as we are in a flourishing context, which must ultimately refer to one's own life. But, of course, *our* solution does not seem to be talking about the victim. By the same token, LeBar needs some concrete example of giving authority to give us reasons that is not a special form of authority as in the smoking case, and which prevents one from just considering effects upon oneself. For that reason, LeBar calls upon rights theory to illustrate what it means to give the sort of respect needed here. Apparently, the language of rights is strong enough, publicly intuitive enough, and other-directed enough to carry the weight needed for countering Plato's misplaced focus.

With LeBar, for Mary to attack William unprovoked is a failure on her part to respect William, and that is clearly implied in saying that Mary violated William's rights. The giving, by one person to another, of the authority to give back to the first person reasons for acting in certain ways, is part of what LeBar understands as underlying a rights relationship. Suffice it to say that we have, from a non-constructivist form of perfectionism, also given an explanation of rights in *Norms of Liberty*.[11] Our view, however, does not involve giving others the authority to give us reasons. Rather, it sees the nature of social and political life, where the object is to protect the possibility of moral action itself, as the basis for making rights claims. Since the focus here is not our alternative account of rights, however, it is enough to note that, while we imagine rights to involve respect in some form, that respect does not come from reasons given to us by others to act in certain ways. The reason we hold for respecting rights is that such forms of behavior are necessary to get the moral

---

[11] Douglas B. Rasmussen and Douglas J. Den Uyl, *Norms of Liberty: A Perfectionist Basis for Non-Perfectionist Politics* [hereafter *NOL*] (University Park: Pennsylvania State University Press, 2005).

enterprise off the ground when others are present. In this regard, LeBar sometimes speaks as if he agrees. As for the punchline of why we should cede such authority over us to others, the answer seems neither to require giving, nor even to offer much of a distinction from an SRA. To wit: "Why cede this authority to others? . . . The reason we should have the dispositions required by respect is (as with any reason on VE [virtue ethics]) a matter of living well."[12] If I cede authority to others because only by doing so will I live well, then the reason for not harming another does seem to be a form of an SRA. But, of course, the response would be that one's ceding of authority is to promote the flourishing of others as well as oneself, so one is not just referring to oneself.[13] And if this is the move, then what we are really committed to, for LeBar, is either a kind of impersonal flourishing, where one's own flourishing matters no more than another's, or flourishing in a Darwallian sense, where flourishing is understood as what is worthy for us to follow (and this is not understood by any appeal to what is good for one). So, the question still is: Why should this agent be moved by generalized or worthy flourishing? "Living well" does, indeed, seem to be the answer; but that is because, for us, only individuals "live well," thus making the final appeal to the individual agent. Why would LeBar's individual "give authority" to others for the sake of generalized or worthy "living well?"

LeBar's response to our last point would be to identify that his argument occurs on two levels, and thus that "our attitudes of respect for others and our reasons for having such attitudes are importantly distinct."[14] In this regard, our reason for having certain attitudes—namely, living well—would, after all, be a kind of SRA. It is our end of wanting to live well that gives us the context for respecting others and giving them the authority to give us reasons for certain types of behaviors. Because of this, our actual attitude toward others is not one of seeing how any given action the other may do contributes to one's own living well, but rather one of showing respect for *them* by acting in ways appropriate to *them* as final ends in themselves. Now

---

[12] LeBar, *VLW*, p. 317.

[13] In Darwallian fashion, it is possible that LeBar could be saying that "flourishing" is independent of self and others, much like "worth" is for Darwall. "Flourishing," then, would be a standard independent of self- or other-giving reasons, and the basis for measuring both. From our point of view, such a move would make matters worse, as it further removes flourishing from the individual. See below.

[14] LeBar, *VLW*, p. 325.

the (potential) victim does enter into the picture, because now we are not trying to explain our conduct toward the other in terms of how it affects us, but rather in terms of an attitude that is fully focused on the other. Rights are a good way of formalizing that show of respect for others. As one can see, LeBar's approach marries the Kantian notions of respecting persons to the eudaimonist principle of living well. It is not exactly a match made in heaven, however. In the first place, depending on how one understands "distinct" in this context, it divorces our attitudes from our reasons for having them. If nothing else, this separation is a recipe for motivational heteronomy which, in the sort of perfectionism we advocate, is ultimately a failure of integrity. Our attitudes should be a function of, and reflect, our reasons for having them, such that we can tell something of the reasons for certain attitudes by witnessing the attitudes themselves.[15] Of course, if "distinct" does not mean separable in this context, we can certainly distinguish actions for the sake of others from those which might use others simply or primarily for one's own ends. That sort of distinction, however, simply begs for an indication of what the agent's own larger framework of integrating self- and other-oriented forms of action into a coherent nexus[16] of practical reasoning looks like. This sort of "what kind of person are you" or "how well are you flourishing" is still a form of SRA, even if at a more abstract level than that of concrete motivation. In short, the distinction LeBar proposes may keep constructivism alive, since the reasons for having certain attitudes do not yet seem to specify the reasons for certain types of treatment. However, it also either implies that those reasons can arguably stand outside one's own nexus—in which case, we do not need a concept of "flourishing," as we suspect Kant rightly concluded; or it does finally appeal to some form of the state of the agent's "soul," however appropriate it may be to notice the difference in conduct between instrumentalizing others and treating them with respect.

---

[15] LeBar sometimes sounds like this as well. At one point, he tells us that "we *don't* ask first whether or not they have given us authority to set ends for them, or given them reasons nor do they. They simply assume (and assume rightly) that we are accountable to them for our treatment of them (and vice versa), period. These moral relations are inescapable and ordinarily allow of no exemptions" (ibid., p. 331). Here the distinction seems almost to disappear; but LeBar wants to keep it, because *eudaimonia* is supposed to fit our reasons for having certain attitudes, thus keeping it in the picture.

[16] See our discussion in Chapters 1 and 5.

Yet, the main problem with the marriage is less the distinction itself than its perpetuation of the "myth of respect" so common among contemporary moralists, especially when thinking of the appropriate way to understand rights. The myth of respect is what we believe makes it so difficult to see what is really the marginal dimension of big morality that makes it so compelling. That marginal difference—what we have pressed for all along in this work—is individualism. The point here is not difficult to see. If Mary refrains from attacking William, and does so in ways normally considered rights-respecting, it is not because Mary respects William. At most, it might be because Mary respects some generic aspect of William, perhaps William's personhood (P-hood). But Mary is not respecting William here, for the simple reason that John, Thomas, Fred, and so on can be substituted for William. There is no William, John, Thomas, Fred, etc. in these acts of "respect." Only possessors of P-hood. That is, William does not matter. William is only a someone, a placeholder for anyone possessing the generic characteristic of P-hood. As we have argued in *NOL*, there are good reasons to develop norms (for example, rights) for a context of someones, but that is a far cry from Mary respecting William. For Mary to respect William, Mary would have to be taking into account what is unique to William and its distinction from what is unique to John, and so on. That is definitely not what is going on here, and the language of respect ends up obscuring what is important for properly thinking about what rights are and are not doing.

We might note at this juncture that we have argued in section 2 of Chapter 2, "Ethics versus Politics and Law: The Importance of Liberal Political Order," that the problem rights address is a different sort of problem than the problem of morality generally. This is because rights, on our view, concern the social/political conditions for making morality possible. The problem with respect as a basis for all this is that it does not discriminate between the levels of morality and the norms necessary for morality to function. Hence, LeBar is left with the question of why we would cede authority to persons P in general, and not just to this or that specific P (as in the smoking case). To our way of thinking, the sort of respect owed to persons in a rights context is different from that in the normal moral case. In the former, one gets a kind of respect for the kind of being they are—in the latter, for what they do with themselves. In a way, as Kant again saw (though for perhaps different reasons), rights do not even require the presence of another person—only the potential presence. What one is actually respecting is not persons, but the generic property of personhood, as just noted. It is not that this sort of respect is unimportant. The myth is not that there is no respect here, but rather that there is a respect for *persons*. As we have maintained throughout this work, persons are more than their generic properties, and significant portions of the moral enterprise—indeed, the most significant—are those non-generic characteristics. To say that respecting rights is respecting a person is about like telling a friend that your relationship with her is completely captured by your generic need for friendship.[17]

The response to what we have said is perhaps to employ, as LeBar repeatedly does, the language of seeing others as "final ends." And while we are sympathetic to the rhetorical value of this and would use such language ourselves as shorthand for a longer explanation, the locution does not help. For if Mary is not respecting William as William, per above, then Mary is not seeing William as a final end either. What is unique to William, once again, makes no difference to Mary, for reasons already mentioned. Now, in response, it is likely that each of us as individuals has a stake in the form of treatment that is "rights-respecting"; and thus it would seem fair to say that we are respecting *the individual* when we treat her in a rights-respecting way, because that is how she herself would want to be treated. However plausible such a response might be—and it is plausible to assume that each individual wants to be treated in a rights-respecting way—we are still no closer to respecting individuals. Again, it does not matter to Mary whether William wants to be treated this way or not. William as William is still irrelevant to Mary's appropriate conduct, because anyone and everyone can be substituted for William. William matters as an instance of a principle one should respect— namely, the presence of P-hood. But William does not matter as William; and because of that, he is not a final end in himself, though he is a final end *for* himself. The being a final end for himself is the teleological basis upon which rights are built, as it does express a truth about personhood generally. But for William to be a final end

---

[17] LeBar certainly recognizes this as well: "A friend does not act for the sake of friendship; a friend acts for the sake of the friend him- or herself" (*VLW*, p. 324). This is all fine, but it simply begs the question of why this is *my* friend, which has to be established if one is going to act the recommended way. His proposed distinction does not get him to the "myness" of the issue because, while it tries to recognize the end of there being an other that is individual, it fails to see that that individuality has to be recognized by another individual or it remains just a set of properties.

in himself *for Mary* would require that William *as William* matter to Mary; and nothing in the "final-endedness" of William in a rights context does that. As we have maintained from the start, morality never finally rests at the generic or universal level, however important that level may be, as indeed it is when speaking about rights.

So, we are now ready to return to our issue of big morality. What can account for the horrendous character of some of the most notorious acts of inhumanity we have witnessed in the last century alone? All would certainly agree on at least two things—namely, the nature of the very acts themselves and the scope of their execution. Of course, within a context of a theory of flourishing, such brutalities clearly thwart any possibility for flourishing. Yet, as we have suggested above, a threat to an abstract notion of general flourishing does not account for the horror of it all. When we search for the causes of our repulsion, certainly the mere contemplation of the nature and scope of the acts themselves would evoke a significant sentiment of horror and disgust. But if these sorts of events can be comprehended at all in the depth of their evil, what might be the marginal difference beyond the brutality of the acts themselves that is so horrifying? We would submit that it is the utter and thorough disregard of individuality that is the marginal difference between these acts and other acts of evil, especially since they are usually performed in the name of some impersonal universal abstraction such as the "race," the "Fatherland," "progress," or "the people." The "bigness" of this sort of immorality is precisely its complete obliteration of the relevance of, and possibility for, the individual.[18] If the moral enterprise is essentially concerned with what one is to make of one's life, the idea of actions that regard one's life as completely unimportant, even for oneself, could not be more horrific. Notice, it is not the act of killing per se that is the problem here. In arguably legitimate forms of killing, such as self-defense or punishment, it is precisely the *presence* of individuality—namely, the particular circumstances and intentions of the particular agent—that not only justifies what is done, but also eases our contemplation of it. Notice, too, that on the positive side of big morality, it is almost a hyper form of individuality that is displayed and impresses us. The acts of heroism, generosity,

---

[18] Our discussion of LeBar above by no means suggests that here we are placing him in disagreement with our conclusions. Our ways of arriving at those conclusions may at times differ, but we suspect those conclusions are not dissimilar in their content.

excellence, charity, and the like are admired because the agents of these acts stand out *so* distinctly as individuals.

Morality understood only in terms of universal or generic properties, even when those are the "good" ones, is at least prone to distortion, if not to becoming the path of immorality itself. The fact that modern technology allows one to do something on a massive scale does not thereby justify doing "good" on such a basis. It does not follow, in other words, that because something can be done on a massive scale, only evil doings should be avoided, and only "good" ones done. As we have argued all along, goodness is a phenomenon of individuals, thereby implying that it is a perversion of "do good and avoid evil" to suppose that the individuality that is ignored in big *im*morality can also be ignored in big morality. From Adam Smith's "man of system" to clichés about "good intentions," the truth is that the pursuit of generalized good is often the path to generalized evil. Hence, our insistence upon individuality was not simply a matter of trying to get the ontology right, but also a reminder of the link between metanorms and metaethics. The perfectionist turn is not a turning away from metanorms. And in reminding ourselves that metanorms are norms for the possibility of individual moral action, we are reminded also that it is, indeed, individuals who must do the acting—and with them that ultimate responsibility must lie. Because of that, Plato was right that it is a corrupted soul (one not in proper order) which regards individuals as instances of universals, even if they are of the "good" kind of universals, or which disregards individuals altogether. That type of soul is prone to do harm even when, and perhaps especially when, what is done is done in the name of some good. Consequently, it is to that particular soul to which one must directly appeal in the last analysis—however much the other should be independently considered—because it is the nature and quality of that particular soul which will produce the actions that are to become the objects of moral concern. It is possible to avoid that conclusion if one holds that, in the final analysis, there is only the social, and that individuals are themselves social constructs. Yet, with Plato, we have held the reverse. The final appeal must be to the state of one's own soul, because that is one's chief and only inescapable responsibility.

Index

abstraction, 29, 42, 66, 68–9, 72,
72n11, 74–5, 77, 79, 81–2, 87–9,
94, 101, 101n16, 134, 178, 273,
299, 331
  modern view of, 72n11
  non-precisive (without precision), 72,
73n14, 74–5
  precisive (with precision), 72–3,
73n14, 74
  Thomist moderate realist view of,
72, 89
  as tool of cognition or practical
reason, 66, 72–3, 77, 86–7
Ackrill, J. L., 38n14, 39
activity, 43, 45, 51–2, 55–6, 59, 62–3,
93, 122, 178, 180, 199, 199n57,
217–18, 227, 232, 237–8, 241,
249–52, 255–7, 261, 263–4, 268,
280–1, 288–9, 301, 308
actualization, 38n13, 43–6, 89,
147n29, 149, 172–4, 174n4, 175,
178, 193, 193n43, 194, 194n45,
196, 199, 214, 216–20, 224, 233,
237, 245, 249, 273, 276, 281–2;
see also potentiality
agent, 17, 24, 46, 52, 64, 89, 226, 241,
249, 251, 252, 257, 259, 282,
284n1, 299, 301, 306, 324
  agent-centered, 23–4, 24n42, 84,
124, 128; see also agent-relative
  agenthood, 67, 70, 75
  agent-independent, 248, 248n3,
257, 267n39, 284, 284n1; see also
agent-neutral
  agent-neutral, 27, 34–5, 35n4, 36,
57–8, 60, 83, 85, 128–9, 177,
179, 186–7, 253, 260–1, 263,
264n33, 266, 284n1; see also
impersonalism
  agent-relative, 34–5, 35n4–6, 36–7,
37n10–11, 41–3, 54, 58, 64, 69n6,
83–5, 92, 128, 131–3, 174n3,

233, 249, 249n7, 252–3, 260–2,
264n33, 276, 285, 311; see also
personalism
  agent-specific, 69n6; see also agent-
relative
  moral agent, 7, 315
  wise agent, 277–8
analytic, 209, 209n26, 210, 238n92
Annas, Julia, 9–10, 10n20, 27, 27n47,
195, 199n57, 268–9
Anscombe, G. E. M., 39n15, 239,
258n22
anthropomorphism, fallacy of, 196,
225, 268
Aquinas, 9, 14, 38n13, 40, 66, 70,
72, 72n11, 90, 90n35, 212, 217,
217n50, 218–19, 228n67, 237,
243, 249n8, 256, 257n21
Ariew, André, 195n48, 197n51
Aristotle, 8–9, 14, 16, 27n47,
38n13–14, 39, 45, 48–9, 51,
51n42–43, 52–4, 54n52, 55–6,
60, 63, 69–70, 72–5, 87n30, 178,
184, 190, 197n51, 197n53, 218,
218n51, 226, 232n80, 241, 250n8,
264, 269, 290n11, 302, 302n30,
309, 318, 321
  Aristotelian, 20n35, 33–4, 46,
49n39, 56, 58, 69, 89, 111,
111n30, 112, 112n31, 114, 138,
175, 183, 190–1, 200, 262–4,
264n33, 286n4, 296, 320; see also
neo-Aristotelian
  Aristotelian–Thomistic, 207, 214,
216, 239n95
atomism, 24n43, 61

Badhwar, Neera K., 59n55
Balagangadhara, S. N., 151n44
Balme, D. M., 197n51
because, 201, 203–5, 206, 216, 228,
242–4, 270

Bedau, Mark, 198
Berlin, Isaiah, 98, 182
Besser-Jones, Lorraine, 59n55
biocentric context of
 human good, 44
 practical reason, 250
Black, Max, 203n5, 211n34
Blackburn, Simon, 213, 213n40–2,
 227n65
Bloomfield, Paul, 42n20, 76n15,
 196n50, 208n22, 213n42, 236n88,
 243n104, 295n20
Bok, Sissela, 6
Bosanquet, Bernard, 147
Boyle, Robert, 225n60
Bradie, Michael, 197n53
Brewer, Talbot, 4n4, 10–11, 11n23,
 37n10, 175n5, 176n9, 227n65,
 238n92m, 239n95
Brink, David O., 210
Brody, Baruch, 244n106
Brown, Stephen R., 206n15, 225n61
Brunner, Karl, 318
Buchanan, James, 47–51, 100n12, 117,
 117n37, 299–300, 304–5, 310,
 315
Butchvarov, Panayot, 210n28, 212,
 214n44, 215n47, 241

categorical imperative, 77–8, 81, 236,
 285
causality, 196–7, 197n51, 210, 237,
 240, 242, 251, 275–6, 279n71; see
 also conflation of: final causes with
 efficient causes
 efficient, 197n51, 222n57, 223, 242,
 250–1
 final, 70, 197n51, 217, 222n57, 223,
 250–1
 formal, 250–1
 immanent, 221
 material, 197n51
 transient, 221
choice-worthiness, 15, 43–5, 78, 84,
 179, 202, 232, 243, 247–8, 249
Christian, 100, 110, 113, 115
Claerhout, Sarah, 151n44
claim and command, 154–8; see also
 template of respect
communism, 297, 297n24
community, 42n21, 53–4, 87, 90n35,
 111, 113, 115n34, 124, 131, 153,
 160, 160n59, 161–3, 165, 168

comprehensive philosophy, 13–14, 28,
 94, 96, 96n1, 97, 98, 99, 100–1,
 101n15, 101n17, 102–4, 104n20,
 105–16, 116n35, 117, 135–7, 216,
 228,
conflation of
 abstractions with realities, 79
 consensus with justification, 103
 distinct with separable, 101n15,
 111n29; see also rationalism
 ethics or morality with law, 57,
 115n34
 ethics with politics, 139n11, 158; see
 also statecraft as soulcraft
 final causes with efficient causes,
 197n51
 logical necessity with psychological
 necessity, 258
 mode of cognition with reality, 76,
 81; see also Modernist fallacy;
 rationalism
 morally binding demands of justice
 with morally and legally binding
 demands of justice, 140
 natural teleology with
 anthropocentric and providential
 accounts of nature, 225
 reasoning with reality, 101n15,
 258
 social with political, 153
 universality with objectivity, 84n26
consequentialism, 22, 40, 124, 125n60,
 214, 248, 251–3
constraints, 27, 27n47, 47–8, 66,
 101–2, 156, 199n57, 277–8, 302,
 313, 317
 the Four Constraints, 66, 89, 94–5
constructivism, 29, 47, 79n20, 81,
 112, 117, 214n43, 230n74, 246,
 258, 268–71, 275–8, 282, 322–3,
 325–6, 328
Cooper, John, 51
Copleston, F. C., 257n21
Csíkszentmihályi, Mihály, 62n57
Curzer, Howard J., 293n16

Dancy, Jonathan, 69n6
Darwall, Stephen, 15n30, 19, 137,
 159, 159n57–8, 160, 160n59,
 161–2, 162n64, 163–4, 164n69,
 165–6, 166n70, 167, 167n72, 168,
 208n20, 234n83, 246–8, 248n3,
 249, 249n7, 250, 250n9, 251–3,

253n12–13, 254–60, 261n27, 262, 262n32, 263–4, 264n33, 265, 265n36, 266, 267n39, 268, 282, 284, 286, 323, 325, 327n13
Darwallian, 262, 327, 327n13
Davitt, Thomas, 38n13
de Lazari-Radek, Katarzyna, 45, 47n34
De Roover, Jakob, 151n44
definition, 208–11
  nominal, 208
  real, 207n16, 208, 210–11, 231–3
Delbrück, Max, 198n56
Den Uyl, Douglas J., 23n39, 24n43, 33n1, 35n5, 42n21, 65n1, 90n32–3, 93n40, 94n41, 120n45, 130n74, 134n87, 156n51, 159n57, 161n62, 278n68, 303n31
deontology, 4–5, 7n9, 13, 13n26, 14, 18, 22, 83n24, 141, 162n65, 249n7, 285; see also Kant, Immanuel: Kantian
descriptive, 4, 21, 45, 118, 185, 203, 203n7, 204–5, 224–7, 227n65, 228, 230–1, 234–5, 240, 270, 276; see also prescriptive
design, 312–14
desire, 18, 28, 37, 43–4, 59, 217–18, 235–9, 261n27, 263, 281, 316
  rational, 58n55, 241
  right, 44, 237
Devitt, Michael, 230n73
Dewey, John, 121
dichotomy, 209n26; see also separation of
dignity, 6n5, 17, 17n33, 18–19, 100, 107, 160, 163–4, 164n69, 165, 192, 257, 297, 314, 314n42
divine essence and eternal law, 218
doctrine of the mean, 309
Dorsey, Dale, 184n26
Dreier, James, 212n37, 213n41
Dworkin, Ronald, 97

economics, 47, 133, 287, 291, 304, 316, 319
  economic egalitarianism, 125
egoism, 9, 14–15, 36, 53
end, 33, 45, 47, 55, 72, 78–9, 172, 182, 194, 217–18, 251, 279; see also means and ends; telos
  categorical end, 236n88
  as dispositional propensity or goal, 64, 293, 312

dominant end, 38–9, 48, 64, 198, 252
end in itself, 16, 39, 55, 59, 157, 233n81, 324, 327, 330
end-oriented, 279, 281
end-realization, 263
ethical end, 50, 200
final end, 27, 38, 48–9, 49n39, 50, 64, 198–200, 282, 287, 327, 330–1
hierarchy of ends, 193n43, 277
inclusive end, 38–9, 39n15, 48, 198
inherent end, 263
natural end, 45, 47, 51–2, 198–9, 225, 227n66, 236, 263, 269, 279, 279n71, 280–2
not mere means, 6n5
ultimate end, 33, 38, 193, 193n43, 219, 252, 268, 280–2
entrepreneur, 29, 268, 284, 286, 286n4, 287, 287n5–6, 288, 288n7, 289–90, 290n11, 291–3, 295–313, 315, 317–19
equinormativity see ethics, ethical norm, equinormative
ergon, 45, 172, 184, 243 see function
essence vs meaning, 210, 213
essentialism, 200n58
ethics, vi–vii, 1–2, 2n2, 4–5, 9–10, 12–14, 14n29, 15–16, 24–6, 28–9, 55, 57, 62, 65–71, 77, 80, 85, 88, 93–4, 118n40, 138, 174, 179, 185, 190, 232–4, 241, 243, 254, 270, 284–5, 287–9, 291–3, 296, 298–303, 306–9, 312, 316, 318–20; see also objectivity; sociality: socialization; socialized ethics or morality
  ancient ethics, 10, 12, 14, 27, 85
  Aristotelian ethics, 20n35, 38n14, 49n39, 262
  discourse ethics, 122
  ethical framework, 3; see also template of respect; template of responsibility
  ethical model: evaluational (or evaluative), 58, 284–6, 289, 296, 312, 318; juridical, vi, 58, 166–8, 272, 284–6, 289, 297, 302–3, 312–14, 317–18; legislative, 27, 29, 64, 66, 89, 137, 140, 156–7, 318; responsibility, 297

essentialism (*cont.*)
  ethical norm, vi, 1, 3, 16, 25, 89,
    93, 93n39, 98n8, 141, 162n65,
    190, 258–9, 269–70, 295, 298:
    equinormativity, 93n39, 99n8,
    112, 303n31; metanormative,
    35n5; *see also* metanorm
  ethical opportunity, 291, 292n16,
    293–4; *see also* objectivity: of
    ethical opportunity
  ethical order, 90, 141; *see also*
    politics: political order; sociality:
    social order
  eudaimonistic ethics, 321–2
  Kantian ethics, 78, 80, 83n24,
    236n88
  as means of defining relations among
    persons, 26
  modern or contemporary ethics, 4, 9,
    18, 21, 47, 60, 69, 84n26, 89, 138,
    168, 284, 318
  neo-Aristotelian ethics, 27, 34, 37,
    49, 84, 110, 138–9, 140, 166, 173,
    198, 200, 292n16, 295n21
  perfectionist ethics, vi–vii, 27, 45, 63,
    229n72, 232, 241, 244, 287, 320
  as real vs theoretical construct, 1,
    1n1
  rule-governed ethics, 88, 315,
    315n43
  as self-contained, 302
  social reasoning ethics, 142n15
  as tool for guiding and regulating
    interests and purposes of agents,
    26
  as tool of social management and
    control, 11, 25, 61, 89, 154,
    267n38, 285, 314, 316, 317
  as tool of successful living, 89
  utilitarianism, 4, 9n16, 14, 19, 22,
    26n45, 47, 49, 85n28, 97, 103,
    110, 125, 141, 285; *see also*
    sociality: social utility
  virtue ethics, 4, 138–40, 327
ethics and politics, vi–vii, 27–8, 89–92,
    92n38, 93–5, 139n11, 141, 156,
    158–9, 162; *see also* conflation of:
    ethics with politics
  liberating ethics from politics, 28, 66,
    91, 95, 107, 137, 156, 159
eudaimonia, 27, 33–4, 38–40, 40n16,
    51, 51n43, 58–9, 62, 162, 187,
    189, 232n80, 268, 275, 282,

291–2, 304, 320, 321–2, 328,
    328n15; *see also* flourishing;
    happiness
Euthyphro question, 43, 237, 278
evaluative, 29, 41, 45, 118, 124, 132,
    189, 195, 203, 203n7–8, 204,
    216n48, 224–7, 227n65, 228, 240,
    260, 285; *see also* ethical model:
    evaluational; factual; prescriptive
E-world *see* world of E
experience machine, 43
expressivism, 213n42

fact, 7, 37n10, 47, 101n17, 109n16,
    114, 119, 120n47, 123, 157,
    202–3, 203n8, 204–5, 227, 235,
    241, 243n104, 249, 261n27, 263,
    271–2, 275–6, 305; *see also* value
  "bald facts," 189–92
  fact–value separation, 205, 209n26,
    107, 227n64; *see also* gap:
    ontological or fact–value
  fact–value union, 59, 123, 205,
    227–8, 228n68
factual, 29, 190, 203–4, 235n86, 240,
    243n104, 244; *see also* descriptive;
    evaluative
Feser, Edward, 239n95
Finnis, John, 38n13, 41, 41n19
first and second nature, 189, 189n35,
    190–3, 194n45, 199n57, 231n77,
    281–2
Flanagan, Owen, 59n55
flourishing, 20, 27, 33–4, 37–45,
    50–5, 58–9, 62, 64, 67–9, 69n6,
    70–3, 75–6, 84–5, 87–9, 91–4,
    134, 171–4, 176, 180, 182, 186,
    199, 199n57, 236–7, 240, 242–3,
    249–52, 282, 287–8, 291–2, 295,
    303n31, 306–7, 316, 320, 327,
    331; *see also eudaimonia*; good
    and goodness; happiness; *telos*
  as do-it-yourself-job, 52, 281
  as individualized, 34, 41–3, 53–4, 69,
    73, 76, 84, 92, 174n3, 182, 307,
    320
  -at-large or -for-some-person, 35, 37
Foot, Philippa, 9, 10n21, 40n18, 86,
    177, 177n10, 193–5, 207, 212n36,
    219–20, 220n55, 228, 229n72,
    230n74–75, 232, 233n81, 244
form of life, 64, 100, 185, 194, 196,
    220

"forms of life," 231, 231n77
Frank, Robert, 294n17
Frankena, William K., 209n27
free and equal persons, 108, 138–9, 141–2, 142n15, 151n44
freedom, 83, 98n7, 102n18, 125n61, 139, 142–5, 147–50, 150n42, 152, 253–4, 256–7, 282, 287; *see also* liberty
function, 45–6, 52n47, 125n61, 172, 175–6, 183–4, 184n26, 185, 195, 197, 220–1, 224n58, 225–6, 227n66, 242–3, 250–1, 303n31, 306; *see also ergon*

"G" question, 176–7, 180, 192–3, 216, 219
gap, 206, 206n15; *see also* separation
epistemological, 203, 215n46, 222, 224–8, 234
logical, 201–2, 203n6, 206
motivational, 202, 206, 208n20, 235, 241–3
ontological or fact–value, 33, 46–7, 201, 203, 203n6, 204–6, 209n26, 216, 227n64, 244, 247
semantic, 206–7, 207n16, 216–17
Garcia, J. L. A., 24n42
Gaus, Gerald, 19, 137–8, 138n5, 139, 139n11, 140, 140n12–13, 141–3, 143n16–17, 144, 144n18, 145–7, 147n30, 148–54, 154n48, 155n50, 156n51–2, 157, 157n53, 158, 167, 247, 315n45
Gaussian: free moral person, 144; Rule-following Punishers, 148
George, Robert, 41, 41n19
Gibbard, Alan, 204n11, 208n20, 234n83
Gill, Christopher, 68n5, 85
Glassen, P., 175, 175n5
good and goodness, 10–11, 16, 27, 29–30, 33, 35, 38n11, 40, 50, 52, 56–8, 60, 68, 76, 87, 90, 112–15, 141, 171–3, 175–6, 176n7, 176n9, 177, 177n10, 179, 181–3, 192–5, 200n58, 207–10, 213–15, 215n46, 216, 216n48, 217, 217n50, 218–22, 224–6, 228–9, 232, 234, 237–8, 242–3, 259, 262, 288, 308, 311, 318–19; *see also* agent-centered; agent-neutral; agent-relative; flourishing;

goods and virtues; human good; *telos*
Aristotelian–Thomistic goodness, 207, 214–16, 216n48
as abstract or general or universal, 42, 54n52, 193
as actual rather than potential, 215, 217, 219, 224, 237, 301, 307
-at-large or -for-some-person, 35
basic goods; *see also* goods and virtues
common good, 42n21, 90n35
as conformity to one's nature, 216, 222, 239n95
ethical or moral good, 90–1, 93, 263
good of and good for, 27, 33, 35, 37, 37n10–11, 54n52, 67, 76, 129, 171, 173, 174n3, 175–6, 176n7–9, 177, 179, 183, 192–3, 194n45, 195–6, 199, 216–17, 219–26, 230, 232, 243, 261n27, 269, 276, 281, 309, 311, 325, 327
good without qualification, 54n52
goods and virtues, 54, 57, 74, 178, 234: basic or generic, 38, 38n13, 41–2, 45, 53–4, 59, 67, 69, 73–5, 79, 86–7, 174, 174n4, 178, 184–6, 198, 230, 234, 243, 262, 266–7, 267n39; constituent, 33, 40–2, 54, 73–4, 178, 243
human good, 29, 33–5, 37, 39n15, 42, 44, 46, 59, 64, 68, 70, 75–6, 174, 174n3, 176–9, 193, 195, 197–8, 219, 229–32, 241, 243, 249, 252, 256–7, 264, 280, 282, 286n4, 296; *see also* agent-centered; flourishing; impersonalism
as impersonalist, 85n27–28
as inclusive end, 38–9, 39n15, 198
as indefinable, 207, 211, 211n34, 212, 214–15, 215n47, 216
as individualized, 42, 43n23, 55, 60, 67, 76, 156, 174, 178–9, 233, 249, 269, 281, 319
as intersubjective, 43n23
as intrinsic or autonomous, 177n10
Moorean or neo-Moorean goodness, 35n4, 206–8, 210–11, 211n34, 212, 212n37, 213, 213n39, 214, 214n43, 215n47, 216, 216n48, 247–9, 253

good and goodness (*cont.*)
  natural good, 177n10, 193, 216–17,
    219–20, 220n55, 221, 225, 227–9,
    232, 233n81, 238, 242, 242n101,
    245
  as naturalistically grounded, 207,
    216
  as non-naturalistic, 47n35; *see also*
    Moore, G. E.
  as non-reductively naturalistic, 214,
    226
  as non-relational or absolute, 37n11,
    85n28, 213n39
  as norm for human conduct, 247–9
  not an ordinary property, 215
  not worth or worthiness, 253
  as objective or subjective, 43n23
  as ontological and relational, 215,
    217–18
  as perfectionist, 215–16, 219
  as person-relative, 37n10
  as property of will or intention, 5–6,
    78, 310, 332
  as requiring desirability and
    evaluation, 217, 226, 237
  self-direction as central good, 61
  as supervenient, 212–13, 213n39,
    214–15
  as teleological, 17
  ultimate good, 33, 37, 98n7, 252; *see
    also* end; *telos*
Gotthelf, Allan, 196n50
Grant, Ruth W., 153n46

Habermas, Jürgen, 122, 122n51,
    122–4, 126
Hacker-Wright, John, 189n35, 229n72
Haidt, Jonathan, 44, 53n49, 307
happiness, 9n15, 33, 38n14, 40n16, 58,
    78, 181–3, 186–90, 257n21, 265,
    275, 299n28; *see also eudaimonia*;
    flourishing
Hardcastle, Valerie Gray, 175, 175n5
Harris, George W., 10n21, 20n35
Haybron, Daniel M., 172n1, 173, 175,
    175n5, 176n7–8, 179–80, 180n15,
    181–4, 186–8, 193
Hayek, F. A., 130–1, 286n4, 297–300,
    300n29
hero, 286, 315, 331; *see also* morality:
    moral exemplar
Hobbes, Thomas, 145–7
honor, 20, 39, 162–4, 164n69, 165

honor society, 164–5; *see also*
    liberalism: liberal order
Hospers, John, 80
human being; *see also* good and
    goodness: human good
  capacities or capabilities of, 97, 125,
    125n61, 133–4, 134n87, 173,
    180–2, 187, 190n37
  cognition or reason of, 81–3, 108,
    135, 235, 242, 250n8, 256,
    256n18, 257, 280
  nature of, vii, 33, 41, 46, 48, 54,
    136, 173–4, 177–8, 187–9,
    189n35, 190–2, 199n57, 200n58,
    219, 228, 230n74, 231–3, 236,
    236n88, 241, 243, 243n104,
    249–50, 267, 291, 325
  as rational animal, 22, 46, 49, 78,
    80, 82, 149, 231, 254, 279
  as social animal, 11, 24, 61, 69, 140,
    162, 188, 259, 307
Hume, David, 14, 201–3, 203n6, 224,
    227n64, 235, 235n86, 236n87,
    318
Humean, 235–6, 240
Hurka, Thomas, 37n10, 45n30, 47n34,
    176n7
Hursthouse, Rosalind, 229n72,
    233n81
hypothetical imperative,
  assertoric, 78, 236, 236n88, 240n95,
    257n21
  problematic, 78, 235

impersonalism, vii, 17, 20n35, 34,
    34n3, 35n6, 37n11, 57, 60, 64,
    83–5, 85n27–8, 92, 128–34, 327,
    331; *see also* agent-neutral
impositionality, 132
inclusive, 19–20, 34, 38–9, 39n15,
    40–3, 48, 52, 57–8, 64, 92, 174n4,
    198, 217, 252, 288
incommensurability, 33n1
individual, 6, 8, 17
  individualism, vi, 18, 24n43, 29,
    42, 61, 130–1, 134, 173, 175,
    197, 199n57, 219, 303–4, 309,
    315–8, 329; *see also* perfectionism:
    individualistic perfectionism (IP)
  individuality, 34, 41, 42n20, 67, 76,
    129–30, 134, 134n87, 177, 182,
    186, 194, 221, 267n38, 330n17,
    331–2

individualized, 34, 41–3, 43n23, 53–5, 61, 64, 67, 69n6, 72–3, 76, 84, 92, 154, 156, 174, 174n3, 178–9, 182, 184–6, 229n72, 233, 249, 269, 281, 305, 307, 319–20
instrumental, 38, 40, 55, 59–60, 197, 246, 248, 251, 303, 307, 307n35, 323, 328
integrated diversity, political problem of, 91; *see also* liberalism: liberalism's problem
integrity, 20, 20n35, 21, 38, 58–9, 67, 162, 174, 221, 228, 290, 290n9, 295, 302, 306, 308, 328
interpersonal, 16, 20, 57, 86, 98n8, 127, 130, 141, 144, 259–60, 277, 307, 309
Irwin, Terence, 10n21

Jacobs, Jonathan, 201n1, 240
Jensen, Steven J., 244n105
Jesus, 320
Jews, 113, 115
justice, 11, 108, 114, 125,
comparative judgments of, 126–7, 130–1, 134
demands of, 90, 126, 140

Kant, Immanuel, 5–7, 26, 77, 77n16, 78–83, 83n24, 89, 115n34, 129, 140, 143n17, 154, 165, 236n87–8, 240, 256, 257n21, 279, 284n1, 318, 318n47, 328–9
Kantian, 5–6, 6n5, 14, 23–4, 58, 81, 94n41, 100n12, 107, 109–10, 113–14, 127, 128n69, 129n72, 192, 236, 236n88, 257, 275, 285, 325–6, 328; *see also* deontology; neo-Kantian; principle of universalizability
Kateb, George, 7n10, 17n33
Kelly-Gagnon, Michel, 154n47
Khawaja, Irfan A., 85n27
Kirzner, Israel, 287, 287n6, 299, 308n37
Koons, Robert C., 43n23, 46n32
Korsgaard, Christine, 204n12, 271
Kraut, Richard, 37n11, 38n14, 54n52, 85n28, 213n39, 271–3, 275

Larmore, Charles, 97–8, 98n7, 108, 108n24

LeBar, Mark, 3n3, 172n1, 173, 173n2, 214n43, 246, 268–77, 277n62, 278, 278n66, 279, 279n71, 280–2, 309n38, 322–7, 327n13, 328, 328n15, 329–30, 330n17, 331n18
Lenman, James, 239
Lennox, James, 46n32, 195n48
Lewens, Tim, 230n75
liberalism, 28, 70, 90–1, 93–4, 97–9, 107–9, 112, 115n34, 116, 139–40, 154, 159–61, 161n62, 162, 164–6
liberal order, 94, 98, 109, 151, 156, 163–5; *see also* honor: honor society
liberal social and political project, 139
liberalism's problem (LP), 91–2; *see also* integrated diversity, political problem of
liberty, 90–1, 126, 145, 145n23, 287n4; *see also* freedom; rights
demands of equal liberty, 126
negative liberty or freedom, 125n61, 145n23, 147
positive liberty or freedom, 125n61, 147
life-form, 29, 54, 174, 177, 194–6, 199, 199n57, 220–2, 222n57, 224, 230–2, 237
Locke, John, 72n11, 145, 147, 147n30, Lockean, 145
Lott, Micah, 231n75
L-world; *see also* World of L

MacDonald, Scott, 39n15, 53
McDowell, John, 172n1, 189, 189n35, 191–2, 205n14, 206
Machan, Tibor R., 226, 232n78, 280
MacIntyre, Alasdair, 9, 138
Mack, Eric, 36n9, 83n25, 143n16
Mackie, J. L., 29, 201, 203, 205–6, 228, 242, 244, 270, 277, 279, 279n69
maximand, 48–9, 49n39, 50, 198, 200
meaning, 6, 44, 115–16, 116n35, 119, 141, 209n25, 210, 213
means and ends, 250n8, 257n21, 287, 313
means-end reasoning, 55–6
Meno problem, 102, 104, 104n20
metaethics, 28, 47, 65, 120n47, 242, 244, 246, 268, 332

metanorm, vi, 23n39, 93–4, 162n65, 295, 332; *see also* ethics: ethical norm, metanormative; rights

metanormativity *see* ethics: ethical norm, metanormative

meta-persons, 17; *see also* template of respect

impartial spectators, 17, 124

noumenal selves, 17, 80, 82, 130, 165, 236n88, 258, 281, 284n1; *see also* self

social utility calculators, 17

Meyer, Jared, 287n5

Mill, John Stuart, 148–9, 266, 319, 319n48

Millean, 94

Miller, Jr., Fred D., 51n41, 139, 196n50, 197n53

Mises, Ludwig von, 286n4

Mitchell, Sandra D., 197n54

Modernist fallacy, 81; *see also* conflation of: mode of cognition with reality

monism, 54, 90, 98, 100n13, 118n40, 138, 138n5, 151n43, 155n50, 252

Moore, G. E., 47n35, 203n8, 206–7, 207n16, 208–11, 211n34, 212, 212n37, 213, 213n39, 214, 214n43–4, 215n47, 216, 216n48, 224, 247–8, 253

Moorean, 35n4, 249; *see also* neo-Moorean

morality, 29, 66, 83, 94, 138, 138n5, 145, 155, 155n49–50, 158, 161, 222, 236, 296, 329, 331–2

big morality, 320–2, 329, 331–2

demands of, 142, 144–5, 147, 160n59

Modernity's approach to, 138

moral community, 160, 160n59, 161–2, 165

moral exemplar, 57, 64, 285, 302, 318, 320; *see also* hero

moral norms, 21, 62, 106, 117n37, 165, 297

moral obligation, 33, 35n6, 41–2, 69n6, 159–62, 166, 168

moral pluralism, 138, 150–1, 155n50, 311

moral point of view, 34, 83, 85; *see also* impersonalism

moral psychology, 58, 58n55, 59

moral realism, 120, 120n47

moral relations, 158, 328n15: essentially claims and commands, 154–8; essentially encouragements and persuasion, 158

moral virtue, 58, 174, 206, 233–4, 252

as self-legislated, 149n38

social morality, 137–8, 138n5, 139, 140n13, 141–2, 142n15, 143, 143n17, 144, 144n18, 146, 149n38, 150, 153–4, 155n50, 156, 156n52, 157, 157n53, 158

supervenient role of, 152

Murdoch, Iris, 9n15

Muslims, 113, 115

Nagel, Thomas, 35–6

natural kinds, 193n42

naturalism, vii, 18, 29, 46n33, 133–4, 165, 172–3, 175, 188, 200, 203n8, 206n14, 207, 213, 216, 216n48; *see also* perfectionism: naturalistic perfectionism; teleology

ethical, 27, 120, 205n14, 232

narrow, 198

non-reductive, 1n1, 175, 203n8, 214, 214n45, 226

teleological, 18

naturalistic fallacy, 15n30, 28, 147n29, 193, 205, 205n14, 206–7, 216, 234, 244

nature, conception of

anthropocentric, 225

providential, 196, 225

neo-Aristotelian, 27, 34, 37, 49, 81, 84, 101n15, 110, 138–40, 166, 173, 179, 198, 200, 257, 292n16, 295n21

neo-Kantian, 20n35

neo-Moorean, 35n4

nexus, 20, 41, 49–50, 54, 56, 67, 70, 75, 79, 86, 87n30, 93, 129, 132, 185, 198, 231, 290, 328

Nielsen, Kai, 34n3

Nietzsche, 191

Nietzschean, 190–1

non-cognitivism, 204n11, 212, 236

non-consequentialistic, 6, 162n65

non-constructivist, 322, 325

non-naturalism, 47n35, 203n8, 207, 211, 213, 216,

non-perfectionist, 156n52, 181

normative theory, 33, 40, 104, 205, 229, 233n81
normativity, vi–vii, 247, 249, 253–4, 261n27, 267–9, 277
  evaluational form of, 58, 284–6, 289, 296, 318
  juridical form of, vi, 58, 115n34, 160n59, 166–8, 282, 284–5, 285n3, 286, 289, 297, 302–3, 312–14, 317–18
Norms of Liberty (NOL), vi, 23n39, 24n43, 33n1, 35n5, 42n21, 61, 65, 65n2, 70, 89, 90n32–3, 93n39–40, 94n41, 99n8, 100, 100n14, 101, 130n74, 156n51, 159n57, 161n62, 162n63, 162n65, 233n81, 298, 303n31, 326, 329
Norton, David, 58, 266, 267n39, 292
Nozick, Robert, 12, 12n24, 13, 13n26, 18, 23–4, 43–4, 131
  four layers of ethics, 12n24
  moral pushes and pulls, 12–13, 23–4
Nuccetelli, Susana, 214n45
nudging, 102, 313
Nussbaum, Martha, 6n5, 19, 96, 97, 97n5, 98, 98n7, 99, 99n10, 100, 100n12–13, 101n15, 102, 102n18, 103–4, 104n20, 105, 107–8, 108n24, 116–17, 134n87, 139

O'Callaghan, John P., 228n67
objectivity, 27, 34, 42–3, 43n23, 44, 57, 64, 66, 70, 76, 84, 84n26, 85–6, 92, 118–19, 130–1, 133–4, 226, 256, 278, 291, 295
  of ethical opportunity, 293–4
  in ethics, 23, 86, 118–20, 120n47, 123, 133–4: demands of, 118
  in ethics and political philosophy, 123, 126, 128, 135
  in morality, 46–7
obligation, 5, 23n39, 27, 29, 33, 40, 69n6, 161–2, 166–8, 252, 255, 309
Oderberg, David S., 193n42, 220, 230n73
"one's own," 8, 10–11, 33–6, 51, 53, 55, 57, 59–62, 83, 86, 116, 132, 140, 145–6, 156, 158, 162, 175, 180, 259, 259n24, 260, 261n27, 291, 291n14, 293, 307, 316, 318–19, 324, 326–8, 332

open-ended, 24, 26, 54, 64, 92, 92n37, 130–1, 185, 191n39, 312, 315
open-question argument (OQA), 207–8, 208n20, 209, 209n27, 210–11, 213, 214n45, 234n83, 247–8, 253–4, 257
other-giving reasons, 324–7, 327n13
other-oriented, 11, 53, 259, 314, 328
Owens, Joseph, 73n14

Pap, Arthur, 210n28
Parfit, Derek, 22n38
Paul, Jeffrey, 147n29
perfectibility, vii, 171
perfectionism, vii, 11, 27, 29, 33–4, 41–2, 64, 97, 109n26, 110–12, 172–3, 175, 178–9, 193, 193n41, 203n8, 205–7, 215–16, 219, 235, 302, 321; *see also* self: self-perfection
  ethical perfectionism, vi, 27, 45, 63, 229n72, 232, 241, 244, 320
  individualistic perfectionism (IP), vi, 9, 27–9, 35, 35n5, 38, 40–2, 44, 48–9, 53, 55–6, 60–2, 64, 94–5, 139n11, 174, 177, 184, 203n8, 206, 232–3, 233n81, 244, 246, 249, 268, 311–12, 315–16; *see also* individual: individualism
  naturalistic perfectionism, 46, 232, 234, 236, 241; *see also* naturalism
  perfectionism with a capital P, 176n8
  perfectionism without transcendence, 177
  teleological perfectionism, 27, 45, 287; *see also* teleology
perfectionist turn, 14, 28, 332
person, 2, 4–6, 6n5, 8, 34, 41n19, 49, 57, 65n2, 83–4, 86, 89, 93, 99, 157–8, 165, 173–4, 176, 186, 190, 249, 252, 261n27, 262, 264, 286, 294, 329–30
  personhood (P-hood), 5–6, 80, 163–5, 329–30; *see also* self: selfhood
personalism, vii, 40, 52, 57, 64, 69, 79, 83, 85–6, 89, 110, 117, 123, 128, 130–4, 162, 183, 187, 221, 234, 254, 282–3, 302–3; *see also* agent: agent-relative
phronēsis, 250n8; *see also* practical wisdom
Pietarinen, Ahti Veikko, 120n45

Pigden, Charles, 202–3
Plato, 14, 89, 91, 104, 104n20,
    155n50, 171, 212, 237, 293,
    322–3, 326, 332
  Platonic, 46, 71, 120, 177, 273, 323
pleasure, 19, 38–9, 67, 78, 174, 186,
    190n37, 227, 233, 242, 264–5
pluralism, 33, 89–91, 98, 119, 135,
    138, 150–1, 155, 182, 198–200,
    309, 311
polis, 53–4, 90, 92n37, 321; see also
    sociality: society
politics, vi–vii, 28, 57, 70, 76, 91–2,
    92n38, 96, 96n1, 97, 98n7–8,
    99–101, 101n15, 104–5, 107, 117,
    117n37, 135, 152, 152n45, 156–8,
    159n57, 161, 287n4, 317; see also
    conflation of: ethics with politics;
    ethics and politics
  demands of political philosophy, 142
  as ethics writ large, 90
  political community, 42n21, 90n35
  political norms, 100, 317
  political order, 35n5, 61, 65, 65n2,
    89–91, 105–6, 108–9, 111,
    139–41, 15–3, 155–6, 156n52,
    158, 162–3, 285; see also ethics:
    ethical order; sociality: social order
  political/legal order, 28, 35n5, 61,
    65n2, 90–2, 100, 127, 130–1, 141,
    145n23, 150, 159n57, 162
  as self-contained or self-sufficient,
    27n47, 96, 96n1
  social/political order, 163, 285
Pols, Edward, 251n10
position-dependent, 132
position-relative, 132
potentiality, 37, 38n13, 45–6, 53,
    171–4, 174n4, 175, 178, 193,
    193n43, 194, 194n45, 196,
    199, 214–15, 215n46, 217–20,
    224–5, 227n66, 237, 241, 244–5,
    249–50, 263, 273, 276; see also
    actualization
practical rationality, 82, 269, 271,
    278–9, 280–2
practical reasoning, 20n35, 29, 40,
    55–7, 59–60, 77–9, 85, 85n28, 87,
    87n30, 126, 134, 185, 231, 233,
    236n88, 238, 240, 243, 247–9,
    249n8, 250–6, 256n19, 271–2,
    275, 279–81, 292, 316, 318–9,
    323–4, 328

practical wisdom, 27, 29, 33, 35n5,
    40–1, 51n42, 52n45, 54–9, 61–4,
    67, 69, 75, 80, 86, 89, 131, 174,
    184–5, 193n41, 199, 234, 234n82,
    250n8, 252, 273, 289, 295–6,
    306–8, 310, 312, 316, 323–5; see
    also phronēsis
prescriptive, 15–16, 93, 105, 110, 153,
    187, 204, 240, 285, 311; see also
    descriptive
principle of universalizability, 35n6, 80,
    127–8, 128n69, 129
procedure-independent, 123
public reasoning, 17, 117, 123–35,
    142n15, 143n16, 145–7, 147n30,
    148–55, 155n50, 157–8, 279n68
punishment, 139, 148, 154, 315, 331
Putnam, Hilary, 118, 118n40, 119,
    119n42, 119n44, 120, 120n46–7,
    121, 121n50, 122, 122n51, 123,
    126n65, 130, 133, 135, 146n26,
    205n13, 228n68

Quine, W. V. O., 210n29
Quinn, Warren, 240n97, 242

Railton, Peter, 208n20, 234n83
Rand, Ayn, 220n55, 256n18
Randall, Jr., John Herman, 225n60,
    226
Rasmussen, Douglas B., 23n39, 24n43,
    33n1, 35n5, 42n21, 65n1, 73n14,
    82n23, 90n32–3, 93n40, 94n41,
    119n44, 120n44, 122n51, 130n74,
    134n87, 156n51, 159n57, 161n62,
    193n42, 205n13, 210n33, 278n68,
    287n4, 303n31
rational caring, 258–61; see also
    standpoint: second-person
rationalism, 25, 33, 59n55, 101n15,
    111n29, 135, 286n4; see also
    conflation of: distinct with
    separable; conflation of: mode of
    cognition with reality
  concept rationalism, 75
  ethical rationalism, 42, 57, 75
rationality, 23–5, 122–3, 149, 151n43,
    199, 199n57, 215n46, 231–2, 238,
    240, 242, 280–1; see also human
    being: as rational animal; practical
    rationality
Rawls, John, 13n27, 19, 96, 97, 98n7,
    102n18, 107–8, 110, 112–15,

115n34, 116–17, 117n37, 123–4,
126, 130, 142n15, 143n17, 158
Rawlsian, 111–12, 112n31, 114–17,
123, 324
Raz, Joseph, 33n1, 98
Reid, Thomas, 82
respect, 2n2, 3, 3n3, 5–6, 6n5, 7, 11,
12n24, 18–19, 22, 63, 89, 99–100,
122, 151n44, 152, 160, 163–6,
286, 297–8, 307n35, 314, 314n42,
315, 319, 322–30; see also
template of respect
appraisal respect, 19, 163–4
as basically relational, 2n2
equal respect, 5, 6n5, 99, 100,
100n12–13, 101–4, 107
myth of respect, 329
recognition respect, 19, 163–4
respect-based ethics, 7n9, 12n24, 14,
61, 97, 140, 162, 162n64, 254,
262, 284, 286n3
response-dependent, 269
responsibility, 2n2, 3, 7–8, 18, 20–1,
30, 94, 96, 155n49, 158, 162,
256, 261n27, 319, 332; see also
template of responsibility
as basically agent-centered, 2n2
primacy of personal responsibility,
283
responsibility-based ethics, 2n2, 7n9,
9, 140, 162, 262, 284, 286n3, 296,
317
Ridley, Mathew, 131n77
rights, 156, 159–62, 164, 166, 195,
229, 326, 329–31
Darwallian rights, 159–61
egocentrism of rights, 17n33
equal rights, 233n81
as framework of American Founders,
104
generic and universal rights, 162
individual and negative rights,
12n24, 23n39, 65, 65n2, 89, 94,
145, 145n23, 147, 233n81
legal or juridical rights, 160n59
Lockean rights, 145
as means of formalizing respect, 328
as metanorms, 23n39, 162n65
as norms, 162n65, 329
as not being general moral
obligations, 161, 166, 168
as political expression of liberalism,
94, 161

property rights, 152
rights respecting, 93n40, 152, 156,
326, 329, 330
as special moral obligations, 166
Robinson Crusoe, 157n53
Rogers, Kelly, 53n50
Ronow-Rasmussen, Toni, 176n9
Rosati, Connie S., 35n4, 84n26
Rose, David C., 294, 294n17
Rousseau, Jean-Jacques, 140, 147n30,
149, 154
Russell, Daniel C., 63n58, 172n1,
173, 173n2, 176, 176n8, 182n20,
186–90, 192–3, 234n82, 309n38
Ryle, Gilbert, 240

Scheffler, Israel, 209n27
Scherkoske, Greg, 20n35
Schroeder, Mark, 204n11, 217n49
Schumpeter, Joseph, 287n6, 305,
308n37
Scott, Robert B., 205n14
Seay, Gary, 214n45
self, 7–9, 9n15, 11, 18, 20, 24, 35,
56, 60–2, 140, 182, 254–6,
296, 320, 327n13, 331; see also
person; personhood; responsibility:
primacy of personal responsibility
Aristotelian conception of, 58
coherency of, 21
dialectical self, 8
noumenal self, 17, 80, 82, 130, 165,
236n88, 258, 281, 284n1
phenomenal self, 284n1
self-centered, 321–2, 326; see also
self: self-referring
self-defense, 331
self-development, 8, 262–3, 268; see
also self: self-fulfillment
self-directed, 29, 33–4, 45, 51,
51n43, 52–3, 61–2, 64, 91–2,
94, 94n41, 156, 156n51, 162,
200, 229n72, 232, 238, 242, 250,
250n9, 251–2, 256, 270, 280, 287
self-flourishing, 322; see also self:
self-fulfillment
self-focused, 322; see also self: self-
referring
self-fulfillment, 11, 181
self-giving reasons, 322–6, 327n13;
see also self: self-referring
selfhood, 61; see also person:
personhood

self (*cont.*)
  self-improvement, 199; *see also* self:
    self-fulfillment
  self-interested, 11, 100n12, 103–4,
    117n37, 146, 259, 266, 291–2
  self-justifying, 277
  self-oriented, 328; *see also* self: self-
    referring
  self-perfection, 11, 38n13, 52, 60–2,
    64, 75, 155, 172, 172n1, 174,
    174n4, 186, 193n41, 200, 234,
    241–2, 252, 282, 315
  self-realization, 60; *see also* self: self-
    fulfillment
  self-referring, 324
  self-referring argument (SRA), 323–4,
    326–8
  self-validating, 230n74; *see also* self:
    self-justifying
Sen, Amartya, 19, 96, 117–18, 118n40,
    119–24, 124n56, 124n60,
    125, 125n61, 126, 126n65–6,
    127–32, 132n82, 132n85, 133–4,
    134n86–7, 135, 142n15, 146n26,
    158
separation of *see* gap
  agent and what is good, worthy, or
    obligatory, 253n13
  attitudes and reasons for having
    them, 328
  description and evaluation, 227–8
  directive and procedural dimensions,
    110
  epistemic and ethical, 102n18
  fact and value, 206, 209n26, 227,
    227n64
  first and second natures, 190
  good and good for, 193, 220
  good and right, 11, 11n23, 13,
    112–13
  human capacities and ethical norms,
    190
  individuative considerations and
    generic considerations, 187
  performance value and success
    value,181
  speculative and practical reason,
    249n8
  well-being and duties, 11
Shafer-Landau, Russ, 47n35, 213,
    213n42
Shane, Scott, 287, 290, 290n11, 296,
    308–10

Sidgwick, Henry, 11, 128–9, 129n72,
    175n5
Sidgwickean, 11
Singer, Peter, 45, 47n34
skepticism, 81, 270
Smith, Adam, 8, 14, 62, 124, 126,
    160–3, 164n68–9, 304, 307, 310,
    318, 321, 332
smuggling undefended assumptions
    into political philosophy, 101–2,
    102n18, 105, 136, 216n48; *see
    also* untethering
  "equal respect" as often loaded with
    tacit normative content, 101
  "veil of ignorance," 101–2, 108,
    142,
Snow, Nancy, 58n55
socialism, 286n4, 297, 297n24,
    319
sociality, 34, 53–4, 60–1, 89, 92,
    92n37, 320, 325; *see also* human
    being: as social animal; morality:
    social morality
  social contract, 101, 101n17, 102,
    107, 109–11, 114, 116–17, 123,
    147, 147n29, 294
  social order, 25, 91, 115, 156n52,
    162–4, 285, 297–8; *see also* ethics:
    ethical order; politics: political
    order
  social reasoning, 142n15, 144, 148,
    151: Social Reasoner's Dilemma,
    142, 142n15, 144n18
  social utility, 17, 22, 26n45, 285; *see
    also* meta-persons
socialization, 155n49, 157: oneself
    as socialized, 319; socialized ethics
    or morality, 61, 155n49, 156,
    157n53, 318; socialized norms,
    61
society, 4, 53, 90; *see also* polis
Socrates, 43, 70, 72–5, 171–2, 178,
    199, 224, 226, 228, 266, 320
Socratic, 241
Spector, Horacio, 203n6
speculative or theoretical
  knowledge, 67, 70
  reasoning, 56, 86–7, 231, 247,
    248–9, 249n8, 250n9, 251, 256,
    256n19, 280
  science, 66
  wisdom, 51n42, 56, 199
Spinoza, 218n52, 318

standpoint, 165, 260
  first-person, 248–9, 253, 253n13,
    260, 264, 326
  second-person, 19, 159, 165, 247,
    249n7, 253, 253n13, 254, 257–8,
    323; *see also* rational caring;
    template of respect
  third-person, 323
statecraft as soulcraft, 89–90; *see also*
  conflation of ethics with politics
Stephen Pinker, 116
Sternberg, Elaine, 290n9, 295n21
Stoics, 14
Strawson, P. F., 138
summum bonum, 42
Sumner, L. W., 43, 175, 175n5
supervenience, 22, 47n35, 152, 213,
    213n42, 214, 214n43, 215–16,
    216n48, 235n86, 275–7
  Admission of Supervenience, 212,
    213n39, 214, 216

Taylor, Charles, 8n13
Taylor, Gabriele, 239n95
teleology, 27, 29, 45–7, 49, 191,
    194–5, 197–200, 218, 220–1,
    230, 237–8, 240n95, 241–3,
    250–1, 276, 281, 291, 304, 330;
    see also perfectionism: teleological
    perfectionism
  Aristotelian and Platonic models, 46,
    197n53
  natural teleology, 28, 45–7, 47n34,
    59n55, 195–8, 203n8, 220, 225,
    225n60–1, 226, 279, 279n69,
    281
telos, 33, 37, 45–6, 49, 55, 60–3, 172,
    194, 220, 228, 238, 240, 243,
    251–2, 267, 292–3, 319, 323, 325;
    see also end; flourishing; good and
    goodness; ultimate good
Temkin, Larry S., 85n28
template (or framework) of respect,
    2, 2n2, 3–5, 7–8, 8n12, 10–14,
    15n30, 16–20, 21n36, 22–6, 140,
    246, 317; *see also* meta-persons
  reliance upon appeals to "public
    reason" and "views from
    nowhere," 17
  separation of good and right, 11,
    11n23, 112–13, 115
template (or framework) of
  responsibility, 2, 2n2, 3, 3n3, 4,
    7–8, 8n12, 9–10, 10n21, 11–14,
    17–18, 20, 21n36, 22–3, 23n39,
    24, 24n42, 25–7, 140, 261n27,
    317, 319
  four structural pillars, 27
  unity of good and right, 11–13
tethering, 94, 96–7, 101–2, 107,
    110–12, 114–17, 120, 134–7; *see*
    also untethering
thick evaluative concepts, 128n69,
    203n7, 227, 227n65, 228
thin moralities, 98, 101, 104, 106–7,
    109
Thompson, Michael, 195–6, 230n74,
    231n77
Thoreau, Henry David, 21n37
truth
  necessary, 209–10, 210n33
  self-evident, 209

ultimate good, 33, 37, 98n7, 216–17;
    see also end; *eudaimonia*; *telos*
universal, 1, 18, 22, 23n39, 28, 51, 65,
    67, 69–71, 75–6, 81, 86–7, 87n30,
    88–9, 91–2, 94, 162, 179, 210n31,
    263, 274, 296
universalization, 22, 23n39, 28,
    35n6, 57–8, 71n9, 76–81, 84–5,
    87, 127–8, 128n69, 129, 140,
    153, 157, 178–9, 260, 285,
    290, 311; *see also* principle of
    universalizability
untethering, 96–7, 97n1, 100–1,
    101n15, 105–8, 135; *see also*
    smuggling undefended assumptions
    into political philosophy
utilitarianism *see* ethics; utilitarianism

value, 4–5, 36–7, 115, 123, 157, 190,
    198, 206, 228, 306–8, 319; *see*
    also fact: fact-value separation,
    fact-value union; gap: ontological
    or fact-value
  performance value and success value,
    180, 180n15, 181–2
  as pluralistic, 33n1
  standard of value, 200
Van Schoelandt, Chad, 143n16
Veatch, Henry B., 43, 51, 72n13, 178,
    208n22, 209n26, 210n31, 214–15,
    215n46–7, 216, 216n48, 227,
    227n64, 227n66, 232n80, 235n86,
    239n95, 241n100, 285n2

veil of ignorance, 101–2, 108,
142n15
Velleman, J. David, 239n95
Venkataraman, S., 287, 287n6, 290,
290n11, 296, 308, 308n37,
309–10
virtue, 55, 58–9, 174, 199n57, 269,
289, 290n11, 293n16; *see also*
good and goodness: goods and
virtues
unity of the virtues, 292n16
virtues and visions, 138; *see also*
template of responsibility

Walsh, Denis, 46n32, 195n48, 230n73
Weber, Max, 2n2
Weithman, Paul, 108, 108n24, 109
White, Morton G., 210n29
Whiting, Jennifer, 53n47
Wiesel, Elie, 321, 321n3
Wilkes, Kathryn V., 184
Williams, Bernard, 207, 226, 226n64
world of E, 311–18
world of L, 311–18
worthiness, 15, 15n30, 16, 16n31,
17–21, 103, 163–4, 164n68, 251,
253, 257, 259–60, 283; *see also*
choice-worthiness